무지개보카

고등 중급편

목차

Chapter 1.

1	**humble**	[ˈhʌm.bəl]	a. 겸손한, 자기를 낮추는
2	**subsidy**	[ˈsʌb.sɪ.di]	n. 보조금(pl. subsidies)
3	**shovel**	[ˈʃʌv.əl]	n. 삽 v. 삽으로 푸다
4	**subside**	[səbˈsaɪd]	v. 가라앉다, 침전하다; 진정되다
5	**vintage**	[víntidʒ]	n. 포도주, 포도 수확연도 a. 오래됨, 오래된
6	**cacography**	[kəkάgrəfi]	n. 악필
7	**school supplies**	[səplái]	p. 학용품
8	**detente**	[deitάːnt]	n. 긴장 완화
9	**reprimand**	[réprəmænd]	v. 비난하다, 질책하다
10	**frugal**	[ˈfruː.ɡəl]	a. 절약하는, 검소한
11	**affluent**	[ˈæf.lu.ənt]	a. 풍부한
12	**the masses**		p. 대중
13	**tactful**	[ˈtækt.fəl]	a. 재치있는
14	**contravene**	[ˌkɒn.trəˈviːn]	v. 반대하다; 위반하다
15	**altruism**	[ˈæl.tru.ɪ.zəm]	n. 이타주의, 이타심
16	**void**	[vɔɪd]	a. 텅 빈 / n. 공간
17	**suboptimal**	[sʌbάptəməl]	a. 차선의
18	**append**	[əˈpend]	v. 덧붙이다, 추가하다
19	**heterosexual**	[ˌhet.ər.əˈsek.ʃu.əl]	a. 이성애의
20	**herd**	[hɜːd]	n. 무리, 떼
21	**roam**	[rəʊm]	v. 배회하다, 돌아다니다
22	**adorn**	[əˈdɔːn]	v. 꾸미다, 장식하다
23	**plumb**	[plʌm]	n. 추 v. 재다; 납으로 봉하다
24	**lick**	[lɪk]	v. 핥다
25	**mooch**	[muːtʃ]	v. 배회하다, 살금살금 거닐다; 빌붙다
26	**the real deal**		n. 실질적인 것, 진짜
27	**plum**	[plʌm]	n. 자두
28	**transgress**	[trænzˈgres]	v. 넘다, 벗어나다; 위반하다, 어기다
29	**marinate**	[ˌmær.ɪˈneɪd]	v. 양념장에 재워두다, 절이다
30	**erode**	[ɪˈrəʊd]	v. 침식하다
31	**take up**		p. ~을 맡다
32	**serve to do**		p. ~하는 데 도움이 되다
33	**slip away**		p. 사라지다, 없어지다
34	**make A a regular habit**		p. A하는 습관을 들이다
35	**opposed to N**		p. ~에 반대하는
36	**at a 형 pace**		p. ~한 속도로
37	**at one time**		p. 한꺼번에, 동시에; 일찍이, 한 때
38	**be detached from**		p. ~에서 분리되다
39	**take place**		p. 일어나다, 발생하다
40	**take leave**		p. 작별을 고하다

1

humble

[ˈhʌm.bəl]

a. 겸손한, 자기를 낮추는

humbly adv. 겸손하게
humbleness n. 겸손함, 변변치 않음
humility n. 겸손

어원	-hum, -humili : earth 땅 → '땅에 가까운 겸손'
유의어	Modest, unpretentious, meek, self-deprecating, down-to-earth
반의어	Arrogant, pretentious, boastful, self-important, egotistical
영영	having or showing a modest or low estimate of one's importance
예문	She lived in a humble apartment, but it was clean and comfortable. 그녀는 초라한 아파트에 살았지만 깨끗하고 편안했습니다.

2

subsidy

[ˈsʌb.sɪ.di]

n. 보조금(pl. subsidies)

submarine n. 잠수함
reside v. 거주하다
subsidize v. ~에게 보조금을 지급하다
subsidiary a. 보조의, 부차적인

어원	-sub : under + -sid : sit → '아래 깔려 있는 돈이니 보조금'
유의어	Grant, financial aid, assistance, support, handout
반의어	Tax, burden, cost, fee, expense
영영	a sum of money granted by the government or a public body to assist an industry or business
예문	Low-income families may qualify for a housing subsidy to help with rent payments. Korean 저소득 가정은 집세 지불을 돕기 위한 주택 보조금을 받을 수 있을 것입니다.

3

shovel

[ˈʃʌv.əl]

n. 삽 v. 삽으로 푸다

shove v. 밀다, 밀어내다
shover n. 밀어 넣는 사람
scoop v. 스쿱; 뜨다

어원	-sha, -shi, -she, -sho : cut → '땅을 자르는 삽'
유의어	Spade, scoop, dig, excavate, clear
반의어	Plant, bury, cover, fill, conceal
영영	a tool with a broad flat blade and typically a slightly curved handle, used for moving, lifting, and throwing loose material such as soil, coal, or snow
예문	She used a shovel to move the dirt and rocks out of the way. 그녀는 흙과 바위를 치우기 위해 삽을 사용했습니다.

4

subside

[səbˈsaɪd]

v. 가라앉다, 침전하다; 진정되다

submerge v. 잠기다, 가라앉히다
subsidence n. 가라앉음, 침전

어원	-sub : under + -sid : sit → '밑으로 가라앉다'
유의어	Abate, lessen, decrease, dwindle, taper off
반의어	Intensify, escalate, increase, worsen, amplify
영영	become less intense, violent, or severe
예문	The pain in my ankle will subside with time and rest. 발목 통증은 시간과 휴식을 통해 가라앉을 것이다.

5

vintage

[víntidʒ]

n. 포도주, 포도 수확연도 a. 오래됨, 오래된

vinegar n. 식초

어원	-vine 포도나무, 덩굴 식물 + -age → '포도를 수확하고서 숙성한 연도' , '포도를 수확하고 오래 숙성을 해야 포도주'
유의어	Classic, old-fashioned, antique, retro, timeless
반의어	Modern, contemporary, new, trendy, current
영영	the year or place in which wine, especially wine of high quality, was produced
예문	The vintage wine was aged for 30 years in oak barrels. 그 빈티지 와인은 30년 동안 오크통에서 숙성되었습니다.

6

cacography

[kəkάgrəfi]

n. 악필

cacophony n. 불협화음
caca n. 응가

어원	-caco 추한, 나쁜 + -graph 쓰다 → '추하게 쓰다'
유의어	Bad handwriting, illegible script, scrawl, scribble, chicken scratch
반의어	Neat handwriting, calligraphy, penmanship, legible script, cursive
영영	bad handwriting or spelling
예문	Cacography is deliberate comic misspelling or bad handwriting. Cacography는 웃기기 위한 미스스펠링이나 읽기 어려운 손 글씨이다.

7

school supplies

[səplái]

p. 학용품

supply v. 공급하다
take a supplement p. 영양제를 복용하다

어원	-school 학교 + -supply 공급 물품 → '학교 생활을 위한 공급 물품이 학용품'
유의어	Educational materials, student tools, learning necessities, classroom essentials
반의어	Leisure items, entertainment tools, toys, hobbies
영영	materials used in schools, such as books, pens, pencils, and notebooks
예문	The store has a wide selection of school supplies for students of all ages. 그 가게에는 모든 연령대의 학생들을 위한 다양한 학교 용품이 있어요.

8

detente

[deitά:nt]

n. 긴장 완화

n. tension 긴장
n. hypertension 고혈압

어원	-de : down + -ten, -tent : tense 긴장 → '긴장을 낮추니 긴장 완화'
유의어	Relaxation of tension, easing of hostilities, truce, ceasefire, thaw
반의어	Escalation, conflict, war, hostility, aggression
영영	the easing of hostility or strained relations, especially between countries
예문	The detente between the two countries has led to increased trade and cooperation. 두 나라 간의 긴장 완화로 무역과 협력이 증가했습니다.

9

reprimand

[réprəmænd]

v. 비난하다, 질책하다

print n. 인쇄
reprimand for n. ~때문에 질책하다
reprimander n. 견책자
reprimandingly adv. 견책하면서, 견책하듯

어원	-re : again + -prim, -prin : press (F) → '계속해서 누르며 비난하다'
유의어	Rebuke, scold, lecture, criticize, admonish
반의어	Praise, commend, compliment, encourage, applaud
영영	a rebuke, especially an official one
예문	The teacher had to reprimand the student for talking during class. 선생님은 수업 중에 말하는 학생을 질책해야 했습니다.

10

frugal

['fru:.gəl]

a. 절약하는, 검소한

fruitful a. 생산적인, 수확이 많은
fulfill v. 이행하다, 충족하다

어원	-fruit 열매, 결실 → '긍정적 결실을 위해 지금 절약하는'
유의어	Thrifty, economical, mindful, saving, budget-conscious
반의어	Extravagant, wasteful, spendthrift, lavish, impulsive
영영	sparing or economical with regard to money or food
예문	The restaurant offers a frugal menu for those on a budget. 식당은 예산이 부족한 사람들을 위해 검소한 메뉴를 제공합니다.

11

affluent

['æf.lu.ənt]

a. 풍부한

fluent a. 유창한
affluently adv. 부유하게
affluential n. 막대한 부의 영향력을 가진 사람
maffluent n. 주식 부호들

어원	-af : to + -flu : flow → '~에 흘러 넘치니 풍부한'
유의어	Wealthy, rich, prosperous, well-off, abundant
반의어	Poor, impoverished, destitute, needy, lacking
영영	having a great deal of money; wealthy
예문	The affluent neighborhood was filled with mansions and luxury cars. 부유한 동네는 맨션과 고급 자동차로 가득 차 있었습니다.

12

the masses

p. 대중

mass n. 질량
massive a. 거대한
maximize v. 최대화하다
maximum n. 최대

어원	-mass 덩어리 → '덩어리처럼 뭉쳐 있는 대중'
유의어	Crowd, people, common folk, general public, population
반의어	Elite, aristocracy, privileged few, upper class, leaders
영영	the ordinary people; the common people
예문	The masses were excited about the new movie. 대중들은 새로운 영화에 대해 흥분했습니다.

13	어원	-ti, -tig, -ting, -tag, -tac, -tan, -ten : touch + -full → '손만 대면 일이 해결되는 능력이 가득하니 재치있는
tactful	유의어	Diplomatic, sensitive, considerate, discerning, discreet
	반의어	Blunt, insensitive, rude, tactless, abrasive
[ˈtækt.fəl]	영영	having or showing tact; diplomatic
a. 재치있는		
tactile a. 촉각의	예문	He gave a tactful response to the criticism. 그는 비판에 재치 있는 답변을 내놨습니다.

14	어원	-contra : against + -ven : come → '반대 방향에서 오니 위반'
contravene	유의어	Violate, disobey, transgress, break, defy
	반의어	Abide by, comply with, respect, obey, conform
[ˌkɒn.trəˈviːn]	영영	violate the prohibition or order of (a law, treaty, or code of conduct)
v. 반대하다; 위반하다		
contradict v. 반박하다 contrast n. 대조, 대비	예문	The company's actions contravened the regulations. 그 회사의 행동은 규정을 위반했습니다.

15	어원	-al, -alien, -alter, altru : other 다른(L) + -sm 사상 → '다른 이를 먼저 생각하는 사상이 이타주의'
altruism	유의어	Selflessness, generosity, kindness, compassion, empathy
	반의어	Selfishness, egoism, greed, indifference, cruelty
[ˈæl.tru.ɪ.zəm]	영영	the belief in or practice of disinterested and selfless concern for the well-being of others
n. 이타주의, 이타심		
altruistic a. 이타적인 altruistically adv. 이타적으로 alternative n. 대안, 양자택일 alter v. 바꾸다, 변경하다	예문	She had to alter some of her plans. 그녀는 그녀의 계획의 일부를 변경해야만 했다.

16	어원	-van, -vain, -void, -vac : empty 빈
void	유의어	Empty, hollow, vacant, null, invalid
	반의어	Full, occupied, filled, valid, substantial
[vɔɪd]	영영	not valid or legally binding
a. 텅 빈 / n. 공간		
voided a. 공백이 된, 무효가 된 voidable a. 무효로 할 수 있는, 비울 수 있는 devoid a. ~이 빠진, 전혀 없는 vacant a. 빈 자리의	예문	He felt a void in his life after his wife passed away. 아내가 세상을 떠난 후 그는 삶에 공허함을 느꼈습니다.

17	어원	-sub : under + -optim 최고 → '최고의 아래니 차선의'
suboptimal	유의어	Less than ideal, not the best, substandard, mediocre, inferior
	반의어	Optimal, excellent, ideal, superior, top-notch
[sʌbɑ́ptəməl]	영영	less than optimal; not as effective or efficient as possible
a. 차선의		
optimistic a. 낙관적인 pessimistic a. 비관적인	예문	The results were suboptimal due to poor planning. 잘못된 계획으로 인해 결과가 차선책이었습니다.

18	어원	-ap : on + -pend, -pen : attach or hang → '~에 덧붙이니 추가하다'
append	유의어	Add, attach, join, affix, supplement
	반의어	Remove, detach, separate, disconnect, subtract
[əˈpend]	영영	add (something) to the end of a written document
v. 덧붙이다, 추가하다		
n. appendix 부록; 맹장 n. appendage 첨가물, 부속물, 종속물 a. appendant 부수하는, 부대적인; 부속물 v. depend 의존하다 / n. pendulum 진자	예문	He appended his name to the list of attendees. 그는 참석자 명단에 이름을 추가했습니다.

19

heterosexual

[ˌhet.ər.əˈsek.ʃu.əl]

a. 이성애의

heterodox n. 다른 생각; a. 이단의, 비전통의

어원	-hetero 다른 (G) + -sex 성 → '다른 성이니 이성애의' - homogeneous : 동질적(*-gen 낳다) / heterogeneous : 이질적(*-gen 낳다)
유의어	Straight
반의어	Homosexual, bisexual, lesbian, gay
영영	sexually attracted to people of the opposite sex
예문	I don't think he's heterosexually inclined. 나는 그가 이성애적인 경향이 있다고 생각하지 않는다.

20

herd

[hɜːd]

n. 무리, 떼

shepherd n. 양치기

어원	-herd 무리, 떼(같은 종)
유의어	Flock, group, crowd, swarm, pack, shoal, pride
반의어	Individual, lone, solitary, isolated, detached
영영	a large group of animals, especially hoofed mammals, that live, feed, or migrate together
예문	She pushed her way through a herd of lunchtime drinkers. 그녀는 점심 때 한잔 하러 나온 사람들 사이를 뚫고 앞으로 나갔다.

21

roam

[rəʊm]

v. 배회하다, 돌아다니다

road n. 길
roadbed n. 노면, 노상
rough a. 거친; 대충한, 개략적인
roughly adv. 대략

어원	-roa : road + -m : move → '길거리를 돌아다니다' * 휴대전화의 로밍 서비스를 생각
유의어	Wander, rove, travel, explore, drift
반의어	Stay put, settle down, fixate, anchor, remain
영영	move about or travel aimlessly or unsystematically, especially over a wide area
예문	The dogs roamed around the park. 개들이 공원을 돌아다니며 산책했습니다.

22

adorn

[əˈdɔːn]

v. 꾸미다, 장식하다

adornment n. 장식, 치장
adorable a. 사랑스러운
ornate a. 화려하게 장식한
ornament n. 장식품

어원	-ad : to + -orn 새 깃털; 꾸미다, 갖추다 → '컨셉에 맞춰 새 깃털처럼 화려하게 꾸미다'
유의어	Decorate, embellish, beautify, enhance, enrich
반의어	Strip, denude, simplify, impoverish, diminish
영영	decorate or add beauty to
예문	She adorned her room with flowers and pictures. 그녀는 방을 꽃과 그림으로 장식했습니다.

23

plumb

[plʌm]

n. 추 v. 재다; 납으로 봉하다

plumber n. 배관공
plumbum n. 납
plum n. 자두

어원	-plumb 끈에 매달린 납 덩어리 / 납 원소 기호 : Pb → '끈에 매달린 납 덩어리로 추로 측량하다' * plum 자두 처럼 생긴 납 덩어리
유의어	Measure, investigate, explore, delve into, examine
반의어	Ignore, overlook, neglect, dismiss, avoid
영영	measure the depth of (a body of water)
예문	He plumbed the depths of his emotions and found a new level of understanding. 그는 감정의 깊이를 탐구하고 새로운 이해의 수준을 찾았습니다.

24

lick

[lɪk]

v. 핥다

n. liberty 자유
n leisure 여가

어원	-lick : pass the tongue over 혀를 스치다 → '혀를 스치듯이 핥다' * lip 입술을 벌리고 혀로 핥다
유의어	Lap up, devour, consume, ingest, gulp down
반의어	Spit out, reject, refuse, discard, expel
영영	an act of licking something with the tongue
예문	The dog licked his owner's face in greeting. 개가 인사로 주인의 얼굴을 핥았습니다.

25	어원	-mo, -mot, -mob, -mop, -mut 이동하다, 움직이다(L) → '움직이며 배회하다'
mooch [muːtʃ] v. 배회하다, 살금살금 거닐다; 빌붙다 v. move 움직이다	규의어	Freeload, Scrounge, Sponge, Beg, Cadge, Borrow, Panhandle, Leach, Parasitize, Plead
	반의어	Pay, Contribute, Donate, Give, Offer, Provide, Purchase, Buy, Invest, Share
	영영	ask for or obtain (something) without paying for it
	예문	He mooched off his friends for food and money. 그는 친구들에게 음식과 돈을 얻어냈습니다.

26	어원	-real 진짜의 + -deal 거래 → '진짜 거래가 될만한 것'
the real deal n. 실질적인 것, 진짜 strike a deal p. 계약을 맺다 new deal p. 뉴딜 정책 deal in p. 장사하다 a great deal of p. 많은, 다량의	규의어	Authentic, genuine, legitimate, true, bona fide
	반의어	Fake, counterfeit, phony, imitation, impostor
	영영	the genuine or true quality of something
	예문	This is the real deal, not a fake or imitation. 이것은 가짜나 모방이 아닌 진짜입니다.

27	어원	-plum 자두 * plump 통통한(→ '통통한 자두가 맛있어')
plum [plʌm] n. 자두 plumb n. 추 plumbum n. 납	규의어	Prize, reward, benefit, jewel, advantage
	반의어	Dud, disadvantage, burden, liability, drawback
	영영	a fruit with a stone in the middle and juicy flesh surrounding it
	예문	The plum tree bore many ripe plums. 그 자두나무에는 많은 익은 자두가 열렸습니다.

28	어원	-tran, -trans : across + -gress : go → '담을 넘어가니 위반하다'
transgress [trænzˈgres] v. 넘다, 벗어나다; 위반하다, 어기다 transmit v. 전송하다 agresss v. 공격하다 transgression n. 위반, 죄 transgressive a. 위반하기 쉬운, 죄를 범하기 쉬운	규의어	Violate, disobey, break, defy
	반의어	Abide by, comply with, respect, obey, conform
	영영	infringe or go beyond the bounds of (a moral principle or other established standard of behavior)
	예문	He transgressed the boundaries of acceptable behavior. 그는 용납할 수 없는 행동의 경계를 넘었습니다.

29	어원	-mar : water + -in : in → '물 안에 담궈두는 행동이니 양념장에 재우다'
marinate [ˌmær.ɪˈneɪd] v. 양념장에 재워두다, 절이다 n. submarine 잠수함 n. marination 양념에 재우기 a. marinated 양념에 재운, 절인	유의어	Soak, steep, infuse, imbue
	반의어	Dehydrate, dry out, parch, desiccate, wither
	영영	soak (meat, fish, or other food) in a marinade
	예문	The meat was marinated in a mixture of oil and vinegar. 고기는 기름과 식초 혼합물에 절여졌습니다.

30	어원	-e : out + -rod 갉아먹다 → '표면 밖으로 갉아내니 침식'
erode [ɪˈroʊd] v. 침식하다 v. corrode 부식하다 a. rodent 설치류의 n. erosion 침식	유의어	Wear away, crumble, decay, disintegrate, deteriorate
	반의어	Build up, strengthen, solidify, solidify, reinforce
	영영	gradually wear away (soil, rock, or land)
	예문	The constant flow of water caused the riverbank to erode over time. 물의 지속적인 흐름으로 인해 시간이 지남에 따라 강둑이 침식되었습니다.

31

take up

p. ~을 맡다

take up the issue p. 그 문제를 상정하다
take the side of p. ~의 편을 들다
be taken back p. 당황하다, 허를 찌르다

어휘	-take 취해서 up -끝까지 맡다
유의어	Occupy, engage, absorb, engross, enrapture
반의어	Leave, release, vacate, abandon, relinquish
영영	begin to study, practice, or do (a hobby or activity)
예문	She decided to take up the offer and start working for the company. 그녀는 제안을 받아들이고 회사에서 일하기로 결정했습니다.

32

serve to do

p. ~하는 데 도움이 되다

serve in the ranks p. 사병으로 복무하다
serve as p. ~의 역할을 하다
servant n. 하인, 부하, 공무원
servile a. 노예의, 비굴한

어원	-serv, -serve : keep 지키다, 보호하다 → '지키고 있으니 일을 하는 데 도움이 되다'
유의어	Facilitate, enable, assist, help, promote
반의어	Hinder, impede, obstruct, prevent, thwart
영영	contribute to or promote the accomplishment of a purpose
예문	The purpose of this meeting is to serve to do our best to achieve our goals. 이 회의의 목적은 우리의 목표를 달성하기 위해 최선을 다하는 것입니다.

33

slip away

p. 사라지다, 없어지다

slippery a. 미끄러운
slog v. 힘겹게 나아가다
sleeve n. 소매, 소맷자락
slant n. 경사, 비탈

어휘	-sli, -sla, -slo, -sle : sled + -away → '미끄러져 멀리 사라지다'
유의어	Disappear, vanish, fade away, elude, escape
반의어	Appear, emerge, come into view, materialize, materialize
영영	leave furtively or unnoticed
예문	He slipped away from the party without saying goodbye. 그는 인사도 하지 않고 파티에서 슬그머니 빠져나왔습니다.

34

make A a regular habit

p. A하는 습관을 들이다

make the point that p. ~이라는 주장을 하다
make a change p. 변경사항을 만들다
make a correction p. 수정하다
make up p. ~을 꾸며내다

어원	-make 만들다 + -regular habit 규칙적인 습관 → 'A라는 규칙적 습관을 만들다'
유의어	Establish a routine, Cultivate a habit, Form a regular practice
반의어	Break a habit, Abandon a routine, Discontinue a practice
영영	to incorporate an activity into your routine, doing it consistently and repeatedly.
예문	The feeling also grows when you make giving a regular habit, regardless of the size of the contributions. 당신이 주는 것을 정기적인 습관으로 하면 기부의 규모에 상관없이, 그러한 기분은 또한 커진다.

35

opposed to N

p. ~에 반대하는

opposing a. 마주보는
as opposed to p. ~과는 대조적으로
opponent n. 상대, 적
depot n. 저장소; 정거장

어원	-op, -ob : against + -pon, -pos : place → '반대편에 서서 마주보는'
유의어	Against, contrary to, at odds with, inconsistent with, incompatible with
반의어	In agreement with, consistent with, compatible with, in harmony with
영영	in conflict or disagreement with
예문	He is opposed to the idea of nuclear weapons. 그는 핵무기의 개념에 반대합니다.

36

at a 형 pace

p. ~한 속도로

at a 형 speed p. ~한 속도로
at a 형 price p. ~한 가격으로
at a 형 charge of p. ~의 비용 부담으로
at a discount p. 할인하여

어휘	-at 점 + -pace 속도 → '지정한 속도로'
유의어	At a 형 rate, 형 quickly, 형 swiftly, 형 rapidly, 형 speedily
반의어	At a 형 slow pace, 형 slowly, 형 sluggishly, 형 lazily, 형 leisurely
영영	at a certain speed or rate
예문	The car rat at a good pace. 차는 상당한 속도로 달렸다.

37

at one time

p. 한꺼번에, 동시에; 일찍이, 한 때

all the time p. 항상
by the time p. ~할 즈음에
all the same time p. 동시에
in the nick of time p. 아슬아슬하게 맞춰

어원	-at 지점 + -one + -time → '한 지점 한 시간에 모이니 한꺼번에'
유의어	Formerly, previously, once upon a time, in the past, in days gone by
반의어	Now, currently, presently, contemporaneously, contemporaneously
영영	at some point in the past
예문	At one time, many men wanted to date me. 한때는 남자들을 꽤 좇아오던 시절이 있었지요.

38

be detached from

p. ~에서 분리되다

detachment n. 분리, 탈착
attachment n. 부착

어원	-de : away + -tach, -tak 말뚝, 막대; 들러붙게 하다 → '말뚝에서 멀리 분리하다'
유의어	Be independent of, be separate from, be disconnected from, be dissociated from, be isolated from
반의어	Be connected to, be related to, be associated with, be affiliated with, be joined to
영영	not emotionally involved or connected
예문	He is detached from the world and lives in his own world. 그는 세상과 단절되어 자신만의 세계에서 살고 있습니다.

39

take place

p. 일어나다, 발생하다

take over p. 넘겨 받다; 장악하다
take possession of p. ~을 점유하다
take sides p. 편을 들다
take the liverty to do p. 실례를 무릅쓰고 ~하다

어원	-take 취하다 + -place 장소 → '장소에서 사건을 취하니 일이 발생'
유의어	Happen, occur, materialize, transpire, come to pass
반의어	not happen, not occur, not materialize, not transpire, not come to pass
영영	occur; happen
예문	The concert will take place next week. 콘서트는 다음 주에 열릴 예정입니다.

40

take leave

p. 작별을 고하다

take over p. 넘겨 받다; 장악하다
take initiative p. 주도권을 잡다
take sides p. 편을 들다
take on p. ~을 취하다, ~을 태우다

어원	-take 취하다 + -leave 떠나다 → '떠남을 취하니 작별을 고하다'
유의어	Depart, leave, go away, say goodbye, bid farewell
반의어	Arrive, come, reach, show up, appear
영영	go away or depart, especially permanently
예문	With a nod and a smile, she took leave of her friends. 고개를 끄덕이고 미소를 지으며, 그녀가 친구들에게 작별을 고했다.

Chapter 2.

41	rivulet	[rívjulit]	n. 시내, 개울
42	raze	[reɪz]	v. 완전히 파괴하다
43	relinquish	[rɪˈlɪŋ.kwɪʃ]	v. 포기하다, 양도하다, 단념하다
44	luster	[lʌstər]	n. 광택
45	enjoin	[ɪnˈdʒɔɪn]	v. ~에게 명령하다; 금하다
46	barley	[ˈbɑː.li]	n. 보리
47	garment	[ˈgɑː.mənt]	n. 의류, 옷가지
48	tease	[tiːz]	v. 놀리다, 못살게 굴다
49	natal	[ˈneɪ.təl]	a. 태어난 (고향의), 출생의
50	tangible	[ˈtæn.dʒə.bəl]	a. 만질 수 있는, 유형의
51	deceive	[disíːv]	v. 속이다, 기만하다
52	subtle	[ˈsʌt.əl]	a. 미묘한, 감지하기 힘든, 교묘한
53	notwithstanding	[ˌnɒt.wɪðˈstæn.dɪŋ]	c. ~에도 불구하고
54	grievance	[ˈgriː.vəns]	n. 불만
55	mirage	[mɪˈrɑːʒ]	n. 신기루
56	sojourn	[ˈsɒdʒ.ɜːn]	v. 묵다, 체류하다
57	carnivore	[ˈkɑː.nɪ.vɔːr]	n. 육식동물
58	odometer	[əʊˈdɒm.ɪ.tər]	n. 주행기록장치
59	quantum physics		n. 양자 물리학
60	kin	[kin]	n. 친척, 친족; 친족인
61	contour	[ˈkɒn.tɔːr]	n. 윤곽, 외형; 지형선, 등고선
62	peculiar	[pɪˈkjuː.li.ər]	a. 특유의, 특이한
63	sage	[seɪdʒ]	n. 현자
64	ample	[ˈæm.pəl]	a. 충분한
65	archaeology	[ˌɑː.kiˈɒl.ə.dʒi]	n. 고고학
66	aspirator	[ǽspərèitər]	n. 흡인기
67	imperative	[ɪmˈper.ə.tɪv]	a. 반드시 해야하는, 필수적인; 강제적인, 긴급한
68	theology	[θiˈɒl.ə.dʒi]	n. 신학
69	holocaust	[ˈhɒl.ə.kɔːst]	n. 대량학살
70	blunt	[blʌnt]	a. 무딘, 퉁명스러운
71	be skilled in		p. ~에 능숙한
72	make the point that		p. ~이라는 주장을 하다
73	take precaution		p. 조심하다
74	act as		p. ~역할을 하다, ~로 행동하다; ~로 작용하다
75	at home		p. 국내에서
76	control over		p. ~에 대한 통제력
77	move around		p. 이러저리 옮기다
78	venture into		p. ~로 과감히 들어가보다
79	aggressive to N		p. ~에게 공격적인
80	reaction to N		p. ~에 대한 반응

41	어원	-riv : river → '강으로 이어지는 시내나 개울'
	유의어	Stream, brook, creek
rivulet	반의어	Flood, deluge
[rívjulit]	영영	a small stream
n. 시내, 개울		
reverine a. 강변의 delive v. 비롯되다, 유래하다, 유도하다 delive from p. ~에서 유래하다 rival n. 경쟁, 경쟁자	예문	The water from the mountain flowed down as a small rivulet. 산에서 내려온 물은 작은 개울이 되어 흘렀다.
42	어원	-ras, -raz 긁어 내다 → '긁어내듯이 완전히 파괴하다'
	유의어	Demolish, destroy, level
raze	반의어	Build, construct, erect
[reɪz]	영영	to destroy completely
v. 완전히 파괴하다		
n. razor 면도기	예문	The old building was razed to the ground. 오래된 건물은 완전히 파괴되어 땅바닥에 주저앉았다.
43	어원	-re : back + -linqu : leave → '내 것을 뒤로 하고 떠나며 포기하다'
	유의어	Surrender, abandon, renounce
relinquish	반의어	Retain, keep, hold onto
[rɪˈlɪŋ.kwɪʃ]	영영	to give up something
v. 포기하다, 양도하다, 단념하다		
relinquishment n. 포기, 양도 relic n. 유물, 유적 delinquent a. 체납된, 연체된	예문	He decided to relinquish his position as a CEO. 그는 CEO 자리를 포기하기로 결정했다.
44	어원	-lucid : light → '빛이 나는 광택'
	유의어	Shine, brilliance, radiance
luster	반의어	Dullness, tarnish, dimness
[lʌstər]	영영	brightness or shine
n. 광택		
luxury n. 사치, 쾌락 deluxe a. 고급의	예문	The diamond had a beautiful luster. 그 다이아몬드는 아름다운 광채를 가지고 있었다.
45	어원	-en : on + -join, -junc, -junct 합치다(L) → '임무를 더해주는 것이니 명령하다' * join, junc(t) '서로 만나서 합침' VS ser(t) '밀어 넣어서 합침'
	유의어	Command, order, instruct
enjoin	반의어	Allow, permit, authorize
[ɪnˈdʒɔɪn]	영영	to order or command someone to do something
v. ~에게 명령하다; 금하다		
adjoin v. 인접하다 disjoint v. 해체하다	예문	The judge enjoined the jury to find the defendant guilty. 판사는 배심원들에게 피고가 유죄라고 판결하도록 명령했다.
46	어원	-bar : bere 보리(E) → '맥주의 원료인 보리'
	유의어	Grain, cereal, wheat
barley	반의어	None (Barley is a specific type of grain)
[ˈbɑː.li]	영영	a type of grain that is used to make beer and some breads
n. 보리		
n. beer 맥주 n. wheat 밀	예문	The farmer planted barley in the field. 농부는 밭에 보리를 심었다.

47

garment

[ˈɡɑː.mənt]

n. 의류, 옷가지

guard n. 경호원

어원	-gar : protect → '몸을 보호해 주는 옷'
유의어	Clothing, attire, apparel
반의어	Nakedness, undress
영영	an article of clothing
예문	She wore a beautiful garment for the party. 그녀는 파티를 위해 아름다운 옷을 입었다.

48

tease

[tiːz]

v. 놀리다, 못살게 굴다

어원	-tease 놀리다 → '놀리면서 못살게 굴다' * 티저(teaser) 영상 : 놀리듯이 살짝만 보여주는 영상
유의어	Taunt, provoke, mock
반의어	Please, compliment, praise
영영	to make fun of someone in a playful way
예문	He teased her about her hair color. 그는 그녀의 머리카락 색을 놀렸다.

49

natal

[ˈneɪ.təl]

a. 태어난 (고향의), 출생의

a. naïve 순진한
a. nasty 끔찍한, 고약한

어원	-na, -nat, -gna : born 낳다, 태어나다 → '태어난 고향의'
유의어	Birth, native, original
반의어	Postnatal, acquired, non-native
영영	relating to birth
예문	The natal home of the president is located in Seoul. 대통령의 생가가 서울에 위치해 있다.

50

tangible

[ˈtæn.dʒə.bəl]

a. 만질 수 있는, 유형의

a. tactile 촉각의
a. tactful 재치있는

어원	-ti, -tig, -ting, - tag, -tac, -tan, -ten : touch + -ible → '만질 수 있으니 유형의'
유의어	Concrete, palpable, real
반의어	Abstract, intangible, unreal
영영	able to be touched or perceived by the senses
예문	The tension between them was almost tangible. 그들 사이의 긴장이 거의 손에 만져질 것 같은 정도였다.

51

deceive

[dɪsíːv]

v. 속이다, 기만하다

v. receive 받다, 수신하다
v. preconceive 선입견을 가지다
n. deception 속임수

어원	-de : away + -ceive : take → 'take away 빼앗으려고 속이다' * 디셉티콘 : 영화 '트랜스포머'에서 나쁜 무리의 우두머리'
유의어	Mislead, trick, cheat
반의어	Inform, clarify, reveal
영영	to trick or mislead someone
예문	The tangible evidence of the crime was found in the room. 범죄의 실체적인 증거가 방에서 발견되었다.

52

subtle

[ˈsʌt.əl]

a. 미묘한, 감지하기 힘든, 교묘한

subtly adv. 미묘하게
subtilize v. 미세하게 만들다
little a. 작은
brittle a. 부서지기 쉬운

어원	-sub : under + -tle 직물, 실 → '가치가 떨어지는 얇은 실로 짜서 알아차리기 어려운 미묘함'
유의어	Crafty, elusive, delicate
반의어	Obvious, blatant, overt
영영	difficult to notice or understand
예문	The subtle difference between the two colors was difficult to notice. 두 색의 미묘한 차이를 알아차리기 어려웠다.

53

notwithstanding

[ˌnɒt.wɪðˈstæn.dɪŋ]

c. ~에도 불구하고

어원	-not + -with + -standing → '함께 서 있음에도 불구하고 안 되는'
유의어	Nevertheless, nonetheless, despite
반의어	Therefore, hence, thus
영영	in spite of
예문	Notwithstanding the rain, the concert went on as planned. 비에도 불구하고 콘서트는 계획대로 진행되었다.

54

grievance

[ˈɡriː.vəns]

n. 불만

gravity n. 중력; 진지함
grief n. 슬픔

어원	-grav, -griev : heavy 무거움; 고통 → '고통 때문에 생긴 불만'
유의어	Complaint, grievance, resentment
반의어	Satisfaction, contentment, approval
영영	a complaint or problem
예문	The employees expressed their grievances to the management. 직원들은 경영진에게 불만을 표현했다.

55

mirage

[mɪˈrɑːʒ]

n. 신기루

mirror n. 거울
admire v. 존경하다

어원	-mir 보다 → '불투명한 대기로 인해 거울 이미지가 보이는 현상(G) * miracle 기적 같은 신기루
유의어	Illusion, hallucination, apparition
반의어	Reality, actuality, truth
영영	an illusion or something that appears to be something else
예문	The mirage of a waterfall appeared in the desert. 사막에서 폭포의 신기루가 나타났다.

56

sojourn

[ˈsɒdʒ.ɜːn]

v. 묵다, 체류하다

n. journey 여행
v. adjourn 휴회하다; 연기하다

어원	-so, -sub : under + -journ : day → '~ 아래서 며칠을 보내니 체류하다'
유의어	Stay, visit, stopover
반의어	Departure, journey, migration
영영	a temporary stay in a place
예문	His sojourn in my place was thankfully short. 나의 집에서 그의 체류는 고맙게도 짧았다.

57

carnivore

[ˈkɑː.nɪ.vɔːr]

n. 육식동물

carnival n. (브라질) 축제
carnation n. 카네이션, 담홍색
carnivorous 육식성의
carnage n. 살육, 대량 학살

어원	-carn, -caro : flesh 살, 고기; 피부; 과육 + -vore 먹다 → '고기를 먹는 육식동물'
유의어	Meat-eater, predator, carnivorous animal
반의어	Herbivore, vegetarian
영영	an animal that eats meat
예문	The lion is a carnivore that feeds on meat. 사자는 고기를 먹는 육식동물이다.

58

odometer

[əʊˈdɒm.ɪ.tər]

n. 주행기록장치

period n. 주기, 기간
exodus n. 탈출, 이주
anode n. 양극

어원	-od : hodos 길(G) + meter : measure 재다, 측정하다 → '길을 측정하는 것이니 주행기록장치'
유의어	Mileage counter, mileometer
반의어	None (Odometer typically does not have a direct opposite)
영영	a device that measures the distance a vehicle has traveled
예문	The odometer shows the distance your car travels. 거리측정기는 당신의 차가 얼마나 멀리 운행하였는지 보여준다.

59

quantum physics

n. 양자 물리학

quantity n. 양, 수량

어원	-quantum : how much + -physics 물리학 → '얼마나 많이 이산적으로 계산하는 양자 물리학'
유의어	None (Specific scientific field)
반의어	Classical physics
영영	the branch of physics that deals with the smallest particles and forces in nature
예문	Quantum physics is a branch of physics that deals with the behavior of matter and energy at the atomic and subatomic level. 양자 물리학은 원자와 아원자 수준에서 물질과 에너지의 행동을 다루는 물리학의 한 분야입니다.

60

kin

[kin]

n. 친척, 친족; 친족인

akin a. 친척의; 유사한
kinship n. 친족, 연대감
kindergarten n. 유치원, 유아원
kidnap v. 유괴하다, 납치하다

어원	-kin, -kind, -kid : birth → '한 집안에서 태어난 친척'
유의어	Family, relatives, kindred
반의어	Strangers, non-relatives
영영	family or relatives
예문	My kin are all living in the countryside. 나의 친척들은 모두 시골에서 살고 있다.

61

contour

[ˈkɒn.tɔːr]

n. 윤곽, 외형; 지형선, 등고선

tournament n. 토너먼트
detour n. 우회로

어원	-con : together + -tour, -torn : turn → '외곽을 돌며 그린 윤곽선이 지형선'
유의어	Outline, shape, form
반의어	Flatness, smoothness, featurelessness
영영	the outline of something
예문	The contour of the mountain was very clear in the morning mist. 아침 안개 속에서 산의 윤곽이 선명하게 보였다.

62

peculiar

[pɪˈkjuː.li.ər]

a. 특유의, 특이한

adv. peculiarly 특이하게
n. peculiarity 특이함

어원	-pecul, -pecun : particular person → '특별한 사람이나 집단에게'
유의어	Strange, unusual, unique
반의어	Common, ordinary, typical
영영	strange or unusual
예문	Isn't he peculiar? 그 사람 사차원 아냐?

63

sage

[seɪdʒ]

n. 현자

saint n. 성인
sabotage v. 파괴하다

어원	-sage : clarus 맑은 눈(L) → '맑은 눈을 가진 현자'
유의어	Wise, knowledgeable, judicious
반의어	Foolish, ignorant, naïve
영영	a wise person
예문	The old sage had many wise sayings. 그 노인은 많은 현명한 말을 했다.

64

ample

[ˈæm.pəl]

a. 충분한

amplify v. 증폭시키다

어원	-ampl : contain 담고 있다 → '담고 있는 것이 충분한' * 앰프 소리가 충분히 큰 / sample이 충분한
유의어	Abundant, plentiful, generous
반의어	Insufficient, inadequate, scant
영영	plenty of
예문	There was ample food for everyone at the party. 파티에는 모든 사람이 먹을 수 있는 충분한 음식이 있었다.

65

archaeology

[ˌɑːkiˈɒl.ə.dʒi]

n. 고고학

archaic a. 낡은, 오래된
archaeologist n. 고고학자

어원	-archae, -archaeo 오래된 (L) + -logy : logos 연구 → '오래된 것들을 연구하는 학문'
유의어	Antiquities, excavation, study of ancient cultures
반의어	Modern history, contemporary studies
영영	the study of past human cultures through their remains
예문	Archaeology is the study of ancient human societies. 고고학은 고대 인간 사회를 연구하는 것이다.

66

aspirator

[æspərèitər]

n. 흡인기

inspire v. 고무하다
expire v. 만기가 되다, 끝나다

어원	-a : against + -spire : breath + -or 것 → '숨을 반대로 흡입하는 것이 흡인기'
유의어	Suction device, vacuum pump
반의어	Blower, expeller
영영	a device that sucks up liquid or gas
예문	rchaeology is the study of human history through the excavation and analysis of artifacts. 고고학은 유물의 발굴과 분석을 통해 인간의 역사를 연구하는 학문이다.

67

imperative

[ɪmˈper.ə.tɪv]

a. 반드시 해야하는, 필수적인; 강제적인, 긴급한

prepare v. 준비하다
repair v. 수리하다

어원	-im : not + -pera : prepare → '준비할 새도 없이 긴급하니 반드시 해야하는'
유의어	Crucial, essential, necessary
반의어	Optional, unnecessary, dispensable
영영	essential or necessary
예문	It is imperative to follow the safety guidelines while working with chemicals. 화학물질을 다룰 때는 안전 지침을 따르는 것이 필수적이다.

68

theology

[θiˈɒl.ə.dʒi]

n. 신학

theism n. 신론
atheism n. 무신론
theologian n. 신학자

어원	-theo, -thus : god+ -logos 연구 → '신을 연구하는 학문'
유의어	Religious studies, divinity, philosophy of religion
반의어	Atheism, secularism
영영	the study of God and religion
예문	Theology is the study of God and religion. 신학은 신과 종교를 연구하는 학문이다.

69

holocaust

[ˈhɒl.ə.kɔːst]

n. 대량학살

holistic a. 전체론적인, 종합적인
caustic a. 부식성의

어원	-hol : whole 전체 (G) + -cause 태우다 → '동물을 통째로 불에 태워 신에게 바치는 유대인 의식' → '2차 세계대전을 거치면서 독일의 유대인 대학살을 지칭'
유의어	Genocide, mass destruction, annihilation
반의어	Salvation, preservation, rescue
영영	the destruction of a large group of people, especially Jews by the Nazis
예문	The holocaust of World War II was one of the darkest moments in human history. 제2차 세계대전의 홀로코스트는 인류 역사상 가장 어두운 순간 중 하나였다.

70

blunt

[blʌnt]

a. 무딘, 퉁명스러운

blunder n. 실수 v. 실수하다
blur a. 흐릿한

어원	-blunt : blind 눈이 먼 → '눈이 먼 것처럼 상대를 안 하니 무딘'
유의어	Dull, obtuse, straightforward
반의어	Sharp, pointed, keen
영영	direct and to the point, sometimes in a rude way
예문	The knife was too blunt to cut the bread. 칼이 너무 무뎌서 빵을 자를 수 없었다.

71	어원	-skill 기술 + -in → '기술이 내재해 있으니 능숙한'
be skilled in	유의어	Excel in, master, proficient in
	반의어	Inexperienced in, unskilled in, inept in
p. ~에 능숙한	영영	to be good at something
	예문	She is skilled in playing the guitar. 그녀는 기타 연주에 능숙하다.

72	어원	-make 만들다 + -point → '포인트를 만들어 주장하다'
make the point that	유의어	Emphasize, assert, argue
	반의어	Minimize, downplay, ignore
p. ~이라는 주장을 하다	영영	to emphasize something
make a change p. 변경사항을 만들다 make a correction p. 수정하다 make up p. ~을 꾸며내다 make A a regular habit p. A하는 습관을 들이다	예문	He made the point that hard work is necessary for success. 그는 성공을 위해서는 노력이 필요하다는 것을 강조했다.

73	어원	-take 취하다 + -precaution 예방책 → '예방책을 취하니 조심하다'
take precaution	유의어	Be cautious, be careful, take care
	반의어	Be reckless, be incautious, ignore precautions
p. 조심하다	영영	to be careful
	예문	It is important to take precaution when driving in bad weather. 악천후에 운전할 때는 예방 조치를 취하는 것이 중요하다.

74	어원	-ac, -act, -ag, -ig : do 행하다, act 작용하다, drive 몰다(L) → 'as 이하로서 행동하다'
act as	유의어	Serve as, function as, play the role of
	반의어	Cease to be, stop being
p. ~역할을 하다, ~로 행동하다; ~로 작용하다	영영	to behave in a particular way
action n. 활동, 움직임	예문	She was asked to act as the spokesperson for the company. 그녀는 회사의 대변인 역할을 하도록 요청받았다.

75	어원	-home 집 → '집이 있는 국내에서'
at home	유의어	Comfortable, familiar, adept
	반의어	Uncomfortable, unfamiliar, inept
p. 국내에서	영영	comfortable and relaxed
homegrown a. 토착의, 국내의 homemaker n. (전업) 주부 come home to p. 가슴에 뼈저리게 사무치다	예문	I feel at home when I am with my family. 나는 가족과 함께 있을 때 편안함을 느낀다.

76	어원	-cont : counter 반대 + -rot, -rol : roll (L) → '구르던 것을 반대로 굴려 통제하다'
control over	유의어	Authority over, command, mastery
	반의어	Lack of control, powerlessness, submission
p. ~에 대한 통제력	영영	the ability to make decisions about something
	예문	The company has control over the production of the product. 회사는 제품 생산에 대한 통제권을 가지고 있다.

77	어원	-mo, -mot, -mob, -mop, -mut : move(L) + -around → '주변으로 이리저리 옮기다'
move around	유의어	Wander, roam, travel
	반의어	Stay still, remain stationary, settle
p. 이러저리 옮기다	영영	to go from one place to another.
	예문	It might fit in the living room if we move some furniture around. 몇몇 가구를 일저리 옮긴다면 거실에 맞을지도 몰라요.

78	어원	-vent : come + -into → '내게 오는 모험에 과감히 들어가보다' * adventure 위험X VS venture 위험 O
venture into	유의어	Explore, embark on, delve into
	반의어	Avoid, retreat from, shun
p. ~로 과감히 들어가보다	영영	to go somewhere that is dangerous or unknown
	예문	He ventured into the unknown territory with a map and a compass. 그는 지도와 나침반을 가지고 미지의 영토에 모험을 걸었다.

79	어원	-ag : to + -gress 올라가다, 단계 → '단계를 올라가기 위해 공격적인'
aggressive to N	유의어	Hostile to, confrontational, belligerent toward
	반의어	Friendly to, amicable toward, peaceful toward
p. ~에게 공격적인 non-aggressive a. 공격적이지 않은 aggression n. 공격, 공격성 aggresiveness n. 적극성, 진취 regress v. 후퇴하다	영영	likely to attack or harm someone
	예문	The dog was aggressive to strangers. 그 개는 낯선 사람들에게 공격적이었다.

80	어원	-re : back + -act + -to → '행동으로 돌려주니 반응하다'
reaction to N	유의어	Response to, feedback on, reply to
	반의어	Nonreaction to, indifference to, lack of response to
p. ~에 대한 반응	영영	the way someone responds to something
	예문	The reaction to the new product was very positive. 새로운 제품에 대한 반응은 매우 긍정적이었다.

Chapter 3.

81	allure	[əlúər]	v. 유혹하다, 매혹하다
82	adjoin	[əˈdʒɔɪn]	v. 붙어 있다, 인접하다
83	incidence	[ˈɪn.sɪ.dəns]	n. 발생률, 빈도
84	tropic	[ˈtrɒp.ɪk]	n. 회귀선, 열대 지방 a. 열대 지방의
85	repulse	[rɪˈpʌls]	v. 퇴짜놓다, 거절하다
86	brace	[breɪs]	v. 떠받치다 n. 버팀목, 버팀대; 치아 교정기
87	mortify	[ˈmɔː.tɪ.faɪ]	v. 굴욕감을 주다, 몹시 당황하게 만들다
88	ranch	[rɑːntʃ]	n. 목장
89	gut	[gʌt]	n. 창자, 장 a. 본능적인, 근본적인
90	heterodox	[ˈhet.ər.ə.dɒks]	n. 다른 생각 a. 이단의, 비전통의
91	embed	[ɪmˈbed]	v. 꽂아 넣다, 깊이 박다
92	oath	[əʊθ]	n. 맹세, 서약, 선서; 욕설
93	acquit	[əˈkwɪt]	v. 석방하다, 무죄로 하다; 행동하다, 처신하다
94	intrude	[ɪnˈtruːd]	v. 강요하다; 간섭하다, 방해하다
95	spouse	[spaʊs]	n. 배우자
96	ingrain	[ingréin]	a. 깊이 배어든, 뿌리 깊은
97	congregate	[ˈkɒŋ.grɪ.geɪt]	v. 모이다, 집합시키다
98	casualty	[ˈkæʒ.ju.əl.ti]	n. 사상자, 피해자
99	memorabilia	[ˌmem.ər.əˈbɪl.i.ə]	n. 기념품
100	afflict	[əˈflɪkt]	v. 괴롭히다, 들볶다
101	humanitarian	[hjuːmænitέəriən]	n. 인도주의자 a. 인도주의적인, 인간애의
102	interdict	[ˈɪn.tə.dɪkt]	v. 금지하다, 제지하다
103	acrobat	[ˈæk.rə.bæt]	n. 곡예사, (정치적 의견, 주의 등의) 변절자
104	intermit	[ìntərmít]	v. 일시 멈추다, 중단되다
105	polarity	[pəˈlær.ə.ti]	n. 양극성, 상반되는 대립
106	impregnate	[imprégneit]	v. 임신시키다; 주입하다
107	behalf	[bihǽf]	n. 이익, 원조, 자기편; 지지
108	missionary	[ˈmɪʃ.ən.ri]	n. 전도사, 선교사
109	antebellum	[ˌæn.tiˈbel.əm]	a. 전쟁 전의
110	dullard	[ˈdʌl.əd]	n. 얼간이, 멍청이, 바보
111	at a glance		p. 한 눈에, 즉시
112	at pleasure		p. 하고 싶은 대로, 내키는 대로
113	take a supplement		p. 영양제를[알약을] 복용하다
114	admit to N		p. ~한 것을 인정하다
115	contribute to N		p. ~에 기여하다, ~의 원인이 되다
116	delegate A to B		p. A를 B에게 위임하다
117	lay off		p. ~을 해고하다
118	pin back		p. (고정핀으로) 뒤로 당겨서 묶다, 고정시키다
119	confer with		p. ~과 협의하다
120	bear with		p. ~을 견디다

81

allure

[əlúər]

v. 유혹하다, 매혹하다

어원	-al : to + -lure 미끼 → '미끼로 유혹하다'
유의어	Attraction, Charm, Appeal
반의어	Repel, Deter, Repulse
영영	to attract or tempt someone with something that seems exciting or desirable
예문	The scent of flowers allured the bees to the garden. 그 꽃의 향기는 벌들을 정원으로 유혹했다.

82

adjoin

[əˈdʒɔɪn]

v. 붙어 있다, 인접하다

joint n. 관절
disjoint v. 해체하다

어원	-ad : to + -join, -junc, -junct 합치다(L) → '~로 합치니 인접하여 붙어 있다' * join, junc(t) '서로 만나서 합침' VS ser(t) '밀어 넣어서 합침'
유의어	Border, Abut, Touch
반의어	Separate, Distance, Detach
영영	to be next to or connected to something
예문	The house adjoins the park. 그 집은 공원과 인접해 있다

83

incidence

[ˈɪn.sɪ.dəns]

n. 발생률, 빈도

incident n. 고의적 사건
accident n. 우연한 사건

어원	-in : on + -cid : fall + -ent 명접 → '근접해 떨어진 부수적인 사건의 발생률'
유의어	Occurrence, Frequency, Rate
반의어	Rarity, Infrequency, Absence
영영	the number of times something happens
예문	The incidence of cancer in the population is increasing. 인구의 암 발생률이 증가하고 있다

84

tropic

[ˈtrɒp.ɪk]

n. 회귀선, 열대 지방 a. 열대 지방의

tropical a. 회귀선의, 열대 지방의
subtropical a. 아열대의
heliotrope n. 해바라기

어원	-trop 돌아오다 → 지구의 반환점이 걸쳐 있어 태양빛을 가장 많이 받는 열대 지방' * 음료 트로피카나
유의어	Tropical, Equatorial, Torrid
반의어	Polar, Arctic, Frigid
영영	a region of the Earth near the equator where the sun is directly overhead at least once a year
예문	The tropic of Cancer is the imaginary line that circles the earth at its widest point. 북회귀선은 지구의 가장 넓은 지점을 따라 원을 그리는 가상의 선이다.

85

repulse

[rɪˈpʌls]

v. 퇴짜놓다, 거절하다

repulsive a. 혐오스러운, 불쾌한
repulsion n. 배척, 거부
pulse n. 맥박, 진동
repel v. 격퇴하다

어원	-re : again + -pu : push → '반대로 밀어내니 거절하다'
유의어	Rebuff, Reject, Drive away
반의어	Attract, Welcome, Accept
영영	to drive or force someone or something away
예문	The enemy was repulsed by our strong defense. 적은 우리의 강력한 방어에 의해 격퇴되었다.

86

brace

[breɪs]

v. 떠받치다 n. 버팀목, 버팀대; 치아 교정기

bracing a. 기운나는, 상쾌한
braces n. 구강 교정기
embrace v. 껴안다
bracelet n. 팔찌

어원	-brace 팔 → '팔을 지지하거나 고정하는 장치'
유의어	Support, Strengthen, Prop up
반의어	Weaken, Debilitate, Undermine
영영	to prepare or strengthen oneself for something difficult or unpleasant
예문	She put her arm around me and braced herself against the wind. 그녀는 내 팔을 두르고 바람에 대비해 몸을 지탱했다.

87

mortify

[ˈmɔːtɪfaɪ]

v. 굴욕감을 주다, 몹시 당황하게 만들다

mortification n. 수치심, 굴욕감
mortifying a. 창피한, 굴욕적인
mortal a. 죽을 운명인, 치명적인
immortal a. 불멸의, 죽지 않는

어원	-mort : death + -fy : make → '죽을 결심을 할 정도로 굴욕감을 주다'
유의어	Humiliate, Embarrass, Shame
반의어	Praise, Encourage, Applaud
영영	to cause someone to feel ashamed or humiliated
예문	He was mortified when he realized he had made a mistake. 그는 실수를 했다는 것을 깨닫고 굴욕감을 느꼈다.

88

ranch

[rɑːntʃ]

n. 목장

rancher n. 목축업자, 목장주
ranching n. 목축업, 목작경영
ranchland n. 목장 지역, 목초지
wrangler n. 목장 일꾼, 마구간 일꾼

어원	-ranch : range → '범위 내에서 가축을 기르는 목장'
유의어	Farm, Plantation, Estate
반의어	Urbanize, Develop, City
영영	a large farm where cattle, horses, or other livestock are raised
예문	The family runs a large cattle ranch in the countryside. 그 가족은 시골에서 큰 소 목장을 운영한다

89

gut

[gʌt]

n. 창자, 장 a. 본능적인, 근본적인

guts n. 배짱, 용기
gutless a. 소심한, 용기 없는
gutted a. 내부가 파괴된, 갈아엎힌
engulf v. 삼켜버리다

어원	-guz 배 → '배 내장물이 gut' * the large gut 대장, the small gut 소장, the blind gut 맹장, gut feeling 직감
유의어	Empty, Clean out, Eviscerate
반의어	Fill, Stock, Preserve
영영	the digestive system of a person or animal
예문	The fire destroyed the entire building, leaving only the gutted remains. 화재는 건물 전체를 파괴하고, 내부가 파괴된 잔해만 남겼다.

90

heterodox

[ˈhet.ər.ə.dɒks]

n. 다른 생각 a. 이단의, 비전통의

paradox n. 역설, 모순
heterosexual a. 이성애의
heterodoxy n. 이단, 이교
heterodoxical a. 이단적인, 이교의

어원	-hetero 다른 (G) + -dox 의견 → '다른 의견을 내니 다른 생각'
유의어	Unorthodox, Heretical, Dissenting
반의어	Orthodox, Conventional, Traditional
영영	not in agreement with the generally accepted beliefs or opinions of a particular group or society
예문	His opinion is distinctly heterodox. 그의 의견은 특유하게 다른 의견이다.

91

embed

[ɪmˈbed]

v. 꽂아 넣다, 깊이 박다

embedded a. 내장된, 포함된
embedding n. 내장, 포함
embedment n. 내장, 포함
embolden v. 격려하다

어원	-em, -en : in + -bed 놓다 → '안에 깊숙히 꽂아 넣다'
유의어	Imbed, Implant, Encase
반의어	Extract, Remove, Detach
영영	to insert or incorporate something into something else
예문	The soldiers were ordered to embed themselves in the local community. 군인들은 현지 주민들과 동화되도록 명령받았다.

92

oath

[oʊθ]

n. 맹세, 서약, 선서; 욕설

oathbound a. 맹세한, 서약으로 묶인
oathbreaker n. 맹세를 어기는 사람
oathkeeping n. 맹세 지키기, 서약 준수하기
oathspeaker n. 맹세하는 사람

어원	-oath : swear → '맹세하는 서약'
유의어	Pledge, Vow, Promise
반의어	Denial, Refusal, Renunciation
영영	a solemn promise or declaration
예문	The judge administered an oath to the witnesses before they testified. 판사는 증인들이 증언하기 전에 선서를 하도록 했다.

93

acquit

[əˈkwɪt]

v. 석방하다, 무죄로 하다; 행동하다, 처신하다

acquisition n. 획득, 습득
acquittal n. 무죄 선고, 석방
acquitted a. 무죄인, 석방된

어원	-ac : to + -quit : free → '죄를 끝내고 자유롭게 해주다'
유의어	Absolve, Clear, Exonerate
반의어	Convict, Condemn, Blame
영영	to declare someone not guilty of a crime
예문	The jury acquitted the defendant of all charges. 배심원단은 피고에게 모든 혐의에 대해 무죄를 선고했다.

94

intrude

[ɪnˈtruːd]

v. 강요하다; 간섭하다, 방해하다

v. introduce 소개하다
v. protrude 내밀다, 튀어나오다
n. intruder 방해자, 침입자

어원	-in : in + -trud : thrust → '안에다 억지로 밀어넣어 방해하다'
유의어	Invade, Encroach, Trespass
반의어	Retreat, Withdraw, Avoid
영영	to come into a place or situation without being invited or wanted
예문	The guests were asked not to intrude on the couple's privacy during their honeymoon. 손님들은 신혼여행 동안 부부의 사생활을 침해하지 않도록 부탁받았다.

95

spouse

[spaʊs]

n. 배우자

espouse v. 지지하다, 옹호하다
spousal a. 배우자의, 결혼의
spouseless a. 배우자가 없는

어원	-spond, -spon : promise 약속하다 → '미래를 약속한 배우자'
유의어	Partner, Husband/Wife, Mate
반의어	Single, Solo, Bachelor/Bachelorette
영영	a person's husband or wife
예문	The couple have been married for 30 years and are still deeply in love with each other and their spouse. 이 부부는 결혼한 지 30년이 지났지만 여전히 서로와 배우자를 깊이 사랑하고 있다.

96

ingrain

[ingréin]

a. 깊이 배어든, 뿌리 깊은

ingrained a. 깊이 배어든
grain n. 낱알, 곡물
granola n. 그래놀라

어원	-in 안 + -grain, -gran : seed 알갱이 → '씨 뿌린 곳 뿌리까지 깊이 배어든'
유의어	Imprint, Instill, Infuse
반의어	Erase, Remove, Eliminate
영영	to make something a permanent part of something else
예문	The habit of saving money is ingrained in her character. 저축하는 습관은 그녀의 성격에 깊이 배어 있다.

97

congregate

[ˈkɒn.grɪ.geɪt]

v. 모이다, 집합시키다

n. congregation 교회 회중, 집회
a. congregational 교회 회중의, 의회의
n. congregationalism (미국의) 개혁파 교회 철학
n. aggregation 집합

어원	-con : together + -greg : flock 무리; 모이다 → '함께 몰려들다'
유의어	Assemble, Gather, Collect
반의어	Disperse, Scatter, Separate
영영	to come together in a group
예문	The people congregated in the square to watch the parade. 사람들은 퍼레이드를 보기 위해 광장에 모였다.

98

casualty

[ˈkæʒ.ju.əl.ti]

n. 사상자, 피해자

a. casual 무심한, 건성의
n. causality 인과 관계

어원	-cas : fall → '포탄이 떨어져 생긴 피해자나 사상자'
유의어	Victim, Fatality, Loss
반의어	Survivor, Escaper, Unharmed
영영	a person who is killed or injured in an accident, war, or other disaster
예문	The accident resulted in several casualties. 그 사고로 여러 명의 사상자가 발생했다.

99

memorabilia

[ˌmem.ər.əˈbɪl.i.ə]

n. 기념품

Memorial day p. 현충일
memoir n. 회고록
commemorate v. 기념하다
immemorial a. 기억에 없는, 옛날의

어원	-memor 기억(L) + -able + -a 명접 → '추억을 기억하도록 만든 기념품' * 메노신Memnosyne(로마) : 가이아(gaia)와 우라노스(Uranus)의 딸로 기억의 여신
유의어	Souvenirs, Mementos, Reminiscences
반의어	Forgettable items, Disposable items
영영	objects or items that are kept as reminders of something
예문	The baseball player autographed a ball for his fans and sold it along with other memorabilia. 그 야구 선수는 팬들에게 공에 사인을 해주고 다른 기념품과 함께 팔았다.

100

afflict

[əˈflɪkt]

v. 괴롭히다, 들볶다

affliction n. 고통, 고통의 원인
afflicted a. 괴로워하는, 고통받는
afflictive a. 괴로운, 고통스러운
conflict n. 갈등, 충돌

어원	-af : to + -flic, -flict : strike 때리다 → '~쪽으로 가 때리며 괴롭히다'
유의어	Torment, Trouble, Suffer
반의어	Comfort, Console, Soothe
영영	to cause someone to suffer or experience pain or distress
예문	The disease afflicts many people in the region. 그 질병은 그 지역의 많은 사람들에게 고통을 주고 있다.

101

humanitarian

[hjuːmænitέəriən]

n. 인도주의자 a. 인도주의적인, 인간애의

humanism n. 인간 중심주의, 인문주의
humanize v. 인간화하다
humanity n. 인류, 인간애
humanly a. 인간적으로

어원	-human 사람 + -nitar : nature + -ian 사람 → '인간의 본성을 사랑하는 사람이니 인도주의자'
유의어	Philanthropic, Charitable, Altruistic
반의어	Selfish, Inhuman, Uncharitable
영영	relating to or concerned with human welfare
예문	The humanitarian organization is working to provide aid to refugees 인도주의 단체는 난민들에게 원조를 제공하기 위해 노력하고 있습니다

102

interdict

[ˈɪn.tə.dɪkt]

v. 금지하다, 제지하다

n. interdiction 금지, 차단, 방지
n. interdictor 금지하는 사람
n. interdental 이음, 이음소리
n. jurisdiction 재판권; 관할권

어원	-inter : between + dict : speak → '~사이에서 하지 말라고 제지하니 금지하다'
유의어	Prohibit, Forbid, Ban
반의어	Allow, Permit, Authorize
영영	to prevent something from happening
예문	The government issued an interdict against the use of fireworks during the national holiday. 정부는 국경일 동안 불꽃놀이 사용을 금지하는 금지령을 발표했다.

103

acrobat

[ˈæk.rə.bæt]

n. 곡예사, (정치적 의견, 주의 등의) 변절자

acrophobia n. 고소공포증
ominous a. 불길한, 흉조의
monster n. 괴물
abominate v. 혐오하다, 증오하다

어원	-acro : peak + -bat : beat → '높은 곳에서도 목표를 때리는 곡예를 보여주는 곡예사'
유의어	Aerialist, Gymnast, Tumbler
반의어	Clumsy person, Non-athlete
영영	a person who performs acrobatic stunts
예문	The acrobat performed a daring stunt on the tightrope. 그 곡예사는 줄 위에서 대담한 묘기를 선보였다.

104

intermit

[ɪntərmít]

v. 일시 멈추다, 중단되다

intermission n. 중지, 막간, 휴식
intermittent a. 간헐적인
mission n. 임무
missionary n. 전도사

어원	-inter : between + -mit, -miss, -mess : send(L) → '중간에 신호를 보내서 일시 멈추다'
유의어	Suspend, Cease, Pause
반의어	Continue, Persist, Uninterrupted
영영	to stop or pause for a period of time
예문	The rain intermitted for a while, but then started again. 비는 잠시 멈췄다가 다시 내리기 시작했다.

105	어원	-pole 장대; 끝지점이 먼 극 → '장대처럼 거리가 먼 극으로 상반되는 대립'
polarity	유의어	Oppositeness, Divergence, Contrast
[pəˈlær.ə.ti]	반의어	Similarity, Sameness, Uniformity
n. 양극성, 상반되는 대립	영영	the state of being opposite or contrary
polar a. 북극의 polarize v. 양극화하다 polarized a. 양극화된 polarization n. 양극화	예문	The two opposing political parties have different views on the issue of taxation. 두 개의 반대되는 정당은 세금 부과 문제에 대해 다른 견해를 가지고 있다.

106	어원	-im, -in : intensive + -pregna, -pregnant 임신한 → '임신한 것처럼 씨를 주입하다'
impregnate	유의어	Saturate, Infuse, Permeate
[imprégneit]	반의어	Dry, Drain, Dehydrate
v. 임신시키다; 주입하다	영영	to fill something with something else
pregnant a. 임신한	예문	The farmer's fields were impregnated with fertilizers to improve the crop yield. 농부의 밭은 농작물 생산량을 높이기 위해 비료로 토양을 비옥하게 했다.

107	어원	-behalf : by half 옆에서 → '옆에서 지지하는 자기편이 있어 이익'
behalf	유의어	Interest, Advantage, Support
[bihǽf]	반의어	Detriment, Disadvantage, Opposition
n. 이익, 원조, 자기편; 지지	영영	for the benefit or advantage of someone else
behave v. 행동하다 beholder n. 구경하는 사람	예문	The lawyer spoke on behalf of his client. 변호사는 고객을 대신하여 말했다.

108	어원	-miss, -mess : send → '여기저기 보내지는 사절단의 임무가 전도'
missionary	유의어	Evangelist, Preacher, Proselytizer
[ˈmɪʃ.ən.ri]	반의어	Non-believer, Heathen, Unconverted
n. 전도사, 선교사	영영	a person who is sent to spread a religion or belief in another country or region
missionize v. 전도하다 remission n. 완화, 면제 missile n. 미사일, 발사체 emissive a. 방사된, 방출의	예문	The missionary traveled to Africa to spread the gospel. 선교사는 아프리카로 가서 복음을 전파했다.

109	어원	-ante : before + -bel, -belli, -bella : war → '전쟁 전의' * Bellona 로마 신화에 나오는 싸움의 여신
antebellum	유의어	Pre-war, Before the war
[ˌæn.tiˈbel.əm]	반의어	Post-war, After the war
a. 전쟁 전의	영영	existing or happening before a war
anterior a. 앞의, 선행하는 antebate v. 앞서다, 앞당기다 postbellum a. 전쟁 후의 interbellum n. 전쟁 기간, 전쟁 사이	예문	The Civil War began in 1861, just a few years after the end of the antebellum period. 남북 전쟁은 1861년에 시작되었는데, 이는 전운기가 끝난 지 몇 년 후였다.

110	어원	-dull : doll 인형 + -ard 극단적으로 ~하는 사람 → '인형처럼 극단적으로 무딘 얼간이' * 덜 떨어져 무딘 바보
dullard	유의어	Dolt, Simpleton, Blockhead
[ˈdʌl.əd]	반의어	Genius, Intellectual, Savant
n. 얼간이, 멍청이, 바보	영영	a stupid or slow-witted person
n. dullness 둔함, 무감각함, 지루함 v. dullify 지루하게 만들다, 둔화시키다 n. dullnesses 어리석음, 멍청함	예문	The dullard failed to understand the simplest of mathematical concepts. 그 얼간이는 가장 간단한 수학 개념도 이해하지 못했다.

111

at a glance

p. 한 눈에, 즉시

gaze v. 응시하다
glare v. 노려보다
glimpse a. 잠깐 보다

어휘	-at + -gli, -glit, -glo : glow 빨간 빛 → '빛나는 곳을 찍어 한 눈에 즉시 보다'
유의어	Quickly, Rapidly, Swiftly
반의어	Closely, Carefully, Thoroughly
영영	by looking quickly or briefly
예문	You can see what e-mails you have received at a glance and decide which ones to read. 어떤 이메일을 받았는지 한 눈에 확인하고 어떤 것을 읽을지 결정하실 수 있습니다.

112

at pleasure

p. 하고 싶은 대로, 내키는 대로

pleasure n. 기쁨, 즐거움

어휘	-at 지점 + -pla, -plac, -plas, -pleas, -plead 기쁘게 하다 → '기쁜 지점에 멈춰 하고 싶은 대로'
유의어	At will, Freely, Voluntarily
반의어	Compulsory, Obligatory, Coerced
영영	whenever one wants or feels like it
예문	You may come or go at pleasure. 오든 가든 마음대로다.

113

take a supplement

p. 영양제를[알약을] 복용하다

supplement n. 보충제
supplementation n. 보충, 추가
school supplies p. 학용품
comply v. 준수하다, 따르다

어휘	-take 취하다 + -supplement 영양제 → '영양제를 취하니 복용하다'
유의어	Consume an addition, Ingest an extra
반의어	Abstain, Refrain, Avoid supplementation
영영	to eat or drink something in addition to one's usual diet
예문	If a diet is balanced, most people need not take vitamin supplements. 균형 잡힌 식사를 한다면, 대부분의 사람들은 비타민 영양제를 복용할 필요가 없다.

114

admit to N

p. ~한 것을 인정하다

어휘	-ad : to + -mit, -miss, -mess : send(L) → '(비난·사람 등을)(안으로) 들여보낸 것을 인정하다'
유의어	Confess, Acknowledge, Allow into
반의어	Deny, Refute, Reject from
영영	to confess or acknowledge that one is N
예문	Don't be afraid to admit to your mistakes. 자기 실수를 인정하기를 두려워하지 말아.

115

contribute to N

p. ~에 기여하다, ~의 원인이 되다

tribute n. 헌사, 공물
contributive a. 기여하는, 이바지 하는
contribute A to B p. A를 B에게 기부하다
make a contribution to N p. 이바지하다

어휘	-con : together + -tribu : assign → '모두에게 할당될 수 있도록 기여하다', '모든 일에 할당되는 원인'
유의어	Donate to, Give to, Provide for
반의어	Withhold from, Keep from, Deprive of
영영	to help to cause or create N
예문	The company contributed to the community by sponsoring local events and charities. 회사는 지역 행사와 자선단체를 후원하여 지역사회에 기여했습니다.

116

delegate A to B

p. A를 B에게 위임하다

어휘	-de : down + -leg, -leag, -loy : law 법률, 위임하다 → '법적 권한을 A에게서 내려 B에게 위임'
유의어	Assign, Entrust, Transfer
반의어	Retain, Keep, Hold onto
영영	to give (control, responsibility, authority, etc.) to someone
예문	Some managers find it difficult to delegate authority to their successors. 일부 관리자들은 후임들에게 권한을 위임하는 것을 힘들어 한다.

117 **lay off** p. ~을 해고하다	어원	-lay 놓다 + -off 떨어뜨려 → '직장에서 떨어뜨려 놓으니 해고'
	유의어	Terminate, Dismiss, Suspend
	반의어	Retain, Keep, Continue employment
	영영	to dismiss or terminate someone's employment
	예문	The company had to lay off several employees due to financial difficulties. 회사는 재정적 어려움으로 인해 직원 몇 명을 해고해야 했습니다.

118 **pin back** p. (고정핀으로) 뒤로 당겨서 묶다, 고정시키다	어원	-pin 핀; 꽂다 + -back → '뒤로 당겨서 핀을 꽂아 묶다'
	유의어	Fasten, Secure, Clamp
	반의어	Release, Unpin, Free
	영영	to hold something back or restrain it
	예문	The nurse pinned back the patient's hair to check for any signs of infection. 간호사는 감염의 징후가 있는지 확인하기 위해 환자의 머리카락을 뒤로 고정했습니다.

119 **confer with** p. ~과 협의하다 conference n. 협의 differ v. 다르다	어원	-con 함께 + -fer : carry(L) + -with → '함께 의견을 주고 받으며 협의하다'
	유의어	Consult, Discuss, Deliberate with
	반의어	Ignore, Disregard, Exclude from discussion
	영영	to talk to someone about something
	예문	The manager conferred with his team to discuss the best way to approach the project. 매니저는 팀과 함께 프로젝트에 접근하는 가장 좋은 방법을 논의하기 위해 회의를 했습니다.

120 **bear with** p. ~을 견디다	어원	-bear 애를 낳다 + -with → '애를 낳는 고통을 함께 하며 견디다' * bear-bore-born
	유의어	Tolerate, Endure, Patience with
	반의어	Reject, Resist, Refuse to tolerate
	영영	to tolerate or put up with something
	예문	The audience was asked to bear with the performer as they worked through their technical difficulties. 관객들은 기술적인 어려움을 해결하는 동안 연주자를 참고 기다려 달라는 요청을 받았습니다.

Chapter 4.

121	cane	[keɪn]	n. 줄기; 지팡이
122	pauper	[ˈpɔː.pər]	n. 극빈자, 빈민
123	belligerent	[bəˈlɪdʒ.ər.ənt]	a. 적대적인, 공격적인
124	bewilder	[biwíldər]	v. 어리둥절하게 만들다
125	intrepid	[ɪnˈtrep.ɪd]	a. 대담한
126	corpse	[kɔːrps]	n. 시신, 시체
127	spatial	[ˈspeɪ.ʃəl]	a. 공간의, 공간적인
128	brevity	[brévəti]	n. 짧음; 간결
129	remnant	[rémnənt]	n. 나머지, 잔여, 자취
130	decay	[dɪˈkeɪ]	v. 썩다, 부식하다; 쇠퇴하다
131	riverine	[rívəràin]	a. 강변의
132	induct	[ɪnˈdʌkt]	v. 취임시키다, 입문시키다; 전수하다
133	vigor	[ˈvɪɡə]	n. 활기, 활력
134	falter	[ˈfɒl.tər]	v. 말을 더듬다, 흔들리다
135	joint	[dʒɔɪnt]	a. 관절, 공동의
136	infant	[ínfənt]	n. 유아
137	contagious	[kənˈteɪ.dʒəs]	a. 전염성의
138	embody	[ɪmˈbɒd.i]	v. 구체화 하다; 포함하다
139	brute	[bruːt]	n. 짐승, 야수 a. 힘에만 의존하는
140	naturalize	[ˈnætʃ.ər.əl.aɪz]	v. 귀화시키다
141	march	[mɑːtʃ]	v. 나아가다, 행진하다 n. 3월
142	mutually exclusive		a. 상호 배타적인
143	blast	[blæst]	n. 돌풍, 센바람
144	feint	[feɪnt]	n. 거짓 꾸밈, 가장
145	impute	[ɪmˈpjuːt]	v. ~의 탓으로 하다
146	fetch	[fetʃ]	v. 가져오다
147	tribute	[ˈtrɪb.juːt]	n. 헌사, 공물
148	orchestrate	[ˈɔː.kɪ.streɪt]	v. 조직하다; 오케스트라용으로 편곡하다
149	virtuosic	[vəːrtʃuɑ́sik]	a. 거장다운, 거장의
150	convict	[kənˈvɪkt]	v. 유죄를 선고하다 n. 죄수
151	make no mistake about		p. ~은 분명하다
152	by the same token		p. 같은 이유로
153	make a commotion		p. 소동을 일으키다
154	at all cost		p. 기어코, 어떠한 희생을 치르더라도
155	at fault		p. 잘못이 있는, 책임이 있는
156	at one's expense		p. ~의 부담으로
157	at the outset		p. 처음부터, 처음에
158	in a split second		p. 눈깜짝할 사이에
159	bring to the table		p. ~을 제공하다, ~을 제시하다
160	except to do		p. ~을 제외하고

121

cane

[keɪn]

n. 줄기; 지팡이

candy n. 사탕
canoe n. 카누
canebrake n. 대나무 숲

어원	-cane : kanna 갈대 → '갈대 같은 줄기; 지팡이'
유의어	Stick, Staff, Walking stick
반의어	Limb, Branch, Twig
영영	a long, slender stick, typically made of wood, used as a support for walking or as a weapon
예문	The old man used a cane to help him walk. 그 노인은 걷는 데 도움을 받기 위해 지팡이를 사용했다.

122

pauper

[ˈpɔːpər]

n. 극빈자, 빈민

pauperism n. 가난한 삶, 빈곤
pauperize v. 가난하게 만들다
pauperization n. 가난화, 빈곤화
poverty n. 가난

어원	-pover, -pauper : poor + -er 사람 → '가난한 이들이니 극빈자'
유의어	Beggar, Destitute, Mendicant
반의어	Wealthy, Affluent, Rich
영영	a person who is extremely poor
예문	The pauper was living in a homeless shelter. 그 거지는 노숙자 보호소에서 살고 있었다.

123

belligerent

[bəˈlɪdʒ.ər.ənt]

a. 적대적인, 공격적인

belligerency n. 전쟁 상태, 교전 상태
belligerently adv. 호전적으로, 적대적으로
belligerence n. 호전성, 적대성
bellicose a. 호전적인

어원	-bel, -belli, -bella : war + -ent 형접 → '전쟁을 일으키니 공격적이고 적대적인' * Bellona 로마 신화에 나오는 싸움의 여신
유의어	Hostile, Aggressive, Combative
반의어	Peaceful, Friendly, Non-aggressive
영영	aggressive or warlike
예문	The belligerent child threw a tantrum when he didn't get his way. 그 호전적인 아이는 자신의 뜻대로 되지 않자 떼를 썼다.

124

bewilder

[biwíldər]

v. 어리둥절하게 만들다

bewildered a. 당황한, 멍한
bewildering a. 당황스러운, 혼란스러운
bewilderment n. 당황, 혼란
unwilder v. 혼란에서 벗어나게 하다

어원	-be : make + -wild 사나운, 거친 → '마음을 거칠게 만드니 어리둥절하게 만들다'
유의어	Confuse, Perplex, Baffle
반의어	Clarify, Explain, Enlighten
영영	to confuse or puzzle someone
예문	The sudden change in plans bewildered everyone. 갑작스러운 계획 변경에 모두가 당황했다.

125

intrepid

[ɪnˈtrep.ɪd]

a. 대담한

intrepidity n. 대담함, 용기
intrepidly adv. 대담하게, 용감하게
intrepidness n. 대담함, 용감함
terror n. 테러, 공포

어원	-in : not + -trep, -ter, -tre, -trepid : fear, terror → '두려워 하지 않으니 대담한'
유의어	Fearless, Brave, Courageous
반의어	Timid, Cowardly, Fearful
영영	brave or fearless
예문	The intrepid explorer braved the dangers of the unknown jungle. 그 용감한 탐험가는 미지의 정글의 위험을 무릅썼다.

126

corpse

[kɔːrps]

n. 시신, 시체

corporal a. 육체의, 신체의
corporation n. 기업, 회사
corps n. 부대, 군단

어원	-corp, -corpor : body → '몸 뿐인 시체'
유의어	Cadaver, Dead body, Remains
반의어	Living, Alive, Survivor
영영	a dead body
예문	The police found the corpse of the murdered man in the alley. 경찰은 골목길에서 살해된 남자의 시체를 발견했다.

127

spatial

[ˈspeɪʃəl]

a. 공간의, 공간적인

spatially adv. 공간적으로
space n. 공간, 장소

어원	-spa : space 공간 + -ial 형접 → '공간의'
유의어	Geographic, Relating to space, Dimensional
반의어	Non-spatial, Non-dimensional
영영	relating to space or occupying space
예문	The artist's use of color and space created a unique and spatial effect. 그 예술가는 색상과 공간을 활용하여 독특하고 공간적인 효과를 만들어냈다.

128

brevity

[brévəti]

n. 짧음; 간결

breviate v. 요약하다, 축약하다
breviary n. 기도문서
briefing n. 브리핑

어원	-brev : short → '짧으니 간결'
유의어	Conciseness, Shortness, Briefness
반의어	Lengthiness, Long-windedness, Verbosity
영영	the quality or state of being brief or concise
예문	The speaker's brevity made it difficult for the audience to follow the presentation. 연설자의 간결함 때문에 청중이 프레젠테이션을 따라가기 어려웠다.

129

remnant

[rémnənt]

n. 나머지, 잔여, 자취

v. remain 남다, 머무르다
n. mansion 대저택, 저택

어원	-re : back + -min, -man : stay → '뒤에 남아있는 나머지'
유의어	Residue, Remainder, Leftover
반의어	Whole, Entirety, Totality
영영	a small remaining part of something
예문	The remnant of the old civilization can still be seen in the ruins of the ancient city. 고대 도시의 유적지에서는 옛 문명의 흔적을 여전히 볼 수 있다.

130

decay

[dɪˈkeɪ]

v. 썩다, 부식하다; 쇠퇴하다

decayed a. 부패한
decaying a. 부패하고 있는
cavity n. 구멍; 충치
decadence n. 퇴폐

어원	-de : down + -cay : fall → '썩어 내려가니 부식하고 쇠퇴하다'
유의어	Decomposition, Rot, Deterioration
반의어	Growth, Flourishing, Preservation
영영	to deteriorate or decompose
예문	The decay of the old building was causing structural problems. 오래된 건물의 부식으로 인해 구조적인 문제가 발생하고 있었다.

131

riverine

[rívəràin]

a. 강변의

rivulet n. 시내, 개울
delive v. 비롯되다, 유래하다, 유도하다
delive from p. ~에서 유래하다
rival n. 경쟁, 경쟁자

어원	-riv : river → '강 주위의 강변'
유의어	Related to rivers, Riparian
반의어	Inland, Non-aquatic
영영	relating to or situated on a river
예문	The riverine ecosystem is home to a variety of aquatic plants and animals. 강 생태계는 다양한 수생식물과 동물의 서식지이다.

132

induct

[ɪnˈdʌkt]

v. 취임시키다, 입문시키다; 전수하다

inductance n. 유도
inductee n. 입문자
induction n. 유도
seduce v. 나쁜 길로 유혹하다

어원	-in : in + -duc : lead → '조직 안으로 이끄니 입문 후 기술 전수'
유의어	Install, Initiate, Admit
반의어	Exclude, Oust, Remove
영영	to formally introduce someone into a position or organization
예문	The new CEO was inducted into the company's board of directors. 신임 CEO는 회사의 이사회에 합류했다.

133	어원	-vid, -viv, -vit, -vig, -veget : live 살다, life : 생명(L) * bigger 더 큰 활력이니 활기찬
	유의어	Energy, Vitality, Strength
vigor	반의어	Weakness, Fatigue, Lethargy
[ˈvɪɡə]	영영	energy or vitality
n. 활기, 활력		
vigorous a. 강력한 invigorate v. 활기를 불어넣다 invigorating a. 활기를 불어넣는 vigil n. 철야, 불침번, 밤샘	예문	The athlete's vigor and energy were evident in his impressive performance. 그 선수의 활력과 에너지는 인상적인 경기에서 분명히 드러났다.
134	어원	-fals, -fal, -fail, -faul : deceie : wrong 잘못된(L) → '잘못한 것이 있어 맘이 흔들리니 말을 더듬다'
	유의어	Hesitate, Waver, Stumble
falter	반의어	Proceed, Advance, Persevere
[ˈfɒl.tər]	영영	to hesitate or waver
v. 말을 더듬다, 흔들리다		
faltering a. 주춤하는, 망설이는 falteringly adv. 주저하며, 미안하게 unfaltering a. 동요하지 않는, 확고한 infalterable a. 동요하지 않는	예문	The runner faltered at the finish line, but managed to cross it in first place. 그 선수는 결승선에서 비틀거렸지만, 1위로 통과했다.
135	어원	-join, -junc, -junct 합치다(L) → '뼈가 만나는 관절' * join, junc(t) '다른 것이 만나 합침' VS ser(t) '밀어 넣어서 합침'
	유의어	Connection, Articulation, Junction
joint	반의어	Disconnection, Separation, Disjointed
[dʒɔɪnt]	영영	a connection or junction between two or more things
a. 관절, 공동의		
disjoint v. 해체하다, (관절을) 삐게 하다 disjointed a. 연결이 안 되는, 흐트러진 junction n. 접합, 교차점 conjunction n. 결합, 접속사	예문	The doctor recommended a joint replacement surgery for the patient's knee. 의사는 환자의 무릎에 관절 교체 수술을 권했다.
136	어원	-in : not + -fa, -fan : speak → '말하지 못하는 유아'
	유의어	Baby, Newborn, Toddler
infant	반의어	Adult, Grown-up, Mature
[ínfənt]	영영	a young child
n. 유아		
a. infantile 어린애 같은, 유치한 n. infancy 유아기 n. fairy 요정, 마녀 n. fable 우화, 전설	예문	The infant was sleeping soundly in its crib. 아기는 침대에서 곤히 자고 있었다.
137	어원	-con : together + -tag : touch → '서로 접촉해서 병이 옮는'
	유의어	Infectious, Transmittable, Spreadable
contagious	반의어	Non-contagious, Non-infectious
[kənˈteɪ.dʒəs]	영영	capable of being transmitted from one person or thing to another
a. 전염성의		
contagiously adv. 전염되어, 전염성으로 aontagiousness n. 전염됨, 전염성임 contact v. 접촉하다 contiguous a. 인접한, 연속된	예문	The virus was highly contagious and quickly spread throughout the community. 바이러스는 전염성이 매우 높아 빠르게 지역사회에 퍼져나갔다
138	어원	-em, -en : in + -body : corps 몸, 신체 → '~안에 실체를 만들어 구현하니 구체화하다'
	유의어	Incorporate, Personify, Manifest
embody	반의어	Disembody, De-incarnate, Divest
[ɪmˈbɒd.i]	영영	to represent or symbolize something
v. 구체화 하다; 포함하다		
corpse n. 시체 incorporate v. 통합하다, 합병하다 embodiment n. 구체화, 형상화 reembody v. 재구성하다	예문	The artist's painting embodied the spirit of the era. 그 예술가의 그림은 시대의 정신을 구현했다.

139

brute

[bruːt]

n. 짐승, 야수 a. 힘에만 의존하는

a. brutal 잔인한, 야만적인
adv. brutally 잔인하게, 무자비하게
n. brutality 잔인성, 무자비함
n. Beauty and the Beast 미녀와 야수

어원	-brute : beast 야수 → '야수처럼 힘에만 의존하는'
유의어	Beast, Animal, Savage
반의어	Human, Civilized, Gentle
영영	a cruel or brutal person
예문	The brute was known for his violent temper and aggressive behavior. 그 짐승은 폭력적인 성격과 공격적인 행동으로 유명했다.

140

naturalize

[ˈnætʃ.ər.əl.aɪz]

v. 귀화시키다

naturalization n. 귀화, 천연화
naturopathy n. 자연요법

어원	-na, -nat, -gna : born 낳다, 태어나다 + -ize 동접 → '태어난 고향 그곳으로 귀화시키다'
유의어	Acclimatize, Adapt, Assimilate
반의어	Alien, Unnaturalize, Isolate
영영	to confer citizenship on someone
예문	The immigrant was granted citizenship after naturalizing his status. 그 이주민은 국적을 취득한 후 시민권을 받았다.

141

march

[mɑːtʃ]

v. 나아가다, 행진하다 n. 3월

n. marcher 전쟁; 행군을 하는 군인
n. marching 행진, 진군
n. marcus 전쟁, 전사

어원	-march 빠른 걸음 → '빠른 걸음으로 당당하게 걷는 행진', '걸음을 빨리 시작해야 하는 3월 입학 시기' * 마치 마차처럼 빠르게 걷는 행진
유의어	Walk, Parade, Advance
반의어	Retreat, Withdraw, Reverse
영영	to walk with a regular, measured tread
예문	The soldiers marched in formation down the street. 군인들은 질서정연하게 거리를 행진했다.

142

mutually exclusive

a. 상호 배타적인

어원	* mutually(-mut : change → '바꾸기로 상호간 합의') * exclusive(-ex : out + -clu → '밖을 닫아 배타적인')
유의어	Incompatible, Contradictory, Irreconcilable
반의어	Compatible, Harmonious, Coexistent
영영	not able to exist together
예문	The two options are mutually exclusive and cannot be chosen at the same time. 두 가지 옵션은 상호 배타적이며 동시에 선택할 수 없습니다.

143

blast

[blæst]

n. 돌풍, 센바람

blasted a. 지독한, 황폐한
balsting n. 폭파, 분쇄
blastoma n. 종양
blastula n. 분신

어원	-blizzard, -blast : bhle, bhel : blow, swell → '부는 바람이 거세니 돌풍'
유의어	Explosion, Detonation, Burst
반의어	Whisper, Murmur, Silence
영영	to explode or detonate
예문	The explosion caused a blast of heat and smoke that filled the room. 폭발로 인해 방 안에 열과 연기가 가득 찼다.

144

feint

[feɪnt]

n. 거짓 꾸밈, 가장

feign v. ~인 체하다, 위조하다
feigned a. 가장한
faint a. 기절한, 희미한

어원	-feint : fake 가짜 공격, 동작 → '가짜로 공격하니 거짓 동작' * 슛 모션 전에 페인트 동작
유의어	Deception, Pretense, Sham
반의어	Genuine move, Sincere action
영영	a deceptive or misleading movement
예문	The boxer used a feint to distract his opponent and then delivered a powerful punch. 복서는 상대를 현혹시키기 위해 페인트를 사용한 후 강력한 펀치를 날렸다.

145

impute

[ɪmˈpjuːt]

v. ~의 탓으로 하다

imputable a. 돌릴 수 있는, 전가할 수 있는
imputation n. 전가, 돌리기, 지우기
dispute v. 반박하다, 논쟁하다
repute v. 평가하다, 생각하다

어원	-im, -in : in + -put 놓다 → '굳이 책임을 안에 끼워 넣어 탓으로 돌리다'
유의어	Attribute, Ascribe, Credit
반의어	Absolve, Exonerate, Disclaim
영영	to attribute something to someone or something
예문	Some people impute their success to luck, while others attribute it to hard work and determination. 어떤 사람들은 성공을 운으로 돌리고, 다른 사람들은 노력과 결단력으로 돌린다.

146

fetch

[fetʃ]

v. 가져오다

n. fetcher 가져오는 사람
a. fetching 마음을 사로잡는, 매혹적인
adv. fatchingly 매혹적으로
v. refetch 재검색하다

어원	-foot, -feet, -fet 발 → '발로 가지러 가서 가져오다'
유의어	Retrieve, Bring, Get
반의어	Leave, Abandon, Depart
영영	to go and get something
예문	The dog was trained to fetch the ball when it was thrown. 그 개는 공을 던지면 물어오는 훈련을 받았다.

147

tribute

[ˈtrɪbjuːt]

n. 헌사, 공물

contribute v. 기부하다
contribution n. 기부, 기여, 공헌
contributive a. 기여하는, 이바지하는
contributable a. 기부할 수 있는

어원	-trib, -tribut : assign, give → 부족의 족장이 나누어 주는 활동이 헌사, 공물 * tribe 부족(-tri : three + -be → 고대 로마는 3부족)
유의어	Homage, Admiration, Respect
반의어	Insult, Disrespect, Contempt
영영	a gift or offering made as a sign of respect or admiration
예문	The artist paid tribute to his mentor by including his influence in his latest work. 그 예술가는 자신의 최근 작품에 스승의 영향을 담아 스승에게 경의를 표했다.

148

orchestrate

[ˈɔːkɪˌstreɪt]

v. 조직하다; 오케스트라용으로 편곡하다

orchestra n. 오케스트라, 관현악단
orchestrated a. 체계적인, 조직화된
chorus n. 합창단; 코러스
choir v. 합창하다 n. 성가대

어원	-orchestra 오케스트라 + -ate 동접 → '관현악단을 조직하다'
유의어	Organize, Arrange, Coordinate
반의어	Disorganize, Scatter, Disperse
영영	to arrange or plan something carefully
예문	The conductor carefully orchestrated the music to create a beautiful and harmonious sound. 지휘자는 아름다운 소리를 만들기 위해 음악을 신중하게 조율했다.

149

virtuosic

[vəːrˈtʃuɑ́sik]

a. 거장다운, 거장의

n. virtuosity 예술적 솜씨
n. virtu 가치
n. virtue 장점; 덕

어원	-virtu 우수(L) + -sic 형접 → '우수한 실력을 가진 거장의'
유의어	Masterful, Skilled, Accomplished
반의어	Incompetent, Untalented, Unskilled
영영	highly skilled or accomplished
예문	The pianist's virtuosic performance left the audience in awe. 피아니스트의 뛰어난 연주에 관객들은 놀라움을 금치 못했다.

150

convict

[kənˈvɪkt]

v. 유죄를 선고하다 n. 죄수

conviction n. 유죄 판결; 설득, 납득; 확신
convicted a. 유죄가 선고된
convincing a. 설득력 있는
victory n. 승리

어원	-con : intensive + -vict : victory → '완전히 법적 싸움에서 이기고 유죄를 선고하는 죄수'
유의어	Criminal, Offender, Inmate
반의어	Innocent, Acquitted, Free
영영	to find someone guilty of a crime
예문	The jury convicted the defendant of theft and sentenced him to ten years in prison. 배심원단은 피고에게 절도죄를 선고하고 10년 징역형을 선고했다.

151

make no mistake about

p. ~은 분명하다

어원	-make 만들다 + no mistake + -about → '그것 만큼은 실수가 없으니 분명하다'
유의어	Be Clear, Be Certain, Be Sure
반의어	Be Confused, Be Uncertain, Be Doubtful
영영	to be certain of something
예문	Make no mistake about it, this is a serious matter. 이것은 심각한 문제라는 점을 분명히 말씀드립니다.

152

by the same token

p. 같은 이유로

어원	-same + -token : sign → '같은 징표가 되니 같은 이유로'
유의어	Likewise, Similarly, Also
반의어	Conversely, On the Contrary, In Contras
영영	for the same reason
예문	By the same token, you should also be careful when driving. 마찬가지로 운전할 때도 주의해야 합니다.

153

make a commotion

p. 소동을 일으키다

commotional a. 소란의, 소동의
promote v. 촉진하다, 장려하다, 승진시키다
demote v. 강등하다, 강제로 내리다

어원	-make 만들다 + -commotion 소동 → '소동을 만드니 일으키다' * commotion(-com + -mot : move → 함께 움직이는 소동)
유의어	Stir Up, Create a Disturbance, Cause a Ruckus
반의어	Quiet Down, Settle, Calm
영영	to cause a disturbance or stir
예문	The crowd made a commotion when the celebrity arrived at the event. 유명인이 행사에 도착하자 군중들은 소란을 떨었다.

154

at all cost

p. 기어코, 어떠한 희생을 치르더라도

costly adv. 대가가 큰
costa n. 늑골
at a loss p. 어쩔 줄을 모르는
at no time p. 결코 ~하지 않다

어원	-all + -cost → '모든 비용을 들여서라도'
유의어	Regardless of the Cost, No Matter What
반의어	Avoiding Cost, Economically
영영	regardless of the consequences
예문	The team was determined to win the game at all cost. 팀은 무슨 수를 써서라도 경기에서 승리하기로 결심했습니다.

155

at fault

p. 잘못이 있는, 책임이 있는

어원	-at 지점 + -fals, -fal, -fail, -faul : deceie : wrong 잘못된(L) → '잘못된 지점을 보니 책임이 있는'
유의어	Responsible, Blameworthy, Guilty
반의어	Innocent, Blameless, Faultless
영영	responsible for something wrong
예문	The driver was at fault for causing the accident. 운전자는 사고를 일으킨 책임이 있었다.

156

at one's expense

p. ~의 부담으로

at the expense of p. ~을 희생하면서
expend v. (돈, 시간, 노력)을 쓰다
expense n. 비용, 지출, 경비
expendable a. 소모용의

어원	-at 지점 + -expense 비용 → '비용이 들어가는 지점이니 ~의 부담으로'
유의어	Paid by Someone, Funded by Another
반의어	At One's Own Expense, Self-financed
영영	to one's own detriment
예문	The company was trying to save money by cutting costs at the employee's expense. 회사는 직원의 비용을 절감하여 비용을 절약하려고 했습니다.

157	어원	-at 지점 + -out : outside + -set → '밖에 최초로 내놓아 착수한 지점이니 처음부터'
at the outset	유의어	Initially, at the beginning
	반의어	Eventually, Finally, Ultimately
	영영	at the beginning
p. 처음부터, 처음에		
outset n. 착수, 시작 onset n. 착수; 공격 set A apart from B p. A와 B를 구별하다 set A asdie p. A를 제쳐 두다	예문	At the outset, it was unclear how the project would be successful. 처음에는 프로젝트가 성공할지 여부가 불분명했습니다.
158	어원	-split : divide + -second 초 → '초를 나눌 정도로 눈깜짝할 사이에' * 다리 찢기 split
in a split second	유의어	Instantaneously, Immediately, Suddenly
	반의어	Gradually, Slowly, Over time
	영영	very quickly or instantly
p. 눈깜짝할 사이에		
	예문	The decision was made in a split second, without any hesitation. 결정은 망설임 없이 순식간에 내려졌다.
159	어원	-bear, -bir, -bri 나르다, 가져오다, 데려오다 → '테이블 위로 제안서를 들고와 제시하다'
bring to the table	유의어	Contribute, Offer, Provide
	반의어	Withhold, Keep back, Retain
	영영	to contribute or offer something
p. ~을 제공하다, ~을 제시하다		
bring A to bear p. A에 집중하다 bring on p. ~을 야기하다, 초래하다 bring A up to speed p. A에게 최신 정보를 주다 bring up p. 기르다, 교육하다	예문	The team brought to the table a variety of skills and expertise. 팀은 다양한 기술과 전문 지식을 가지고 있었습니다.
160	어원	-ex : out + -cept : take → 'take out 밖으로 빼서 제외하고' * except, but, save는 접속사로 to V나 동사원형을 취할 수 있다
except to do	유의어	Exclude, Omit, Leave out
	반의어	Include, Incorporate, Encompass
	영영	other than doing something
p. ~을 제외하고		
	예문	The athlete was determined to win the race, except to do anything illegal. 그 운동선수는 불법적인 행동을 하지 않고 경기에서 승리하기로 결심했습니다.

Chapter 5.

161	dazzle	[ˈdæz.əl]	v. 눈이 부시게 하다 n. 눈부심, 황홀함
162	suspend	[səˈspend]	v. 일시 중지하다; 정직시키다; 연기하다; 매달다
163	superfluous	[suːˈpɜː.flu.əs]	a. 불필요한, 여분의
164	perpetual	[pəˈpetʃ.u.əl]	a. 끊임없이 계속되는, 영원한; 빈번한
165	resilience	[rizíljəns]	n. 탄력성, 회복력
166	recede	[rɪˈsiːd]	v. 물러나다, 희미해지다, 약해지다
167	proponent	[prəpóunənt]	n. 지지자
168	dwell	[dwel]	v. 거주하다, 살다
169	hierarchy	[ˈhaɪə.rɑː.ki]	n. 계급, 위계
170	disparage	[dɪˈspær.ɪdʒ]	v. 비방하다, 경시하다, ~을 얕보다
171	repel	[rɪˈpel]	v. 물리치다, 쫓아버리다
172	apprehend	[ˌæp.rɪˈhend]	v. 이해하다, 염려하다; 체포하다
173	rebel	[ˈreb.əl]	n. 반역자, 반항아 v. 반란을 일으키다
174	scavenger	[ˈskæv.ɪn.dʒər]	n. 쓰레기 뒤지는 사람, 죽은 동물을 먹는 동물
175	conspicuous	[kənˈspɪk.ju.əs]	a. 눈에 띄는, 현저한
176	mingle	[ˈmɪŋ.gəl]	v. 섞이다, 어우러지다
177	pendulum	[ˈpen.dʒəl.əm]	n. (시계의) 추, 진자
178	reprehend	[ˌrep.rɪˈhend]	v. 꾸짖다, 비난하다
179	necessitous	[nəsésətəs]	a. 가난한, 궁핍한, 필연적인
180	courtship	[ˈkɔːt.ʃɪp]	n. 구애, 구혼, 약혼 전의 교재
181	dispense	[dɪˈspens]	v. 나누어 주다, 분배하다; 조제하다
182	cringe	[krɪndʒ]	n. 비굴한 태도 v. 굽실대다
183	indigenous	[ɪnˈdɪdʒ.ɪ.nəs]	a. 토착의, 원주민의
184	antinomy	[ænˈtɪn.ə.mi]	n. 모순; 이율 배반
185	controversy	[ˈkɒn.trə.vɜː.si]	n. 논쟁
186	diminish	[dɪˈmɪn.ɪʃ]	v. 줄이다, 축소하다, 감소시키다
187	diabetes	[ˌdaɪ.əˈbiː.tiːz]	n. 당뇨병
188	credulous	[ˈkredʒ.ə.ləs]	a. 너무 잘 믿는(속기 쉬움)
189	spine	[spaɪn]	n. 척추, 등뼈; 가시
190	gravel	[ˈgræv.əl]	n. 자갈
191	make one's way to		p. ~로 나아가다
192	take A further		p. A추가적인 조치를 취하다
193	on closer inspection		p. 더 자세히 살펴보면
194	prove a point		p. 반드시 ~하다
195	carry away		p. 가져가 버리다; 넋을 잃게 하다
196	at variance with		p. ~와 상충하는 / 모순되는
197	with regard to		p. ~과 관련하여, ~에 대해
198	triumph over		p. ~에게 승리하다
199	at the expense of		p. ~을 희생하면서
200	come out ahead		p. 결국 이득을 보다

161

dazzle

[ˈdæz.əl]

v. 눈이 부시게 하다 n. 눈부심, 황홀함

dazzlement n. 눈부심
bedazzle v. 압도하다, 현혹하다
dizzy a. 어지러운, 아찔한
daze n. 멍한 상태 v. 멍하게 하다

어원	* -da : day 빛 + -zzle : puzzle → '날이 너무 밝아 빛이 혼란스러울 정도로 눈이 부시게 하다'
유의어	Bedazzle, amaze, impress
반의어	Dull, bore, disappoint
영영	impress or overwhelm with brilliance or splendor.
예문	The fireworks display dazzled the crowd with its vibrant colors and explosive energy. 불꽃놀이는 화려한 색채와 폭발적인 에너지로 군중을 눈부셨습니다.

162

suspend

[səˈspend]

v. 일시 중지하다; 정직시키다; 연기하다; 매달다

suspension n. 중단, 정지
suspensible a. 중단 가능한
compensate v. 보충하다, 보상하다
pendulum n. 추, 진자

어원	-sus, -sub : under + -pend : hang → '아래로 매달아 일시 중지시키다'
유의어	Halt, interrupt, cease
반의어	Continue, resume, proceed
영영	temporarily stop or postpone something.
예문	The teacher suspended the student for a week for disruptive behavior. 교사는 학생의 방해 행위로 인해 1주일 동안 징계했습니다.

163

superfluous

[suːˈpɜː.flu.əs]

a. 불필요한, 여분의

superfluity n. 여분, 불필요한 물건
superfluence n. 과잉, 초과
afluent a. 풍부한
fluctuate v. 변동하다

어원	-super : over + -flu : flow → '~위에 흘러 넘치니 불필요한 여분의'
유의어	Excessive, redundant, unnecessary
반의어	Essential, necessary, crucial
영영	unnecessary or excessive.
예문	Removing the superfluous details made the report much easier to read. 불필요한 세부 사항을 제거하면 보고서를 읽기 훨씬 쉽게 만들었습니다.

164

perpetual

[pəˈpetʃ.u.əl]

a. 끊임없이 계속되는, 영원한; 빈번한

perpetuate v. (악습, 실수 등을) 계속하게 하다
perpetuity n. 영원함, 불멸성
repeat v. 반복하다
compete v. 경쟁하다

어원	-per : 완전히 통하여 + -pet 가서 찾는 → '완전히 찾을 때까지 끊임없는'
유의어	Eternal, everlasting, continuous
반의어	Temporary, finite, intermittent
영영	lasting forever or for a very long time.
예문	She longed for a life of perpetual happiness and sunshine. 그녀는 영원한 행복과 햇살이 가득한 삶을 갈망했습니다.

165

resilience

[riziljəns]

n. 탄력성, 회복력

resilient a. 탄력성이 있는, 잘 회복하는
resile v. 튕기다, 되돌아오다
assail v. 공격하다
salient a. 두드러진, 현저한

어원	-re : again + -sil, -sal : leap → '다시 뛰어 오를 정도로 탄력성이 있어 잘 회복하는'
유의어	Flexibility, toughness, adaptability
반의어	Fragility, weakness, inflexibility
영영	the ability to bounce back from difficulties or challenges.
예문	Despite facing numerous challenges, the community showed remarkable resilience and bounced back stronger than ever. 수많은 어려움에 직면했음에도 불구하고, 지역 사회는 놀라운 회복력을 보여주고 이전보다 더 강해졌습니다.

166

recede

[rɪˈsiːd]

v. 물러나다, 희미해지다, 약해지다

recede from v. ~에서 물러나다
precede v. 선행하다, 앞서다
exceed v. 초과하다

어원	-re : back + -cede : go → '뒤로 물러나니 약해지다'
유의어	Retreat, withdraw, regress
반의어	Advance, approach, progress
영영	move or withdraw backward.
예문	The tide receded, leaving a trail of seaweed and shells behind. 조수가 빠지면서 다시마와 조개 껍데기의 흔적이 남았습니다.

167

proponent

[prəpóunənt]

n. 지지자

propose v. 제안하다
repose v. 쉬다
depose v. 폐위시키다

어원	-pre : before + -pon : put + -ent 사람 → '~앞에 대놓고 지지하니 지지자'
유의어	Advocate, supporter, champion
반의어	Opponent, critic, adversary
영영	someone who supports or defends a particular cause or idea.
예문	The proponent of the new tax law argued that it would help to stimulate the economy. 새로운 세법의 지지자는 이 법이 경제를 활성화하는 데 도움이 될 것이라고 주장했습니다.

168

dwell

[dwel]

v. 거주하다, 살다

dwelling n. 거주, 주거지
dwell on v. 곰곰이 생각하다
dwindle v. 줄어들다, 감소하다

어원	-d : away + -well : spring or turn, move → '움직임이 멈췄으니 거주하다'
유의어	Reside, live, inhabit, lodge, remain, sojourn
반의어	Depart, vacate, leave
영영	live or stay in a place for a long time.
예문	She dwells on the past, unable to move on from her childhood trauma. 그녀는 어린 시절의 트라우마를 극복하지 못하고 과거에 머물러 있습니다.

169

hierarchy

[ˈhaɪ.ə.rɑː.ki]

n. 계급, 위계

hierarchical a. 계급에 따른
anarchy n. 무정부 상태, 무질서

어원	-hier, -hiero 성스러운 + -arches, -archy : rule 통치하다 → '성스러운 hero들의 통치 순위 체계니 계급'
유의어	Ranking, order, structure
반의어	Anarchy, disorder, chaos
영영	a system of organization with different levels of authority.
예문	The company's hierarchy is very rigid, with a clear chain of command. 이 회사의 계층 구조는 매우 경직되어 있으며 명확한 명령 계통이 있습니다.

170

disparage

[dɪˈspær.ɪdʒ]

v. 비방하다, 경시하다, ~을 얕보다

disparaging a. 얕보는, 험담하는, 헐뜯는
disparagingly adv. 깔보는 듯이, 폄하여
diparagement n. 비난, 비방, 경멸
disparity n. 차이, 불균형

어원	-dis : away + -par : peer, equal → '친구 사이가 멀어져 비방하는'
유의어	Belittle, criticize, demean
반의어	Praise, commend, laud
영영	criticize or speak disrespectfully of someone or something.
예문	The politician disparaged his opponent's character, calling him a liar and a cheat. 정치인은 상대방의 인격을 비하하며 그를 거짓말쟁이이자 사기꾼이라고 불렀습니다.

171

repel

[rɪˈpel]

v. 물리치다, 쫓아버리다

repellency n. 반발성, 격퇴성
propel v. 추진하다, 밀어내다
compel v. 강요하다, 억지로 ~시키다
repeal v. ~을 취소하다, 폐지하다

어원	-re : back + -pel, -peal, -pul : drive 몰다 → '뒤로 후퇴하도록 물리치다'
유의어	Reject, resist, drive away
반의어	Attract, welcome, embrace
영영	push back or drive away with force.
예문	The strong smell of the garbage repelled the flies. 쓰레기의 강한 냄새가 파리를 쫓아냈습니다.

172

apprehend

[ˌæp.rɪˈhend]

v. 이해하다, 염려하다; 체포하다

apprehensive a. 염려하는
apprehension n. 체포, 이해, 염려
apprehensible a. 이해할 수 있는, 인지할 수 있는
reprehend v. 꾸짖다, 비난하다

어원	-ap : upon + -prehen, -pren, -pregn, -pris : seize → '앞서 의미를 잡아 이해하는'
유의어	Arrest, capture, understand
반의어	Release, free, misunderstand
영영	capture or arrest someone.
예문	The police apprehended the suspect after a brief chase. 경찰은 짧은 추격 끝에 용의자를 체포했습니다.

173	어원	-re : against + -bel, -belli, -bella : war → '대항해서 전쟁을 일으키니 반항, 저항' * Bellona 로마 신화에 나오는 싸움의 여신
rebel ['reb.əl] n. 반역자, 반항아 v. 반란을 일으키다	유의어	Revolt, resist, defy
	반의어	Obey, submit, conform
	영영	someone who opposes or resists authority or control.
rebellion n. 반항, 저항 rebellious a. 반항적인, 반대하는 rebelliously adv. 반항적으로, 반역적으로 belligerent a. 적대적인, 공격적인	예문	The people rebelled against the tyrannical government. 사람들은 폭군 정부에 반란을 일으켰습니다.
174	어원	-sca : scan 살피다 + -ven : come → '살피러 와서 쓰레기 더미를 뒤지다'
scavenger ['skæv.ɪn.dʒər] n. 쓰레기 뒤지는 사람, 죽은 동물을 먹는 동물	유의어	Forager, scavenging animal, collector
	반의어	Predator, hunter, gatherer
	영영	an animal that feeds on dead or waste organic matter.
scavenge v. 쓰레게 더미를 뒤지다, 죽은 고기를 먹다 scavengeable a. 회수 가능한, 재활용 가능한 venue n. 장소; 범행지	예문	The vulture is a scavenger that feeds on dead animals. 독수리는 사체를 먹는 청소부입니다.
175	어원	-con : together + -sper, -spar, -spair : see → '모두 보이도록 비추니 눈에 띄는'
conspicuous [kən'spɪk.ju.əs] a. 눈에 띄는, 현저한	유의어	Obvious, noticeable, prominent
	반의어	Inconspicuous, hidden, subtle
	영영	easily seen or noticed.
conspicuously adv. 두드러지게, 현저히 conspicuousness n. 눈에 잘 띔, 뚜렷함 despise v. 경멸하다	예문	The woman's bright red dress was conspicuous in the crowd. 그 여성의 밝은 빨간 드레스는 군중 속에서 눈에 띄었습니다.
176	어원	-mingle : mix → '섞여서 어우러지다'
mingle ['mɪŋ.ɡəl] v. 섞이다, 어우러지다	유의어	Mix, blend, combine
	반의어	Separate, segregate, divide
	영영	mix or socialize with other people.
mingle with v. ~와 섞다 comingle v. 혼합하다 commingle v. ~을 혼합하다, 뒤섞이다	예문	The guests mingled at the party, enjoying each other's company. 손님들은 파티에서 서로 어울리며 즐거운 시간을 보냈습니다.
177	어원	-pend, -pens, -pond : hang 매달다, weigh 무게를 달다 → '매달린 추' * pend(d,s)은 '매달리다', grav는 '고통'의 의미
pendulum ['pen.dʒəl.əm] n. (시계의) 추, 진자	유의어	Swinging device, oscillator
	반의어	Fixed, stationary
	영영	a weight swinging from a fixed point, used in clocks or to regulate the timing of something.
expensive a. 비싼 pendant v. 펜던트, 목걸이 pendent a. 매달린, 미결의, 드리워진 pend v. 미결인 채로 두다, 결정을 미루다	예문	The pendulum swung back and forth, marking the passage of time. 진자가 좌우로 흔들리며 시간이 흘러가는 것을 알렸습니다.
178	어원	-re : back + -prehen, -pren, -pregn, -pris : seize → '뒤에서 약점만 잡아 비난하다'
reprehend [ˌrep.rɪ'hend] v. 꾸짖다, 비난하다	유의어	Rebuke, criticize, reprimand
	반의어	Praise, applaud, commend
	영영	criticize or express disapproval of someone's behavior.
reprehension n. 비난, 질책 reprehensible a. 비난 받을 만한 apprehend v. 이해하다; 체포하다 comprehend v. 이해하다	예문	The teacher reprimanded the student for talking in class. 교사는 수업 시간에 떠든 학생을 질책했습니다.

179

necessitous

[nəsésətəs]

a. 가난한, 궁핍한, 필연적인

necessity n. 필수품; 필요

어원	-necess : necessary 필요한 → '도움이 반드시 필요할 정도로 가난하고 궁핍하니 필연적인'
유의어	Needy, impoverished, deprived
반의어	Affluent, wealthy, prosperous
영영	needing something essential or important.
예문	The poor family was in a necessitous situation, struggling to make ends meet. 가난한 가족은 생계를 이어가는 데 어려움을 겪으며 어려운 상황에 처했습니다.

180

courtship

['kɔːt.ʃɪp]

n. 구애, 구혼, 약혼 전의 교재

court n. 궁정, 법원, 코트
courteous a. 공손한, 정중한
escort n. 호위, 안내

어원	-court 법정, 귀족의 궁정(F) + -ship 명접 → '궁정의 관습을 따라 상대에게 연애 과정을 위한 구애'
유의어	Wooing, dating, romance
반의어	Rejection, avoidance, indifference
영영	Romantic relationship development with potential for marriage or commitment, involving shared activities and gestures.
예문	The couple's courtship was long and drawn-out, but it eventually led to marriage. 그 커플의 연애는 길고 지루했지만 결국 결혼으로 이어졌습니다.

181

dispense

[dɪˈspens]

v. 나누어 주다, 분배하다; 조제하다

dispensable a. 불필요한
indispensable a. 필수적인
dispensary n. 조제실, 양국
dispensation a. 분배, 분배품, 체제

어원	-dis : away + -pens, -ponder : weigh → '무게를 재고 내어주다'
유의어	Distribute, allocate, administer
반의어	Withhold, retain, keep
영영	give out or distribute something.
예문	The doctor dispensed medicine to the patient. 의사는 환자에게 약을 나누어 주었습니다.

182

cringe

[krɪndʒ]

n. 비굴한 태도 v. 굽실대다

cringer n. 굽실거리는 사람
creep v. 기어가다
crawl v. 기어가다
cripple n. 불구자

어원	-creep, -cra, -cri, -rep 기다, 구브리다 → '기어가며 비굴한 태도로 굽실대다'
유의어	Shrink, recoil, flinch
반의어	Stand tall, confront, embrace
영영	shrink back or flinch in fear or disgust.
예문	The child cringed in fear as the dog growled at him. 그 아이는 개가 자신을 으르렁거리자 두려움에 몸서리쳤습니다.

183

indigenous

[ɪnˈdɪdʒ.ɪ.nəs]

a. 토착의, 원주민의

n. indigene 원주민, 토착민
v. indigenize 원주민화하다, 국내화하다
a. indigent 빈곤한, 궁핍한

어원	-indi : indian + -gen : birth → '인디언들이 태어난 곳이니 토착의'
유의어	Native, original, local
반의어	Foreign, alien, non-native
영영	native to a particular place.
예문	The indigenous people of the island have lived there for centuries. 그 섬의 토착민들은 수세기 동안 그곳에 살았습니다.

184

antinomy

[ænˈtɪn.ə.mi]

n. 모순; 이율 배반

antinomical a. 모순적인, 양립할 수 없는
antinomist n. 율법성 반대론자
antinomianism n. 율법성 반대론
autonomous a. 자율적인

어원	-anti : against + -nom : law 법칙 → '법칙에 반대하니 모순이고 이율 배반'
유의어	Contradiction, paradox, conflict
반의어	Harmony, agreement, consistency
영영	a contradiction that arises from the apparent validity of two opposing principles or statements.
예문	The antinomy of free will and determinism states that free will and determinism are both true, but they cannot be true at the same time. 자유 의지와 결정론의 모순은 자유 의지와 결정론이 모두 참이지만, 동시에 참일 수 없다고 주장합니다.

185

controversy

[ˈkɒn.trə.vɜː.si]

n. 논쟁

controversial a. 논쟁의 소지가 있는
controversion n. 논쟁, 논의
contravert v. 논쟁하다, ~에 반박하다
pervert v. 타락시키다, 왜곡하다

어원	-contra : against + -verge, -vers, -vert : turn → '반대로 말하는 논쟁'
유의어	Dispute, disagreement, contention
반의어	Agreement, consensus, harmony
영영	a strong disagreement or argument about something.
예문	The new tax law is controversial, with some people supporting it and others opposing it. 새로운 세법은 논란의 여지가 있으며, 일부 사람들은 이를 지지하고 다른 사람들은 반대합니다.

186

diminish

[dɪˈmɪn.ɪʃ]

v. 줄이다, 축소하다, 감소시키다

diminutive a. 자그마한, 왜소한
diminution n. 축소, 감소
diminishment n. 감소, 약화
dim a. 흐릿한, 희미한

어원	-de, -di : apart + -min, -mini, -minim 작은 (L) / 돌출하다 → 멀리 떨어져 보이는 것처럼 작아지게 줄이다
유의어	Reduce, decrease, lessen
반의어	Increase, grow, expand
영영	make something smaller or less.
예문	The value of the dollar has diminished in recent years. 달러의 가치는 최근 몇 년 동안 떨어졌습니다.

187

diabetes

[ˌdaɪ.əˈbiː.tiːz]

n. 당뇨병

diabetic a. 당뇨병의
diagnose v. 진단하다

어원	-dia : across + -betes : go → ' 당이 몸을 가로질러 가서 소변으로 배출되는 당뇨병'
유의어	High blood sugar, Hyperglycemia, Diabetic condition Glucose disorder
반의어	Normal blood sugar levels, Euglycemia, Healthy metabolic state, Non-diabetic condition
영영	a chronic disease that affects how your body regulates blood sugar.
예문	Diabetes is a chronic disease that affects the way your body regulates blood sugar. 당뇨병은 신체가 혈당을 조절하는 방식에 영향을 미치는 만성 질환입니다.

188

credulous

[ˈkredʒ.ə.ləs]

a. 너무 잘 믿는(속기 쉬움)

credulously adv. 쉽게 믿어서
credulousness n. 쉽게 믿음, 곧잘 속음
credit card n. 신용카드
creed n. 신조, 신념

어원	-cre, -cred, -creed : believe 믿다(G) + -ous 형접 → '믿기만 하니 속기 쉬운'
유의어	Gullible, trusting, naïve
반의어	Skeptical, cautious, distrustful
영영	easily believing what you are told, even if it is not true.
예문	The witness was credible, and her testimony was accepted by the jury. 그 증인은 믿을 만하였고, 그 증언은 배심원들에 의해 받아들여졌습니다.

189

spine

[spaɪn]

n. 척추, 등뼈; 가시

spiny a. 가시가 많은
spindle n. 축, 굴대
spanking a. 매우 민첩한
spike n. 대못, 철책; 스파이크

어원	-spine : spike 못 → '못처럼 뾰족한 등뼈가 모인 척추'
유의어	Backbone, vertebral column
반의어	None (Spine doesn't have a direct opposite in this context)
영영	the backbone of an animal.
예문	The lion used its spine to break the neck of its prey. 사자는 등뼈를 사용하여 먹잇감의 목을 부러뜨렸습니다.

190

gravel

[ˈɡræv.əl]

n. 자갈

a. granular 알갱이 모양의, 입자상의
v. granulate 알갱이 형태로 만들다
n. granola 씨리얼
n. grain 낱알, 곡물

어원	-grain, -gran : seed 알갱이 → '알갱이가 큰 자갈'
유의어	Pebbles, crushed rock, grit
반의어	Smooth surface, pavement
영영	small stones or pebbles.
예문	The road was covered in gravel, making it difficult to drive. 그 길은 자갈로 덮여 있어 운전하기가 어려웠습니다.

191
make one's way to

p. ~로 나아가다

make for p. ~에 기여하다
make it to p. ~에 도착하다, 이르다
make the point that p. ~라는 주자을 하다
be made up of p. ~로 구성되어 있다

어원	-make 만들다 + -way → '길을 만들어 나아가다'
유의어	Journey to, travel to, proceed to
반의어	Depart from, leave, avoid
영영	go to a particular place.
예문	The hikers made their way to the top of the mountain. 하이커들은 산 정상으로 향했습니다.

192
take A further

p. A추가적인 조치를 취하다

far from p. 전혀 ~이 아닌
further adv. 더 멀리
furthermore adv. 게다가, 더욱이

어원	-take 취하다 + -further 더 → '더 취했으니 추가 조치'
유의어	Proceed with, continue, advance
반의어	Halt, stop, regress
영영	go a little further than A.
예문	The researcher took his research a further step by conducting experiments on animals. 그 연구원은 동물을 대상으로 실험을 수행함으로써 연구를 한 단계 더 발전시켰습니다.

193
on closer inspection

p. 더 자세히 살펴보면

inspect v. 조사하다
inspector n. 조사관, 감독관
inspection n. 검사, 점검
self-inspection n. 자기 점검

어원	-on 접촉 + -closer 더 가까이 + -spect : look → '더 가까이 붙어서 보니 자세히 살펴보면'
유의어	Upon examination, with careful scrutiny
반의어	Superficially, at a glance, without scrutiny
영영	when you look at something more carefully.
예문	On closer inspection, the painting turned out to be a fake. 자세히 살펴보니 그 그림은 가짜로 밝혀졌습니다.

194
prove a point

p. 반드시 ~하다

make a point p. 강조하다; 주장을 밝히다
point of view n. 관점
point out p. 가리키다, 지적하다
at some point p. 어느 시점에서

어원	-prove 증명하다 + -point → '요점을 증명했으니 반드시 ~하리라 주장하다'
유의어	Demonstrate, confirm, substantiate
반의어	Disprove, refute, invalidate
영영	show that something is true or correct.
예문	The lawyer proved his point by presenting evidence. 그 변호사는 증거를 제시함으로써 자신의 주장을 입증했습니다.

195
carry away

p. 가져가 버리다; 넋을 잃게 하다

carry on p. 계속 수행하다
carry out p. ~을 수행하다
carry weight p. ~을 중요하게 여기다
miscarry v. 유산하다

어원	-carry 나르다 + -away → '멀리 가져가 버리니 넋을 잃게 하다'
유의어	Transport, sweep away, captivate
반의어	Leave behind, reject, repel
영영	take someone away with strong emotions or excitement.
예문	The music carried him away, and he forgot all about his troubles. 그 음악은 그를 사로잡았고, 그는 모든 어려움을 잊어버렸습니다.

196
at variance with

p. ~와 상충하는 / 모순되는

v. vary 다르다, 달라지다

어원	-at 지점 + -variance 변화 + -with → '변화하는 지점에서 모순되고 상충하는'
유의어	In disagreement with, conflicting with
반의어	In agreement with, aligned with
영영	different from or in disagreement with.
예문	The findings of the study were at variance with the previous research. 그 연구 결과는 이전 연구와 일치하지 않았습니다.

197	어원	-with + -regard 관심 → '관심과 함께 있으니 계속 ~와 관련하여'
with regard to	긍의어	Concerning, regarding, in relation to
	반의어	Irrelevant to, unrelated to, regardless of
p. ~과 관련하여, ~에 대해	영영	concerning or relating to something.
with regard to p. ~와 관련하여, ~에 대해 regale v. 매우 즐겁게 하다 regarding prep. ~에 관하여 disregard v. 무시하다	예문	With regard to the recent controversy, I have nothing to say. 최근 논란에 대해서는 할 말이 없습니다.
198	어원	-trumpet (G) 디오니서스 신의 찬양 + -over : more than → 'trumpet나팔을 불며 진 상대에게 승리를 알리다' * 미국 트럼프 전 대통령
triumph over	긍의어	Conquer, prevail over, overcome
	반의어	Surrender to, yield to, succumb to
p. ~에게 승리하다	영영	defeat someone or something in a competition or struggle.
triumph n. 나팔, 승리 / v. 승리를 알리다 triumphant a. 크게 성공한, 큰 승리를 거둔 triumphantly adv. 위풍당당하게, 의기양양하여 trumpet n. 으뜸패, 승리의 나팔	예문	The athlete triumphed over adversity to win the race. 그 선수는 역경을 극복하고 경기에서 우승했습니다.
199	어원	-at 지점 + -expense 비용 → '비용이 들어간 지점이니 ~을 희생하면서'
at the expense of	긍의어	To the detriment of, sacrificing, costing
	반의어	Without cost to, at the benefit of
p. ~을 희생하면서	영영	causing harm or disadvantage to someone or something else in order to achieve something.
at one's expense p. ~의 부담으로 expend v. (돈, 시간, 노력)을 쓰다 expense n. 비용, 지출, 경비 expendable a. 소모용의	예문	The company made a profit at the expense of its workers. 그 회사는 노동자들의 희생을 바탕으로 이익을 남겼습니다.
200	어원	-come out 나오다 + -ahead 앞서서 → '앞서 나오니 결국 이득을 보다'
come out ahead	긍의어	Succeed, prosper, win
	반의어	Fall behind, lose, fail
p. 결국 이득을 보다	영영	be successful or win in a competition or situation.
come across p. 우연히 발견하다 come in handy p. 쓸모가 있다 come true p. 실현되다 come to do p. ~하게 되다	예문	The investor came out ahead despite the market crash. 그 투자자는 시장 폭락에도 불구하고 이익을 남겼습니다.

Chapter 6.

201	acne	[ˈæk.ni]	n. 여드름
202	poverty	[ˈpɒv.ə.ti]	n. 가난
203	contend	[kənténd]	v. 주장하다, 논쟁하다; 다투다
204	bosom	[búzəm]	n. (여자의) 가슴; 단란함
205	fluctuate	[ˈflʌk.tʃu.eɪt]	v. 변동하다
206	garb	[gɑːb]	n. 복장
207	acquisitiveness	[əˈkwɪz.ɪ.tɪv.nəs]	n. 물욕, 탐욕
208	amass	[əˈmæs]	v. 모으다, 축적하다
209	ensue	[ɪnˈsjuː]	v. 계속해서 일어나다
210	solitary	[ˈsɒl.ɪ.tər.i]	a. 고독한, 혼자의
211	audiovisual	[ˌɔː.di.əʊˈvɪʒ.u.əl]	a. 시청각의
212	picket	[ˈpɪk.ɪt]	v. 피켓 시위를 하다
213	voyage	[ˈvɔɪ.ɪdʒ]	n. 항해, 여행
214	disparate	[díspərit, dispǽ-]	a. 이질적인
215	connote	[kəˈnəʊt]	v. 암시하다, 함축하다, 내포하다
216	suffrage	[ˈsʌf.rɪdʒ]	n. 투표권, 선거권
217	disperse	[dɪˈspɜːs]	v. 흩어지게 하다; 분산시키다
218	feasible	[ˈfiː.zə.bəl]	a. 실행 가능한, 그럴듯한
219	ethanol	[ˈeθ.ə.nɒl]	n. 에탄올
220	jurisdiction	[ˌdʒʊə.rɪsˈdɪk.ʃən]	n. 재판권; 관할권
221	pediatric	[ˌpiː.diˈæt.rɪk]	a. 소아과의
222	premonitory	[priˈmɒn.ɪ.tər.i]	a. 예고의, 전조의
223	endear	[ɪnˈdɪər]	v. 애정을 느끼게 하다
224	specimen	[ˈspes.ə.mɪn]	n. 견본, 표본
225	pox	[ˈpɒks]	n. 천연두
226	underdog	[ˈʌndərdɔ.g]	n. 약체, 약자
227	telling	[ˈtel.ɪŋ]	a. 효과적으로 보여 주는; 효과적인, 효험이 있는
228	utensil	[juːˈten.səl]	n. 도구, 기구
229	standfast	[stǽndfæst]	n. 바른, 확고한 위치
230	arithmetic	[əˈrɪθ.mə.tɪk]	n. 산수, 연산
231	at the rate of		p. ~의 비율로
232	at a distance		p. 멀리서[거리를 두고]
233	take stock		p. (찬찬히) 살펴보다, 점검하다; 재고 조사하다
234	at the best		p. 잘해봐야
235	rise to the bait		p. 미끼를 물다
236	come on		p. 시작하다; ~이 닥쳐오다
237	at first glance		p. 처음에는[언뜻 보기에는], 처음 봐서는
238	at the age of		p. ~의 나이로
239	factor in		p. ~을 고려하다, ~을 계산에 넣다
240	in the abstract		p. 추상적으로, 관념적으로

201	어원	-ac, -aci, -acu 뾰족한, 날카로운 → '뾰족하게 솟은 여드름'
acne [ˈæk.ni] n. 여드름	유의어	Pimple, blemish, zit
	반의어	Clear skin, flawless complexion
	영영	a skin condition characterized by pimples
acneigenic a. 여드름 유발성인 acid a. 산, 신맛의	예문	She suffered from acne on her face. 그녀는 얼굴에 여드름이 났다.

202	어원	-pov, -pau 약간, 조금 → '조금 밖에 없으니 가난한'
poverty [ˈpɒv.ə.ti] n. 가난	유의어	Destitution, indigence, penury
	반의어	Wealth, affluence, prosperity
	영영	the state of being poor
impoverish v. 가난하게 하다, 고갈시키다 pauper n. 빈민 penury n. 궁핍	예문	Many people live in poverty in developing countries. 개발도상국에서는 많은 사람들이 가난하게 살고 있다.

203	어원	-con : together + -ten, -tens : stretch → '같이 손을 뻗어 다투다'
contend [kənténd] v. 주장하다, 논쟁하다; 다투다	유의어	Compete, vie, struggle
	반의어	Concede, yield, surrender
	영영	to compete or argue
a. contentious 논쟁적인, 분쟁을 일으키는 n. contest 대회, 시합, 경쟁 v. distend 팽창시키다	예문	The two teams will contend for the championship. 두 팀은 챔피언 자리를 놓고 경쟁할 것이다.

204	어원	-blizzard, -blast : bhle, bhel : blow, swell → '바람이 들어간 것처럼 부푼 가슴' * 보솜 보솜 단란한 분위기
bosom [búzəm] n. (여자의) 가슴; 단란함	유의어	Chest, breast
	반의어	Back, spine
	영영	the chest
busom a. 안락한, 편안한 abdomen n. 복부	예문	She hugged him tightly to her bosom. 그녀는 그를 가슴에 꼭 안았다.

205	어원	-flu, -flo : flow 흐르다(L) + -ate 동접 → '흐르는 물은 계속 변동한다'
fluctuate [ˈflʌk.tʃu.eɪt] v. 변동하다	유의어	Vary, oscillate, change
	반의어	Stabilize, remain, constant, steady
	영영	to vary or change irregularly
fluctuation n. 변동, 흔들림 influx n. 유입 confluence n. 합류, 융합, 연결점	예문	The price of oil fluctuates depending on the market conditions. 석유 가격은 시장 상황에 따라 변동한다.

206	어원	-gar : protect → '몸을 보호해 주는 옷'
garb [gɑːb] n. 복장	유의어	Attire, outfit, clothing
	반의어	Undress, strip, disrobe
	영영	clothing
guard n. 경호원	예문	He wore a suit and tie, which was his usual garb for formal occasions. 그는 정장과 넥타이를 입었는데, 그것은 격식을 갖춘 자리에서 그가 입는 평소 옷차림이었다.

207

acquisitiveness

[əˈkwɪz.ɪ.tɪv.nəs]

n. 물욕, 탐욕

v. acquire 얻다, 획득하다
n. acquisition 획득, 취득
a. acquisitive 얻으려고 하는, 욕심 많은

어원	-a : to + -quir, -quer, -quest, -quisit : seek 구하다 → '~쪽으로 계속 구하려는 물욕이나 탐욕' * acquirement 개인의 노력을 통한 성과 VS acquisition 기계적인 장치를 이용한 데이터
유의어	Greed, avarice, covetousness
반의어	Generosity, contentment, selflessness
영영	the desire to acquire something
예문	His acquisitiveness led him to accumulate a large amount of wealth. 그의 욕심은 그를 많은 재산을 모으게 했다.

208

amass

[əˈmæs]

v. 모으다, 축적하다

mass n. 질량
massive a. 거대한
maximize v. 최대화하다
maximum n. 최대

어원	-a : to + -mass 덩어리 → '한 덩어리로 모으다'
유의어	Accumulate, gather, collect
반의어	Scatter, disperse, distribute
영영	to gather or collect a large amount of something
예문	He amassed a fortune through his business ventures. 그는 사업을 통해 많은 재산을 모았다.

209

ensue

[ɪnˈsjuː]

v. 계속해서 일어나다

sequence n. 연속 사건
sequential a. 연속되는
consequence n. 결과
pursue v. 추구하다

어원	-en : upon + -sue : follow → '일이 붙어 일어나니 계속'
유의어	Follow, result, occur
반의어	Precede, antecede
영영	to follow or result from something
예문	After the accident, several injuries ensued. 사고 후에는 여러 부상이 뒤따랐다.

210

solitary

[ˈsɒl.ɪ.tər.i]

a. 고독한, 혼자의

solitude n. 고독
soliloquy n. 독백
isolate v. 격리하다
solo n. 솔로

어원	-sol, -soli, -sun : 태양, alone 혼자(L) + -ary 형접 → '태양처럼 혼자 있으니 고독한' * 태양은 유일한 것. 그래서 신도 하나라 생각
유의어	Alone, lonely, isolated
반의어	Social, companionable, gregarious
영영	alone or isolated
예문	He spent most of his time in solitary confinement. 그는 대부분의 시간을 독방에서 보냈다.

211

audiovisual

[ˌɔː.di.əʊˈvɪʒ.u.əl]

a. 시청각의

auditor n. 청취자, 방송인
auditory a. 청각의, 귀의
audiometer n. 청력계
acoustic a. 청각의

어원	-audio 듣다 + -visual 보다 → '듣기도 보기도 하니 시청각의'
유의어	Multimodal, multimedia, sensory
반의어	Nonvisual, nonauditory
영영	relating to both sound and vision
예문	The presentation included a variety of audiovisual aids. 발표에는 다양한 시청각 자료가 포함되었다.

212

picket

[ˈpɪk.ɪt]

v. 피켓 시위를 하다

pricky a. 가시가 많은, 성가신
pricking n. 따끔하게 찌르기
picky a. 까다로운
pungent a. 신랄한

어원	-pick, -punc, -pung : prick 찌르다(F) → '땅에 찔러 박고 피켓 시위를 하다'
유의어	Demonstrate, protest, strike
반의어	Support, endorse, advocate
영영	a person who stands in a public place to protest or demonstrate
예문	The workers organized a picket outside the factory. 노동자들은 공장 밖에서 시위를 조직했다.

213

voyage

[ˈvɔɪ.ɪdʒ]

n. 항해, 여행

vehicle n. 탈 것, 운반수단

어원	-vi, -via, -vey, -voy 길(L) → '길을 만들어 가는 항해로 여행'
유의어	Journey, trip, expedition
반의어	Stay, remain, stagnation
영영	a long journey by sea or air
예문	They set sail on a voyage around the world. 그들은 세계 일주 여행을 시작했다.

214

disparate

[díspərit, dispǽ-]

a. 이질적인

n. parasite 기생충

어원	-dis : not + -para 옆에, 나란히 (L) → '나란히 같지 않으니 이질적인'
유의어	Different, distinct, diverse
반의어	Similar, alike, uniform
영영	very different
예문	The two groups had vastly disparate views on the issue. 두 그룹은 이 문제에 대해 매우 다른 견해를 가지고 있었다.

215

connote

[kəˈnoʊt]

v. 암시하다, 함축하다, 내포하다

connotation n. 함축, 내포
notation n. 표기법
annotate v. 주석을 달다

어원	-con : together + -no, -not : mark 표시하다, know 알다(L) → '아는 것을 다 내포하니 함축'
유의어	Imply, suggest, indicate
반의어	Denote, specify, state explicitly
영영	to suggest or imply something in addition to the literal meaning of the word
예문	The word "freedom" connotes many different meanings depending on the context. "자유"라는 단어는 문맥에 따라 다양한 의미를 내포한다.

216

suffrage

[ˈsʌf.rɪdʒ]

n. 투표권, 선거권

suffragist n. 여성 선거권론자
franchise n. 선거권

어원	-suf, -sub : under + -frag : crash → '밑에 있던 계급이 부딪쳐 쟁취한 투표권'
유의어	Voting rights, franchise, enfranchisement
반의어	Disenfranchisement, disfranchise
영영	the right to vote
예문	Women were granted the right to vote in 1920, thanks to the efforts of suffragettes. 여성들은 1920년에 여성 참정권 운동가들의 노력 덕분에 투표권을 부여받았다.

217

disperse

[dɪˈspɜːs]

v. 흩어지게 하다; 분산시키다

dispersal n. 분산, 살포, 해산
intersperse v. 흩뿌리다, 점재시키다
sparkling a. 불꽃을 튀기는
sparse a. 드문드문한, 부족한, 희박한

어원	-dis : away + -spers, -spars, -sparg : scatter → '서로 떨어지도록 흩뜨려 뿌리다'
유의어	Scatter, distribute, dissipate
반의어	Gather, collect, congregate
영영	to scatter or spread out
예문	The crowd dispersed after the police arrived. 경찰이 도착한 후 군중은 흩어졌다.

218

feasible

[ˈfiː.zə.bəl]

a. 실행 가능한, 그럴듯한

feasibly adv. 실현 가능하게
feasibility n. 실현 가능성
unfeasible a. 실현이 어려운
feat n. 업적

어원	-feat 이뤄내다 + -ible 할 수 있는 → '이뤄낼 수 있으니 실현 가능한'
유의어	Achievable, possible, viable
반의어	Impractical, unattainable, unrealistic
영영	possible to do or achieve
예문	It is feasible to build a new subway line in the city. 도시에 새로운 지하철 노선을 건설하는 것은 가능하다.

219

ethanol

[ˈeθ.ə.nɒl]

n. 에탄올

어원	-ethan 에탄 + -alcohol 수분 → '에탄에 수분이 포함된 에탄올'
유의어	Ethyl alcohol, grain alcohol
반의어	Water
영영	an alcohol produced by the fermentation of sugars or starches
예문	Ethanol is a type of alcohol that is used as a fuel. 에탄올은 연료로 사용되는 알코올의 일종이다.

220

jurisdiction

[ˌdʒʊə.rɪsˈdɪk.ʃən]

n. 재판권; 관할권

jurisdictional a. 관할권의, 사법권의
judge n. 판사, 심판
jury n. 배심원단

어원	-ju : right + -dict : say → '옳게 판단하여 말해야 하는 재판권'
유의어	Authority, control, power
반의어	Subjection, submission, obedience
영영	the power to make legal decisions or judgments
예문	The court has jurisdiction over all criminal cases in the city. 법원은 도시 내 모든 형사 사건에 대한 관할권을 가지고 있다.

221

pediatric

[ˌpiː.diˈæt.rɪk]

a. 소아과의

pediatrics n. 소아과
pediatrician n. 소아과 의사
psychiatry n. 정신의학

어원	-ped 아이, 가르치다 (G) + -iatros 의사 → '아이를 치료하는 의사가 있는 소아과' * -ped(L) : foot / pedestrian 보행자
contour	Child health, pediatrician
반의어	Geriatric, adult
영영	relating to children's medical care
예문	The hospital has a pediatric ward for children. 병원에는 어린이들을 위한 소아과 병동이 있다.

222

premonitory

[priˈmɒn.ɪ.tər.i]

a. 예고의, 전조의

monitor n. 감시자, 관찰자
premonish v. 미리 경고하다, 예고하다
admonish v. 훈계하다, 충고하다

어원	-pre : before + -moni : advise → '미리 조언하니 전조의' * '미리 moster가 나타났다고 경고하니 예감'
유의어	Warning, predictive, prophetic
반의어	Reassuring, calming, comforting
영영	giving warning or indication of something that is to come
예문	There were some premonitory signs that the storm was coming. 폭풍이 올 것이라는 징후가 몇 가지 있었다.

223

endear

[ɪnˈdɪər]

v. 애정을 느끼게 하다

darling n. 자기, 여보

어원	-en : make + -dear 사랑하는 → '사랑의 감정을 만들어 애정을 느끼게 하다'
유의어	Charm, captivate, attract
반의어	Repel, alienate, discourage
영영	to make someone or something more attractive or likable
예문	His kindness and humor endeared him to everyone. 그의 친절과 유머는 모든 사람들에게 사랑받았다.

224

specimen

[ˈspes.ə.mɪn]

n. 견본, 표본

species n. 종, 종류
specified a. 명시된
specification n. 열거, 명세사항
speculate v. 추측하다

어원	-spec 보다 → '보이는 특성대로 나누어 놓은 견본'
sample	Sample, example, model
반의어	Aberration, anomaly, irregularity
영영	a sample or example of something
예문	The scientist collected a specimen of the rare plant. 과학자는 희귀 식물의 표본을 수집했다.

225	어원	-po : poison 독 → '작은 독 덩어리'
pox [ˈpɒks] n. 천연두		Rash, blisters, sores
	반의어	Health, wellness, soundness
	영영	a contagious disease characterized by pustules
poxy a. 불쾌한, 불결한, 하찮은 pustule n. 사마귀, 여드름	예문	The child had a bad case of chicken pox. 그 아이는 심한 수두에 걸렸다.

226	어원	-under + -dog 개 → '개보다 못한 약자'
underdog [ˈʌndərdɔ.ɡ] n. 약체, 약자	유의어	Outsider, disadvantaged, dark horse
	반의어	Favorite, top contender, frontrunner
	영영	a person or group that is considered to be less likely to succeed
outsider n. 외부인 dogma n. (독단적인) 신조 a dog's breakfast p. 쓰레기 더미, 더러운 것 donation n. 기부, 기부금	예문	The team was considered the underdog in the competition. 그 팀은 대회에서 약자로 여겨졌다.

227	어원	-tell, -tal 말하다 (E) → '말이 계속 이어질 정도로 강력하고 효과적인'
telling [ˈtel.ɪŋ] a. 효과적으로 보여 주는; 효과적인, 효험이 있는	유의어	Compelling, convincing, persuasive
	반의어	Ineffective, weak, unconvincing
	영영	revealing or informative
tale n. 이야기 untold a. 무한한	예문	The telling of the story was very moving. 그 이야기의 전달은 매우 감동적이었다.

228	어원	-us, -ut : use(L) + -sil : fit → '사용하기에 알맞은 물건들'
utensil [juːˈten.səl] n. 도구, 기구	유의어	Tool, implement, instrument
	반의어	Raw material, resource, compone
	영영	a tool or implement used in cooking or other household tasks
utilitarian a. 실용적인, 공리주의의 utility n. 공익 설비	예문	She picked up a spoon and fork from the utensil drawer. 그녀는 수저 서랍에서 숟가락과 포크를 집어들었다.

229	어원	-stand 서 있는 + -fast 고정된 → '흔들림 없이 서 있으니 확고한'
standfast [stændfæst] n. 바른, 확고한 위치	유의어	Persist, endure, persevere, stand firm
	반의어	Yield, surrender, give up, capitulate
	영영	firm or unyielding in one's beliefs or principles
standby n. 예비물, 대기신호 standee n. 입석 standpoint n. 입장, 견지, 관점 fasten v. 고정하다	예문	The soldiers stood fast in the face of enemy fire. 군인들은 적의 공격에 맞서 굳건히 서 있었다.

230	어원	-arith 셈하다, 평가하다(G) + -metic : measure 측정하다 → '셈을 측정하는 수학'
arithmetic [əˈrɪθ.mə.tɪk] n. 산수, 연산	유의어	Math, calculation, figures, mathematics
	반의어	Algebra, geometry, advanced math
	영영	the branch of mathematics that deals with numbers
n. algorithm 알고리즘, 계산 과정 n. geometry 기하학	예문	He was good at arithmetic and could solve complex equations quickly. 그는 수학을 잘했고 복잡한 방정식을 빠르게 풀 수 있었다.

231

at the rate of

p. ~의 비율로

rate n. 비율, 속도 v. 평가하다
ratio n. 비율
at the rate of p. ~의 비율로
in the ratio of p. ~의 비율로

어원	-at 지점 + -rate 비율 → '지정한 비율로'
be skilled 유의어 반의어	According to, based on, in proportion to Irrespective of, regardless of, uniformly
영영	in a certain amount for each unit of time
예문	The car was going at the rate of 60 miles per hour. 그 차는 시속 60마일의 속도로 달리고 있었다.

232

at a distance

p. 멀리서[거리를 두고]

at all cost p. 기어코, 무슨 수를 써서라도
at an angle p. 비스듬히
at first glance p. 처음에는, 언뜻 보기에는
at a loss p. 어쩔 줄을 모르는

어원	-at 점 + -distant 먼 → '먼 지점까지 거리를 두고'
유의어 반의어	Far away, remotely, distantly, from a distance Up close, nearby, closely
영영	from a distance
예문	The mountain looked small at a distance. 산은 멀리서 보니 작게 보였다.

233

take stock

p. (찬찬히) 살펴보다, 점검하다; 재고 조사하다

어원	-take + -stock 재고 → '재고를 취할 때마다 찬찬히 살펴보며 점검하다'
유의어 반의어	Assess, evaluate, appraise, inventory Neglect, ignore, overlook, dismiss
영영	to assess or evaluate a situation
예문	We need to take stock of our situation and make some decisions. 우리는 상황을 파악하고 결정을 내려야 한다.

234

at the best

p. 잘해봐야

at no cost p. 공짜로
at no time p. 결코 ~하지 않다
at one's option p. ~의 마음대로
at peace p. 평화롭게

어원	-at 지점 + -best 최고 → '최고 지점이 정해져 있으니 잘해봐야'
유의어 반의어	Ideally, optimally, under the best circumstances Worst-case scenario, at the worst, under adverse conditions
영영	under the most favorable circumstances
예문	At the best, we can only hope for a miracle. 기껏해야 우리는 기적을 바랄 수 있을 뿐이다.

235

rise to the bait

p. 미끼를 물다

bait n.미끼, 유혹
bay n. 만, 후미
abetment n. 선동, 교사
abettor n. 선동자

어원	-rise 오르다 + -bait 미끼 → '뛰어 올라 미끼를 물다'
at home 반의어	Take the bait, fall for the trap, respond to provocation Resist temptation, ignore provocations, stay unaffected
영영	to react to a provocation
예문	The fish didn't rise to the bait, so we had to try another approach. 물고기가 미끼를 물지 않아서 우리는 다른 방법을 시도해야 했다.

236

come on

p. 시작하다; ~이 닥쳐오다

come across p. 우연히 발견하다
come in handy p. 쓸모가 있다
come true p. 실현되다
come out ahead p. 결국 이득을 보다

어원	-come 오다 + -on → '일에 붙었으니 시작'
control over 반의어	Approach, advance, move forward Retreat, withdraw, step back
영영	an exclamation used to encourage or urge someone to do something
예문	Come on, let's go already! 자, 이제 그만 가자!

237	어원	-at 지점 + -first + -glance 흘깃 봄 → '흘깃 처음 봐서는'
	유의어	Initially, at the outset
at first glance	반의어	Upon closer inspection, upon further consideration
	영영	from a quick or superficial examination
p. 처음에는[언뜻 보기에는], 처음 봐서는		
at no cost p. 공짜로 at no time p. 결코 ~하지 않다 at one's option p. ~의 마음대로 at peace p. 평화롭게	예문	At first glance, the painting seemed simple, but upon closer inspection, it was much more complex. 첫눈에 그 그림은 간단해 보였지만 자세히 살펴보니 훨씬 더 복잡했다.
238	어원	-at 지점 + -age 나이 → '정해진 지점의 나이로'
	유의어	When, at the time of, during
at the age of	반의어	Before the age of, after the age of, later in life
	영영	when one is a certain age
p. ~의 나이로		
at no cost p. 공짜로 at no time p. 결코 ~하지 않다 at one's option p. ~의 마음대로 at peace p. 평화롭게	예문	She became a doctor at the age of 30. 그녀는 30세에 의사가 되었다.
239	어원	-factor 요인 + -in 안 → '요인들을 모두 범주 안에 넣고 고려하다'
	aggressive to	Take into account, consider, include
factor in	반의어	Overlook, neglect, ignore
	영영	to take into account or consider something
p. ~을 고려하다, ~을 계산에 넣다		
factor n. 요소, 요인 by a factor of p. ~배로	예문	We need to factor in the cost of transportation when planning our budget. 예산을 계획할 때 교통비를 고려해야 한다.
240	어원	-abs : away + -trac, -tract, -trai, -tray, -treat : draw(L) → '멀리 끌어가는 생각이니 추상적인', 추상적으로 핵심만 모아 놓은 개요'
	유의어	Theoretically, conceptually, in theory
in the abstract	반의어	In reality, practically, concretely
	영영	in a general or theoretical way, without considering specific details
p. 추상적으로, 관념적으로		
attract v. 끌어들이다 tractor n. 트랙터 retract v. 철회하다, 거부하다	예문	The idea of love is often discussed in the abstract, but it can be difficult to define in concrete terms. 사랑이라는 개념은 추상적으로 논의되는 경우가 많지만 구체적인 용어로 정의하기는 어렵다.

Chapter 7.

241	rhetorical	[rɪˈtɒr.ɪ.kəl]	a. 수사적인, 미사여구식의, 과장이 심한
242	carton	[ˈkɑː.tən]	n. 상자
243	arrogate	[ˈær.ə.geɪt]	v. 침해하다, 가로채다
244	domineer	[dàməníər]	v. 권력을 휘두르다
245	tariff	[ˈtær.ɪf]	n. 관세, 요금표
246	pulp	[pʌlp]	n. 걸쭉한 것; (과일·채소) 과육
247	outage	[ˈaʊ.tɪdʒ]	n. 정전, 단수
248	indignant	[ɪnˈdɪg.nənt]	a. 분개한, 성난
249	junction	[ˈdʒʌŋk.ʃən]	n. 접합, 교차점, 분기점
250	reign	[reɪn]	n. 통치 기간 v. 통치하다
251	comprehend	[ˌkɒm.prɪˈhend]	v. 이해하다
252	intact	[ɪnˈtækt]	a. 완전한, 손상되지 않은
253	pardon	[ˈpɑː.dən]	n. 용서 v. 용서하다
254	abuse	[əˈbjuːz]	v. 학대하다; 남용하다, 오용하다
255	posterity	[pɒsˈter.ə.ti]	n. 자손, 후대
256	avert	[əˈvɜːt]	v. (불행한 일을) 피하다, 막다; 돌리다
257	fuss	[fʌs]	n. 공연한 소란
258	acclimate	[ˈæk.lɪ.meɪt]	v. 새 풍토에 길들이다
259	embryo	[ˈem.bri.əʊ]	n. 태아, 배
260	archive	[ˈɑː.kaɪv]	n. 기록, 자료 수집
261	adjudicate	[əˈdʒuː.dɪ.keɪt]	v. 판결하다, 선고하다
262	algebra	[ˈæl.dʒə.brə]	n. 대수학
263	alleviate	[əˈliː.vi.eɪt]	v. 경감시키다, 완화시키다
264	surge	[sɜːdʒ]	v. 밀어닥치다, 쇄도하다; 급등하다 n. 큰 파도, 격동
265	wavelength	[weiˈvleɪ̩ŋθ]	n. 주파수, 파장
266	consort	[kənˈsɔːt]	v. 사귀다, 어울리다 n. 배우자
267	moron	[ˈmɔː.rɒn]	n. 바보 천치, 멍청이
268	gymnasium	[dʒɪmˈneɪ.zi.əm]	n. 체육관, (실내) 경기장
269	abolish	[əˈbɒl.ɪʃ]	v. 폐지하다, 없애다
270	anguish	[ˈæŋ.gwɪʃ]	n. 극심한 고통, 고뇌
271	double back on oneself		p. 왔던 길로 되돌아가다
272	pin down		p. ~을 정확히 밝히다
273	take a measure		p. 조치를 취하다
274	short of breath		p. 숨이 가쁜, 숨을 쉴 수 없는
275	at hand		p. 당면한
276	by a factor of		p. ~ 배로
277	pull out		p. 철수하다, 빼다, 벗어나다
278	close call		p. 위기일발
279	an array of		p. 많은
280	at its highest		p. 절정에

241

rhetorical

[rɪˈtɒr.ɪ.kəl]

a. 수사적인, 미사여구식의, 과장이 심한

rhetoric n. 연설술, 용변술

어원	-rheto 대중 연설(L) → 대중 연설을 위해 수사법으로 말을 꾸미니 미사여구식의'
유의어	Oratorical, expressive, persuasive
반의어	Literal, straightforward, non-rhetorical
영영	Used for effect or to ask a question for emphasis rather than to get an answer.
예문	His question was purely rhetorical, intended to make a point rather than elicit a genuine response. 그의 질문은 순전히 수사적이었으며 실제 응답을 유도하는 것이 아니라 어떤 점을 강조하기 위한 것이었다.

242

carton

[ˈkɑː.tən]

n. 상자

cartoon n. 만화
carry v. 나르다

어원	-card 두꺼운 종이 → '두꺼운 종이로 만든 상자'
유의어	Box, container, package
반의어	Unpackaged, loose, individual item
영영	A cardboard box typically used for packaging goods.
예문	She carried a carton of eggs from the grocery store. 그녀는 식료품 가게에서 계란 한 상자를 들고 왔다.

243

arrogate

[ˈær.ə.geɪt]

v. 침해하다, 가로채다

arrogance n. 오만, 거만, 자만
arrogantly adv. 거만하게
arrogant a. 오만한
abrogate v. 폐지하다, 철회하다

어원	-ar : to + -rog : ask → '남의 것을 내 것이라고 요구하며 침해'
유의어	Seize, usurp, claim
반의어	Relinquish, yield, surrender
영영	To claim or seize something without justification or right.
예문	The dictator attempted to arrogate more power to himself by suppressing dissent. 독재자는 이의 억압을 통해 자신에게 더 많은 권력을 차지하려고 했다.

244

domineer

[dàməníər]

v. 권력을 휘두르다

dominate v. 지배하다
domain n. 영토

어원	-dom 지배하다 (L) → 둥근 천장 → 건축양식 → '지배 범위 내에서 권력을 휘두르다' * dom '지배' VS man, main '살다'
유의어	Bully, oppress, tyrannize
반의어	Submit, yield, cooperate
영영	To control or influence someone in a forceful or overbearing way.
예문	The manager had a tendency to domineer over his subordinates, making it difficult for them to express their opinions. 그 매니저는 부하직원들에게 지배적인 태도를 보여 자신들의 의견을 표현하기 어렵게 만들었다.

245

tariff

[ˈtær.ɪf]

n. 관세, 요금표

a. tariffless 관세가 없는, 관세가 면제된

어원	* tariff : 16세기 스페인 요새 Tarifa에서 유래, 해적들은 해협을 지나는 화물선에서 공물을 강제로 수탈
유의어	Duty, tax, customs
반의어	Exemption, rebate, discount
영영	A tax on goods imported or exported.
예문	The government imposed a new tariff on imported goods to protect domestic industries. 정부는 국내 산업을 보호하기 위해 수입품에 대한 새로운 관세를 부과했다.

246

pulp

[pʌlp]

n. 걸쭉한 것; (과일·채소) 과육

a. pulpy 걸쭉한; 유연한

어원	-pulp 걸쭉한 것 * pull 나무 등의 섬유 식물에서 뽑아낸 것
유의어	Mash, mush, paste
반의어	Solid, whole, intact
영영	Soft, moist matter made from crushed wood or fruit.
예문	The paper was recycled into pulp to be used in the production of new paper products. 종이는 새로운 종이 제품의 생산에 사용하기 위해 펄프로 재활용되었다.

247

outage

[ˈaʊ.tɪdʒ]

n. 정전, 단수

outcry n. 비명
out of the blue p. 느닷없이

어원	-out + -age 기간 → '기간이 끝났으니(out) 정전이나 단수'
유의어	Blackout, interruption, failure
반의어	Continuity, stability, operation
영영	A sudden and temporary interruption in the supply of a service or utility.
예문	The power outage left the entire neighborhood in darkness for several hours. 정전으로 전체 동네가 몇 시간 동안 어둠 속에 놓여 있었다.

248

indignant

[ɪnˈdɪg.nənt]

a. 분개한, 성난

dignity n. 위엄, 존엄

어원	-in : not + -dign, -dain : worth → '가치가 없다고 하여 분개한'
유의어	Angry, outraged, resentful
반의어	Pleased, content, indifferent
영영	Feeling or expressing anger or outrage at something unjust or wrong.
예문	She felt indignant at the unfair treatment she received. 그녀는 받은 불공평한 대우에 분개했다.

249

junction

[ˈdʒʌŋk.ʃən]

n. 접합, 교차점, 분기점

juncture n. 접합
conjunction n. 결합, 접속사
joint a. 관절, 공동의
conjunction n. 결합, 접속사

어원	-join, -junc, -junct 합치다(L) → '다른 길이 서로 만나는 교차점' * join, junc(t) '다른 것이 만나 합침' VS ser(t) '밀어 넣어서 합침'
유의어	Intersection, connection, meeting point
반의어	Separation, disconnection, divergence
영영	A place where two or more roads, paths, or boundaries meet.
예문	The traffic was congested at the junction of two major highways. 두 대형 고속도로의 교차로에서 교통이 막혔다.

250

reign

[reɪn]

n. 통치 기간 v. 통치하다

n. regent 통치자
a. regal 군주적인, 왕다운
n. regime 정권

어원	-rig, -rec, -rect, -reg, -reig, -roy 올바른(L), rule 통치하다(F) → '올바르게 통치한 기간'
유의어	Rule, sovereignty, dominance
반의어	Submission, defeat, overthrow
영영	The period of time during which a monarch or other ruler is in power.
예문	The king's reign was marked by prosperity and cultural development. 왕의 통치 시기는 번영과 문화 발전으로 특징지어졌다.

251

comprehend

[ˌkɒm.prɪˈhend]

v. 이해하다

comprehensive a. 포괄적인, 함축적인
comprehension n. 이해, 이해력
comprehensible a. 이해할 수 있는
apprehend v. 체포하다, 이해하다

어원	-com : together + -prehen, -pren, -pregn, -pris : seize → '모든 개념을 잡았으니 포괄적으로 이해'
유의어	Understand, grasp, perceive
반의어	Misunderstand, confuse, overlook
영영	To understand something fully.
예문	It took her a while to comprehend the complexity of the scientific theory. 그녀는 과학 이론의 복잡성을 이해하는 데 시간이 걸렸다.

252

intact

[ɪnˈtækt]

a. 완전한, 손상되지 않은

intangible a. 만질 수 없는, 비물질적인

어원	-in : not + -tac 닿다 → '아직 손이 닿지 않아 온전한'
유의어	Unbroken, undamaged, whole
반의어	Broken, damaged, fragmented
영영	Whole and undamaged.
예문	Despite the accident, the package arrived at its destination intact. 사고에도 불구하고, 소포는 목적지에 그대로 도착했다.

253	어원	-par, -per 완전히 + -don : give → '완전한 자유를 주니 용서하다'
pardon	유의어	Forgive, excuse, absolve
[ˈpɑː.dən]	반의어	Condemn, blame, accuse
n. 용서 v. 용서하다	영영	To forgive someone for a crime or offense.
pardonable a. 용서할 수 있는 donation n. 기부금, 기증 condolence n. 애도, 조의	예문	The president issued a pardon to the political prisoner, allowing him to be released from prison. 대통령은 정치 죄수에게 사면을 발표하여 그를 감옥에서 석방시켰다.

254	어원	-ab : away + -us : use → '올바른 사용에서 멀어져 남용하는'
abuse	유의어	Mistreatment, maltreatment, misuse
[əˈbjuːz]	반의어	Respect, honor, use properly
v. 학대하다; 남용하다, 오용하다	영영	To treat someone or something with cruelty or violence.
n. usage 사용, 용도 n. disuse 폐지	예문	The teacher warned the students against the abuse of school property. 선생님은 학교 재산 남용에 대해 학생들에게 경고했다.

255	어원	-post : after + -er 비교급 → '더 뒤에 있는 후손'
posterity	유의어	Descendants, offspring, future generations
[pɒsˈter.ə.ti]	반의어	Ancestors, forebears, past generations
n. 자손, 후대	영영	Future generations of people.
postmortem n. 시체 해부 posthumous a. 사후의	예문	Many historical figures strive to leave a positive legacy for the benefit of posterity. 많은 역사적 인물들이 후대의 이익을 위해 긍정적인 유산을 남기려 노력했다.

256	어원	-a, -ab : from + vert : turn → '다른 쪽으로 돌려 불행을 피하다'
avert	유의어	Prevent, avoid, deflect
[əˈvɜːt]	반의어	Allow, permit, accept
v. (불행한 일을) 피하다, 막다; 돌리다	영영	To prevent something from happening.
averse a. 싫어하는 aversion n. 혐오, 반감, 기피 vertigo n. 현기증 subvert v. 전복시키다, 뒤집다	예문	She tried to avert her gaze to avoid eye contact with the suspicious stranger. 그녀는 의심스러운 낯선 사람과 눈을 마주치지 않기 위해 시선을 피했다.

257	어원	-fus, -fut, -fund : melt 녹이다; pour 붓다 → '소리를 퍼부으니 공연한 소란' * 버스(bus)에서 소란을 떨다
fuss	유의어	Commotion, uproar, disturbance
[fʌs]	반의어	Calm, tranquility, silence
n. 공연한 소란	영영	An excessive amount of worry or bother about something unimportant.
make a fuss p. 수선을 떨다 confuse v. 혼동시키다, 당황하게 하다 refuse v. 거절하다, 사절하다 transfuse v. 헌혈하다	예문	There was a fuss in the office when the fire alarm went off accidentally. 화재 경보가 실수로 울리자 사무실에서 소란이 났다.

258	어원	-ac : to + climate 기후 → '새로운 환경에 맞추는'
acclimate	유의어	Adapt, adjust, accustom
[ˈæk.lɪ.meɪt]	반의어	Resist, reject, oppose
v. 새 풍토에 길들이다	영영	To become adjusted to a new environment or situation.
acclimation n. 새 환경에의 적응 microclimate n. 미세기후 climatology n. 기후학 adhere v. 들러붙다, 부착되다	예문	It takes time to acclimate to a new climate, especially when moving to a different country. 특히 다른 나라로 이사할 때 새로운 기후에 적응하는 데는 시간이 걸린다.

259

embryo

[ˈem.bri.əʊ]

n. 태아, 배

embryonic a. 배아의, 발생 초기의
brute n. 짐승 a.잔인한; 신체적

어원	-em, -en : in + -bryo : swell → '배 안에서 부풀어 오르며 성장하는 태아'
유의어	Fetus, incipient, rudimentary
반의어	Adult, mature, developed
영영	An organism in the early stages of development before it is born or hatched.
예문	The scientist studied the development of the embryo to understand early stages of life. 과학자는 생명의 초기 단계를 이해하기 위해 태아의 발달을 연구했다.

260

archive

[ˈɑː.kaɪv]

n. 기록, 자료 수집

n. architect 건축가
n. technique 기술, 기법

어원	-archive 그리스 지방 관리자 아르콘(Archon)의 집 → '이 집에는 공식적인 문서와 기록들이 보관'
유의어	Record, repository, storage
반의어	Delete, discard, erase
영영	A collection of historical documents or records.
예문	The historical documents were carefully preserved in the archive for future reference. 역사적 문서들은 미래 참고를 위해 보관소에서 신중하게 보존되었다.

261

adjudicate

[əˈdʒuː.dɪ.keɪt]

v. 판결하다, 선고하다

judge n. 판사, 심판
jury n. 배심원단

어원	-ac : to + -judic : judge → '판결의 방향으로 선고하다'
유의어	Judge, decide, settle
반의어	Disregard, ignore, neglect
영영	To act as a judge or arbitrator in a dispute.
예문	The judge will adjudicate the case to determine a fair resolution. 판사는 사건을 심판하여 공정한 해결책을 결정할 것이다.

262

algebra

[ˈæl.dʒə.brə]

n. 대수학

altruistic a. 이타적인
algorithm n. 알고리즘
alternative n. 대안, 양자택일
alter v. 바꾸다, 변경하다

어원	-aljabr 대수 → '수를 대신한 기호의 학문이 대수학' * -al, -alien, -alter, altru : other 다른(L) + ge : birth
유의어	Mathematical, symbolic, variable
반의어	Arithmetic, numerical, concrete
영영	A branch of mathematics dealing with symbols and their operations.
예문	In algebra, variables and equations are used to solve mathematical problems. 대수학에서는 변수와 방정식이 수학적 문제를 해결하는 데 사용된다.

263

alleviate

[əˈliː.vi.eɪt]

v. 경감시키다, 완화시키다

levitate v. 공중에 떠오르다, 부양시키다
relieve v. 경감시키다
lever n. 지렛대, 레버
levity n. 경솔

어원	-al : to + -levi : light → '가볍게 하니 완화시키다'
유의어	Relieve, ease, mitigate
반의어	Aggravate, intensify, worsen
영영	To make something less severe or painful.
예문	Medication can help alleviate the symptoms of a cold. 약물은 감기의 증상을 완화하는 데 도움이 될 수 있다.

264

surge

[sɜːdʒ]

v. 밀어닥치다, 쇄도하다; 급등하다 n. 큰 파도, 격동

surf v. 파도 타기를 하다
source n. 근원, 출처

어원	-surg, -sour 솟아나다 (L) → '솟아오른 파도처럼 일이 밀어닥치다'
유의어	Rush, flood, swell
반의어	Recede, ebb, decline
영영	A sudden, sharp increase in something.
예문	The hospital experienced a surge in patients during the flu season. 병원은 독감 시즌에 환자 수가 급증했다.

265	어원	-wave 파동 + -length 길이 → '파동의 길이인 파장으로 주파수 파악'
wavelength	유의어	Frequency, vibration, resonance
[weiˈvleˌŋθ]	반의어	Disharmony, discord, mismatch
n. 주파수, 파장	영영	The distance between two corresponding points on a wave.
n. wave 파도	예문	The two friends were on the same wavelength, understanding each other without many words. 두 친구는 말이 많이 필요하지 않고 서로를 이해하는 데 동일한 물결 길이에 있었다.
266	어원	-con : together + -sort 부류 → '부류별로 어울리며 사귀다가 배우자까지'
consort	유의어	Associate, partner, companion
[kənˈsɔːt]	반의어	Competitor, adversary, opponent
v. 사귀다, 어울리다 n. 배우자	영영	A spouse or companion of a high-ranking person.
consortium n. 컨소시엄; 국제협회 assort v. 분류하다	예문	The queen chose her consort to be her partner in ruling the kingdom. 여왕은 왕비를 국가 통치의 파트너로 선택했다.
267	어원	-moron 느린, 굼뜬, 바보같은(G) * moron 모르는 바보 천치
moron	유의어	Fool, idiot, imbecile
[ˈmɔːrɒn]	반의어	Genius, intellect, prodigy
n. 바보 천치, 멍청이	영영	A person with very low intelligence.
	예문	Using offensive language to describe someone as a moron is not respectful. 누군가를 모른으로 묘사하는 데 무례한 언어를 사용하는 것은 예의 없다.
268	어원	-gymnos 맨몸의 + -nastos 선수 → '맨몸의 운동 선수가 운동하는 체육관'
gymnasium	유의어	Fitness center, workout facility, health club
[dʒɪmˈneɪ.zi.əm]	반의어	Sedentary, inactive, lethargic
n. 체육관, (실내) 경기장	영영	A large room or building equipped for indoor sports and physical exercise.
gymnastics n. 체조; 체육학 gymnast n. 체조선수 gymnophobia n. 체육 공포증	예문	The school built a new gymnasium for students to engage in physical activities. 학교는 학생들이 신체 활동에 참여할 수 있도록 새로운 체육관을 건설했다.
269	어원	-ab : away + -ol : odor 냄새, 악취 → '악취를 멀리 보내니 제거하다'
abolish	유의어	Eliminate, eradicate, annul
[əˈbɒl.ɪʃ]	반의어	Establish, institute, retain
v. 폐지하다, 없애다	영영	To formally end or put an end to something.
abolition n. 폐지, 폐지주의 abolitionist n. 폐지주의자 aberrant a. 정도를 벗어난, 변태적인 abort v. 낙태하다, 유산하다; 중단하다	예문	The government decided to abolish the outdated law to make way for more progressive policies. 정부는 더 진보적인 정책을 위해 구식인 법률을 폐지하기로 결정했다.
270	어원	-ang, -anx : choke, 고통(L) + -ish 명접 → '질식할 정도로 누르기 고통'
anguish	유의어	Suffering, torment, agony
[ˈæŋ.gwɪʃ]	반의어	Contentment, joy, happiness
n. 극심한 고통, 고뇌	영영	Severe mental or physical pain or suffering.
a. angry 화난 a. anxious 걱정하는, 갈망하는	예문	The family experienced great anguish when they received news of the tragic accident. 그 가족은 비극적인 사고에 대한 소식을 받고 큰 고통을 겪었다.

271

double back on oneself

p. 왔던 길로 되돌아가다

v. double-bag 두 겹으로 봉투에 담다
adv. doubly 이중으로
a. dual 둘의
v. doubt 의심하다

어원	-double : two + -back → '스스로 뒤를 돌아보는 두 번의 여정으로 돌아가다'
유의어	Retrace one's steps, backtrack, reverse course
반의어	Move forward, continue straight ahead
영영	To return to a previous place or position.
예문	Realizing he had taken the wrong path, he had to double back on himself to find the right way. 잘못된 길을 선택한 것을 깨닫고, 그는 올바른 길을 찾기 위해 자신의 길을 되돌아가야 했다.

272

pin down

p. ~을 정확히 밝히다

pin n. 핀 v. 꽂다
pin back p. 뒤로 당겨서 묶다

어원	-pin 꽂아 + -down 아래 → '핀을 원하는 대상에 꽂아 정확히 원인을 밝히다'
유의어	Identify, specify, define
반의어	Vague, generalize, uncertain
영영	To identify or fix something exactly.
예문	It's challenging to pin down the exact cause of the problem without further investigation. 추가 조사 없이 문제의 정확한 원인을 정확히 결정하는 것은 어렵다.

273

take a measure

p. 조치를 취하다

measure v. 측정하다, 평가하다
take measures p. 조치를 취하다
measure up with p. ~와 겨루다

어원	-take 취하다 + -measure 측정하다 → '사건의 크기를 측정하고 조치를 취하다'
유의어	Assess, evaluate, gauge
반의어	Ignore, neglect, overlook
영영	To take action to achieve something.
예문	Before implementing changes, it's essential to take a measure of the current situation. 변경 사항을 시행하기 전에 현재 상황을 측정하는 것이 중요하다.

274

short of breath

p. 숨이 가쁜, 숨을 쉴 수 없는

catch one's breath p. 숨을 고르다
take a deep breath p. 심호흡하다
breathless a. 숨이 가쁜, 숨을 쉴 수 없는
breathtaking a. 숨막히는, 아슬아슬한

어원	-short + -breath 숨 → '숨이 짧으니 가쁜'
유의어	Breathless, panting, winded
반의어	Breathable, at ease, relaxed
영영	Having difficulty breathing.
예문	After running for miles, he was short of breath and needed a moment to recover. 몇 마일을 뛰어서 그는 숨이 차고 회복하는 데 순간이 필요했다.

275

at hand

p. 당면한

on one hand p. 한편으로는
second-hand p. 간접적으로
hand down p. ~을 물려주다
near at hand p. 가까이에

어원	-at ~에 + -hand 손 → '손에 닿을 정도니 곧 이르는'
유의어	Nearby, close, within reach
반의어	Distant, far away, out of reach
영영	Close by or readily available.
예문	Keep your tools at hand so that you can quickly access them when needed. 필요할 때 빠르게 액세스할 수 있도록 도구를 손안에 두세요.

276

by a factor of

p. ~ 배로

factor n. 요소, 요인
factor in p. ~을 고려하다, ~을 계산에 넣다

어원	-factor 비율; 요인 → '비율만큼 ~ 배로'
유의어	Multiplied by, increased by
반의어	Divided by, decreased by
영영	A way to express a multiplication by a certain number.
예문	The production efficiency increased by a factor of two after implementing the new technology. 새로운 기술을 도입한 후에 생산 효율이 두 배로 증가했다.

277

pull out

p. 철수하다, 빼다, 벗어나다

pull A out p. A를 인출하다
pull over p. 끌어당기다
pull down p. 허물다

어원	-pull 당기다 + -out → '밖으로 잡아당겨 빼니 철수하다'
유의어	Withdraw, extract, remove
반의어	Insert, put in, stay in
영영	To remove something from a place or position.
예문	The company decided to pull out of the market due to increased competition. 회사는 경쟁이 치열해진 것을 이유로 시장에서 철수하기로 결정했다.

278

close call

p. 위기일발

call after p. ~을 따라 이름짓다
call back p. ~을 취소하다
call for p. ~을 요구하다, 구하다
call off p. 취소하다, 중지하다

어원	-close 가까운 + -call → '콜을 불러야 할 위기 상황과 가까우니 위기일발'
유의어	Near miss, narrow escape, close shave
반의어	Safe distance, no risk, clear victory
영영	A situation in which something dangerous or unpleasant was narrowly avoided.
예문	It was a close call, but the driver managed to avoid the collision at the last moment. 그것은 위험했지만, 운전자는 마지막 순간에 충돌을 피할 수 있었다.

279

an array of

p. 많은

array n. 대형, 배치
disarray n. 혼란, 혼잡

어원	- ar : to + -ray, -rei : order → '순서에 맞춰 정렬된 것이 많은'
유의어	A variety of, a range of, a multitude of
반의어	A few, a lack of, a scarcity of
영영	A large number or variety of something.
예문	The buffet offered an array of delicious dishes from various cuisines. 뷔페는 다양한 요리에서 나온 맛있는 음식들을 제공했다.

280

at its highest

p. 절정에

at no cost p. 공짜로
at no time p. 결코 ~하지 않다
at one's option p. ~의 마음대로
at peace p. 평화롭게

어원	-at 지점 + -highest → '가장 높은 지점이니 절정에'
유의어	At its peak, at its maximum, at its zenith
반의어	At its lowest, at its minimum, at its nadir
영영	At the greatest or most intense level.
예문	The temperature is expected to be at its highest in the afternoon, so stay hydrated. 온도는 오후에 가장 높을 것으로 예상되므로 수분 섭취에 주의하세요.

Chapter 8.

281	dwindle	[ˈdwɪn.dəl]	v. 줄어들다, 감소하다, 작아지다
282	prehensile	[prɪˈhen.saɪl]	a. 잡기에 적합한; 이해력이 있는
283	barter	[ˈbɑː.tər]	n. 물물 교환 v. 물건을 교환하다
284	confucius	[kənˈfjuː.ʃəs]	n. 공자(유교의 창시자)
285	archaic	[ɑːˈkeɪ.ɪk]	a. 낡은, 오래된
286	regime	[reiʒíːm]	n. 정권, 제도, 체제
287	apparel	[əˈpær.əl]	n. 옷, 복장, 의류
288	decry	[dɪˈkraɪ]	v. 비난하다
289	atypical	[eitípikəl]	a. 불규칙의, 비정형의, 이례적인
290	homage	[ˈhɒm.ɪdʒ]	n. 경의; 존경의 표시
291	antedate	[ˌæn.tiˈdeɪt]	v. ~에 앞서다, 날짜를 앞당기다
292	malefactor	[ˈmæl.ɪ.fæk.tər]	n. 죄인, 악인
293	snuff	[snʌf]	v. 코를 킁킁거리다; (촛불 같은 것을) 끄다
294	guile	[gaɪl]	n. 간교한 속임수
295	transmittance	[trænsmítəns]	n. 투과율
296	erratic	[irǽtik]	a. 별난, 괴상한, 불규칙한
297	allege	[əˈledʒ]	v. 주장하다, 단언하다
298	parish	[ˈpær.ɪʃ]	n. 교구; 행정구
299	fatal	[ˈfeɪ.təl]	a. 치명적인; 결정적인, 중대한
300	auxiliary	[ɔːgˈzɪl.i.ə.ri]	a. 보조의
301	calculus	[kǽlkjuləs]	n. 미적분학; 계산법; 석탄
302	splendid	[ˈsplen.dɪd]	a. 정말 좋은, 훌륭한
303	suffocate	[ˈsʌf.ə.keɪt]	v. 숨을 막다, 질식시키다
304	stiff	[stif]	a. 뻣뻣한, 딱딱한; 치열한; 강한 n. 시체
305	scrutinize	[ˈskruː.tɪ.naɪz]	v. 세밀히 조사하다
306	amnesia	[æmˈniː.zi.ə]	n. 기억상실증
307	ludicrous	[ˈluː.dɪ.krəs]	a. 우스운
308	incur	[ɪnˈkɜːr]	v. 초래하다; (손실을) 입다, (빚을) 지다
309	punctual	[pʌŋkʧuəl]	a. 시간을 엄수하는, 기한을 지키는
310	corrode	[kəˈrəʊd]	v. 부식하다
311	line of attack		p. 대처 방안
312	creep over		p. (공포 따위가) ~을 엄습하다
313	take up the issue		p. 그 문제를 상정하다
314	rooted in		p. ~에 뿌리를 둔
315	goods and services		p. 재화와 용역
316	fit A like a glove		p. A에 맞춘 듯이 꼭 맞아떨어지다
317	wipe out		p. 멸종시키다
318	know A by sight		p. A와 안면은 있다
319	as ever		p. 변함없이
320	at length		p. 오랫동안, 상세히

281	어원	-dwindle 사라지다 → '사라지는 것처럼 줄어들어 작아지다' * -d : down + wind → '바람에 날려 양이 줄어들다'
dwindle	유의어	Decrease, diminish, shrink, wane.
[ˈdwɪn.dəl]	반의어	Increase, grow, expand, swell.
v. 줄어들다, 감소하다, 작아지다	영영	To become gradually smaller or fewer.
a. dwindling 적어지는, 저하하는 v. diminish 감소시키다, 줄이다, 약화시키다 v. decline 쇠퇴하다, 감소하다, 기울다	예문	The number of visitors to the museum has dwindled over the years. 박물관 방문객 수가 몇 년 동안 감소했다.
282	어원	-pren : seize + -able → '잡을 수 있는 지식 때문에 이해력이 있는'
prehensile	유의어	Grasping, clutching, seizing.
[prɪˈhen.saɪl]	반의어	Nonprehensile, ungrasping, non-grasping.
a. 잡기에 적합한; 이해력이 있는	영영	Capable of grasping or holding onto objects.
prehension n. 파악, 잡기, 포착 comprehend v. 이해하다 reprehend v. 꾸짖다, 비난하다	예문	The monkey has prehensile tail that it uses to grab things. 그 원숭이는 물건을 잡는 데 사용하는 물건을 잡는 꼬리를 가지고 있다.
283	어원	-barter 물물교환 * 바트(태국 화폐)로 물물교환
barter	유의어	Trade, exchange, swap, negotiate.
[ˈbɑː.tər]	반의어	Buy, sell, purchase, trade.
n. 물물 교환 v. 물건을 교환하다	영영	The exchange of goods or services for other goods or services without using money.
n. barley 보리	예문	In the past, people often bartered goods and services for other goods and services. 과거에는 사람들이 종종 상품과 서비스를 다른 상품과 서비스와 교환하곤 했다.
284	어원	- confu : kung fu 철학 마스터 → '철학 마스터인 공자'
confucius	유의어	Kong Fuzi, Kongzi, Kong Qiu.
[kənˈfjuː.ʃəs]	반의어	
n. 공자(유교의 창시자)	영영	A Chinese philosopher and teacher known for his teachings on ethics, morality, and social relationships.
confucian a. 공자의, 유교의 Confucianism n. 유교 Confucianism n. 유교	예문	Confucius is a famous philosopher in Chinese history. 공자(孔子)는 중국 역사상 유명한 철학자이다.
285	어원	-archae, -archaeo 오래된 (L) → '오래 되니 낡은'
archaic	유의어	Outdated, antiquated, obsolete, ancient.
[ɑːˈkeɪ.ɪk]	반의어	Modern, contemporary, current, up-to-date.
a. 낡은, 오래된	영영	Relating to a very old or ancient time; no longer in common use.
archaeology n. 고고학 archaeologist n. 고고학자	예문	The language used in the old book is archaic and difficult to understand. 그 오래된 책에 사용된 언어는 고풍스럽고 이해하기 어렵다.
286	어원	-rig, -rec, -rect, -reg, -reig, -roy 올바른(L), rule 통치하다(F) → '올바르게 통치하는 정권과 제도'
regime	유의어	Government, administration, rule, leadership.
[reiʒíːm]	반의어	Opposition, resistance, rebellion, insurgency.
n. 정권, 제도, 체제	영영	A system of government or management, often with a particular set of rules or principles.
n. regent 통치자 a. regal 군주적인, 왕다운 a. royal 왕의, 왕립의	예문	The regime in North Korea is known for its strict control over its citizens. 북한 정권은 시민들에 대한 엄격한 통제로 유명하다.

287

apparel

[əˈpær.əl]

n. 옷, 복장, 의류

appear v. ~처럼 보이다
disappear v. 사라지다

어원	-appar: appearance 모습 → '겉모습을 만드는 옷이나 복장이 의류'
유의어	Clothing, attire, garments, dress.
반의어	Nude, undress, uncover, strip.
영영	Clothing or garments worn by people.
예문	She bought new apparel for her trip to Europe. 그녀는 유럽 여행을 위해 새 옷을 샀다.

288

decry

[dɪˈkraɪ]

v. 비난하다

outcry n. 비명
descry v. 발견하다

어원	-de : down + -cry 소리치다 → '아래로 내려다보며 소리치니 비난하다'
유의어	Denounce, condemn, criticize, disparage.
반의어	Praise, applaud, commend, laud.
영영	To publicly criticize or denounce something.
예문	Many people decry the use of plastic bags because they are harmful to the environment. 많은 사람들이 환경에 해롭기 때문에 비닐 봉지의 사용을 비난한다.

289

atypical

[eitípikəl]

a. 불규칙의, 비정형의, 이례적인

p. typical of ~의 전형인
adv. typically 일반적으로, 보통

어원	-a, -an : not + -typical → '전형적이지 않은'
유의어	Unusual, abnormal, uncommon, unconventional.
반의어	Typical, normal, standard, ordinary.
영영	Not conforming to the usual or typical pattern or behavior.
예문	The patient's symptoms were atypical and difficult to diagnose. 환자의 증상은 비정형적이어서 진단하기 어려웠다.

290

homage

[ˈhɒm.ɪdʒ]

n. 경의; 존경의 표시

homosexual a. 동성애의
homeostasis n. 항상성
honest a. 솔직한

어원	-homo 사람 + -omage 존경 (F) → '사람에 대한 존경' * 오마주 : 감독이나 작가에 대한 존경의 표시로 영화의 대사나 장면을 인용하는 일
유의어	Respect, honor, reverence, tribute.
반의어	Disrespect, dishonor, scorn, contempt.
영영	A show of respect or honor, often in the form of a tribute or acknowledgment.
예문	The team paid homage to their late coach by wearing special jerseys. 그 팀은 고인이 된 감독에게 경의를 표하기 위해 특별한 유니폼을 입었다.

291

antedate

[ˌæn.tiˈdeɪt]

v. ~에 앞서다, 날짜를 앞당기다

anterior a. 이전의
anthropology n. 인류학

어원	-ant, -ante 이전 + -date 날짜 → '앞으로 날짜를 당기다'
유의어	Precede, precede in time, come before.
반의어	Postdate, follow, come after.
영영	To precede or come before in time.
예문	The painting was found to antedate the artist's previously known works. 그 그림은 화가의 이전에 알려진 작품들보다 더 오래된 것으로 밝혀졌다.

292

malefactor

[ˈmæl.ɪ.fæk.tər]

n. 죄인, 악인

malevolent a. 사악한
malice n. 악의, 원한
malign a. 유해한, 악성인

어원	-mal : bad(L) +-fac : do + -or 사람 → '나쁜 일을 하는 사람이니 죄인, 악인'
유의어	Criminal, wrongdoer, offender, lawbreaker.
반의어	Innocent, law-abiding, righteous.
영영	A person who commits a crime or wrongdoings.
예문	The malefactor was sentenced to life in prison for his crimes. 그 범죄자는 범죄로 인해 종신형을 선고받았다.

293	어원	-snort 코골이 * -sn은 주로 코와 관련
snuff	유의어	Extinguish, put out, douse, quench.
	반의어	Ignite, light, kindle.
[snʌf]	영영	To extinguish or put out, often referring to a candle or flame.
v. 코를 킁킁거리다; (촛불 같은 것을) 끄다		
sneeze v. 재채기하다 sniffs n. 콧구멍 snobbish a. 잘난 척 하는 snub v. 모욕하다	예문	The candle went out after being snuffed by the wind. 촛불은 바람에 꺼져 버렸다.

294	어원	-guil, -guile : guilty 유죄 → '유죄를 받을 정도로 교활한 속임수'
guile	유의어	Deception, cunning, craftiness, slyness.
	반의어	Honesty, straightforwardness, candor.
[gaɪl]	영영	Cunning or deceitful behavior.
n. 간교한 속임수		
beguile v. 속이다, 즐겁게 하다 guileful a. 교활한 guileless a. 악의 없는, 순진한 guilty a. 죄책감이 드는, 유죄의	예문	He used guile to get the better of his opponent in the game. 그는 교활한 방법을 써서 경기에서 상대방을 이겼다.

295	어원	-trans : across + -mit : send → '건너서 보내는 투과율'
transmittance	유의어	Transmission, conveyance, passage, transfer.
	반의어	Absorption, obstruction, blocking.
[trænsmítəns]	영영	The ability to transmit or pass through, often used in the context of light or signals.
n. 투과율		
transmit v. 보내다, 전송하다 omit v. 생략하다, 빠뜨리다 remission n. 용서, 면제	예문	The transmittance of the radio signal was poor due to the heavy rain. 폭우로 인해 라디오 신호의 전달이 좋지 않았다.

296	어원	-err, -error : wander → ' 오류가 있는 것처럼 보이니 별나고 괴상한'
erratic	유의어	Unpredictable, irregular, inconsistent, unstable.
	반의어	Predictable, steady, regular, stable.
[irǽtik]	영영	Not following a regular or predictable pattern; irregular.
a. 별난, 괴상한, 불규칙한		
error n. 실수, 오류 errneous a. 잘못된 errand n. 심부름, 잡일	예문	His behavior has been erratic lately, and no one knows what he's going to do next. 최근 그의 행동은 변덕스러워져서 아무도 그가 다음에 무엇을 할지 모른다.

297	어원	-al : to + -leg, -litigare : law → '~방향으로 법적인 주장'
allege	유의어	Assert, claim, declare, contend.
	반의어	Deny, refute, disprove, contradict.
[əˈledʒ]	영영	To claim or assert without providing proof or evidence.
v. 주장하다, 단언하다		
allegation n. 혐의 제기 allergy n. 알러지 litigate v. 제소하다, 소송하다	예문	The witness alleged that the defendant had stolen the money. 증인은 피고가 돈을 훔쳤다고 주장했다.

298	어원	-par, -para : beside + -ish, -oikos : house → '옆의 이웃을 사랑하는 교회의 교구'
parish	유의어	District, locality, community, township.
	반의어	Metropolis, city, urban area.
[ˈpær.ɪʃ]	영영	A local administrative district, often used in the context of religious congregations.
n. 교구; 행정구		
parody n. 패러디 parasite n. 기생충	예문	The parish priest is responsible for the spiritual needs of the local community. 교구 목사는 지역 사회의 영적인 요구에 책임이 있다.

299

fatal

['feɪ.təl]

a. 치명적인; 결정적인, 중대한

fatally adv. 치명적으로
fatality n. 치사성, 사망, 사망자
fate n. 운명, 숙명
infatuate v. 열광시키다, 미쳐버리다

어원	-fa, -fe, -fess, -phe : talk 말하다 → '신의 말씀이니 치명적이고 중요한' * 팜므파탈 femme 여성 fatale 치명적인 '치명적 매력의 여성'
유의어	Lethal, deadly, mortal, life-threatening.
반의어	Nonfatal, harmless, survivable.
영영	Resulting in death; deadly.
예문	The accident was fatal and the driver was killed instantly. 그 사고는 치명적이었고 운전자는 즉사했다.

300

auxiliary

[ɔːgˈzɪl.i.ə.ri]

a. 보조의

audio a. 녹음의
audience n. 청중, 관객
audit v. 청강하다

어원	* aux - 오디오 관련 장치에서 aux라고 표시된 단자 : auxiliary의 약자로 보조로 다른 장치를 추가해서 연결
유의어	Supplementary, additional, extra, backup.
반의어	Main, primary, central, essential.
영영	Providing additional support or assistance; secondary.
예문	The auxiliary verb "to be" is used to form the present tense of regular verbs. 조동사 "to be"는 규칙 동사의 현재 시제를 만드는 데 사용된다.

301

calculus

[kælkjuləs]

n. 미적분학; 계산법; 석탄

calibration n. 눈금 매기기; 눈금
calculate v. 계산하다
calendar n. 달력

어원	-calculus 작은 돌(L) → '옛날 양치기가 양의 수를 셀 때 작은 돌을 이용했다'
유의어	Mathematical calculation, computation.
반의어	Algebra, arithmetic, basic math.
영영	A branch of mathematics that deals with rates of change and accumulation, often used in calculus equations.
예문	Calculus is a branch of mathematics that deals with rates of change and slopes of curves. 미적분학은 변화율과 곡선의 기울기 등을 다루는 수학의 한 분야이다.

302

splendid

['splen.dɪd]

a. 정말 좋은, 훌륭한

special a. 특별한
spectacles n. 안경
specter n. 망령, 유령

어원	-splendid : shine → '빛이 날 정도로 정말 좋으니 훌륭한' * -sp : spectacular 볼 만할 정도로 훌륭한
유의어	Magnificent, grand, glorious, impressive.
반의어	Mediocre, ordinary, plain, unremarkable.
영영	Extremely impressive or magnificent.
예문	The view from the top of the mountain was splendid. 산 정상에서 본 경치는 장관이었다.

303

suffocate

['sʌf.ə.keɪt]

v. 숨을 막다, 질식시키다

suffocation n. 질식
suffocating a. 숨이 막히는
faucal a. 인후의
faucet n. 수도꼭지

어원	-suf, -sub : under + -foc, -fauc : throat → '목 아래를 눌러 질식시키다'
유의어	Smother, choke, asphyxiate, stifle.
반의어	Breathe, ventilate, oxygenate.
영영	To die or cause someone to die by depriving them of air or oxygen.
예문	The baby was suffocated by the plastic bag that was tied around its head. 아기는 머리에 묶인 비닐 봉지에 질식했다.

304

stiff

[stif]

a. 뻣뻣한, 딱딱한; 치열한; 강한 n. 시체

stiffen v. 경직되다
stifle v. 굳게 하다
stifling a. 억누르는

어원	-sta,-sist, -ste, -st, -stitu, -stin, -sti : stand 서다, 세우다 → '서 있는 자세가 뻣뻣한 시체'
유의어	Rigid, inflexible, unbending, firm.
반의어	Flexible, pliable, supple, loose.
영영	Rigid or not easily bent; also used informally to describe a person who is formal or lacking in flexibility.
예문	The old man walked with a stiff gait due to his arthritis. 그 노인은 관절염 때문에 뻣뻣한 걸음걸이로 걸었

305

scrutinize

[ˈskruː.tɪ.naɪz]

v. 세밀히 조사하다

scrutiny n. 정밀 조사, 철저한 검토
shred v. 찢다, 째다

어원	-scru : shred + -tin : tiny → '조각처럼 작은 부분까지 세세히 조사하는'
유의어	Examine closely, inspect, analyze, study.
반의어	Glance over, skim, overlook.
영영	To examine or inspect closely and thoroughly.
예문	The customs officer scrutinized the passenger's passport carefully. 세관원은 승객의 여권을 꼼꼼히 조사했다.

306

amnesia

[æmˈniː.zi.ə]

n. 기억상실증

amnesty n. 사면, 은사

어원	-a 약한 의미의 부정 + -mne 기억 (G) → '기억이 나지 않으니 기억상실증'
유의어	Memory loss, forgetfulness, blackout.
반의어	Memory retention, recollection.
영영	Loss of memory, often due to injury, illness, or psychological trauma.
예문	The patient suffered from amnesia and couldn't remember anything about his past. 그 환자는 기억상실증으로 고통받았으며 자신의 과거에 대해 아무것도 기억하지 못했다.

307

ludicrous

[ˈluː.dɪ.krəs]

a. 우스운

ludic a. 놀기 좋아하는, 놀이의
lure v. 꾀다, 유혹하다
allure v. 유혹하다, 매혹하다
collude v. 공모하다, 결탁하다

어원	-lud : playful → '놀다보니 우스운'
유의어	Ridiculous, absurd, comical, laughable.
반의어	Serious, sensible, reasonable.
영영	Ridiculous or absurd in a humorous way.
예문	His idea of building a bridge across the river was ludicrous. 강을 가로지르는 다리를 건설하자는 그의 생각은 터무니없었다.

308

incur

[ɪnˈkɜːr]

v. 초래하다; (손실을) 입다, (빚을) 지다

occur v. 발생하다
concur v. 일치하다
recur v. 재발하다

어원	-in : make + -cour, -cur : run → '많은 이들이 달려들도록 초래하다가 손실을 입다'
유의어	Suffer, experience, face, bear.
반의어	Avoid, escape, elude.
영영	To become subject to or experience something undesirable, such as a cost or penalty.
예문	The company incurred a large debt due to its failed investment. 그 회사는 투자 실패로 인해 큰 빚을 지게 되었다.

309

punctual

[pʌŋkʧuəl]

a. 시간을 엄수하는, 기한을 지키는

punctually adv. 제시간에, 늦지 않게
puncture n. 펑크
punctuate v. 중단시키다

어원	-punct, -point 점 → '작은 점인 초까지 맞추니 시간을 엄수하는'
유의어	On time, prompt, timely, exact.
반의어	Late, delayed, overdue.
영영	Being on time or arriving at the scheduled time.
예문	She is always punctual and arrives at work on time. 그녀는 항상 시간을 잘 지키고 제시간에 출근한다.

310

corrode

[kəˈraʊd]

v. 부식하다

n. corrosion 부식
a. corrosive 부식성의
n. erosion 침식

어원	-co 함께 + -rod, -ros : 갉아먹는 → '다 함께 갉아 먹으니 썩는'
유의어	Rust, decay, deteriorate, erode.
반의어	Preserve, protect, maintain, strengthen.
영영	To gradually wear away or deteriorate through a chemical reaction, often used in the context of metal rusting.
예문	The metal pipes corroded over time and had to be replaced. 금속 파이프는 시간이 지나면서 부식되어 교체해야 했다.

311

line of attack

p. 대처 방안

counterattack n. 역습, 반격

어원	* line of attack 펜싱에서 공격이 들어오는 선수의 상체 부위 → '들어오는 공격에 대한 대처 방안'
유의어	Strategy, plan, approach, tactic.
반의어	Retreat, withdrawal, surrender.
영영	A strategy or approach used to achieve a particular goal or objective.
예문	The coach drew up a new line of attack for the team's next game. 감독은 팀의 다음 경기를 위해 새로운 공격 전술을 세웠다.

312

creep over

p. (공포 따위가) ~을 엄습하다

creepy a. 오싹한, 소름끼치는
creeping n. 포복 a. 천천히 나아가는
reptile n. 파충류(기어다니는 짐승)
creed n. 신조, 신념

어원	-creep 기다 → '귀신이 기어오듯 공포가 엄습하다'
유의어	Infiltrate, sneak, encroach, trespass.
반의어	Retire, recede, withdraw.
영영	To move quietly or stealthily over a surface.
예문	The feeling of fear slowly crept over me as I realized what was happening. 무슨 일이 일어나고 있는지 깨달으면서 두려움이 서서히 밀려왔다.

313

take up the issue

p. 그 문제를 상정하다

take up p. ~을 맡다
take the side of p. ~의 편을 들다
be taken back p. 당황하다, 허를 찌르다

어원	-take 취하다 + -up 위로 + -issue 문제 → '문제를 취해서 쟁점으로 올리니 상정하다'
유의어	Address, tackle, deal with, confront.
반의어	Ignore, avoid, neglect.
영영	To address or deal with a specific problem or topic.
예문	The government has decided to take up the issue of climate change and work towards finding solutions. 정부는 기후 변화 문제를 해결하기 위해 노력하기로 결정했다.

314

rooted in

p. ~에 뿌리를 둔

root crop p. 뿌리 작물

어원	-root 뿌리 + -in → '정해진 범위 안에 뿌리를 둔'
유의어	Based on, grounded in, originated in, derived from.
반의어	Detached from, unrelated to, disconnected from.
영영	Having its origins or foundation in something.
예문	The tradition of celebrating Christmas is rooted in the Christian religion. 크리스마스를 축하하는 전통은 기독교 신앙에 뿌리를 두고 있다.

315

goods and services

p. 재화와 용역

n. goods 물건, 제품

어원	-good 좋은 상품 + -service 서비스 → '좋은 상품인 재화와 서비스를 제공하는 용역'
유의어	Commodities, products, merchandise.
반의어	Products and assistance
영영	Products and actions offered for sale or exchange in an economy.
예문	The market for goods and services has been growing steadily over the past decade. 지난 10년간 상품과 서비스 시장은 꾸준히 성장해 왔다.

316

fit A like a glove

p. A에 맞춘 듯이 꼭 맞아떨어지다

fit in p. ~에 잘 들어맞다
fit into p. 적합하다, 어울리다
fitter n. 설비 기술자

어원	-fit 맞추다 + -glove 장갑 → '장갑을 맞춘듯이 꼭 맞아떨어지다'
유의어	Perfect fit, suit perfectly, match perfectly.
반의어	Ill-fitting, mismatched, incompatible.
영영	To be a perfect match or fit for something.
예문	The new pair of gloves fit me like a glove. 새 장갑은 내게 꼭 맞는다.

317

wipe out

p. 멸종시키다

n. wiper 와이퍼

어원	-wipe 닦다 + -out → '흔적을 닦아서 완전히 없애니 멸종시키다'
유의어	Eradicate, eliminate, obliterate, annihilate.
반의어	Preserve, protect, save.
영영	To completely destroy or eliminate something.
예문	The tsunami wiped out entire villages along the coast. 쓰나미는 해안가의 마을 전체를 휩쓸어 버렸다.

318

know A by sight

p. A와 안면은 있다

p. know better than to do ~할 정도로 어리석지 않다.

어원	-know 알다 + -by sight 시선 → '시선만 맞춘 적이 있어 안면은 있다
유의어	Recognize, identify, be familiar with.
반의어	Be unfamiliar with, not recognize.
영영	To recognize or be familiar with someone or something based on appearance.
예문	I know him by sight, but I don't know his name. 나는 그를 얼굴만 알고 이름은 모른다.

319

as ever

p. 변함없이

a. even 균등한, 대등한

어원	-ev : long → '오랫동안이니 항상, 언제나'
유의어	As usual, as always, consistently.
반의어	Occasionally, rarely, sporadically.
영영	As always or as has been the case consistently.
예문	He is as ever, full of energy and enthusiasm. 그는 여전히 에너지와 열정이 넘친다.

320

at length

p. 오랫동안, 상세히

lengthen v. 길어지다
linger v. 오래 머무르다; 지속되다

어원	-at 고정 + -long, -leng,-ling : long 긴 / want 갈망하다 → '오랫동안 고정하고 살피니 상세히'
유의어	In detail, extensively, thoroughly, comprehensively.
반의어	Briefly, concisely, shortly.
영영	In great detail or for a long period of time.
예문	After much discussion, we finally reached a decision at length. 많은 논의 끝에 우리는 마침내 긴 시간에 걸쳐 결정을 내렸다.

Chapter 9.

321	trousers	[ˈtraʊ.zəz]	n. (남성용) 바지
322	rodent	[ˈroʊ.dənt]	a. 설치류의 n. 설치류 동물, 쥐
323	assumedly	[əsúːmidli]	adv. 아마
324	rustic	[ˈrʌs.tɪk]	a. 시골풍의
325	progeny	[ˈprɒdʒ.ə.ni]	n. 자손
326	unison	[ˈjuː.nɪ.sən]	n. 일치, 조화
327	tactile	[ˈtæk.taɪl]	a. 촉각의
328	snore	[snɔːr]	v. 코를 골다
329	asterisk	[ˈæs.tər.ɪsk]	n. 별표
330	frown	[fraʊn]	n. 찡그림 v. 눈살을 찌푸리다
331	confer	[kənˈfɜːr]	v. 주다, 수여하다; 상담하다
332	ail	[eɪl]	v. 괴롭히다, 아프게 하다
333	amenity	[əˈmiː.nə.ti]	n. 예의; 편의시설
334	crook	[krʊk]	n. 구부리다; 사기꾼
335	assimilate	[əˈsɪm.ɪ.leɪt]	v. 동화되다, 동화하다; 소화하다; 이해하다
336	renounce	[rɪˈnaʊns]	v. ~을 포기하다, 버리다; 관계를 끊다
337	loop	[luːp]	n. 고리 (모양); 루프
338	backdrop	[ˈbæk.drɒp]	n. 배경
339	rash	[ræʃ]	n. 발진, 뾰루지 a. 성급한
340	sermon	[ˈsɜː.mən]	n. 설교
341	avocation	[ˌæv.əˈkeɪ.ʃən]	n. 부업; 취미
342	stray	[streɪ]	v. 길을 잃다; 벗어나다
343	falsehood	[ˈfɒls.hʊd]	n. 허위, 거짓말
344	deject	[didʒékt]	v. 낙담시키다
345	timorous	[ˈtɪm.ər.əs]	a. 겁 먹은
346	extrude	[ɪkˈstruːd]	v. 밀어내다, 쫓아내다
347	dipole	[dáipòul]	n. 이중극, 쌍극자
348	oat	[əʊt]	n. 귀리
349	aviation	[ˌeɪ.viˈeɪ.ʃən]	n. 항공(술)
350	reproach	[rɪˈprəʊtʃ]	n. 비난, 책망 v. 비난하다
351	call names		p. 욕하다, 맞욕하다
352	be done with		p. ~을 끝내다
353	grow on		p. 점점 좋아지다, 마음에 들다
354	go well with		p. 잘 어울리다
355	little short of		p. ~와 거의 동일하다, ~에 미치지 못하다
356	hot under the collar		p. 화가 난, 당혹해 하는
357	in a big way		p. 대규모로
358	in any event		p. 아무튼, 어떤 경우에도
359	hold back		p. 막다, 제지하다
360	as far as it goes		p. 그 정도까지

321

trousers

['traʊ.zəz]

n. (남성용) 바지

trouse n. 꽉 끼는 짧은 바지
leggings n. 레깅스
trout n. 송어

어원	-trousers (영국) 신사 바지 * trout 송어가 바지 속으로?
유의어	Pants, slacks
반의어	Skirt, dress
영영	An outer garment covering the body from the waist to the ankles, with a separate part for each leg.
예문	He bought a new pair of trousers for the formal event. 그는 정장 행사를 위해 새로운 바지 한 벌을 샀다.

322

rodent

['roʊ.dənt]

a. 설치류의 n. 설치류 동물, 쥐

n. rat 쥐
v. corrode 부식하다
v. erode 침식하다
v. rot 썩다, 부패하다

어원	-ros, -rod 갉아먹다 → '갉아 먹는 쥐 등의 설치류 동물'
유의어	Mouse, rat
반의어	Predator, prey
영영	A small mammal characterized by sharp incisors for gnawing and a single pair of constantly growing incisors.
예문	Rats and mice are common household rodents. 쥐와 쥐는 흔한 가정용 설치 동물이다.

323

assumedly

[əsú:midli]

adv. 아마

unassuming a. 겸손한
presume v. 가정하다, 추측하다
consume v. 소비하다

어원	-as : to + -sum : take 취하다, 골라 가지다 → '한 방향으로 생각을 취해 보니 아마'
유의어	Presumably, supposedly
반의어	Certainly, definitely
영영	Supposedly or presumably, based on the assumption that something is true.
예문	She will, assumedly, arrive at the airport by 3 PM. 그녀는, 아마도, 오후 3시까지 공항에 도착할 것이다.

324

rustic

['rʌs.tɪk]

a. 시골풍의

rusticity n. 소박함
rusticate v. 시골로 가다
rural a. 시골의, 지방의
rust n. 녹; 녹슬다

어원	-ru, rus 시골, 지방
유의어	Rural, pastoral
반의어	Urban, sophisticated
영영	Characteristic of rural life; simple, plain, or rough in appearance.
예문	The cabin had a rustic charm with its wooden furniture. 그 오두막은 나무 가구로 된 Rustic 매력이 있었다.

325

progeny

['prɒdʒ.ə.ni]

n. 자손

pregnancy n. 임신
impregnate v. 임신시키다; 주입하다

어원	-pro : forth + -gen : birth → '앞 세대에서 낳은 자손'
유의어	Offspring, descendants
반의어	Ancestors, forebears
영영	Offspring or descendants, collectively referring to one's children.
예문	The lioness cared for her progeny in the wild. 암사자는 야생에서 자신의 자손을 돌봤다.

326

unison

['ju:.nɪ.sən]

n. 일치, 조화

unisonance n. 합창, 일치
unisonant a. 일치하는, 합주하는
unisonous a. 일치하는
union n. 결합, 노동조합

어원	-uni : one + -son : sound → '한 목소리를 내니 일치, 조화'
유의어	Harmony, agreement
반의어	Discord, disagreement
영영	Simultaneous action, agreement, or harmony.
예문	The choir sang in perfect unison during the performance. 합창단은 공연 중에 완벽한 유니슨으로 노래했다.

327

tactile

[ˈtæk.taɪl]

a. 촉각의

tactility n. 촉감
tactual a. 촉각의, 만질 수 있는
tactile a. 촉각의
tangible a. 유형의

어원	-ti, -tig, -ting, - tag, -tac, -tan, -ten : touch + -ible → '접촉할 수 있는'
유의어	Tangible, palpable
반의어	Intangible, abstract
영영	Perceptible by touch; relating to the sense of touch.
예문	The artist appreciated the tactile quality of the sculpture. 예술가는 조각의 촉감적인 품질을 감상했다

328

snore

[snɔːr]

v. 코를 골다

snorty a. 공격적인, 경멸스러운
snortingly adv. 코를 불며
snort v. 콧김을 내뿜다, 코웃음 치다
sneeze n. 재채기하다

어원	-sno, -sne : snort 코골이 + -no : noise → '코에서 소음이 나오니 코를 골다'
유의어	Sleep apnea, sawing logs
반의어	Silence, quietness
영영	To breathe with a harsh or noisy sound while sleeping.
예문	He tends to snore loudly when he's in a deep sleep. 그는 깊이 자는 동안 시끄럽게 코를 쉰다.

329

asterisk

[ˈæs.tər.ɪsk]

n. 별표

astral a. 별의
disk n. 디스크
astronomy n. 천문학
disastrous a. 재난을 일으키는, 비참한

어원	-astro, -aster, -cider : little star (G) + -isk 작은 것 → '작은 별의 모습이니 별표'
유의어	Star, mark
반의어	Blank, void
영영	A symbol (*) used to mark printed or written text, typically to indicate a footnote or omission.
예문	The footnote was marked with an asterisk at the bottom of the page. 각주는 페이지 아래에 별표로 표시되었다.

330

frown

[fraʊn]

n. 찡그림 v. 눈살을 찌푸리다

fronwingly adv. 찡그리며
frowy a. 찡그린 듯한, 불쾌한
clown n. 광대
frowsty a. 촌스러운

어원	-frown : snose : nose 코 → '코를 찡그리며 눈살을 찌푸리다'
유의어	Scowl, grimace
반의어	Smile, grin
영영	To furrow the brow in displeasure, concentration, or thought.
예문	She gave him a frown when he arrived late. 그는 늦게 도착했을 때 그녀는 불쾌한 표정을 지었다.

331

confer

[kənˈfɜːr]

v. 주다, 수여하다; 상담하다

conferral n. 수여, 부여
conferment n. 수여, 부여
conferee n. 대상자, 헌신자
differ v. 다르다

어원	-con 함께 + -fer : carry(L) → '함께 의견을 주며 상담하는'
유의어	Consult, discuss
반의어	Ignore, disregard
영영	To consult, discuss, or exchange opinions.
예문	The committee will confer to decide on the best course of action. 위원회는 최선의 대책을 결정하기 위해 협의할 것이다.

332

ail

[eɪl]

v. 괴롭히다, 아프게 하다

ailment n. 질병
ailing a. 아픈, 불쾌한
ailing a. 병든, 약화된
acrid a. 콕 쏘는

어원	-a : ache 통증 + -ill 아픈 → '아픈 통증이 생기도록 괴롭히다' * 'ail 아일 괴롭히며 아프게 하다'
유의어	Suffer, trouble
반의어	Heal, recover
영영	To cause physical or emotional pain; to be unwell.
예문	The change in weather seemed to ail him, as he developed a cold. 날씨 변화가 그에게 영향을 미치는 것 같았다. 그는 감기에 걸렸다.

333

amenity

[əˈmiː.nə.ti]

n. 예의; 편의시설

amor fati s. 운명을 사랑하라
amenable a. 유순한, 쾌적한

어원	-amen : pleasant 기분 좋은 * '아멘'하면 기분 좋은 → '기분 좋은 편의시설'
유의어	Comfort, convenience
반의어	Discomfort, inconvenience
영영	A desirable or useful feature or facility of a building or place.
예문	The hotel offers various amenities, including a pool and gym. 호텔은 수영장과 체육관을 포함한 다양한 편의 시설을 제공한다.

334

crook

[krʊk]

n. 구부리다; 사기꾼

crooked a. 굽은, 구부러진
crouch v. 웅크리다
crank a. 구부러진, 굽은
cripple a. 불구가 된

어원	-croach, -croch : hook → '고리처럼 구부리다', → '마음을 낚아채는 사기꾼'
유의어	Criminal, thief
반의어	Law-abiding citizen
영영	A dishonest or criminal person; a bend or curve.
예문	The detective tried to catch the crook who had committed the robbery. 형사는 강도를 저질렀던 도둑을 잡으려고 노력했다.

335

assimilate

[əˈsɪm.ɪ.leɪt]

v. 동화되다, 동화하다; 소화하다; 이해하다

assimilable a. 동화할 수 있는
assimilation n. 동화, 소화
simulation n. 모의 실험, 가장
association n. 연합, 결연, 협회

어원	-as : to + -simil, -simul : imitate → '진짜처럼 모방하니 동화되다'
유의어	Integrate, absorb
반의어	Reject, resist
영영	To integrate or absorb information, ideas, or cultures.
예문	Immigrants often struggle to assimilate into a new culture. 이민자들은 종종 새로운 문화에 동화되기 어려워 한다.

336

renounce

[rɪˈnaʊns]

v. ~을 포기하다, 버리다; 관계를 끊다

renouncement n. 포기; 부인
renouncer n. 기권자, 포기자
pronounce v. 발표하다; 발음하다
denounce v. 비난하다

어원	-re : back + -nounc, -nuntia : announce → '뒤로 물러나겠다고 발표하고 포기하다'
유의어	Reject, disown
반의어	Embrace, accept
영영	To formally give up or reject a belief, claim, or action.
예문	He decided to renounce his claim to the throne. 그는 왕좌에 대한 청구를 포기하기로 결정했다.

337

loop

[luːp]

n. 고리 (모양); 루프

looping a. 루프 반복, 국선을 그리는
looped a. 루프로 이루어진
looper n. 루프 반복 장치
hoop n. 링, 테

어원	-loop 고리 → '고리 모양으로 도니 순환'
유의어	Circle, circuit
반의어	Straight line, direct path
영영	A shape produced by a curve that bends around and crosses itself.
예문	The rope formed a loop that could be used as a handle. 로프는 손잡이로 사용할 수 있는 루프를 형성

338

backdrop

[ˈbæk.drɒp]

n. 배경

backward a. 뒤쪽의, 후방의; 낙후된
backyard n. 뒷마당, 뒤뜰

어원	-back 뒤 + -drop 사건이 떨어지다, 발생하다 → '사건의 배경'
유의어	Background, setting
반의어	Foreground, focus
영영	The background or setting behind something.
예문	The mountains served as a beautiful backdrop for the picturesque village. 산은 그림 같은 마을의 아름다운 배경이었다.

339

rash
[ræʃ]

n. 발진, 뾰루지 a. 성급한

rashly a. 성급하게, 경솔하게
rashness n. 성급함, 경솔함
rasher n. 훨씬 성급한 사람
radish n. 무(뿌리 식물)

어원	-rad, -rac 뿌리, 혈통, 근본 / rush 서두르는 → '피부 뿌리에 문제가 생기면 발진', '서두르는 성질이니 성급한'
유의어	Hasty, impulsive
반의어	Cautious, deliberate
영영	Acting hastily or without careful consideration; a skin eruption.
예문	Making a decision in haste often leads to rash outcomes. 성급한 결정은 종종 경솔한 결과로 이어진다.

340

sermon
['sɜːmən]

n. 설교

sermonize v. 설교하다
sermonic a. 설교의
assert v. 억지 주장하다
exert v. 행사하다, 쓰다

어원	-ser, -sert 밀어 넣어 합치다 (L) + -mon : mind → '마음에 밀어넣는 설교' * join, junc(t) '서로 다른 것이 만나 합침' VS ser(t) '밀어 넣어 합침'
유의어	Homily, discourse
반의어	Comedy, satire
영영	A religious discourse delivered as part of a church service.
예문	The priest delivered a powerful sermon on forgiveness. 사제는 용서에 관한 강력한 설교를 했다.

341

avocation
[ˌæv.əˈkeɪ.ʃən]

n. 부업; 취미

avocational a. 취미의, 여가 활동의
avocationally adv. 취미로
invoke v. 호출하다, 기원하다
avocatory a. 소환하는, 호출하는

어원	-a, -ab, -abs : away + vocation 본업, 직업, 천직 → '본업과는 떨어져 있는 일이니 부업이나 취미'
유의어	Hobby, pastime
반의어	Profession, vocation
영영	A hobby or secondary occupation pursued for enjoyment.
예문	Gardening became more than a hobby; it became her avocation. 정원 가꾸기는 단순한 취미를 넘어 그녀의 업적이 되었다.

342

stray
[streɪ]

v. 길을 잃다; 벗어나다

strayed a. 길을 잃은
astray a. / adv. 잘못된 길에 빠져
strain v. 견딜 수 없게 하다
stray dog n. 유기견

어원	-str : street + -a : away → '길에서 목적지로부터 멀어지니 길을 잃다'
유의어	Wander, roam
반의어	Stay, remain
영영	To wander off or deviate from a course; a lost or wandering animal.
예문	The lost dog appeared to be a stray with no owner in sight. 길 잃은 개는 주인이 보이지 않는 유기견으로 보였다.

343

falsehood
['fɒls.hʊd]

n. 허위, 거짓말

falsify v. 위조하다
falsification n. 위조, 변조
falsely adv. 거짓으로
brotherhood n. 형제애

어원	-fals, -fal, -fail, -faul : deceive, wrong(L) + -hood 상태, 성질, 관계 → '속이는 상태니 허위고 거짓말'
유의어	Untruth, lie
반의어	Truth, fact
영영	A false statement; the state of being untrue.
예문	Spreading falsehoods can damage one's reputation. 거짓 정보를 퍼뜨리는 것은 명예를 훼손할 수 있다.

344

deject
[didʒékt]

v. 낙담시키다

dejected a. 낙심한, 낙담한, 풀죽은
dejection n. 낙담, 우울, 의기소침
dejectedly adv. 실의에 빠져, 낙담하여
eject v. 추방하다

어원	-de : down + ject : throw → '사기를 밑으로 떨어뜨리며 낙담시키다'
유의어	Discourage, dishearten
반의어	Encourage, uplift
영영	To make dispirited or downcast; to lower in spirits.
예문	The team's loss seemed to deject the players. 팀의 패배는 선수들을 낙담시켰다.

345	어원	-timid : fear → '두려움에 소심한' * -ti : tiger + -mid : middle 중간 → '호랑이들 사이에서 두려운'
timorous	유의어	Fearful, timid
['tɪm.ər.əs]	반의어	Brave, courageous
a. 겁 먹은	영영	Showing fear or lack of confidence; timid.
timorous a. 겁 먹은 timidity n. 소심함 intimidate v. 위협하다, 협박하다 timbre n. 음색	예문	The timorous rabbit hid in the bushes when it sensed danger. 겁 많은 토끼는 위험이 느껴질 때 덤불에 숨었다.
346	어원	-ex : out + -tru : thrust → '바깥으로 밀어내다'
extrude	유의어	Project, protrude
[ɪkˈstruːd]	반의어	Retract, withdraw
v. 밀어내다, 쫓아내다	영영	To force or push out; to shape by pushing through a mold.
a. extrusive 밀어내는; 분출한, 돌출한 n. extrusion 압출 v. protrude 내밀다, 튀어나오다 v. intrude 간섭하다; 강요하다	예문	The machine was designed to extrude plastic into specific shapes. 그 기계는 플라스틱을 특정 모양으로 압출하는 데 사용되었다.
347	어원	-di : two + -pole 장대; 끝지점이 먼 극 → '극이 2개니 이중극의'
dipole	유의어	Antenna, polar molecule
[dáipòul]	반의어	Monopole
n. 이중극, 쌍극자	영영	A pair of electric charges or magnetic poles of equal magnitude but opposite sign.
a. dipolar 이중극의, 쌍극의 n. polo 축구 n. monopole 단극체 n. multipole 다극체	예문	A water molecule is an example of a polar dipole. 물 분자는 극성을 가진 이중 분자의 예시이다.
348	어원	-oat : ate 식물의 한 알갱이 → '고대 북유럽 곡물을 뜻하던 귀리' * 오트밀의 재료인 귀리
oat	유의어	Grain, cereal
[əʊt]	반의어	Dairy, meat
n. 귀리	영영	A cereal grain widely cultivated for its seed.
oaten a. 귀리의 oatcake n. 귀리 케이크 oatgrass n. 귀리풀	예문	Oats are a common ingredient in many breakfast cereals. 귀리는 많은 아침 식사 시리얼의 일반적인 재료이다.
349	어원	-avi, -aus, -au : bird (L) / air → '새처럼 나는 항공술'
aviation	유의어	Aeronautics, flight
[ˌeɪ.viˈeɪ.ʃən]	반의어	Ground, land
n. 항공(술)	영영	The operation of aircraft; the design, development, and production of aircraft.
aviator n. 비행사 aviary n. 새장 aviatrix n. 여성 비행사	예문	The development of aviation has revolutionized global travel. 항공 기술의 발전은 세계적인 여행을 혁신적으로 변화시켰다.
350	어원	-re : against + -proach, -prov, -prob, -proxim 가까이 → '반대편과 가까우니 비난하고 책망하다'
reproach	유의어	Criticize, rebuke
[rɪˈprəʊtʃ]	반의어	Praise, commend
n. 비난, 책망 v. 비난하다	영영	To express disapproval or disappointment; to blame or censure.
reproachable a. 책망당할 만한 reproachful a. 비난하는 approach v. 다가가다 proximity n. 근접	예문	She couldn't hide the reproach in her eyes after the mistake. 그녀는 실수 뒤에 눈에 띄는 비난을 숨길 수 없었다.

351

call names

p. 욕하다, 맞욕하다

call after p. ~을 따라 이름짓다
call back p. ~을 취소하다
call for p. ~을 요구하다, 구하다
call off p. 취소하다, 중지하다

어원	-call 큰 외침(E) + -name 이름 → '누군가를 지칭하며 욕하다'
유의어	Insult, mock
반의어	Praise, compliment
영영	To use offensive or insulting language when addressing someone.
예문	It's not appropriate to call names during a disagreement. 의견 불일치 중에 욕설을 사용하는 것은 적절하지 않다.

352

be done with

p. ~을 끝내다

to do with p. ~와 관계가 있는
do away with p. 폐지하다, 없애다
do one's part in p. 자신의 몫을 다하다
do over p. ~을 다시 하다, 꾸미다

어원	with(함께) + done(끝내다)
유의어	Conclude, finish
반의어	Begin, start
영영	To conclude or finish something.
예문	After the argument, he decided to be done with the relationship. 논쟁 후에, 그는 그 관계를 끝내기로 결정했다.

353

grow on

p. 점점 좋아지다, 마음에 들다

p. grow out of ~을 통해 자라다

어원	-grow 자라다 + on 계속 → '계속 마음이 커지니 점점 좋아지다'
유의어	Appeal, attract
반의어	Repel, discourage
영영	To become more liked or appreciated over time.
예문	The movie might not be impressive at first, but it could grow on you. 처음에는 인상적이지 않을 수 있지만, 나중에 좋아질 수 있다.

354

go well with

p. 잘 어울리다

go with p. 받아들이다; 어울리다
go through p. 통과되다, 성사되다, 해결되다
go over p. 점검하다, 검토하다
go out of one's way p. 굳이 뭔가를 하다

어원	-go 가다 + -well 잘 → '잘 어울려 가다'
유의어	Complement, match
반의어	Clash, mismatch
영영	To complement or match harmoniously.
예문	Red wine often goes well with a rich, savory meal. 레드 와인은 종종 풍부하고 맛있는 식사와 잘 어울린다.

355

little short of

p. ~와 거의 동일하다, ~에 미치지 못하다

p. fall short of ~에 미치지 못하다
p. in short 요약하면
n. shortfall 부족분

어원	-little 적은 + -short 부족한 → '적게 부족하니 미치지 못하는'
유의어	Almost, nearly
반의어	Far from, completely
영영	Almost or nearly, but not completely.
예문	Her efforts were little short of extraordinary in completing the project. 그녀의 노력은 프로젝트를 완수하는 데 있어서 거의 탁월한 것과 비슷했다.

356

hot under the collar

p. 화가 난, 당혹해 하는

collar n. 칼라, 깃, 목걸이
colleague n. 동료
elide v. 생략하다, 무시하다
collect on p. 회수하다

어원	-hot + -collar 깃 → '화가 나서 옷깃도 뜨거워 지니 화가 나거나 당혹해 하는'
유의어	Angry, upset
반의어	Calm, composed
영영	Angry or upset.
예문	He was hot under the collar after hearing the unexpected news. 그는 예상치 못한 소식을 듣고 분개했다.

357

in a big way

p. 대규모로

all the way p. 줄곧, 내내
make one's way p. 나아가다
be in the way p. 방해가 되다

어원	-in + -big 큰 → '큰 규모의 방식으로'
유의어	Significantly, extensively
반의어	Minimally, insignificantly
영영	Significantly or extensively.
예문	The company expanded its operations in a big way, opening multiple new branches. 회사는 대규모로 사업을 확장하여 여러 새 지점을 개업했다.

358

in any event

p. 아무튼, 어떤 경우에도

eventual a. 결국의
intervene v. 중재하다, 개입하다

어원	-any 어떤 + -event 사건 → '어떤 사건이 일어나더라도'
유의어	Anyway, nevertheless
반의어	Moreover, furthermore
영영	Regardless; nevertheless.
예문	In any event, we will need to make a decision by the end of the week. 어떤 경우에도, 우리는 이번 주 끝까지 결정을 내려야 할 것이다.

359

hold back

p. 막다, 제지하다

get hold of p. ~을 구하다, 손에 넣다
hold A in check p. A를 억제하다
hold on p. 붙잡고 있다, 잠시만
hold one's tongue p. 입을 다물다

어원	-hold 잡다 + -back 등 → '등을 잡으며 제지하다'
유의어	Restrain, withhold
반의어	Release, let go
영영	To restrain or withhold.
예문	It's important not to hold back information during the investigation. 조사 중에는 정보를 숨기지 않는 것이 중요하다.

360

as far as it goes

p. 그 정도까지

far from p. 전혀 ~이 아닌
way too far p. 너무 멀리 온, 지나친
take A further p. A추가적인 조치를 취하다

어원	-far 멀리 + -it goes → '갈 수 있는 한 멀리 까지'
유의어	To some extent, partially
반의어	Completely, fully
영영	To a certain extent or limit.
예문	The explanation is accurate as far as it goes, but some details are missing. 설명은 일부 부분에 대해 정확하지만 일부 세부 사항이 빠져 있습니다.

Chapter 10.

361	advert	[ˈæd.vɜːt]	v. 언급하다; 주목하다
362	dilute	[daɪˈluːt]	v. 묽게 하다; 약하게 하다
363	replicate	[ˈrep.lɪ.keɪt]	v. 복제하다; 모사하다 a. 반복된
364	descry	[diskrái]	v. (먼 것을) 발견하다
365	annul	[əˈnʌl]	v. 무효로 하다, 취소하다, 폐지하다
366	lodge	[lɒdʒ]	v. 하숙하다, (일시적으로) 머무르다 n. 오두막집
367	absurd	[əbˈsɜːd]	a. 터무니 없는, 불합리한 n. 부조리, 불합리
368	gill	[gɪl]	n. 아가미
369	entreat	[ɪnˈtriːt]	v. 간청하다
370	levy	[ˈlev.i]	n. 세금 징수 v. 부과하다, 징수하다
371	gaze	[geɪz]	v. 응시하다, 바라보다
372	polytheism	[pɑ́liθiːizm]	n. 다신론, 다신교
373	grin	[grɪn]	v. 활짝 웃다
374	recant	[rɪˈkænt]	v. 취소하다, 철회하다
375	poignant	[pɔ́injənt]	a. 마음 아픈, 신랄한
376	conversant	[kənvə́ːrsənt]	a. ~에 정통한, 잘 알고 있는
377	denounce	[dɪˈnaʊns]	v. ~을 비난하다
378	relic	[ˈrel.ɪk]	n. 유물, 유적
379	artery	[ˈɑː.tər.i]	n. 동맥; 주요 도로
380	reptile	[ˈrep.taɪl]	n. 파충류
381	swarm	[swɔːm]	n. 무리, 떼; 벌 떼 v. 무리를 지어 다니다
382	pasture	[ˈpɑːs.tʃər]	n. 목초지, 방목지, 초원
383	transfuse	[trænsˈfjuːz]	v. 수혈하다
384	facile	[ˈfæs.aɪl]	a. 손쉬운, 수월한
385	despond	[dispɑ́nd	vi. 낙심하다, 실망하다
386	absently	[ˈæb.sənt.li]	adv. 멍하니
387	celerity	[səˈler.ə.ti]	n. 신속, 민첩
388	dismal	[ˈdɪz.məl]	a. 암울한, 음습한
389	subdue	[səbˈdʒuː]	v. 진압하다, 억누르다
390	ruddy	[rʌdi]	a. 붉은, 불그레한; 혈색이 좋은
391	cross one's fingers		p. 행운을 빌다
392	write a good hand		p. 글씨를 잘 쓰다
393	more of		p. ~중에 많이, 더, 더 많이
394	in proportion to		p. ~에 비례하여
395	poke one's nose into		p. 간섭하다, ~을 꼬치꼬치 캐묻다
396	have a hand in		p. ~에 관여하다
397	include out		p. ~을 제외하다, 빼다
398	ᵥe a good head on one's should		p. 머리가 좋다, 분별이 있다
399	by usage		p. 사용에 따라, 관행상
400	to begin with		p. 우선은, 먼저

361

advert

[ˈæd.vɜːt]

v. 언급하다; 주목하다

advertent a. 주의하는
advertise v. 광고하다, 선전하다
adverted a. 주의를 기울인
convert v. 변환하다, 전환하다

어원	-ad : to + -vert : turn → '~쪽으로 관심을 돌리도록 언급하다'
유의어	advertise, promote
반의어	ignore, neglect
영영	to draw attention to something; to announce or mention publicly
예문	The company advertised its new product on TV. 그 회사는 새로운 제품을 TV 광고했다.

362

dilute

[daɪˈluːt]

v. 묽게 하다; 약하게 하다

dilution n. 희석
dilutional a. 희석의
diluent n. 희석제
laundry n. 세탁

어원	-di : away + -lu, -lut, -lau, -laundr : wash → '물로 씻어 멀리 떨어뜨리니 묽게 하다'
유의어	weaken, thin
반의어	concentrate, strengthen
영영	to make a liquid thinner or weaker by adding water or another solvent
예문	The doctor diluted the medicine with water before giving it to the patient. 의사는 환자에게 약을 주기 전에 물로 희석했다.

363

replicate

[ˈrep.lɪ.keɪt]

v. 복제하다; 모사하다 a. 반복된

replica n. 복제품
replication n. 복제, 반복
complicate v. 복잡하게 하다
explicate v. 해명하다

어원	-re : again + -pli, -ply, -ploy, -ploit, -plex : fold(E) → '다시 접어서 똑같이 복제하는'
유의어	duplicate, reproduce
반의어	destroy, eradicate
영영	to duplicate or reproduce; to copy
예문	Scientists were able to replicate the experiment successfully. 과학자들은 실험을 성공적으로 복제할 수 있었다.

364

descry

[diskrái]

v. (먼 것을) 발견하다

description n. 서술
descriptive a. 서술적인
descryer n. 탐지자
decry v. 비난하다

어원	-des, -dis : away + -cry 외치다 → '멀리 떨어진 것을 발견하고 외치는'
유의어	spot, discern
반의어	overlook, ignore
영영	to catch sight of; to discover or detect with the eyes
예문	I could descry a ship on the horizon. 수평선에서 배를 발견할 수 있었다.

365

annul

[əˈnʌl]

v. 무효로 하다, 취소하다, 폐지하다

v. nullify 무효로 만들다
v. annihilate 전멸시키다
syn. invalidate 무효로 하다

어원	-an : to + -nihil, -nul : nothing, no value → '아무것도 없게 만드니 무효로 하다'
유의어	cancel, invalidate
반의어	validate, approve
영영	to declare invalid or void; to cancel or abolish
예문	The judge annulled the marriage due to fraud. 판사는 사기 때문에 결혼을 무효화했다

366

lodge

[lɒdʒ]

v. 하숙하다, (일시적으로) 머무르다 n. 오두막집

lodging n. 숙박
lodgings n. 하숙집
lobby n. 로비

어원	(F) logis 작은 집 → '작은 집에 하숙하다'
유의어	accommodate, house
반의어	evict, expel
영영	to stay temporarily in a place; to provide someone with a place to stay
예문	The hunters lodged in a cabin in the woods. 사냥꾼들은 숲 속의 오두막에 숙소를 잡았다.

367

absurd

[əbˈsɜːd]

a. 터무니 없는, 불합리한 n. 부조리, 불합리

adv. absurdly 불합리하게
n. absurdity 불합리, 모순
a. surreal 초현실적인, 꿈같은
a. surdiform 형태 없는

어원	-ab : away + -surd 안 들리는; 이해하기 어려운 → '떨어져 안 들리는 것처럼 불합리한' * absur(없어) 보일 정도로 불합리한
유의어	ridiculous, nonsensical
반의어	logical, sensible
영영	wildly unreasonable, illogical, or inappropriate
예문	His idea of building a bridge across the ocean was absurd. 바다를 가로지르는 다리를 건설하자는 그의 생각은 터무니없었다.

368

gill

[gɪl]

n. 아가미

gilled a. 아가미가 있는
gillnet n. 그물; 자망으로 잡다
blue gill n. 블루길 : 외래종으로 아가미에 청색 반점이 있음

어원	-gill 아가미 * 질레트(gillette) 면도기로 아가미를 제거
유의어	respiratory organ (in fish)
반의어	
영영	a respiratory organ in fish; also, a unit of liquid measurement
예문	Fish use their gills to breathe underwater. 물고기는 물 속에서 숨을 쉬기 위해 아가미를 사용한다.

369

entreat

[ɪnˈtriːt]

v. 간청하다

entreaty n. 간청, 탄원, 애원
entreating a. 간청하는, 애원하는
intricate a. 복잡한
extricate v. 벗어나다

어원	-en : in + -treat 대접하다 → '안에서 대접하며 간청하다'
유의어	plead, beg
반의어	demand, command
영영	to earnestly request or petition; to plead
예문	She entreated him to help her with the problem. 그녀는 그에게 문제 해결을 도와달라고 간청했다.

370

levy

[ˈlev.i]

n. 세금 징수 v. 부과하다, 징수하다

leviable a. 부과할 수 있는
levier n. 과세자
elevate v. 높이다; 상승
alleviate v. 경감시키다, 완화하다

어원	-lev, -levi : raise (F) → '세금을 올려 부과하다'
유의어	impose, charge
반의어	repeal, abolish
영영	to impose or collect (a tax, fee, or fine)
예문	The government levied a tax on income. 정부는 소득세를 부과했다.

371

gaze

[geɪz]

v. 응시하다, 바라보다

glance v. 흘끗 보다 n. 곁눈질
glare v. 노려보다
glimpse a. 잠깐 보다

어원	-gli, -glit, -glo : glow 빨간 빛 → '빛나는 곳을 응시하다'
유의어	stare, look
반의어	glance, look away
영영	to look steadily and intently, especially in admiration, surprise, or thought
예문	She gazed at the stars in the sky. 그녀는 하늘의 별들을 응시했다.

372

polytheism

[pɑːliˈθiːizm]

n. 다신론, 다신교

polygamy n. 일부다처제
polyglot n. 다국어 구사자
polychromatic a. 다색의, 다양한 색깔의

어원	-poly : many + -the, -theo : god → '여러 신을 믿는 다신론'
유의어	belief in multiple gods
반의어	monotheism (belief in one god)
영영	the belief in or worship of more than one god
예문	In ancient Greece, polytheism was the dominant religion. 고대 그리스에서는 다신교가 지배적인 종교였다.

373	어원	-grin 이를 보이고 웃다 * 그린 것처럼 환한 웃음
grin [grɪn] v. 활짝 웃다	유의어	smile broadly
	반의어	frown, scowl
	영영	to smile broadly, often with the teeth showing
grinner n. 활짝 웃는 사람	예문	He grinned from ear to ear when he heard the news. 그는 그 소식을 듣고 입이 귀에 걸릴 정도로 웃었다.

374	어원	-re : back + -cant : sing → '반대로 부르는 것이니 철회'
recant [rɪˈkænt] v. 취소하다, 철회하다	유의어	retract, renounce
	반의어	affirm, uphold
	영영	to publicly take back or withdraw a statement or belief
n. recantation 취소, 철회 n. incantation 주문, 마술 a. cantankerous 심술궂은, 잘 싸우는	예문	The scientist recanted his earlier claims about the existence of extraterrestrial life. 그 과학자는 외계 생명체의 존재에 대한 이전 주장을 철회했다.

375	어원	-pick, -punc, -pung : prick 찌르다 → '찔린 것처럼 신랄하게 말하니 마음 아픈'
poignant [pɔ́injənt] a. 마음 아픈, 신랄한	유의어	touching, moving
	반의어	dull, insensitive
	영영	evoking a keen sense of sadness or regret; emotionally moving
poignantly a. 가슴에 사무치게, 감동적으로 poignancy n. 날카로움, 매서움 compunction n. 죄의식, 후회 appoint v. 지정하다, 임명하다	예문	The poignant memories of her childhood brought tears to her eyes. 그녀의 어린 시절에 대한 가슴 아픈 기억이 눈물을 자아냈다.

376	어원	-converse 대화하다 + -ant 형접 → '모든 주제에 대화가 가능할 정도로 정통한'
conversant [kənvə́ːrsənt] a. ~에 정통한, 잘 알고 있는	유의어	familiar, knowledgeable
	반의어	unfamiliar, ignorant
	영영	familiar or knowledgeable about a particular subject
converse v. 대화하다 conversely adv. 반대로, 거꾸로 diverse a. 다양한 convert v. 변환하다	예문	He is conversant in several languages. 그는 여러 언어에 능통하다.

377	어원	-de : down + -nounce : tell → '낮춰 말하니 비난하다'
denounce [dɪˈnaʊns] v. ~을 비난하다	유의어	condemn, criticize
	반의어	praise, endorse
	영영	to publicly condemn or criticize; to inform against
v. pronounce 발표하다; 발음하다 v. renounce 포기하다, 버리다 n. denouncement 고발, 비난	예문	The protesters denounced the government's policies. 시위대는 정부의 정책을 비난했다.

378	어원	-re : back + -lic, -linqu : leave → '뒷 세대에 남겨진 유물이나 유적'
relic [ˈrel.ɪk] n. 유물, 유적	유의어	artifact, remnant
	반의어	modern creation, innovation
	영영	an object surviving from an earlier time, especially one of historical or sentimental interest
relict n. 잔존 광물, 잔존 생물 reliquate n. 나머지 reliquary n. 유물을 보관하는 장소 relinquish v. 포기하다, 양도하다	예문	The museum displayed many relics from ancient civilizations. 박물관은 고대 문명의 유물들을 많이 전시했다.

379	어원	-art : air 공기 → '로마인들은 공기가 통하는 관을 통해 동맥의 구조를 이해'
artery	유의어	blood vessel
[ˈɑː.tər.i]	반의어	vein, capillary
n. 동맥; 주요 도로	영영	a blood vessel that carries blood away from the heart
arterial a. 동맥의 arteriole n. 소동맥	예문	The surgeon repaired the damaged artery in the patient's heart. 외과의사는 환자의 심장에 손상된 동맥을 수리했다.

380	어원	-creep, -cra, -cri, -rep 기다, 구브리다 → 기어다니는 짐승
reptile	유의어	snake, lizard
[ˈrep.taɪl]	반의어	mammal, bird
n. 파충류	영영	a cold-blooded vertebrate with scales, such as a snake or lizard
reptilian a. 파충류의; 비열한 reptilia n. 파충류 creep v. 기어가다 crawl v. 기어가다	예문	The zoo had a variety of reptiles, including snakes and lizards. 동물원에는 뱀과 도마뱀을 비롯한 다양한 파충류가 있었다

381	어원	-swarm 무리, 떼(벌 떼) * worm 벌레 무리를 생각
swarm	유의어	multitude, crowd
[swɔːm]	반의어	trickle, few
n. 무리, 떼; 벌 떼 v. 무리를 지어 다니다	영영	a large group of insects, especially bees, moving together
swarmy a. 떼지어 이동하는, 떼를 이룬 swarming a. 쳐들어가는, 몰려드는, 쇄도하는 swarmed a. 몰려들다, 쇄도하다	예문	A swarm of bees buzzed around the flowers. 벌떼가 꽃 주위에서 윙윙거렸다.

382	어원	-past : pastor 목사; 양치기 → '양치기가 양에게 풀을 뜯어 먹이기 위한 공간'
pasture	유의어	grazing land, meadow
[ˈpɑːs.tʃər]	반의어	urban area, city
n. 목초지, 방목지, 초원	영영	land covered with grass and other low plants suitable for grazing animals
depasture v. 방목하다 pastorship n. 목사직 pasture n. 목초지, 방목지, 초원 pastoralist n. 유목민	예문	The cows were grazing in the pasture. 소들이 목장에서 풀을 뜯고 있었다.

383	어원	-trans : across + -fus, -fut, -fund : pour 붓다 → '피를 건네어 부으니 수혈하다'
transfuse	유의어	transfer, infuse
[trænsˈfjuːz]	반의어	withhold, keep
v. 수혈하다	영영	to transfer or inject blood, especially from one person or animal to another
transfusion n. 수혈, 주입 transmit v. 전송하다 diffuse v. 확산시키다, 분산되다 infuse v. 주입하다, 불어넣다	예문	The nurse transfused blood into the patient. 간호사는 환자에게 수혈했다.

384	어원	-fac, -fec, -fic, -fy, -fair : make + -ile 쉬운 → '쉽게 만드니 손쉬운'
facile	유의어	easy, effortless
[ˈfæs.aɪl]	반의어	difficult, challenging
a. 손쉬운, 수월한	영영	easily achieved or effortless; superficial or simplistic
n. facility 시설, 설비; 솜씨; 편의 v. facilitate 촉진하다 n. facilitation 촉진 n. facsimile 모사, 사본	예문	His facile writing style made the book easy to read. 그의 쉬운 글쓰기 스타일은 책을 쉽게 읽을 수 있게 해주었다.

385

despond

[dispάnd]

vi. 낙심하다, 실망하다

despondent a. 낙담한, 풀이 죽은
despondency n. 실망, 낙심
respond v. 응답하다, 대응하다
correspond v. ~와 일치하다

어원	-de : down + -spond : promise → '약속이 무너져 낙심하고 실망하다'
유의어	lose hope, despair
반의어	hope, rejoice
영영	to become disheartened or lose confidence
예문	She despondently looked out the window, feeling sad and hopeless. 그녀는 슬픔과 절망감을 느끼며 낙담한 채 창밖을 바라보았다.

386

absently

[ˈæb.sənt.li]

adv. 멍하니

absence n. 결석, 부재, 결여
absentee n. 결석자, 부재자
absent a. 결석한, 부재 중인
presently adv. 이내, 곧; 현재, 지금

어원	-ab, -a, -abs : away, from (L) + -se, -es : 존재하다 → '생각이 존재하지 않으니 멍하니'
유의어	inattentively, thoughtlessly
반의어	attentively, consciously
영영	inattentively or thoughtlessly
예문	She absently played with her hair while she thought about the problem. 그녀는 문제에 대해 생각하면서 무심결에 머리카락을 가지고 놀았다.

387

celerity

[səˈler.ə.ti]

n. 신속, 민첩

accelerate v. 촉진하다, 가속하다
acceleration n. 촉진, 가속, 가속도
accelerative a. 촉진하는
decelerate v. 감속하다

어원	-celer : swift, speedy → '스피드가 있으니 신속, 민첩한'
유의어	swiftness, speed
반의어	slowness, delay
영영	swiftness of movement or action
예문	He worked with celerity to finish the project on time. 그는 프로젝트를 제시간에 끝내기 위해 신속하게 일했다.

388

dismal

[ˈdɪz.məl]

a. 암울한, 음습한

adv. dismally 암울하게, 음습하게
n. dismay 실망, 낙담
v. dismantle 해체하다, 분해하다

어원	-dis : day + -mal : bad → '나쁘고 악한 날이니 암울하고 음습한'
유의어	gloomy, depressing
반의어	bright, cheerful
영영	depressing, gloomy, or dreary
예문	The weather was dismal, with heavy rain and strong winds. 비가 많이 오고 바람이 강하게 부는 등 날씨가 음침했

389

subdue

[səbˈdʒuː]

v. 진압하다, 억누르다

subdued a. 가라앉은, 완화된, 정복된
unsubdued a. 진압되지 않은, 눌리지 않은
depress v. 낙담시키다
express v. 표현하다

어원	-sup, -sub : under + -du : draw → '아래로 끌어내려 억제하니 진압하다'
유의어	conquer, overcome
반의어	surrender, yield
영영	to bring under control or overcome; to quieten
예문	The police used tear gas to subdue the protesters. 경찰은 시위대를 진압하기 위해 최루탄을 사용했다.

390

ruddy

[rʌdi]

a. 붉은, 불그레한; 혈색이 좋은

ruderal a. 버려진, 폐허 같은
ruddle n. 붉은 대나무, 빨간 진토
rust v. 빨간색으로 녹슬다
cruddy a. 불결한, 지저분한

어원	-rust, -ruddy : reddy 붉은
유의어	reddish, rosy
반의어	pale, wan
영영	having a healthy red color, often used to describe someone's complexion
예문	He had a ruddy complexion and bright blue eyes. 그는 붉은빛이 도는 얼굴과 밝은 파란색 눈을 가지고 있었다.

391

cross one's fingers

p. 행운을 빌다

p. cross to ~로 가로지르다
p. cross at ~을 교차하다
p. cross up 배반, 말썽, 혼란

어원	-cross 꼬다 + -finger 손가락 → '손가락을 꼬아 행운을 빌다'
유의어	hope for luck, wish for success
반의어	wish you a curse
영영	to hope for good luck or success
예문	I'll cross my fingers for you to pass the test. 시험에 합격하길 바라며 행운을 빌어줄게요.

392

write a good hand

p. 글씨를 잘 쓰다

write to p. ~에 가사를 붙이다
write for p. ~에 기고하다
write out p. ~을 또박또박 쓰다, 정서하다
write down p. 평가 절하하다, ~을 적어 두다

어원	-write 쓰다 + -good 좋은 + hand 손 → '좋은 손놀림으로 글씨를 잘 쓰다'
유의어	have good handwriting
반의어	have poor handwriting
영영	to have good handwriting
예문	He writes a good hand, so it's easy to read his handwriting. 글씨를 잘 써서 그의 필체를 읽기 쉬워요.

393

more of

p. ~중에 많이, 더, 더 많이

more often than not p. 대개, 흔히
no more than p. 단지 ~에 지나지 않는, ~일 뿐인
no less than p. 꼭 ~만큼, ~와 마찬가지로

어원	-more 더 + -of ~중에 → '~중에 더 많이'
유의어	additional, extra
반의어	less of, insufficient
영영	a greater quantity or additional amount
예문	Can I have more of this cake? 이 케이크 좀 더 먹어도 될까요?

394

in proportion to

p. ~에 비례하여

portion n. 부분; 몫, 할당
inverse proportion p. 반비례
in direct proportion to p. ~에 정비례해서
in proportion to as p. ~에 비례하여

어원	-pro : forward + -part, -port 부분 → '특별히 나누어 놓은 부분과 비례하여'
유의어	commensurate with, proportional to
반의어	disproportionate to, unrelated to
영영	in relation to; in a balanced or appropriate way
예문	The salary should be in proportion to the amount of work done. 급여는 수행한 업무량에 비례해야 합니다.

395

poke one's nose into

p. 간섭하다, ~을 꼬치꼬치 캐묻다

pricky a. 가시가 많은, 성가신
pricking n. 따끔하게 찌르기
picky a. 까다로운
pungent a. 신랄한

어원	-poke 찌르다 + -nose 코 → '코부터 들이밀고 간섭하다'
유의어	interfere, meddle
반의어	mind one's own business, abstain
영영	to intrude or interfere in someone else's business
예문	Don't poke your nose into other people's business. 남의 일에 참견하지 마세요.

396

have a hand in

p. ~에 관여하다

have a fit p. 화내다
have a point p. 일리가 있다
have a taste for p. ~에 취미가 있다
have a breakdown p. 고장이 나다

어원	-have 갖다 + -hand 손 → '손을 쓰니 ~에 관여하다'
유의어	be involved in, contribute to
반의어	be uninvolved, have no part in
영영	to be involved or participate in
예문	I had a hand in making this cake. 이 케이크 만드는 데 도움을 줬어요.

397

include out

p. ~을 제외하다, 빼다

inclusion n. 포함
inclusive a. 포괄적인
inclusively adv. 전부 통틀어
inclusivity n. 포용성

어원	-in+ -clud, -clude, -clos : close, shut + -out 제외하고 → '~을 제외하고 넣으니 빼다'
유의어	exclude, leave out
반의어	include, incorporate
영영	to exclude or leave out
예문	Include me out. 나를 제외해줘.

398

have a good head on one's shoulders

p. 머리가 좋다, 분별이 있다

have a rude awakening p. 갑자기 불쾌한 일을 깨닫다
have a sneer at p. ~을 비웃다, 냉소하다
have an edge on p. ~보다 유리하다

어원	-have 갖다 + -good head → '좋은 머리라 약삭빠르다'
유의어	be intelligent, be wise
반의어	be foolish, lack wisdom
영영	to be intelligent and sensible
예문	He has a good head on his shoulders and is very smart. 그는 머리가 좋고 매우 똑똑해요.

399

by usage

p. 사용에 따라, 관행상

p. by popular usage 대중의 어법으로
p. by colloquial usage 구어용법으로서
p. by rough usage 거칠게 취급해서

어원	-by 함으로써 + -usage 사용 → '~한 방식으로 사용함으로써'
유의어	conventionally, traditionally
반의어	unusually, atypically
영영	according to common practice or tradition
예문	The word "usage" is often used to refer to the way something is used. "usage"라는 단어는 종종 무언가가 사용되는 방식을 지칭하는 데 사용됩니다.

400

to begin with

p. 우선은, 먼저

being by p. ~으로 시작하다
begin with p. ~으로 시작하다
begin to talk p. 운을 떼다

어원	-be : to make + gin 기계 장치 → '만들기 시작하다'
유의어	initially, originally
반의어	eventually, finally
영영	initially or in the first place
예문	To begin with, let's review the main points of the lecture. 우선, 강의의 주요 요점을 복습해봅시다.

Chapter 11.

401	quantum	[ˈkwɒn.təm]	n. 양자
402	proximity	[praksímɪti]	n. 근접
403	complicit	[kəmˈplɪs.ɪt]	a. 가담한, 공모한, 공범의
404	levity	[ˈlev.ə.ti]	n. 경솔, 변덕, 경솔한 행위
405	cabbage	[ˈkæb.ɪdʒ]	n. 양배추
406	adverse	[ˈæd.vɜːs]	a. 반대의, 역의; 불리한
407	declare	[dɪˈkleər]	v. 단언하다, 공언하다
408	dispute	[dɪˈspjuːt]	v. 반박하다, 논쟁하다; 싸움, 논쟁
409	humiliate	[hjuːˈmɪl.i.eɪt]	v. 굴욕감을 주다, 자존심을 상하게 하다
410	chubby	[ˈtʃʌb.i]	a. 통통한, 토실토실한
411	trump	[trʌmp]	v. 으뜸패를 내다; 이기다
412	aborigine	[æbərídʒəniː]	n. (특히 오스트레일리아의) 원주민, 토착민
413	gross	[ɡrəʊs]	n. 총 a. 중대한; 역겨운
414	absolve	[əbˈzɒlv]	v. 면제하다, 용서하다, 사면하다
415	feast	[fiːst]	n. 연회, 잔치, 축제일 v. 맘껏 먹다, 포식하다
416	exalt	[ɪɡˈzɒlt]	v. (지위·권력·명예 등을) 높이다, 찬미하다
417	juvenile	[ˈdʒuː.vən.aɪl]	a. 젊은
418	intoxicate	[ɪnˈtɒk.sɪ.keɪt]	v. 취하게 하다, 도취시키다
419	authentic	[ɔːˈθen.tɪk]	a. 진정한, 진짜의
420	repeal	[rɪˈpiːl]	v. ~을 취소하다, 폐지하다
421	agony	[ǽɡəni]	n. 몸부림, 고통
422	penitent	[pénətənt]	a. 참회하는, 뉘우치는 n. 참회자
423	pensive	[ˈpen.sɪv]	a. 생각에 잠긴
424	denature	[diːˈneɪ.tʃər]	v. 변성시키다, 성질을 바꾸다
425	maze	[meɪz]	n. 미로; 혼란
426	recess	[rɪˈses]	n. 휴식; 후미진 곳
427	utilitarianism	[juːtilətέəriənizm]	n. 공리주의
428	inflict	[ɪnˈflɪkt]	v. 고통을 가하다, 주다
429	rust	[rʌst]	n. 녹 v. 녹슬다, 부식하다
430	haul	[hɔːl]	v. 끌다, 운반하다
431	make believe		p. 체하다, ~처럼 보이게 하다
432	come off		p. 성공하다, 떨어지다
433	by a hair's breadth		p. 간신히, 겨우, 아슬아슬하게
434	in this regard		p. 이 점에 있어서는
435	lose the day		p. 승부에 지다
436	sort out		p. 해결하다
437	at one's wit's end		p. 어찌할 바를 몰라
438	on the tube		p. 텔레비전에
439	What with A and B		p. A 그리고 B 때문에
440	shelf-stable		p. 상온에서 오래 상하지 않는

401

quantum

[ˈkwɒn.təm]

n. 양자

quantitative a. 양적인, 정량적인
quantization n. 양자화
quantity n. 양, 수량

어원	-quantum : how much → '얼마나 많은지 이산적으로 계산하는 양자'
유의어	amount, quantity, extent
반의어	fraction, part, bit
영영	A discrete quantity of energy proportional to the frequency of the radiation it represents.
예문	The concept of quantum mechanics explores the behavior of particles at the subatomic level. 양자 역학의 개념은 입자의 행동을 소자 수준에서 탐구합니다.

402

proximity

[praksíməti]

n. 근접

proximate a. 가장 가까운, 직전의
proximal a. 기부에 가까운, 기부의
proxima n. 프록시마, 거리는 4.3광년
approximate v. 가까워지다

어원	-proach, -prov, -prob, -proxim 가까이 → '목표로 한 방향 가까워진 근사치니 근접'
유의어	closeness, nearness, adjacency
반의어	distance, remoteness, separation
영영	Nearness in space, time, or relationship.
예문	The proximity of the grocery store to my house makes it convenient for shopping. 식료품 점이 우리 집과 가까워 쇼핑이 편리합니다.

403

complicit

[kəmˈplɪs.ɪt]

a. 가담한, 공모한, 공범의

complicity n. 공모, 연루
complice n. 공범자
complicate v. 복잡하게 하다
replicate v. 복제하다; 모사하다

어원	-com : together + -pli, -ply, -ploy, -ploit, -plex : weave, fold → '함께 엮여 있으니 같은 일에 가담한 공모자이자 공범'
유의어	involved, implicated, accomplice
반의어	innocent, uninvolved, blameless
영영	Involved with others in an illegal activity or wrongdoing.
예문	The accomplice was found to be complicit in the crime and faced charges accordingly. 공범은 그 범죄에 연루되어 있었으며 그에 따라 기소되었습니다.

404

levity

[ˈlev.ə.ti]

n. 경솔, 변덕, 경솔한 행위

levitate v. 공중에 떠오르다, 부양시키다
levitation n. 공중 부양
relieve v. 경감시키다
lever n. 지렛대, 레버

어원	-lev, -levi : raise (F) / light → '기분이 쉽게 업 되니 경솔한'
유의어	lightness, humor, frivolity
반의어	seriousness, gravity, solemnity
영영	Humor or frivolity, especially the treatment of a serious matter with humor or in a manner lacking due respect.
예문	His attempt at levity during the serious meeting was met with disapproval. 심각한 회의 중에 경솔한 웃음을 도입한 시도는 부적절하게 받아들여졌습니다.

405

cabbage

[ˈkæb.ɪdʒ]

n. 양배추

captain n. 선장, 주장, 대위
decapitate v. 참수하다, 머리를 베다

어원	-cab : head → '부풀어 오른 양배추 모습이 사람의 머리를 닮음'
유의어	green, kale, coleslaw
반의어	
영영	A leafy green or purple biennial plant, cultivated as an edible vegetable.
예문	The chef used fresh cabbage to prepare a crunchy coleslaw. 요리사는 신선한 양배추를 사용하여 바삭한 코울 슬로를 준비했습니다.

406

adverse

[ˈæd.vɜːs]

a. 반대의, 역의; 불리한

adversative a. 대조적인, 반대의
adversely adv. 불리하게, 해로운 방식으로
adversary n. 적, 상대
adversity n. 역경, 고난

어원	-ad : to + -verse, -vert : turn → '어떤 일에 등을 돌려 반대하니 부정적인'
유의어	unfavorable, negative, hostile
반의어	favorable, positive, beneficial
영영	Preventing success or development; harmful; unfavorable.
예문	The adverse weather conditions forced the event to be postponed. 불리한 날씨 조건으로 인해 행사가 연기되어야 했습니다.

407

declare

[dɪˈkleər]

v. 단언하다, 공언하다

declaration n. 단언, 공언, 공표
declared a. 공언된, 공표된
declaredly adv. 공표하여, 선언하여
clarity n. 명확성, 깨끗함

어원	-de : completely + -clar : clean → '완전히 투명하게 단언하며 공언하다'
유의어	announce, proclaim, state
반의어	conceal, hide, keep silen
영영	Announce something publicly or formally.
예문	The president will declare a national holiday to celebrate the achievement. 대통령은 성취를 축하하기 위해 국가 공휴일을 선언할 것입니다.

408

dispute

[dɪˈspjuːt]

v. 반박하다, 논쟁하다; 싸움, 논쟁

disputed a. 반박을 받은, 이의가 제기된
disputable a. 논의의 여지가 있는
disputation n. 논쟁, 논의
indisputable a. 부인할 수 없는

어원	-dis : against + -pet, -pete : reckon 셈하다, 평가하다 → '반대로 셈하고 반박하다'
유의어	argue, debate, contest
반의어	agree, concede, harmonize
영영	A disagreement or argument.
예문	The neighbors had a dispute over the property boundary. 이웃 사이에는 부동산 경계에 관한 분쟁이 있었습니다.

409

humiliate

[hjuːˈmɪl.i.eɪt]

v. 굴욕감을 주다, 자존심을 상하게 하다

humiliation n. 굴욕, 수치심
humility n. 겸손
humble a. 겸손한
humid a. 습한, 습기가 많은

어원	-hum, -humili : earth 땅 → '땅으로 숙이게 하여 굴욕감을 주다'
유의어	embarrass, shame, degrade
반의어	praise, honor, elevate
영영	Make someone feel ashamed or foolish.
예문	The intention was not to humiliate anyone but to provide constructive feedback. 의도는 누구도 굴욕스럽게 만드는 것이 아니었지만 건설적인 피드백을 제공하는 것이었습니다.

410

chubby

[ˈtʃʌb.i]

a. 통통한, 토실토실한

chubbily adv. 통통하게, 토실토실하게
chubbiness n. 통통함, 토실토실함

어원	-chub 공, 덩어리 → '둥근 공 모양처럼 통통하고 토실토실한'
유의어	plump, rotund, pudgy
반의어	slim, thin, lean
영영	Plump and rounded in shape.
예문	The baby had a chubby face and chubby little fingers. 아기는 뚱뚱한 얼굴과 뚱뚱한 손가락을 가지고 있었습니다.

411

trump

[trʌmp]

v. 으뜸패를 내다; 이기다

triumph n. 나팔, 승리 / v. 승리를 알리다
triumphant a. 크게 성공한, 큰 승리를 거둔
triumphantly adv. 위풍당당하게, 의기양양하여
trumpet n. 으뜸패, 승리의 나팔

어원	-trumpet (G) 디오니서스 신의 찬양으로 나팔을 불어 승리하다 * 미국 트럼프 전 대통령
유의어	surpass, outdo, excel
반의어	lose, trail, fall behind
영영	To surpass or beat someone by saying or doing something better.
예문	Her achievements in the field of science trumped those of her peers. 그녀의 과학 분야에서의 업적은 동료들을 능가했습니다.

412

aborigine

[æbərídʒəniː]

n. (특히 오스트레일리아의) 원주민, 토착민

aboriginal a. 원주민의, 토착의
aboriginally adv. 토착적으로
aboriginality n. 토착성
orphan n. 고아

어원	ab origine 처음부터 (L) → '17세기 호주 대륙에 거주한 최초의 인간인 호주 원주민'
유의어	native, indigenous person, original inhabitant
반의어	settler, immigrant
영영	An indigenous inhabitant of a place.
예문	The aborigine tribes have a rich cultural heritage passed down through generations. 토착민 지족은 세대를 거치며 전해져온 풍부한 문화 유산을 가지고 있습니다.

413	어원	-gross : large 큰 → '큰 수의 양을 재니 총량', '큰 괴물이 역겨운'
gross	유의어	total, entire, comprehensive
[grəʊs]	반의어	net, partial, individual
n. 총 a. 중대한; 역겨운	영영	Unattractively large or bloated; total income before deductions.
grossly adv. 크게, 심하게 grosser n. 수익을 올리는 것 GDP n. 국내 총생산 grocery n. 식료품, 식료품점	예문	The company's gross profit increased significantly this quarter. 회사의 총 이익은 이 분기에 크게 증가했습니다.
414	어원	-ab: away + -solve 해결 → '(비난 등에서) 멀어지도록 해결하니 사면'
absolve	유의어	forgive, pardon, exonerate
[əbˈzɒlv]	반의어	condemn, accuse, blame
v. 면제하다, 용서하다, 사면하다	영영	Set or declare someone free from blame, guilt, or responsibility.
absolution n. 사면, 용서 absolutism n. 독재주의 dissolve v. 녹이다, 해체하다 resolve v. 결정하다, 해결하다	예문	The apology and sincere efforts to make amends helped absolve him of the wrongdoing. 사과와 진정한 회복을 위한 노력은 그를 잘못에서 벗어나게 도왔습니다.
415	어원	-feast : festival; food → '축제날 맘껏 먹는 음식'
feast	유의어	banquet, celebration, festivity
[fiːst]	반의어	famine, scarcity, deprivation
n. 연회, 잔치, 축제일 v. 맘껏 먹다, 포식하다	영영	A large, elaborate meal, typically one in celebration of something.
feasting n. 잔치, 연회 festival n. 축제	예문	The family gathered for a festive feast to celebrate the special occasion. 가족은 특별한 기념일을 축하하기 위해 화려한 연회를 가졌다.
416	어원	-ex : out + -alt : high → '높은 자리로 보내려 찬미하다'
exalt	유의어	elevate, glorify, uplift
[ɪgˈzɒlt]	반의어	humble, degrade, lower
v. (지위·권력·명예 등을) 높이다, 찬미하다	영영	Hold (someone or something) in very high regard; think or speak very highly of.
exalted a. 고귀한, 지위가 높은 exaltation n. 고양, 승진, 칭찬 altitude n. 고도, 높이 adult n. 성인	예문	The poet sought to exalt the beauty of nature in his verses. 시인은 시에서 자연의 아름다움을 높이 송가하고자 했습니다.
417	어원	-juven : young * 학창 시절 주번을 맡은 젊은 학생들
juvenile	유의어	youthful, adolescent, young
[ˈdʒuː.vən.aɪl]	반의어	adult, mature, grown-up
a. 젊은	영영	Of, for, or relating to young people; a young person.
juvenility n. 어린 나이, 미성숙 rejuvenation n. 회춘, 회복 subjuvene a. 어린, 미성숙한 prejuvenescence n. 청소년기 이전	예문	The juvenile delinquency rate has seen a decline in recent years. 최근 몇 년 동안 청소년 범죄율이 감소했습니다.
418	어원	-in : make + -toxic : poison + -ate 동접 → '독에 취하게 만들다'
intoxicate	유의어	inebriate, enrapture, exhilarate
[ɪnˈtɒk.sɪ.keɪt]	반의어	sober, discourage, depress
v. 취하게 하다, 도취시키다	영영	To poison; excite or stupefy (someone) with alcohol or drugs.
intoxication n. 중독, 음주, 망상 intoxicating a. 황홀감을 주는, 매혹적인 detoxify v. 독소를 제거하다, 디톡스하다 antitoxin n. 항독소	예문	The aroma of the flowers seemed to intoxicate everyone in the room. 꽃의 향기는 방 안의 모든 이를 사로잡은 듯했습니다.

419

authentic

[ɔːˈθen.tɪk]

a. 진정한, 진짜의

authenticity n. 진품성, 진짜임
authenticate v. 진정한 것임을 증명하다
authentically adv. 확실하게, 진짜처럼
authority n. 권한, 권위; 전문가

어원	-auto 스스로 + -hent 되다 → '스스로 원본이 되니 진짜 진품'
유의어	genuine, real, legitimate
반의어	fake, counterfeit, fraudulent
영영	Of undisputed origin; genuine.
예문	The antique store specializes in selling authentic historical artifacts. 그 골동품 가게는 정통 역사 유물을 판매하는 전문점입니다.

420

repeal

[rɪˈpiːl]

v. ~을 취소하다, 폐지하다

repealable a. 취소할 수 있는
repealer n. 폐지론자
appeal v. 호소하다, 항소하다
repel v. 물리치다, 쫓아버리다

어원	-re : back + -peal, -pel : drive → '뒤로 밀어부쳐 취소하다'
유의어	revoke, annul, abolish
반의어	enact, establish, implement
영영	Revoke or annul (a law or congressional act).
예문	The government decided to repeal the controversial law after public outcry. 정부는 대중의 항의 이후 논란이 되고 있는 법률을 폐지하기로 결정했습니다.

421

agony

[ægəni]

n. 몸부림, 고통

agonize v. 고통스럽게 하다, 괴로워하다
agonized a. 고뇌하는, 괴로워하는
angry a. 화난
antagonize v. 화를 내다

어원	-ag, -alg 아픔, 고통(G) / -agon : struggle → '싸움으로 생기는 고통'
유의어	pain, torment, suffering
반의어	comfort, ease, pleasure
영영	Extreme physical or mental suffering.
예문	The athlete experienced agony after sustaining a serious injury during the game. 선수는 경기 중 심각한 부상을 입은 후 고통을 겪었습니다.

422

penitent

[pénətənt]

a. 참회하는, 뉘우치는 n. 참회자

penitential a. 참회의, 개전의
penitentiary n. 교도소
penitence n. 후회, 참회
repent v. 뉘우치다, 회개하다

어원	-pen : penalty 벌칙 → '벌로 고통 받으며 참회하는'
유의어	remorseful, contrite, regretful
반의어	unrepentant, impenitent, defiant
영영	Feeling or showing sorrow and regret for having done wrong.
예문	The penitent criminal expressed remorse for the harm caused by their actions. 회개하는 범죄자는 자신의 행동으로 인한 피해에 대한 후회를 표현했습니다.

423

pensive

[ˈpen.sɪv]

a. 생각에 잠긴

pensively adv. 멍하니 생각에 잠겨
expensive a. 비싼
suspensive a. 정지한, 결단이 서지 않는
ponder v. 곰곰이 생각하다

어원	-pend, -pond : weigh * 펜 씹으며 생각에 잠긴 → '저울질하며 생각하다'
유의어	thoughtful, contemplative, reflective
반의어	carefree, unreflective, thoughtless
영영	Engaged in, involving, or reflecting deep or serious thought.
예문	She sat by the window, looking pensive as she reflected on the past. 그녀는 창가에 앉아 지난 일에 대해 생각하며 수줍게 보였습니다.

424

denature

[diːˈneɪ.tʃər]

v. 변성시키다, 성질을 바꾸다

denatured a. 변성의
natural a. 자연스러운
innate a. 타고난

어원	-de : away + -na, -nat, -gna : born 낳다, 태어나다 → '태어났을 때의 성질과는 거리가 멀도록 바꾸다'(L)
유의어	alter, modify, change
반의어	preserve, maintain, keep unchanged
영영	Take away or alter the natural qualities of.
예문	Heating can denature proteins, altering their structure and function. 가열은 단백질을 비정상적으로 바꾸어 그 구조와 기능을 변경할 수 있습니다.

425

maze

[meɪz]

n. 미로; 혼란

mazy a. 미로같은, 복잡한
maziness n. 미로와 같음
amaze v. 놀라게 하다
amusive a. 즐겁게 하는

어원	-maze, -masian : confuse → '혼란시키는'
유의어	labyrinth, puzzle, confusion
반의어	clear path, straightforward route
영영	A network of paths and hedges designed as a puzzle through which one has to find a way.
예문	The garden had a beautiful maze that visitors enjoyed exploring. 정원에는 방문객들이 즐겨 탐험하는 아름다운 미로가 있었습니다.

426

recess

[rɪˈses]

n. 휴식; 후미진 곳

recession n. 불황, 경기 침체
recessive a. 지배되지 않은
process v. 처리하다, 진행하다
recede v. 물러나다; 희미해지다

어원	-re : back + -cede, -cess : go → '뒤에 후미진 곳으로 가서 휴식'
유의어	break, intermission, pause
반의어	continuation, resumption, activity
영영	A temporary respite or withdrawal from an activity or pursuit.
예문	Students eagerly await recess, a time to play and relax during the school day. 학생들은 수업 중 플레이하고 쉬는 시간인 휴식을 간절히 기다립니다.

427

utilitarianism

[ju:tilətɛəriənizm]

n. 공리주의

utilitarian a. 실용적인, 공리주의의
utility n. 공익 설비
utensil n. 도구, 기구

어원	-us, -ut 사용, 이용(L) + -lie 쉬운 + -sm 사상 → '사용하기 쉬운 실용만 강조하니 공리주의'
유의어	pragmatism, practicality, consequentialism
반의어	idealism, impracticality, non-utilitarianism
영영	The doctrine that actions are right if they are useful or for the benefit of the majority.
예문	Utilitarianism focuses on maximizing overall happiness and well-being in decision-making. 유틸리타리언주의는 의사 결정에서 전반적인 행복과 복지를 극대화하는 데 중점을 둡니다.

428

inflict

[ɪnˈflɪkt]

v. 고통을 가하다, 주다

inflict A on B v. A에게 B를 가하다
infliction n. 고통, 시련
conflict n. 갈등, 충동
afflict v. 괴롭히다, 들볶다

어원	-in + -flic, -flict : strike 때리다 → '마음 속까지 때리며 고통을 주다'
유의어	impose, cause, administer
반의어	prevent, spare, protect
영영	Cause (something unpleasant or painful) to be suffered by someone or something.
예문	It is essential to avoid actions that may inflict harm on others. 다른 사람에게 피해를 입힐 수 있는 행동을 피하는 것이 중요합니다.

429

rust

[rʌst]

n. 녹 v. 녹슬다, 부식하다

rusty a. 녹슨
rustless a. 녹슬지 않은, 녹이 없는
ruddy a. 붉은

어원	-rust, -ruddy : reddy 붉은 → '철의 붉은 코팅이 녹'
유의어	corrosion, oxidation, decay
반의어	polish, protect, preserve
영영	A reddish or yellowish-brown flaky coating of iron oxide that is formed on iron or steel by oxidation.
예문	The old bicycle had started to rust after being exposed to the elements. 낡은 자전거는 날씨에 노출된 후 색이 변하여 녹기 시작했습니다.

430

haul

[hɔːl]

v. 끌다, 운반하다

haulage n. 운송, 운반
hauling n. 끌어당기기, 운반
overhaul 점검하다; 따라잡다
hale v. 잡아끌다

어원	* -ha : hand → '손으로 잡아 끌다'
유의어	pull, drag, transport
반의어	push, leave, abandon
영영	Pull or drag with effort or force.
예문	The fishermen had a successful haul of fish after a day at sea. 어부들은 바다에서 하루를 보낸 후 성공적인 물고기를 잡아왔습니다.

431

make believe

p. 체하다, ~처럼 보이게 하다

make for p. ~에 기여하다
make it to p. ~에 도착하다, 이르다
make one's way to p. ~로 나아가다
be made up of p. ~로 구성되어 있다

어원	-make 만들다 + -believe → '믿게 만드는 것이니 ~처럼 보이게 하다'
유의어	pretend, imagine, simulate
반의어	reality, actuality, truth
영영	Pretend to be doing or using something.
예문	Children often engage in make-believe play, using their imagination to create fantastical scenarios. 어린이들은 종종 상상력을 사용하여 환상적인 상황을 만들어내는 가짜놀이를 합니다.

432

come off

p. 성공하다, 떨어지다

come across p. 우연히 발견하다
come in handy p. 쓸모가 있다
come on p. 시작하다; ~이 닥쳐오다
come out ahead p. 결국 이득을 보다

어원	-come 오다 + -off 떨어져 → '오다 떨어져'
유의어	succeed, achieve, accomplish
반의어	fail, flop, fall short
영영	To happen or take place successfully.
예문	The event was a great success, and everything seemed to come off perfectly. 행사는 큰 성공이었고, 모든 것이 완벽하게 이루어진 것 같았습니다.

433

by a hair's breadth

p. 간신히, 겨우, 아슬아슬하게

hairdo n. 머리 모양
by means of p. ~에 의하여, ~의 도움으로
by no means p. 결코 ~가 아닌
by the same token p. 같은 이유로

어원	-by 차이 + -hair 머리털 + breadth 범위, 폭 → '털끝만한 간격이니 간신히'
유의어	narrowly, barely, almost not
반의어	comfortably, easily, with a wide margin
영영	By a very small margin.
예문	He narrowly escaped the accident by a hair's breadth. 그는 간신히 사고에서 탈출했습니다.

434

in this regard

p. 이 점에 있어서는

in that regard p. 이 점에 있어서는
with regard to p. ~와 관련하여, ~에 대해
regale v. 매우 즐겁게 하다
regarding prep. ~에 관하여

어원	-in 안 + -regard 주의, 관심, 호의 → '관심 속에 있으니 이 점에 있어서는'
유의어	concerning this, with respect to this, in this context
반의어	unrelated to this, not concerning this
영영	In relation to the matter that has just been mentioned.
예문	The new policy will bring positive changes, especially in this regard. 새로운 정책은 특히 이 부분에서 긍정적인 변화를 가져올 것입니다.

435

lose the day

p. 승부에 지다

lose temper p. 화내다
lose oneself in p. 몰두하다; 길을 잃다
lose out p. 지다, 실패하다
lose face p. 체면을 잃다

어원	-lose 지다 + -day 날 → '그날 승부에 지다'
유의어	fail, be defeated, not succeed
반의어	win, succeed, triumph
영영	To be unsuccessful or defeated.
예문	Despite facing challenges, she refused to lose the day to negativity. 도전에 직면했음에도 불구하고, 그녀는 부정적인 상황에 하루를 날려먹지 않기로 했습니다.

436

sort out

p. 해결하다

a sort of p. 일종의
all sorts of p. 모든 종류들의
sort of p. 그런, 같은, 일종의
sorted p. 잘 정리된, 갖춘

어원	-sort 분류하다, 구분하다 + -out 벗어나 → '분류를 끝내고 임무에서 벗어나니 해결'
유의어	resolve, clarify, organize
반의어	confuse, complicate, muddle
영영	Arrange or order systematically.
예문	Let's sit down and sort out the issues before moving forward. 앞으로 나아가기 전에 문제들을 해결하려고 앉아서 얘기해 봅시다.

437

at one's wit's end

p. 어찌할 바를 몰라

witness n. 증인
witty a. 재치 있는, 기지 있는

어원	-wi, -wis, -wit 앎, 현명함 + -end 끝 → '앎이 끝에 이르렀으니 어찌할 바를 몰라'
유의어	perplexed, bewildered, confused
반의어	composed, clear-headed, certain
영영	Extremely worried and not knowing what to do next.
예문	After trying everything, she was at her wit's end on how to solve the problem. 모든 것을 시도한 후에도 문제를 어떻게 해결할지 몰라 마음이 좌절했습니다.

438

on the tube

p. 텔레비전에

test tube p. 시험관
take the tube p. 지하철을 타다
down the tube p. 파멸되어, 못 쓰게 되어

어원	-tube 관 → '초기 텔레비전 세트에서 음극선관을 사용한 것에서 유래'
유의어	on television, on the air
반의어	off the air, not broadcasting
영영	Being broadcast on television.
예문	I caught up on the news while on the tube to work this morning. 오늘 아침 출근길 지하철에서 뉴스를 챙겼습니다.

439

What with A and B

p. A 그리고 B 때문에

what's more p. 더욱이, 게다가
what is knows as p. 소위
what people call p. 소위
the so-called p. 소위

어원	-what 무엇 + -with 함께 → '무엇과 함께 일어난 일이니 ~때문에'
유의어	considering A and B, due to A and B
반의어	regardless of A and B, despite A and B
영영	Considering both A and B; taking into account A and B.
예문	She was exhausted, what with the long hours at work and family responsibilities. 그녀는 업무의 긴 시간과 가족 책임 때문에 지쳐 있었습니다.

440

shelf-stable

p. 상온에서 오래 상하지 않는

p. shelf life 유통기한
p. shelf mark 서가 번호, 서가 기호
n. bookshelf 책장, 책꽂이

어원	-shelf : split piece → '물건을 나누어 꽂는 선반'
유의어	non-perishable, long-lasting, durable
반의어	perishable, short-lived, unstable
영영	Capable of being stored without refrigeration for an extended period.
예문	These canned goods are shelf-stable, meaning they have a long shelf life. 이 캔 제품들은 선반에 오래 두어도 피해가 없다는 뜻인 선반 안정제입니다.

Chapter 12.

441	pollen	[ˈpɒl.ən]	n. 꽃가루, 화분
442	petroleum	[pəˈtrəʊ.li.əm]	n. 석유
443	adjourn	[əˈdʒɜːn]	v. 휴회하다, 중단하다, 연기하다; 자리를 옮기다
444	fame	[feɪm]	n. 명성, 평판
445	awe	[ɔː]	n. 경외심 v. 경외심을 느끼다
446	blossom	[ˈblɒs.əm]	v. 꽃이 피다 n. 개화; 건강한 혈색
447	detain	[dɪˈteɪn]	v. 붙잡아두다
448	pitfall	[ˈpɪt.fɔːl]	n. 함정, 위험
449	stake	[steɪk]	n. 돈, 지분; 말뚝, 기둥; 화형
450	confront	[kənˈfrʌnt]	v. 맞서다, 대항하다; 들이대다
451	impromptu	[imprɑ́mptjuː]	a. 즉석의 adv. 즉흥으로
452	audit	[ˈɔː.dɪt]	n. 회계 감사, 심사; 청강 v. 청강하다
453	parlor	[ˈpɑːr.lə]	n. 응접실, 가게, 거실
454	jest	[dʒest]	n. 농담, 조롱 v. 농담하다
455	nasal	[ˈneɪ.zəl]	a. 코의, 콧소리의
456	redeem	[rɪˈdiːm]	v. ~을 되찾다; 메우다, 보상하다; 구하다
457	heir	[eər]	n. 상속인 , 후계자
458	pungent	[ˈpʌn.dʒənt]	a. 신랄한
459	plea	[pliː]	n. 애원, 간청, 답변
460	intersperse	[ˌɪn.təˈspɜːs]	v. 흩뿌리다; 점재시키다
461	sleeve	[sliːv]	n. 소매, 소맷자락
462	orphan	[ˈɔː.fən]	n. 고아 v. 고아로 만들다
463	mundane	[mʌnˈdeɪn]	a. 일상적인, 재미없는 n. 세속
464	constable	[ˈkʌn.stə.bəl]	n. 치안관, 순경, 경관
465	conspire	[kənspáiər]	v. 음모를 꾸미다; 공모하다
466	trepid	[trépid]	a. 겁내는, 두려워하는
467	meadow	[ˈmed.əʊ]	n. 목초지, 초원
468	calf	[kɑːf]	n. 송아지, 새끼; 종아리
469	longevity	[lɒnˈdʒev.ə.ti]	n. 장수; 수명
470	numb	[nʌm]	a. 감각이 없는, 멍한
471	let on		p. 비밀을 털어놓다
472	make it a rule to do		p. ~하는 것을 규칙으로 삼다
473	lay the foundation		p. 기초 공사를 하다, 기초를 놓다
474	for this once		p. 이번만은
475	in the raw		p. 자연 그대로의, 날것 그대로의, 벌거벗고
476	gain access to		p. ~에 접근하다, ~와 면회하다
477	green thumb		p. 식물 재배의 재능
478	hold onto		p. ~에 매달리다, 꼭 잡다
479	public domain		p. 공유
480	vhat with one thing and anothe		p. 이런 저런 일들 때문에 (바빠서)

441

pollen

[ˈpɒl.ən]

n. 꽃가루, 화분

pollinate v. 수분하다
pollination n. 수분
pollinator n. 꽃가루 매개자
powder n. 분말

어원	-powder, -pollen 먼지, 가루 → '꽃가루가 한자로 화분'
유의어	spore, seed, dust
반의어	clean, purify, sterilize
개념	Fine powdery substance, typically yellow, produced by the male part of a flower.
예문	Bees collect pollen from flowers. 꿀벌은 꽃에서 꽃가루를 모아온다.

442

petroleum

[pəˈtrəʊ.li.əm]

n. 석유

petrify v. 돌로 만들다, 굳게 만들다
petrified a. 굳어진, 둔화된
petrol n. 가솔린
oleaginous a. 기름진, 윤기 있는, 윤활성의

어원	-petra 돌 + -oleum 기름 → '돌에서 발췌한 기름이 석유'
유의어	oil, crude, fossil fuel
반의어	alternative energy, renewable energy
개념	A thick, dark oil obtained from under the ground, from which various substances (e.g., gasoline) are produced.
예문	Most of our energy comes from fossil fuels, including petroleum. 우리의 에너지 대부분은 석유를 포함한 화석 연료에서 나온다.

443

adjourn

[əˈdʒɜːn]

v. 휴회하다, 중단하다, 연기하다; 자리를 옮기다

adjourn for v. ~를 위해 휴회하다
adjournment n. 연기, 폐회
journey n. 여행
sojourn v. 묵다, 체류하다

어원	-ad : to + -journ : diurnum = day → '날짜를 뒤로 늦추다'
유의어	suspend, postpone, recess
반의어	convene, assemble, continue
개념	To suspend or postpone a meeting, legal case, or event to a future time.
예문	The meeting will adjourn until next week. 회의는 다음 주까지 연기될 것이다.

444

fame

[feɪm]

n. 명성, 평판

famed a. 저명한
fameless a. 무명한
famous a. 유명한
infamy n. 악명

어원	-fa, -fe, -fess, -phe : talk 말하다 → '공공연한 이야기를 하는 사람의 명성과 평판'
유의어	celebrity, renown, prestige
반의어	obscurity, anonymity, insignificance
개념	Widespread recognition and reputation, often resulting from notable achievements.
예문	His acting career brought him great fame. 그의 연기 경력은 그에게 큰 명성을 가져다 주었다.

445

awe

[ɔː]

n. 경외심 v. 경외심을 느끼다

awe-inspiring a. 경외심을 자아내는
awful a. 끔찍한 지독한
awesome a. 아주 멋진, 굉장한

어원	* 의성어 / * -awe : away → 멀리 떨어져 경외심을 느끼는'
유의어	admiration, reverence, wonder
반의어	indifference, apathy, disregard
개념	A feeling of reverential respect mixed with fear or wonder.
예문	The majestic mountains filled them with a sense of awe. 웅장한 산들은 그들에게 경외감을 불러일으켰다.

446

blossom

[ˈblɒs.əm]

v. 꽃이 피다 n. 개화; 건강한 혈색

bloom v. 꽃이 피다 n. 개화
bloat v. 팽창시키다
boom n. 호황, 붐

어원	-blizzard, -blast : bhle, bhel : blow, swell → '폭발하는 것처럼 꽃이 피다'
유의어	bloom, flower, flourish
반의어	wither, fade, wilt
개념	The flower or flowers of a plant, especially those of fruit trees.
예문	Spring is the season when flowers blossom. 봄은 꽃이 피는 계절이다.

447

detain

[dɪˈteɪn]

v. 붙잡아두다

detention n. 억류, 구금, 억제
detainee n. 구금된 사람, 억류된 사람
obtain v. 얻다, 획득하다
retain v. 유지하다, 보유하다

어원	-de : down + -tain : hold → '밑에 붙잡아두다'
유의어	imprison, confine, hold
반의어	release, free, liberate
영영	To keep someone in official custody, typically for questioning or investigation.
예문	The police may detain a suspect for questioning. 경찰은 용의자를 심문을 위해 구류할 수 있다.

448

pitfall

[ˈpɪt.fɔːl]

n. 함정, 위험

n. pitcher 투수
n. pit 구덩이
v. peep 훔쳐보다
v. peek (재빨리) 훔쳐보다

어원	-pit, -pitch 밀어내다(E) + -fall 떨어지다 → '밀어서 떨어지게 하는 함정'
유의어	trap, danger, hazard
반의어	advantage, benefit, opportunity
영영	A hidden or unexpected danger or difficulty.
예문	The new project has many potential pitfalls we need to consider. 새로운 프로젝트에는 고려해야 할 많은 잠재적인 위험 요소가 있다.

449

stake

[steɪk]

n. 돈, 지분; 말뚝, 기둥; 화형

stakes n. 배팅
stakeholder n. 지주, 이자 보유자
steak n. 스테이크, 살코기
stakes n. 성공 여부에 걸려 있는 것

어원	-st : stand + -tach, -tak 말뚝, 막대; 들러붙게 하다 → '말뚝처럼 단단히 서 있는 지분이 돈'
유의어	wager, bet, investment
반의어	forfeit, surrender, lose
영영	A sum of money or something else of value, wagered on the outcome of an event.
예문	They had a lot at stake in the outcome of the negotiations. 그들은 협상 결과에 큰 이해관계를 가지고 있었다.

450

confront

[kənˈfrʌnt]

v. 맞서다, 대항하다; 들이대다

confrontation n. 직면, 대립
confrontational a. 대립적인
affont v. 모욕하다
frontal a. 정면의, 전면의

어원	-con : together + -front 정면 → '서로 정면으로 맞서며 들이대다'
유의어	face, encounter, challenge
반의어	avoid, evade, ignore
영영	To face a difficult situation or challenge directly.
예문	It's important to confront challenges rather than avoiding them. 도전에 대면하는 것이 피하는 것보다 중요하다.

451

impromptu

[ɪmprˈæmptjuː]

a. 즉석의 adv. 즉흥으로

adv. promptly 즉각적으로, 신속히
n. prompter 프롬프터
n. promptitude 신속
v. improvise 즉흥적으로 만들다

어원	-im, -in : not + -pro : prepare → '준비할 필요없이 즉흥으로'
유의어	spontaneous, extemporaneous, unrehearsed
반의어	planned, rehearsed, prepared
영영	Done without being planned, organized, or rehearsed.
예문	They made an impromptu decision to go on a road trip. 그들은 즉흥적으로 로드 트립을 가기로 결정했다.

452

audit

[ˈɔː.dɪt]

n. 회계 감사, 심사; 청강 v. 청강하다

auditor n. 청취자, 방송인, 회계감사관
auditable a. 회계 감사할 수 있는
audition n. 심사 v. 오디션을 하다
auditorium n. 강당, 방청석

어원	-aud, -audi, -ey : audire=acou 듣다(L) → '당사자의 말을 들으며 회계 감사'
유의어	examination, inspection, review
반의어	ignore, neglect, overlook
영영	An official inspection of an individual's or organization's accounts.
예문	The company conducts an audit of its financial records annually. 회사는 매년 재무 기록을 감사한다.

453	어원	-parlor, -parl 공식적으로 말하다 (E) → '공식적으로 손님을 대하고 말하는 응접실'
	유의어	lounge, sitting room, salon
parlor	반의어	kitchen, bedroom, outdoors
[ˈpɑːr.lər]	영영	A sitting room in a private house; a lounge.
n. 응접실, 가게, 거실		
parlor game p. 실내 게임 parlor song p. 응접실 노래 parley n. 회담, 협상, 대회 parlance n. 말투, 언어, 표현 방식	예문	The family gathered in the living parlor for a game night. 가족은 게임 나이트를 위해 거실에 모였다.

454	어원	-jok, -jest : joc, ioc 농담 → '농담으로 조롱하다'
	유의어	joke, quip, humor
jest	반의어	seriousness, solemnity, earnestness
[dʒest]	영영	A joke or witty remark; to speak or act in a joking manner.
n. 농담, 조롱 v. 농담하다		
jestful a. 우스꽝스런, 익살스러운 jesting a. 농담하는, 장난치는 jester n. 어릿광대, 광대 gesture n. 제스처, 손짓, 몸짓	예문	He always had a quick jest ready to make people laugh. 그는 항상 사람들을 웃게 하기 위해 빠른 농담을 준비했다

455	어원	-nas : nose 코 → '코로 내는 콧소리의'
	유의어	nasalized, nasal passage, nose
nasal	반의어	oral, non-nasal
[ˈneɪ.zəl]	영영	Relating to the nose; characterized by a sound produced through the nose.
a. 코의, 콧소리의		
nasalize v. 코음화시키다 nasality n. 코음화, 코성 nasally adv. 비음으로, 콧소리로 nose n. 코	예문	A nasal voice can be caused by nasal congestion. 코막힘이 코음을 일으킬 수 있다.

456	어원	-re : again + -em : buy → '잃었던 것을 다시 사다'
	유의어	save, rescue, recover
redeem	반의어	forfeit, lose, surrender
[rɪˈdiːm]	영영	To compensate for the faults or bad aspects of something.
v. ~을 되찾다; 메우다, 보상하다; 구하다		
redemption n. 상환, 회수; 구원 redeemable a. 교환할 수 있는, 환급할 수 있는 preempt v. 점유하다 premium n. 전리품, 보상	예문	He wanted to redeem himself after making a mistake. 그는 실수를 한 후 자신을 바로잡고 싶어했다.

457	어원	-hered, -heir, -herit : 상속 → '상속 받는 사람이 후계자' * hair 머리카락 검사로 친자 확인
	유의어	successor, beneficiary, descendant
heir	반의어	ancestor, predecessor, forebear
[eər]	영영	A person legally entitled to the property or rank of another on that person's death.
n. 상속인 , 후계자		
n. heirship 상속(권) n. inheritance 상속 a. hereditary 유전적인 n. coheir 공동 상속인	예문	The prince is the heir to the throne. 왕자는 왕위의 후계자이다.

458	어원	-pick, -punc, -pung : prick 찌르다 → '찌르는 수법이 신랄한'
	유의어	strong, sharp, intense
pungent	반의어	mild, subtle, bland
[ˈpʌn.dʒənt]	영영	Having a sharply strong taste or smell.
a. 신랄한		
pungency n. 자극, 매움 puncture v. 구멍을 내다, 찌르다 inpugn v. 비난하다, 공격하다 pricky a. 가시가 많은, 성가신	예문	The pungent smell of onions filled the kitchen. 양파의 강렬한 냄새가 부엌에 가득했다.

459

plea

[pliː]

n. 애원, 간청, 답변

plead v. 간청하다, 탄원하다
pleader n. 변론자, 항변자, 변호사
pleading n. 변론, 변명 a. 탄원하는
please v. 기쁘게 하다

어원	-pla, -plac, -plas, -pleas, -plead 기쁘게 하다; 호감을 얻다(L) → '호감을 얻기 위해 간청하다'
유의어	appeal, request, petition
반의어	denial, refusal, rejection
영영	A request made in an urgent and emotional manner.
예문	The defendant entered a guilty plea in court. 피고는 법정에서 유죄를 시인했다.

460

intersperse

[ˌɪn.təˈspɜːs]

v. 흩뿌리다; 점재시키다

interspersion n. 산재, 점재, 흩뿌리기
sparkling a. 불꽃을 튀기는
disperse v. 흩어지게 하다, 분산시키다

어원	-inter : between + -spers, -spars, -sparg : scatter → '서로 떨어지도록 흩뜨려 뿌리다'
유의어	scatter, distribute, sprinkle
반의어	gather, collect, consolidate
영영	Scatter among or between other things.
예문	The artist chose to intersperse bright colors throughout the painting. 예술가는 그림 전체에 밝은 색상을 뒤섞기로 했다.

461

sleeve

[sliːv]

n. 소매, 소맷자락

sleeveless a. 소매 없는, 민소매의
sleevelet n. 작은 소매, 소매 덮개
sleeving n. 보호용 소매
sleeveen a. 부정직한, 속임수를 쓰는

어원	* -sle 미끄러지다 → '옷 속으로 팔이 미끄러져 들어가는 소매'
유의어	cuff, covering, sheath
반의어	bare arm, uncovered
영영	The protective or connecting outer covering of a cable.
예문	She wiped her hands on her sleeve after finishing the messy task. 그녀는 지저분한 작업을 마치고 소매에 손을 닦았다.

462

orphan

[ˈɔːfən]

n. 고아 v. 고아로 만들다

orphans n. 고아
orphanage n. 고아원
orphaned a. 고아가 된, 부모를 잃은
orphical a. 단 한 번밖에 일어날 수 없는

어원	-orph, orpho 아버지의 유산이 없는 + -an 사람 → '아버지의 유산이 없는 아이가 고아'
유의어	parentless, fatherless, motherless
반의어	with parents, not orphaned
영영	A child whose parents are dead.
예문	The orphan found a new family that cared for him deeply. 고아는 그를 심각하게 돌봐주는 새로운 가족을 찾았다.

463

mundane

[mʌnˈdeɪn]

a. 일상적인, 재미없는 n. 세속

n. mundanity 지루함
n. mundification 정화
a. mundificative 정화하는, 깨끗이 하는
n. mundungus 오물

어원	-mundane : mundain 현세의(L), 고귀한, 깨끗한(G) → '세상 사람들이 모두 고귀하니 재미없는, 일상적인' * 뭔데 임마 재미없게~
유의어	ordinary, routine, commonplace
반의어	extraordinary, exceptional, remarkable
영영	Lacking interest or excitement; dull.
예문	The routine tasks may seem mundane, but they are essential. 루틴 작업들은 평범해 보일 수 있지만, 그것들은 중요하다.

464

constable

[ˈkʌn.stə.bəl]

n. 치안관, 순경, 경관

constabulary a. 경찰관의 n. 경찰국, 경찰 조직
constableship n. 경찰 관할권
constant a. 끊임없는, 계속되는
constitution n. 구성, 구조; 헌법

어원	-con : together + -sta : stand → '모두 그대로 제자리에 서서 치안을 유지하는 경찰관'
유의어	officer, policeman, lawman
반의어	criminal, lawbreaker
영영	A peace officer with limited policing authority, typically in a small town.
예문	The constable patrolled the small town to maintain peace. 경찰은 작은 마을을 순찰하여 평화를 유지했다.

465

conspire

[kənspáiər]

v. 음모를 꾸미다; 공모하다

conspiracy n. 음모, 공모
conspirator n. 공모자
inspire v. 고무하다, 격려하다
respire v. 호흡하다, 숨쉬다

어원	-con : together + -spire : breath → '함께 호흡을 같이 하며 공모하다'
유의어	plot, scheme, collaborate
반의어	oppose, resist, thwart
영영	To secretly plan together to commit an illegal or harmful act.
예문	The characters in the novel conspire to overthrow the evil ruler. 소설 속 캐릭터들은 악랄한 지배자를 전복하기 위해 음모를 꾸렸다.

466

trepid

[trépid]

a. 겁내는, 두려워하는

trepidatious a. 두려움에 가득한
trepidatiously adv. 걱정스럽게
trepidation n. 공포, 전율
terror n. 테러, 공포

어원	-trep, -ter, -tre, -trepid : fear, terror → '테러가 두려워 겁내는'
유의어	fearful, anxious, jittery
반의어	calm, composed, confident
영영	Timid, fearful, or nervous.
예문	She felt trepid before giving a speech in front of a large audience. 그녀는 대규모 청중 앞에서 연설하기 전에 불안했다.

467

meadow

['med.əʊ]

n. 목초지, 초원

meadowy a. 초원 같은, 초원에 적합한
meadowland n. 목초지
mow v. 베다, 수확하다

어원	-me : mow 깎다, 베다 → '건초용으로 깎은 풀로 덮인 땅' * meadow 건초를 만드는 공간 VS pasture pastor 양에게 풀을 먹이는 공간
유의어	field, pasture, grassland
반의어	desert, wasteland, barren
영영	A piece of grassland, especially one used for hay.
예문	The cows grazed peacefully in the lush meadow. 소들은 푸르른 목초지에서 평화롭게 풀을 뜯고 있었다.

468

calf

[kɑ:f]

n. 송아지, 새끼; 종아리

calfskin n. 송아지 가죽
calfhood n. 송아지 상태
in calf p. 새끼를 밴

어원	-calf 송아지; 종아리 * 카프킥(Calf kick) : 종아리를 차는 기술
유의어	young cow, bovine, heifer
반의어	adult, mature cow
영영	A young bovine animal, especially a domestic cow or bull.
예문	The baby cow is called a calf. 새끼 소는 송아지라고 불린다.

469

longevity

[lɒnˈdʒev.ə.ti]

n. 장수; 수명

longevous a. 오래 살 수 있는, 장수한
longevities n. 오래 사는 기간, 수명
longitude n. 경도
lengthen v. 길어지다

어원	-long, -leng,-ling : want 갈망하다, long 긴 + -ev : life → '생애가 길게 이어지니 장수'
유의어	long life, duration, permanence
반의어	brevity, short life, transience
영영	Long life or existence; the length of a person's life.
예문	Healthy habits can contribute to a longer longevity. 건강한 습관은 더 긴 수명에 기여할 수 있다.

470

numb

[nʌm]

a. 감각이 없는, 멍한

benumb v. 무감각하게 하다, 얼게 하다
numbness n. 무감각함, 마비
number n. 숫자
denumber v. 제거하다, 수를 뺏다

어원	-num : take + -b 형접 * → '놈(num)한테 감각을 빼앗겨 멍한'
유의어	insensitive, unfeeling, paralyzed
반의어	sensitive, responsive, feeling
영영	Deprived of the power of sensation.
예문	After sitting in the cold, her fingers became numb. 추운 곳에서 앉아서 그녀의 손가락은 무감각해졌다.

471

let on

p. 비밀을 털어놓다

let down p. 기대를 저버리다
let go p. (걱정 근심 등을) 떨쳐버리다
let up p. (강도가) 약해지다
let in p. 들여보내다

어원	-let 허락하다 + -on : about → '~에 관해서 비밀을 털어놓는 것을 허락하다'
유의어	reveal, disclose, admit
반의어	conceal, hide, suppress
영영	To reveal or disclose something.
예문	He didn't want to let on that he knew the surprise. 그는 놀람을 알고 있다는 것을 드러내고 싶지 않았다.

472

make it a rule to do

p. ~하는 것을 규칙으로 삼다

make for p. ~에 기여하다
make it to p. ~에 도착하다, 이르다
make one's way to p. ~로 나아가다
be made up of p. ~로 구성되어 있다

어원	-make 만들다 + -rule 규칙 → '규칙으로 만들다'
유의어	establish a practice, adhere to a guideline
반의어	disregard, ignore, neglect
영영	To establish a practice or habit of doing something regularly.
예문	She decided to make it a rule to do exercise every morning. 그녀는 매일 아침 운동을 하는 것을 규칙으로 정하기로 결정했다.

473

lay the foundation

p. 기초 공사를 하다, 기초를 놓다

p. lay out 펼치다, 늘어놓다
p. lay A on B A를 B에 놓다
v. overlay 덮어씌우다

어원	-lay 놓다, 두다 + -foundation 기초 → '기초를 세우는 것이니 기초 공사를 하다'
유의어	establish, build, ground
반의어	dismantle, destroy, demolish
영영	To establish the basis or groundwork for something.
예문	Education helps lay the foundation for a successful future. 교육은 성공적인 미래를 위한 기초를 마련하는 데 도움이 된다.

474

for this once

p. 이번만은

all at once p. 갑자기, 동시에
once and again p. 여러 번 되풀이하여
once and for all p. 최종적으로
let alone p. ~은 고사하고

어원	-for 기간 + -once 한 번 → '한 번의 기간만 더'
유의어	for this occasion, just this once
반의어	regularly, consistently, always
영영	On this occasion only; not as a regular practice.
예문	I'll let it slide for this once, but don't do it again. 이번 한 번만은 봐줄게, 하지만 다시는 하지 마.

475

in the raw

p. 자연 그대로의, 날것 그대로의, 벌거벗고

p. raw food 생식
p. raw log 원목
p. raw data 미가공 자료
v. crawl 기어가다

어원	-in 안 + -raw 날것의 → '날 것 상태 그대로의'
유의어	naked, exposed, uncovered
반의어	clothed, covered, concealed
영영	In a natural or unprocessed state.
예문	Vegetables are healthiest when eaten in the raw state. 채소는 날것 상태로 먹을 때 가장 건강하다.

476

gain access to

p. ~에 접근하다, ~와 면회하다

v. regain 회복하다, 되찾다
p. with access to 직접 만날 수 있는
p. gain on 침식하다; ~의 마음에 들다
n. accessory 액세서리, 장신구

어원	-gain 얻다 + -access 접근 → '접근 권한을 얻다'
유의어	obtain entry, get into, access
반의어	be denied access, barred
영영	To obtain entry or permission to use or have something.
예문	The keycard allows you to gain access to the building. 키카드를 사용하면 건물에 접근할 수 있다.

477

green thumb

p. 식물 재배의 재능

n. thumbnail 엄지손톱
v. thump 쿵하고 떨어지다, 탁 치다
p. thumb through 휘휘 넘겨보다
p. rule of thumb 경험에 바탕을 둔 방법

어원	-green 식물 + -thumb 엄지 손가락; 최고 → '식물 재배에 있어서 엄지 척'
유의어	gardening skill, plant expertise
반의어	brown thumb, gardening ineptitude
영영	A talent or skill for gardening.
예문	People with a green thumb often have thriving gardens. 원예 소질이 있는 사람들은 종종 번창하는 정원을 가지고 있다.

478

hold onto

p. ~에 매달리다, 꼭 잡다

get hold of p. ~을 구하다, 손에 넣다
hold A in check p. A를 억제하다
hold on p. 붙잡고 있다, 잠시만
hold one's tongue p. 입을 다물다

어원	-hold 잡다 + -onto 붙어 → '딱 붙어 잡으니 ~에 매달리다'
유의어	retain, grasp, keep
반의어	release, let go, relinquish
영영	To keep or retain possession of something.
예문	Hold onto the railing while climbing the stairs. 계단을 올라갈 때 난간을 잡아라.

479

public domain

p. 공유

public relations p. 홍보, 섭외
public speaker p. 대중 연설가
public transportation p. 대중 교통
publicity n. 홍보, 공표

어원	-public 대중의 + -domain 영역, 범위 → '모든 사람들의 영역이니 공유'
유의어	open to the public, unrestricted
반의어	private, restricted, proprietary
영영	The state of being open and unrestricted for public use.
예문	After a certain period, books enter the public domain. 일정 기간이 지나면 책은 공공의 재산이 된다.

480

what with one thing and another

p. 이런 저런 일들 때문에 (바빠서)

what's more p. 더욱이, 게다가
what is knows as p. 소위
what people call p. 소위
what with A and B p. A그리고 B 때문에

어원	-what 무엇 + -with 함께 + one and another 이것 저것 → '이것 저것과 함께 일어난 일들 때문에 바빠서'
유의어	due to various factors, considering everything
반의어	for a single reason, without other factors
영영	Because of various factors or circumstances.
예문	What with one thing and another, I didn't get much sleep last night. 이것저것 있어서 어젯밤에는 잠을 많이 못 잤어.

Chapter 13.

481	ruth	[rú:θ]	n. 슬픔, 비애, 후회: 불운, 재난
482	accession	[əkˈseʃ.ən]	n. 취임, 계승; 동의; 부가, 부가물
483	ponder	[ˈpɒn.dər]	v. 곰곰이 생각하다, 심사숙고하다
484	consolidate	[kənsɑ́lədèit]	v. 합병하다; 강화하다
485	slumber	[ˈslʌm.bər]	n. 잠, 수면 v. 잠자다
486	accede	[əkˈsi:d]	vi. 응하다, 동의하다; 취임하다 (to)
487	reindeer	[ˈreɪn.dɪər]	n. 순록
488	miscarry	[mɪˈskær.i]	v. 실패하다, 유산하다
489	dignity	[ˈdɪg.nə.ti]	n. 위엄, 존엄
490	acrophobia	[ˌæk.rəˈfəʊ.bi.ə]	n. 고소 공포증
491	antidote	[ˈæn.ti.dəʊt]	n. 해독, 소독
492	aggrandize	[əgrǽndaiz]	v. 확대하다, 강화하다, 증대시키다
493	conceit	[kənˈsi:t]	n. 자만심, 자부심
494	dwarf	[dwɔ:f]	n. 난쟁이
495	corridor	[ˈkɒr.ɪ.dɔ:r]	n. 복도
496	contiguous	[kənˈtɪg.ju.əs]	a. 맞닿아 있는, 인접한; 연속된
497	progency	[prɑ́dʒəni]	n. 자식, 자손; 결과
498	pneumonia	[njuːˈməʊ.ni.ə]	n. 폐렴
499	artifice	[ˈɑː.tɪ.fɪs]	n. 계략, 관계, 술책
500	abort	[əˈbɔ:t]	v. [낙태]하다, 유산하다; 중단하다, 실패하다
501	hatch	[hætʃ]	v. 부화하다
502	clamorous	[ˈklæm.ər.əs]	a. 시끄러운
503	solidify	[səlídəfài]	v. 응고하다; 단결하다; 확고해지다
504	eloquent	[ˈel.ə.kwənt]	a. 웅변을 잘하는, 유창한
505	populist	[ˈpɒp.jə.lɪst]	a. 인민주의의, 인민당의 n. 포퓰리스트, 인민주의자
506	virgin	[ˈvɜː.dʒɪn]	n. 처녀, 성모 a. 순수한
507	abhor	[əˈbhɔ:r]	v. 혐오하다
508	deteriorate	[dɪˈtɪə.ri.ə.reɪt]	v. 떨어뜨리다
509	contrive	[kənˈtraɪv]	v. 고안하다, 궁리하다, 꾀하다
510	notorious	[noutɔ́:riəs]	a. 악명이 높은
511	make allowance for		p. 아량을 베풀다
512	of service		p. 쓸모 있는, 유익한
513	draw a deep breath		p. 심호흡을 하다
514	stand out		p. 두드러지다, 눈에 띄다
515	what A like		p. A는 어떠한가?
516	well off		p. 부유한; 충분한
517	look on		p. 구경하다
518	a visit from the stork		p. 아기의 출생
519	rip off		p. 뜯어내다, 훔치다
520	phase in		p. 단계적으로 도입하다

481

ruth

[rúːθ]

n. 슬픔, 비애, 후회; 불운, 재난

ruthless a. 무자비한, 냉정한

어원	-ruth : regret → '후회로 슬퍼하니 불운까지'
유의어	compassion, pity, empathy
반의어	cruelty, harshness, indifference
영영	Compassion or pity towards others.
예문	She showed great ruth towards the stray animals, adopting and caring for them. 그녀는 유기견에 대한 큰 자비심을 보여, 그들을 입양하고 돌봤다.

482

accession

[əkˈseʃ.ən]

n. 취임, 계승; 동의; 부가, 부가물

access n. 접근, 접속
accessible a. 접근하기 쉬운
accessibility n. 접근성
excess n. 초과, 잉여

어원	-ac : to + -ce, -ced, -cess, -cede, -cesler : go → '~조직으로 들어가니 취임 또는 계승'
유의어	addition, increase, augmentation
반의어	reduction, decrease, subtraction
영영	The act of coming into a position of power or authority.
예문	The country celebrated the accession of a new monarch to the throne. 그 나라는 새로운 군주의 즉위를 축하했다.

483

ponder

[ˈpɒn.dər]

v. 곰곰이 생각하다, 심사숙고하다

ponderous a. 무거운, 느린
preponderance n. 우세, 우위
imponderable a. 측정할 수 없는, 의문의
suspend v. 일시 중지하다, 매달다

어원	-pend, -pond : weigh → '저울질하며 심사숙고하다'
유의어	contemplate, meditate, deliberate
반의어	ignore, neglect, dismiss
영영	To think deeply or consider carefully.
예문	Before making a decision, he took some time to ponder the consequences. 결정을 내리기 전에 그는 결과를 숙고하는 시간을 가졌다.

484

consolidate

[kənsɔ́lədèit]

v. 합병하다; 강화하다

consolidated a. 강화된
consolidation n. 합병, 합동
consolidative a. 공고히 하는, 강화하는
solidify v. 응고하다; 단결하다

어원	-con : together + -solid 굳은 → '굳게 서로 합치다'
유의어	integrate, unify, merge
반의어	disperse, scatter, divide
영영	To combine or merge things into a unified whole.
예문	The company decided to consolidate its various branches into a single headquarters. 회사는 여러 지점을 하나의 본사로 통합하기로 결정했다.

485

slumber

[ˈslʌm.bər]

n. 잠, 수면 v. 잠자다

slumbery a. 졸리는, 꾸벅꾸벅 조는, 조용한
slumberous a. 졸리는, 꾸벅꾸벅 조는, 조용한
slumber party n. 파자마 파티
sleepy a. 졸린

어원	-slumber : sleep lightly → '잠자다'
유의어	sleep, rest, repose
반의어	wake, awaken, rous
영영	A state of sleep or deep rest.
예문	After a long day of work, he finally allowed himself to slumber peacefully. 긴 하루 일한 후, 그는 마침내 평화롭게 잠에 빠졌다.

486

accede

[əkˈsiːd]

vi. 응하다, 동의하다; 취임하다 (to)

accede to v. ~에 응하다
accedence n. 동의, 취임, 가입
recede v. 감소하다, 멀어지다
secede v. 탈퇴하다, 탈당하다

어원	-ac : to + -ced : go → '~로 마음이 움직이니 응하다'
유의어	agree, consent, comply
반의어	refuse, deny, reject
영영	To agree or consent to a demand, request, or treaty.
예문	After much negotiation, the two parties finally agreed on the terms of the contract. 긴 협상 끝에 두 당사자는 드디어 계약 조건에 합의했다.

487

reindeer

[ˈreɪn.dɪər]

n. 순록

v. rein 억제하다, 통제하다
n. reins 고삐, 정권, 권력
n. reign 통치 기간 v. 통치하다
n. regime 정권, 제도, 체제

어원	-rig, -rec, -rect, -reg, -reig, -roy rule 통치하다(F) + -deer 사슴 → '통치하에 길들여진 사슴이 순록'
유의어	caribou
반의어	
영영	A type of deer, often associated with Christmas folklore.
예문	In some cultures, reindeer are associated with Christmas and are believed to pull Santa's sleigh. 어떤 문화에서는 순록이 크리스마스와 연관되어 산타의 썰매를 끈다고 믿어진다.

488

miscarry

[mɪˈskær.i]

v. 실패하다, 유산하다

miscarriage n. 유산; 실패, 실책
misguide v. 잘못 지도하다
carriage n. 마차

어원	-mis : wrong + -carry 옮기다 → '잘못 옮겼으니 실패', '씨를 잘못 옮기면 유산'
유의어	fail, abort, flop
반의어	succeed, accomplish, thrive
영영	The failure of a pregnancy, resulting in the loss of the fetus.
예문	Unfortunately, the pregnancy miscarried, leading to great sorrow for the couple. 불행하게도 임신이 낙태되어 그 부부에게 큰 슬픔을 안겼다.

489

dignity

[ˈdɪɡ.nə.ti]

n. 위엄, 존엄

dignify v. 위엄을 갖추다, 고상하게 만들다
dignitary n. 고위 관리, 유력인사
indignation n. 분노, 격노
disdain v. 경멸하다, 거부하다

어원	-dig, -dign, -dain : worth → '가치 있는 위엄이 존엄'
유의어	honor, prestige, respectability
반의어	disgrace, shame, dishonor
영영	The quality of being worthy of honor, respect, or esteem.
예문	She faced the challenges with grace and dignity, earning the respect of her colleagues. 그녀는 도전에 안착하고 품위 있게 대처하여 동료들의 존경을 얻었다.

490

acrophobia

[ˌæk.rəˈfoʊ.bi.ə]

n. 고소 공포증

macrophobia n. 장시간 기다림 공포증
trypanophobia n. 주사공포증
phasmophobia n. 유령공포
acrobat n. 곡예사

어원	-acro : peak + -phobia : fear → '높은 꼭대기에서 느끼는 공포니 고소 공포증'
유의어	fear of heights
반의어	acrophilia (attraction to heights)
영영	An extreme fear of heights.
예문	Those with acrophobia may experience intense fear and anxiety when confronted with heights. 고소공포증을 가진 사람들은 고소에 직면했을 때 강한 두려움과 불안을 경험할 수 있다.

491

antidote

[ˈæn.ti.doʊt]

n. 해독, 소독

antidotal a. 해독의
donate v. 기부하다, 기증하다
antagonist n. 적대자, 반대자

어원	-anti 반대로 + -do : give 주다 → '주어진 독에 반대하여 상쇄하니 해독'
유의어	remedy, cure, solution
반의어	poison, toxin, harm
영영	A substance that counteracts the effects of poison or disease.
예문	The antidote for the venomous snake bite was administered promptly. 독사의 물림에 대한 해독제가 신속히 투여되었다.

492

aggrandize

[əɡrǽndaiz]

v. 확대하다, 강화하다, 증대시키다

n. aggrandizement 증대, 확대
n. aggrandizer 확대하는 사람
n. grandeur 웅장함, 위엄
v. aggravate 악화시키다, 가중시키다

어원	-ag : add + -grand : great → '더해서 크게 확대하다' * 그랜다이저 로보트
유의어	amplify, enhance, boost
반의어	diminish, reduce, decrease
영영	To enhance the power, wealth, or status of someone or something.
예문	The leader was accused of trying to aggrandize his own power at the expense of the people. 그 지도자는 자신의 권력을 확장하려고 하는 것으로 비난받았다.

493	어원	-con : together + -cept, -ceit, -ceive : take 취하다, 잡다 → '모두에게 인정이 취해지니 자부심이 강한'
conceit	유의어	vanity, arrogance, egotism
[kənˈsiːt]	반의어	humility, modesty, selflessness
n. 자만심, 자부심	영영	Excessive pride in oneself or one's abilities.
a. conceited 자부심이 강한 adv. conceitedly 건방지게, 거들먹거리며 n. concept 개념 a. conceivable 상상 가능한	예문	His conceit and arrogance made it difficult for others to work with him. 그의 자만심과 오만함으로 다른 사람들이 그와 협력하기 어려웠다.

494	어원	-dwarf 매우 작은 사람 * -d : down + -ward 방향 → '아래로 키가 향하는 사람'
dwarf	유의어	midget, small person, little person
[dwɔːf]	반의어	giant, colossus, behemoth
n. 난쟁이	영영	A person or creature much smaller than the average size.
dwarfism n. 소인증 dwarfish a. 소인 같은; 미약한 bedwarf v. 작게 만들다 dwindle v. 점점 작아지다, 약화되다	예문	The tiny bonsai tree seemed to dwarf the other plants on the shelf. 작은 분재 나무는 선반 위의 다른 식물들을 작게 보이게 했다.

495	어원	-corridor 긴 통로(F) → '긴 통로의 복도' * -cor : correct → '똑바로 걸어다녀야 하는 복도'
corridor	유의어	hallway, passage, aisle
[ˈkɒr.ɪ.dɔːr]	반의어	open space, courtyard, field
n. 복도	영영	A long, narrow passage in a building.
corridor train p. 복도 열차, 통랑 열차 air corridor p. 공중 회랑 current n. 흐름. 전류 curriculum n. 교육과정	예문	The long corridor led to various rooms in the historic mansion. 긴 복도는 역사적인 저택의 여러 방들로 이어져 있었다.

496	어원	-con : together + -ti, -tig, -tag, -tac : touch → '서로 맞닿아 있으니 인접하여 연속된'
contiguous	유의어	adjacent, neighboring, adjoining
[kənˈtɪɡ.ju.əs]	반의어	distant, separate, isolated
a. 맞닿아 있는, 인접한; 연속된	영영	Sharing a common border or touching.
contiguously adv. 인접하여, 근접하여 contiguousness n. 인접함, 근접함 contact n. 접촉 v. 연락하다 contagious a. 전염성의	예문	The two houses were contiguous, sharing a common wall. 두 집은 서로 접해 있어 공통 벽을 공유했다.

497	어원	-pro : forth + -gen : birth → '앞으로 태어날 자식'
progency	유의어	offspring, descendants, heirs
[prɑ́dʒəni]	반의어	ancestors, forebears, predecessors
n. 자식, 자손; 결과	영영	Offspring or descendants.
a. progenitive 생산적인, 번식에 관련된 v. progernerate 생기게 하다, 생산하다 n. genesis 창조, 발생, 시작 n. profile 프로필, 윤곽	예문	The biologist studied the behavior of the animal's progeny to understand generational patterns. 생물학자는 동물의 후손의 행동을 연구하여 세대 패턴을 이해했다.

498	어원	-pn : air + -eu : eupnea 정상호흡 → '공기로 숨을 쉬는데 문제가 생긴 병이 폐렴'
pneumonia	유의어	lung infection, respiratory illness
[njuːˈməʊ.ni.ə]	반의어	health, wellness
n. 폐렴	영영	A respiratory condition characterized by inflammation of the lungs.
pneumatic a. 공기의; 압축 공기가 채워진 pneumothorax n. 기흉, 폐막증 lung n. 폐 pulmonary a. 폐의, 폐를 침범하는	예문	The patient was hospitalized due to severe pneumonia and respiratory distress. 환자는 심한 폐렴과 호흡 곤란으로 입원되었다.

499

artifice

[ˈɑːtɪfɪs]

n. 계략, 관계, 술책

artificer n. 고안자, 계획자; 기술병
artillery n. 대포, 포병대
artisan n. 장인공
artifact n. 인공물

어원 -art, -arti, -er, -ert 인공; 기술 (L) + -fic : make
→ '인간의 머리로 만든 기술이 계략이고 술책'

유의어 cunning, trickery, deceit
반의어 honesty, sincerity, truthfulness

영영 Clever or cunning strategies or tricks.

예문 His success was based on hard work and talent, not on any deceitful artifice.
그의 성공은 부정직한 계획이나 교활한 수법이 아니라 노력과 재능에 기반했다.

500

abort

[əˈbɔːt]

v. [낙태]하다, 유산하다; 중단하다, 실패하다

abortion n. 낙태
abortive a. (특히 초기에) 실패한, 무산된
abolish v. 폐지하다, 없애다
aberrant a. 정도를 벗어난, 변태적인

어원 -ab : away + -ori, -ort : arise
→ '태어남과 거리가 머니 낙태'

유의어 terminate, cancel, cease
반의어 continue, proceed, persist

영영 To terminate or end prematurely.

예문 The mission had to abort due to unfavorable weather conditions.
불리한 날씨 조건으로 미션은 중단되어야 했다.

501

hatch

[hætʃ]

v. 부화하다

hatches n. 출생, 약혼, 결혼; 사망란
hatchery n. 부화장
hatchet n. 손도끼
hatchback n. 해치백

어원 -hat 모자 → '모자를 벗듯 알에서 껍질을 뚫고 나오는 모양'
* 잠수함 뚜껑도 해치

유의어 incubate, develop, emerge
반의어 extinguish, suppress, stifle

영영 To bring forth from an egg by incubation.

예문 The eggs in the nest began to hatch, and tiny birds emerged.
둥지의 알들이 부화하기 시작했고 작은 새들이 나타났다.

502

clamorous

[ˈklæm.ər.əs]

a. 시끄러운

claim v. 주장하다
claimable a. 요구할 수 있는
exclaim v. 외치다
proclaim v. 선언하다

어원 -claim, -cil : cry out 외치다 / call 부르다
→ '외치기만 하니 시끄러운'

유의어 noisy, loud, boisterous
반의어 quiet, silent, subdued

영영 Characterized by loud and noisy outcry.

예문 The protest outside the government building was clamorous, with people shouting slogans.
정부 건물 외부의 시위는 시민들이 구호를 외치며 시끄러웠다.

503

solidify

[səlídəfài]

v. 응고하다; 단결하다; 확고해지다

solidarity n. 단결, 연대
solidification n. 고체화, 응고
solidity n. 단단함, 튼튼함
consolidate v. 강화하다, 합병하다

어원 solid 고체 + -fy : make
→ '고체로 만드니 응고하다'

유의어 firm up, harden, congeal
반의어 liquefy, melt, soften

영영 To make or become firm, stable, or solid.

예문 The cooling lava began to solidify into a hard, rocky surface.
식어가는 용암은 단단하고 돌 같은 표면으로 고체화되기 시작했다.

504

eloquent

[ˈel.ə.kwənt]

a. 웅변을 잘하는, 유창한

elocution n. 웅변술
elocutionary a. 연설술의, 웅변술의
eloquently adv. 변하듯이, 설득력 있게
analogy n. 유추

어원 -e : out + -log, -loq : speech
→ '밖으로 말을 잘하니 유창한'

유의어 articulate, expressive, persuasive
반의어 inarticulate, mute, speechless

영영 Fluent and persuasive in speaking or writing.

예문 The president delivered an eloquent speech that moved the audience to tears.
대통령은 감동적인 연설을 통해 청중을 눈물짓게 했다.

505

populist

[ˈpɒp.jə.lɪst]

a. 인민주의의, 인민당의 n. 포퓰리스트, 인민주의자

n. populism 인민주의
n. popularity 인기
n. publicity 홍보, 공표, 평판

어원	-popul, -publ 많은 사람들(L) + -ist 사람 → '공동의 사회주의를 제창했던 인민주의자'
유의어	democratic, people-oriented, popular
반의어	elitist, exclusive, undemocratic
영영	Relating to or characteristic of a political approach that strives to appeal to ordinary people.
예문	The politician's populist policies aimed to address the concerns of the common people. 정치인의 대중주의적인 정책은 일반 국민의 우려를 해결하려는 것이었다.

506

virgin

[ˈvɜː.dʒɪn]

n. 처녀, 성모 a. 순수한

virginity n. 처녀성
virginal a. 처녀의, 순수한
virgo n. 처녀자리, 별자리
virtue n. 덕, 미덕

어원	-virgin 어린 여성->처녀(L) * vigor 활력(→ '어린 여성이라 활력 넘치는')
유의어	untouched, pure, pristine
반의어	experienced, deflowered, impure
영영	Inexperienced or untouched by a particular quality or experience.
예문	The untouched forest was described as a virgin landscape, unspoiled by human activity. 손 대지 않은 숲은 인간의 활동에 의해 망가지지 않은 처음 본 듯한 풍경으로 묘사되었다.

507

abhor

[əˈbhɔːr]

v. 혐오하다

a. abhorrent 혐오스러운
n. abrorrence 혐오
a. abhorred 혐오하는
a. horrible 무서운, 불쾌한

어원	-ab : away + -hor, -horror : shudder → '몸서리치며 멀리하니 혐오'
유의어	detest, loathe, despise
반의어	adore, love, cherish
영영	To regard with disgust or hatred.
예문	Many people abhor cruelty to animals and advocate for their rights. 많은 사람들이 동물에 대한 잔혹행위를 혐오하고 그들의 권리를 옹호한다.

508

deteriorate

[dɪˈtɪə.ri.ə.reɪt]

v. 떨어뜨리다

deterioration n. 악화, 하락, 품질 저하
deteriorating a. 악화되는
deteriorative a. 악화하는
interior a. 내부의

어원	-de : down + -terior 비교급 접미어 → '더 떨어지니 품질 저하로 악화'
유의어	decline, worsen, degenerate
반의어	improve, enhance, ameliorate
영영	To become progressively worse over time.
예문	If the infrastructure is not maintained, it will deteriorate over time. 인프라가 유지보수되지 않으면 시간이 지남에 따라 악화될 것이다.

509

contrive

[kənˈtraɪv]

v. 고안하다, 궁리하다, 꾀하다

contrivance n. 고안, 발명
contrived a. 인위적인, 꾸민
contrivingly adv. 계획하여, 설계하여
tribe n. 부족

어원	-con : together + -tri : three(논리, 문법, 수학) → '논리, 문법, 수학 모두를 동원하여 고안하다' * control하기 위한 방법을 고안하며 꾀하다
유의어	devise, plan, concoct
반의어	ruin, destroy, dismantle
영영	To plan or create skillfully and ingeniously.
예문	She managed to contrive a plan to solve the complex problem. 그녀는 복잡한 문제를 해결하기 위한 계획을 만들어냈다.

510

notorious

[noutóːriəs]

a. 악명이 높은

n. notice 알림, 공지
a. noteworthy 주목할 만한
adv. notoriously 악명 높게
a. notorious for ~로 악명 높은

어원	* -not : bad + -ous : famous → '안 좋은 것으로 유명하니 악명높은'
유의어	infamous, disreputable
반의어	reputable, respected, esteemed
영영	Famous or well-known, typically for something negative.
예문	Being cautious, he double-checked all the details before making a decision. 신중한 성격으로, 그는 결정 전에 모든 세부사항을 두 번 확인했다.

511

make allowance for

p. 아량을 베풀다

make for p. ~에 기여하다
make it to p. ~에 도착하다, 이르다
make one's way to p. ~로 나아가다
be made up of p. ~로 구성되어 있다

어원	-make 만들다 + -allowance 수당, 비용, 허용 → '수당을 만들어 주며 아량을 베풀다'
유의어	consider, take into account, accommodate
반의어	ignore, disregard, neglect
영영	To consider or take into account.
예문	In project planning, it's essential to make allowance for unexpected delays. 프로젝트 계획에서는 예상치 못한 지연을 고려하는 것이 중요하다.

512

of service

p. 쓸모 있는, 유익한

serve in the ranks p. 사병으로 복무하다
serve as p. ~의 역할을 하다
servant n. 하인, 부하, 공무원
servile a. 노예의, 비굴한

어원	-serv, -serve : slave / keep 지키다, 보호하다 → '지켜주니 쓸모 있는'
유의어	helpful, useful, beneficial
반의어	unhelpful, useless, detrimental
영영	Providing help or assistance.
예문	The volunteer work was of service to the community, providing valuable assistance. 자원봉사는 지역사회에 유익한 서비스를 제공하여 가치 있는 지원을 했다.

513

draw a deep breath

p. 심호흡을 하다

catch one's breath p. 숨을 고르다
take a deep breath p. 심호흡하다
breathless a. 숨이 가쁜, 숨을 쉴 수 없는
breed v. 번식하다

어원	-draw 당기다 + -deep 깊은 + -breath 숨 → '깊은 숨을 당기니 심호흡 하다'
유의어	inhale deeply, take a deep breath
반의어	exhale, breathe out
영영	To inhale deeply, often as a calming measure.
예문	Before facing the audience, the speaker drew a deep breath to calm nerves. 청중 앞에 나서기 전에 연설자는 신경을 진정시키기 위해 깊게 숨을 들이마셨다.

514

stand out

p. 두드러지다, 눈에 띄다

stand for p. ~을 나타내다, ~을 의미하다
stand up to p. ~에 맞서다, 저항하다
stagger v. 비틀거리다
stagnant a. 침체된, 불경기의

어원	-sta,-sist, -ste, -st, -stitu, -stin, -sti : stand 서다, 세우다 + -out → '밖에서도 눈에 띄다'
유의어	excel, shine, surpass
반의어	blend in, fade, go unnoticed
영영	To be easily noticeable or distinguishable.
예문	Her unique talent helped her stand out among the competitors. 그녀의 독특한 재능은 경쟁자들 사이에서 두드러지게 나타났다.

515

what A like

p. A는 어떠한가?

what's more p. 더욱이, 게다가
what is knows as p. 소위
what people call p. 소위
what with A and B p. A그리고 B 때문에

어원	like(~와 닮은) A는 what(어떠한가?)
유의어	similar to, like, resembling
반의어	unlike, different from, dissimilar to
영영	Unfamiliar phrase; possibly a variation of "what it's like."
예문	Can you tell me what your new neighbor is like? 당신의 새 이웃이 어떤 사람인지 말해 줄 수 있을까요?

516

well off

p. 부유한; 충분한

unwell a. 건강이 좋지 않은
well up p. 샘솟다
well set p. 건장한, 제대로 놓인

어원	-well : good + -off → '잘 살아 떨어지는 것이 없으니 부유한'
유의어	affluent, prosperous, wealthy
반의어	poor, destitute, impoverished
영영	Financially prosperous or comfortable.
예문	After years of hard work, they became well off and could afford a comfortable lifestyle. 수년간의 노력 끝에 그들은 부유해져 편안한 생활을 즐길 수 있었다.

517

look on

p. 구경하다

look after p. 돌보다
be on the lookout for p. ~을 찾고 있다
look over p. 전체를 훑어보다
look through p. ~을 훑어보다

어원	-look 보다 + -on 진행중 → '보는 것만 진행중이니 구경'
유의어	observe, watch, witness
반의어	ignore, overlook, disregard
영영	To observe or watch without active participation.
예문	Instead of intervening, she chose to look on and observe the situation unfold. 개입하지 않고, 그녀는 사태가 전개되는 것을 지켜보기로 했다.

518

a visit from the stork

p. 아기의 출생

n. midwife 산파, 조산사
a. inborn 선천적인, 타고난
v. revisit 재방문하다; 다시 논의하다

어원	-visit 방문 + -strok 황새 → '황새가 아기를 데리고 온다는 설'
유의어	the arrival of a baby, childbirth
반의어	
영영	A humorous or euphemistic way of referring to the arrival of a new baby.
예문	We're excitedly awaiting a visit from the stork as our due date approaches." 출산 예정일이 다가오며, 우리는 아기의 탄생을 기대하고 있습니다.

519

rip off

p. 뜯어내다, 훔치다

rip into p. 비난하다; 거칠게 들어가다
riot n. 폭동
rive n. 벌려진 틈, 균열

어원	-rip 찢다 + -off 떨어져 → '찢어 떨어지도록 뜯어내다'
유의어	swindle, cheat, deceive
반의어	fair deal, honest transaction, integrity
영영	To cheat or deceive, especially by overcharging.
예문	Consumers were warned about the scam that aimed to rip off unsuspecting buyers. 소비자들은 무심코 사는 사람들을 속이려는 사기에 대해 경고받았다.

520

phase in

p. 단계적으로 도입하다

emphasize v. 강조하다, 중요시하다
in phase p. 서로 맞게 돌아가는
a passing phase p. 일시적 현상
phase out p. 단계적으로 폐지하다

어원	-pha,-phan, -phas, -pan, -fan : show 보이다, 보여주다(G) → '보이는 국면이 단계가 나타나는 양상'
유의어	introduce gradually, implement in stages
반의어	phase out, eliminate, remove gradually
영영	To introduce or implement gradually.
예문	The new software will phase in gradually to ensure a smooth transition for users. 새 소프트웨어는 사용자들에게 원활한 전환을 보장하기 위해 점진적으로 도입될 것이다.

Chapter 14.

521	retina	[ˈret.ɪ.nə]	n. 망막
522	gourmet	[ˈɡɔː.meɪ]	n. 미식가
523	heredity	[hɪˈred.ə.ti]	n. 유전
524	relegate	[ˈrel.ɪ.ɡeɪt]	v. ~을 내쫓다, 좌천시키다
525	asperse	[əspə́ːrs]	v. 헐뜯다, 비방하다
526	methodical	[məˈθɒd.ɪ.kəl]	a. 질서 정연한, 조직적인
527	compensate	[ˈkɒm.pən.seɪt]	v. 보충하다; 보상하다
528	plunge	[plʌndʒ]	v. 던져넣다; 뛰어들다; 급락하다
529	discern	[dɪˈsɜːn]	v. 식별하다, 분별하다
530	scant	[skænt]	a. 거의 없는, 부족한
531	crucial	[ˈkruː.ʃəl]	a. 중요한, 결정적인
532	repent	[rɪˈpent]	v. 뉘우치다, 회개하다
533	rehabilitate	[ˌriː.həˈbɪl.ɪ.teɪt]	v. 원상태로 돌리다, 사회에 복귀시키다
534	flesh	[fleʃ]	n. 살, 고기, 육체
535	reparation	[ˌrep.əˈreɪ.ʃən]	n. 보상(금)
536	expire	[ɪkˈspaɪər]	v. 만기가 되다, 끝나다
537	fungus	[ˈfʌŋ.ɡəs]	n. 균류, 곰팡이류; 균상종
538	banish	[ˈbæn.ɪʃ]	v. 명령으로 추방하다
539	vinegar	[ˈvɪn.ɪ.ɡər]	n. 식초
540	marvelous	[mάːrvələs]	a. 훌륭한, 흥미로운
541	seduce	[sɪˈdʒuːs]	v. 부추기다; 매혹시키다
542	haze	[heɪz]	n. 연무, 실안개; 희부연 것 v. 연무로 뒤덮이다
543	liberal	[ˈlɪb.ər.əl]	a. 관대한, 개방적인; 자유주의의
544	interwine	[intərtwaiˈn]	v. 뒤얽히게 하다, 관련지우다, 꼬아 짜다
545	distend	[disténd]	v. 팽창시키다
546	virtu	[vəːrtúː]	n. 가치, 골동적 가치
547	villain	[ˈvɪl.ən]	n. 악인, 악한
548	creep	[kriːp]	v. 서서히 움직이다, 기어가다
549	grudge	[ɡrʌdʒ]	n. 원한, 유감
550	spank	[spæŋk]	v. 찰싹 때리다
551	make my day		p. 좋아, 한 번 해봐
552	wear out		p. 지치게 하다; 닳아서 헤지다
553	miss a beat		p. 순간적으로 주저하다
554	in search of		p. ~을 찾아서
555	leave a mark on		p. ~에 큰 영향을 미치다
556	serve two ends		p. 일거양득이다
557	be pressed for		p. ~이 쪼들리다, 내쫓기다
558	nothing but		p. 오직, 그저 ~일 뿐
559	iron out		p. 해결하다; 다리미질하다
560	track down		p. ~을 추적하다, 찾아내다

521

retina

[ˈret.ɪ.nə]

n. 망막

retinal a. 망막의
retinitis n. 망막염
retinopathy n. 망막병
retinol n. 레티놀(비타민A의 한 종류)

어원	-re : back + -tin : hold → '안구 뒤에서 빛의 감각을 취하는 막'
유의어	optic nerve, ocular tissue, visual receptor
반의어	External, peripheral
영영	The layer at the back of the eye that contains cells sensitive to light, enabling vision.
예문	The retina is responsible for capturing light and sending signals to the brain for visual perception. 망막은 빛을 포착하고 시각 인지를 위해 뇌로 신호를 전송하는 역할을 합니다.

522

gourmet

[ˈgɔː.meɪ]

n. 미식가

gourmand n. 대식가
gourmandise n. 식도락, 미식
gourmandize v. 대식하다, 과식하다
gourmet food n. 고급 음식, 미식 요리

어원	-gour 음식 관련 + -meet → '음식과의 만남을 즐기는 미식가' * gourmet 포도주에 밝은 사람(F)
유의어	epicurean, connoisseur, foodie
반의어	Plain, ordinary, basic
영영	A person who is knowledgeable and discerning in matters of food and drink.
예문	She considers herself a gourmet and enjoys exploring exquisite dishes from different cultures. 그녀는 자신을 미식가로 생각하며 다양한 문화에서의 정교한 요리를 탐험하는 것을 즐깁니다.

523

heredity

[hɪˈred.ə.ti]

n. 유전

hereditary a. 유전적인, 세습되는
hereditable a. 상속할 수 있는
inherit v. 물려받다, 상속하다
heir n. 상속인, 후계자

어원	-hered, -heir, -herit : 상속 + -ity(명접) (L) → '상속되는 유전'
유의어	genetics, inheritance, genetic traits
반의어	Environment, acquired traits
영영	The passing on of physical or mental characteristics genetically from one generation to another.
예문	Traits passed down through heredity include eye color, height, and certain genetic predispositions. 유전을 통해 전해지는 특성에는 눈 색깔, 키, 그리고 특정 유전적 성향이 포함됩니다.

524

relegate

[ˈrel.ɪ.geɪt]

v. ~을 내쫓다, 좌천시키다

relegation n. 좌천, 추방, 위탁
relegable a. 좌천시켜야 할
legitimate a. 합법적인, 정당한
delegate n. 대표자, 대표단

어원	-re : back + -leg : send / legal 임명하다 → '뒤쪽 자리로 임명하고 보내니 좌천시키다'
유의어	demote, downgrade, transfer
반의어	Promote, elevate, upgrade
영영	To consign or dismiss to an inferior rank or position.
예문	After several mistakes, they decided to relegate him to a less demanding role. 여러 차례의 실수 뒤에 그들은 그를 덜 힘든 역할로 격하시키기로 결정했습니다.

525

asperse

[əspáːrs]

v. 헐뜯다, 비방하다

aspersion n. 비난, 중상
aspersement n. 비난, 중상
exasperate v. 몹시 화나게 하다
asperity b. (말투, 성질 등이)거침; 고난

어원	* -a : bad + -spers, -spars, -sparg : scatter → '나쁜 말을 퍼뜨리며 헐뜯고 비방하다'
유의어	slander, defame, malign
반의어	Praise, commend, laud
영영	To slander or criticize someone's reputation.
예문	It is not appropriate to asperse someone's character without evidence. 증거 없이 누군가의 인격을 흐리게 말하는 것은 적절하지 않습니다.

526

methodical

[məˈθɒd.ɪ.kəl]

a. 질서 정연한, 조직적인

methodically adv. 조직적으로
methodlology n. 방법론
methodist n. 감리교도
method n. 방법, 방식; 질서

어원	-met, -meth, -meta 변화하는 (G) + -od, -hod 길 → '변화를 바로 잡는 길이니 조직적이고 질서정연한'
유의어	systematic, organized, orderly
반의어	Haphazard, disorganized, chaotic
영영	Carried out with a systematic and orderly approach.
예문	The scientist followed a methodical approach to conduct the experiment and analyze the results. 과학자는 실험을 수행하고 결과를 분석하기 위해 체계적인 방법을 따랐습니다.

527

compensate

[ˈkɒm.pən.seɪt]

v. 보충하다; 보상하다

compensation n. 배상, 보상, 갚음
compensatory a. 보상의, 보완적인
compensable a. 보상할 수 있는
suspensive a. 정지한, 결단이 서지 않는

어원	-com : together + -pens : weigh → '서로 무게를 달아 부족한 쪽을 보충, 보상'
유의어	reimburse, indemnify, make amends
반의어	Penalize, deprive, withhold
영영	To make up for a loss or deficiency; to provide with something beneficial.
예문	The company decided to compensate employees for their overtime work with additional benefits. 회사는 초과 근무에 대한 보상으로 추가 혜택을 제공하기로 결정했습니다.

528

plunge

[plʌndʒ]

v. 던져넣다; 뛰어들다; 급락하다

plunge in p. 정신없이 뛰어들다
plumbum n. 납
plumber n. 배관공

어원	-plun : plumb 끈에 매달린 납 덩어리 → '납 덩어리를 던진 것처럼 떨어지고 추락하다'
유의어	dive, submerge, plummet
반의어	Ascend, rise, climb
영영	To fall or dive rapidly; to immerse or thrust into something.
예문	Daredevils often take the plunge into extreme sports seeking an adrenaline rush. 대담한 사람들은 종종 아드레날린을 느끼기 위해 극한 스포츠에 도전합니다.

529

discern

[dɪˈsɜːn]

v. 식별하다, 분별하다

disernible a. 인식할 수 있는
discernibly adv. 명료하게, 뚜렷하게
certify v. 증명하다, 보증하다
ascertain v. 확인하다, 규명하다

어원	-dis : apart + -cern : sift → '체로 쳐서 걸러 구분하다'
유의어	perceive, recognize, distinguish
반의어	Overlook, ignore, neglect
영영	To perceive or recognize something with clarity and accuracy.
예문	With experience, she learned to discern between genuine kindness and superficial friendliness. 경험을 통해 그녀는 진정한 친절과 표면적인 우호 간의 차이를 분별하는 법을 배웠습니다.

530

scant

[skænt]

a. 거의 없는, 부족한

scanty a. 부족한, 불충분한
scantness n. 부족, 불충분
scent n. 향기, 냄새
skinny a. 마른, 깡마른

어원	* -scant : short 짧은, 작은, 부족한 → '짧고 부족하니 거의 없는'
유의어	minimal, inadequate, insufficient
반의어	Abundant, plentiful, ample
영영	Insufficient in amount, quantity, or extent.
예문	The evidence was scant, making it difficult to build a strong case. 증거가 부족하여 강력한 사례를 구축하기 어려웠습니다.

531

crucial

[ˈkruː.ʃəl]

a. 중요한, 결정적인

crucible n. 고난, 시련
crucially adv. 결정적으로
crucify v. 십자가에 못박다, 고통을 주다
crystal n. 결정체

어원	-cruc 십자가; 심장 → '십자가에 기도할 만큼 중요한'
유의어	vital, essential, critical
반의어	Insignificant, trivial, unimportant
영영	Extremely important or essential for the resolution of a situation.
예문	In emergency situations, timely medical intervention is crucial for saving lives. 비상 상황에서는 적시의 의료 개입이 생명을 구하는 데 중요합니다.

532

repent

[rɪˈpent]

v. 뉘우치다, 회개하다

repent of p. ~을 회개하다
repentant a. 후회하고 있는, 회개하는
penitent a. 참회하는, 뉘우치는
penalize v. 처벌을 하다

어원	-re : back + -pen : punish 벌 → '일이 끝난 뒤 벌을 받으며 회개하고 뉘우치다'
유의어	regret, remorse, atone
반의어	Rejoice, celebrate, be content
영영	To feel remorse or regret for one's wrongdoing and seek to change.
예문	After realizing the consequences of his actions, he felt deep remorse and decided to repent. 그의 행동의 결과를 깨닫고 깊은 회한을 느낀 후 그는 참회하기로 결정했습니다.

533	어원	-re : again + -hab, -hib, -ab 살다, 유지하다 / have 갖다 → '다시 살 수 있게 회복시키다'
rehabilitate	유의어	restore, recondition
	반의어	Deteriorate, worsen, decline
[ˌriːhəˈbɪlɪteɪt]	영영	To restore to a former condition or to a state of good health.
v. 원상태로 돌리다, 사회에 복귀시키다		
rehabilitation n. 사회 복귀, 복직; 재활 rehab n. 재활 habitat n. 서식지, 거주지 inhabitant n. 거주자	예문	The rehabilitation program helped the athlete recover from the injury and regain strength. 재활 프로그램은 그 선수가 부상에서 회복하고 힘을 되찾는 데 도움이 되었습니다.

534	어원	-flesh 고기 * fresh 신선한 고기
flesh	유의어	tissue, muscle, body
	반의어	Spirit, soul, essence
[fleʃ]	영영	The soft substance consisting of muscle and fat that is found between the skin and bones.
n. 살, 고기, 육체		
fleshly a. 육체적인, 육적인 fleshness n. 육체성, 육적인 fleshy a. 육즙이 많은, 육질의 flay v. (피부를) 벗기다	예문	Muscles, bones, and organs are essential components of the human flesh. 근육, 뼈, 그리고 기관은 인간의 육체의 필수 구성 요소입니다.

535	어원	-re : back + -par, -per 준비하다 → '과거 원래 상태가 되도록 준비하는 보상'
reparation	유의어	compensation, restitution, redress
	반의어	Harm, damage, injury
[ˌrepəˈreɪʃən]	영영	The act of making amends or providing compensation for a wrong or injury.
n. 보상(금)		
reparative a. 보상하는, 수리의 reparable a. 수리할 수 있는 irreparable a. 고칠 수 없는 prepare v. 준비하다	예문	The country offered financial reparations to the victims of the historical injustice. 그 나라는 역사적 불의의 피해자들에게 금전적 보상을 제공했습니다.

536	어원	-ex : out + -spire : breath → '밖으로 마지막 숨을 내뱉으니 끝나다'
expire	유의어	terminate, lapse, end
	반의어	Commence, begin, start
[ɪkˈspaɪər]	영영	To come to an end or to cease to be valid.
v. 만기가 되다, 끝나다		
expiration n. 만료, 만기 expiring a. 만료의, 숨을 거두려 하는 aspire v. 열망하다 inspire v. 고무하다	예문	The contract will expire at the end of the month unless renewed. 계약은 갱신되지 않는 한 이 달 말에 만료될 것입니다.

537	어원	-fungus : mashroom 버섯; 균 → '버섯과 비슷한 생물의 분류군' * fur(털)이 나 있는 균
fungus	유의어	mold, mildew, mycelium
	반의어	Antifungal, antibiotic, sterile
[ˈfʌŋ.gəs]	영영	A type of organism, such as mushrooms or mold, that lacks chlorophyll and obtains nutrients through decomposition.
n. 균류, 곰팡이류; 균상종		
fungi n. 균류, 곰팡이(pl) fungicide n. 곰팡이 제거제, 살균제	예문	Mushrooms are a type of fungus that has various culinary and medicinal uses. 버섯은 다양한 요리 및 의료 용도가 있는 곰팡이의 한 종류입니다.

538	어원	-ban, -band 명령, 법(E) → '명령으로 추방하다'
banish	유의어	exile, expel, oust
	반의어	Welcome, embrace, admit
[ˈbæn.ɪʃ]	영영	To exile or send away, often as a punishment.
v. 명령으로 추방하다		
banishment n. 추방, 퇴거, 유배 ban n. 금지 v. 금하다 abandon v. 단념하다, 포기하다	예문	The king decided to banish the traitor from the kingdom forever. 왕은 배신자를 영원히 왕국에서 추방하기로 결정했습니다.

539

vinegar

['vɪn.ɪ.gər]

n. 식초

vintage n. 포도주; 년식, 오래됨
acetic a. 신랄한, 산뜻한

어휘	-vine 포도나무, 덩굴 식물 + -ar : acer 신 → '포도의 발효과정에서 만들어지는 신 맛의 식초'
유의어	acetic acid, sour liquid, condiment
반의어	Sweetener, honey, syrup
영영	A sour liquid typically used in cooking or as a condiment.
예문	A dash of vinegar can add a tangy flavor to salads and dressings. 조금의 식초는 샐러드와 드레싱에 신맛을 더할 수 있습니다.

540

marvelous

[mɑ́ːrvələs]

a. 훌륭한, 흥미로운

marvel n. 놀라운 일 v. 놀라다
marvelousness n. 경이로움, 놀라운 정도
miracle n. 기적
admirable a. 존경할 만한, 놀랄 만한

어원	-mir, -mar : wonder 놀라다 * 마블 영화를 보며 어벤저스에 놀라는
유의어	fantastic, incredible, extraordinary
반의어	Terrible, awful, dreadful
영영	Extraordinarily good or pleasing; causing wonder or astonishment.
예문	The sunset over the ocean was a marvelous sight, painting the sky with vibrant colors. 바다 위의 일몰은 놀라운 광경이었으며, 하늘에 생생한 색상을 그렸습니다.

541

seduce

[sɪ'dʒuːs]

v. 부추기다; 매혹시키다

seduction n. 유혹, 꼬드기기; 매력, 매혹
seductive a. 매력적인, 유혹적인
induce v. 설득하여 ~하게 하다; 야기하다
conduce v. 도움이 되다, 공헌하다

어원	-se 자르다, 떼어내다 + -duce : lead → 떼어내서 끌고 가다, 나쁜 길로 유혹하다
유의어	entice, allure, tempt
반의어	Repel, deter, discourage
영영	To entice or persuade someone into engaging in sexual activity or some other desired behavior.
예문	The cunning villain tried to seduce the hero's ally to join the dark side. 교활한 악당은 영웅의 동료를 유혹하여 어둠의 편에 합류하려고 했습니다.

542

haze

[heɪz]

n. 연무, 실안개; 희부연 것 v. 연무로 뒤덮이다

in a haze p. (눈이) 흐릿하여
hazy a. 흐린
hazily adv. 연무가 끼어, 흐릿하게
hazard n. 위험

어원	-haze 운 → '운이 어지럽히는 상황같은 옅은 안개'
유의어	mist, fog, smog
반의어	Clarity, clearness, transparency
영영	A state of reduced visibility due to fine particles or moisture in the air.
예문	The morning haze gradually lifted, revealing a clear view of the mountains. 아침 안개가 서서히 걷혀지며 산의 맑은 전망이 드러났습니다.

543

liberal

['lɪb.ər.əl]

a. 관대한, 개방적인; 자유주의의

liberty n. 자유
liberalize c. 자유롭게 하다
liberate v. 자유롭게 하다, 해방하다
libero n. 리베로(축구에서 특정 포지션 없이 자유롭...

어원	-liber, -lic -liver, -lei 나무(L) → '나무처럼 자유롭게 자라는'
유의어	generous, tolerant, open-minded
반의어	Conservative, traditional, orthodox
영영	Open to new behavior or opinions; generous and broad-minded.
예문	She holds liberal views, advocating for social equality and individual freedoms. 그녀는 자유와 사회적 평등을 옹호하는 자유 주의적인 견해를 가지고 있습니다.

544

interwine

[intərtwai'n]

v. 뒤얽히게 하다, 관련지우다, 꼬아 짜다

interwined a. 밀접하게 관련된, 꼬아 합쳐진
interwind v. 한데 감다, 꼬아 짜다
interline v. 어구를 행간에 삽입하다

어원	-inter : between + -wine: wire → '서로를 연결하여 뒤얽히게 하다'
유의어	interlace, intermingle
반의어	Separate, isolate, disconnect
영영	To twist or weave together; to become intricately connected.
예문	The paths of their lives began to intertwine as they shared common experiences. 그들의 삶의 길이 공통적인 경험을 나누며 얽히기 시작했습니다.

545	어원	-dis : away + -ten, -tens : stretch → '멀리 뻗도록 팽창시키다' * tent 텐트를 펼치는 것처럼 팽창시키다
	유의어	expand, inflate, swell
distend	반의어	Shrink, contract, compress
[disténd]	영영	To expand or swell, typically due to pressure from the inside.
v. 팽창시키다		
distended a. 넓어진, 확대한 distendedly adv. 팽창하여, 부풀어 extend v. 확장하다 contend v. 주장하다, 논쟁하다; 다투다	예문	The balloon began to distend as it filled with air. 풍선은 공기로 차면서 팽창하기 시작했습니다.
546	어원	-virtu 우수(L) → '가장 우수해야 할 가치'
	유의어	skill, expertise, mastery
virtu	반의어	Incompetence, ineptitude, lack of skill
[vərtúː]	영영	Skill, expertise, or accomplishment in the arts, especially music.
n. 가치, 골동적 가치		
virtuosity n. 숙련, 역량, 예술적 솜씨 virtuoso n. 예술가 virtue n. 미덕, 덕, 덕행, 덕목 vertual a. 가상의	예문	Her virtu in playing the piano was evident during the concert. 그녀의 피아노 연주에 대한 뛰어난 능력은 콘서트 중에 명백했습니다.
547	어원	-vil : village 나쁜 + -ain 사람 → '농촌 사람 -> 교외 지역에서 나쁜 일을 일삼는 악인'
	유의어	antagonist, wrongdoer, evildoer
villain	반의어	Hero, protagonist, good guy
[ˈvɪl.ən]	영영	A character in a story or play who is known for evil actions or motives.
n. 악인, 악한		
villainy n. 악당의 소행, 비열한 짓 villainous a. 아주 비열한, 극악무도한 villa n. 별장, 대저택 villainage n. 농노제, 농노의 신분	예문	Every good story needs a compelling villain to create conflict and tension. 모든 좋은 이야기에는 충돌과 긴장을 만들기 위한 확실한 악당이 필요합니다.
548	어원	-creep, -cra, -cri, -rep 기다, 구브리다
	유의어	crawl, slither, sneak
creep	반의어	Leap, jump, bound
[kriːp]	영영	To move slowly and quietly, often to avoid being noticed.
v. 서서히 움직이다, 기어가다		
creepy a. 오싹한, 소름끼치는 creeping n. 포복 a. 천천히 나아가는 reptile n. 파충류(기어다니는 짐승) creed n. 신조, 신념	예문	The cat tried to creep closer to the bird without being noticed. 고양이는 발견되지 않게 새에게 더 가까이 다가가려고 했습니다.
549	어원	-grav, -griev : heavy 고통; 무거움 → '고통 때문에 생긴 원한이라 유감' * 그러지 마. 원한 생기잖아
	유의어	resentment, bitterness, animosity
grudge	반의어	Forgiveness, reconciliation, goodwill
[grʌdʒ]	영영	A persistent feeling of ill will or resentment resulting from a past insult or injury.
n. 원한, 유감		
gruding a. 마지 못해 하는, 인색한 grudgingly adv. 마지 못해, 울며 겨자 먹기로 grusome a. 고통스러운 grumble v. 투덜거리다	예문	Holding onto a grudge can negatively impact one's mental well-being. 원한을 품는 것은 개인의 정신적 안녕에 부정적인 영향을 미칠 수 있습니다.
550	어원	-spank : spike 내리 꽂다 → '엉덩이를 내리 꽂아 때리다'
	유의어	paddle, smack, beat
spank	반의어	Praise, reward, commend
[spæŋk]	영영	To strike someone on the buttocks as a form of punishment.
v. 찰싹 때리다		
spanking a. 매우 민첩한 spike n. 대못, 철책; 스파이크 spiny a. 가시가 많은 spindle n. 축, 굴대	예문	Some parents use time-out as a discipline method instead of resorting to spanking. 일부 부모는 처벌로서 매를 대신하여 타임아웃을 사용합니다.

551

make my day

p. 좋아, 한 번 해봐

make for p. ~에 기여하다
make it to p. ~에 도착하다, 이르다
make one's way to p. ~로 나아가다
be made up of p. ~로 구성되어 있다

어원	-make 만들다 + -my day → '나의 날로 만들어봐'
유의어	fulfill my wishes, brighten my day, make me happy
반의어	Ruin my day, spoil my mood, disappoint me
영영	A phrase expressing a desire for something positive or exciting to happen.
예문	Getting a surprise gift would truly make my day. 뜻밖의 선물을 받는 것은 정말로 나의 하루를 행복하게 만들 것입니다.

552

wear out

p. 지치게 하다; 닳아서 헤지다

wear down p. 약화되다, 마모되다
worn out p. 진부한
wield v. 휘두르다, 쓰다

어원	-wear 입다 + -out 상태를 벗어난 → '입다보니 원래 상태를 벗어나 닳아서 헤지다'
유의어	exhaust, fatigue, tire
반의어	Refresh, rejuvenate, revive
영영	To become exhausted or no longer effective due to prolonged use.
예문	Continuous use of the machinery might wear out its components over time. 기계를 계속 사용하면 시간이 지남에 따라 그 구성 요소가 닳아날 수 있습니다.

553

miss a beat

p. 순간적으로 주저하다

debate v. 논쟁하다, 토론하다
upbeat a. 경쾌한, 매우 즐거운
downbeat a. 우울한, 침울한
beat a rhythm p. 장단을 맞추다

어원	-miss 놓치다 + -beat 비트 → '비트를 놓치고 주저하다'
유의어	not react, remain calm, not be surprised
반의어	React, respond, notice
영영	To be momentarily surprised or alarmed; to react unexpectedly.
예문	His confident presentation didn't miss a beat, impressing everyone in the room. 그의 자신감 있는 프레젠테이션은 한 순간도 놓치지 않았으며, 방 안의 모두를 감동

554

in search of

p. ~을 찾아서

search for p. ~을 찾다, 검색하다
searchability n. 검색 가능성

어원	-search : seek 검색하다
유의어	looking for, seeking, searching for
반의어	Found, discovered, located
영영	The act of looking for or seeking something.
예문	Explorers sailed across the oceans in search of new lands and undiscovered treasures. 탐험가들은 새로운 땅과 발견되지 않은 보물을 찾아 해양을 항해했습니다.

555

leave a mark on

p. ~에 큰 영향을 미치다

marker n. 표지, 표시
remark v. 논평하다, 발언하다
make a remark p. 말을 하다
markedly adv. 현저하게, 눈에 띄게

어원	-leave 남기다 + -mark 표시 → '표시를 남길 정도의 큰 영향' * note가 mark보다 좀 더 구체적인 정보를 가지고 있다.
유의어	make an impression on, influence, affect
반의어	Erase, remove, obliterate
영영	To have a lasting impact or influence on something or someone.
예문	Acts of kindness can leave a mark on someone's heart that lasts a lifetime. 친절한 행동은 누군가의 마음에 오래 남는 흔적을 남길 수 있습니다.

556

serve two ends

p. 일거양득이다

serve in the ranks p. 사병으로 복무하다
serve as p. ~의 역할을 하다
servant n. 하인, 부하, 공무원
servile a. 노예의, 비굴한

어원	-serv, -serve : keep 지키다, 보호하다 + - two ends 두 결말 → '두 결말을 다 지켰으니 일거양득이다'
유의어	achieve dual purposes, fulfill two objectives, meet two goals
반의어	Serve one purpose, be unidirectional
영영	To fulfill two purposes or achieve two objectives.
예문	The new policy aims to serve two ends: reduce costs and improve efficiency. 새로운 정책은 두 가지 목표를 달성하려고 합니다: 비용 절감과 효율성 향상.

557

be pressed for

p. ~이 쪼들리다, 내쫓기다

compress v. 압축하다, 꽉 누르다
depress v. 낙담시키다; 불경기로 만들다
depresesd a. 우울한, 의기소침한
depression n. 의기소침; 불경기

어원	-press 누르다 + -for 이유 → '~이유로 압박을 받으니 쪼들리다'
유의어	be short of, lack, be in need of
반의어	Abundant in, surplus, have more than enough
영영	To be in a situation of urgency or shortage.
예문	As the deadline approached, they found themselves pressed for time to complete the project. 마감일이 다가오면서 그들은 프로젝트를 완료하는 데 시간이 부족하다고 느꼈습니다.

558

nothing but

p. 오직, 그저 ~일 뿐

nothing other than p. 단지 ~뿐인
nothing more than p. ~에 불과한
nonetheless adv. 그렇기는 하지만

어원	-nothing 아무것도 + -but → '아무것도 아니지만 그저'
유의어	only, solely, merely
반의어	Everything, all, entirely
영영	Solely, exclusively; indicating there is nothing else except the specified thing.
예문	The room contained nothing but a table and two chairs. 그 방 안에는 탁자와 의자 두 개뿐이었습니다.

559

iron out

p. 해결하다; 다리미질하다

iron age p. 철기 시대
irony n. 아이러니, 풍자, 반어법

어원	-iron 다리미 + - out 밖으로 → '다리미질로 주름을 펴는 것처럼 문제를 밖으로 해결'
유의어	resolve, smooth out, straighten
반의어	Complicate, worsen, exacerbate
영영	To resolve or settle difficulties or problems.
예문	The negotiators worked hard to iron out the details of the agreement. 협상자들은 협정의 세부 사항을 해결하기 위해 노력했습니다.

560

track down

p. ~을 추적하다, 찾아내다

keep track of p. ~을 계속 파악하다
tracker n. 추적기
track to p. ~을 끝까지 추적하다
track back to p. ~로 거슬러 올라가다

어원	-track : trek 걸어서 여행하다 → '걸어서 여행한 흔적을 추적하다'
유의어	locate, find, trace
반의어	Lose track of, misplace, mislay
영영	To locate or find after searching or pursuing.
예문	Private investigators were hired to track down the missing person. 사립 조사관들이 고발된 사람을 찾기 위해 고용되었습니다.

Chapter 15.

561	bellicose	[bélikòus]	a. 호전적인
562	recur	[rɪˈkɜːr]	v. 재발하다, 반복되다
563	faculty	[ˈfæk.əl.ti]	n. 학부, 교수진; 재능
564	varnish	[ˈvɑː.nɪʃ]	n. 니스, 광택제 v. 니스를 바르다
565	savage	[sǽvidʒ]	a. 사나운, 야만적인
566	province	[ˈprɒv.ɪns]	n. 지방,(행정 구역상의) 주/도
567	omen	[ˈəʊ.mən]	n. 징조, 조짐
568	creed	[kriːd]	n. 신조, 신념, 원칙; 교의
569	adjacent	[əˈdʒeɪ.sənt]	a. 인접한
570	nausea	[ˈnɔː.si.ə]	n. 항해 중 고통(배멀미)
571	slay	[sleɪ]	v. 죽이다, 살해하다
572	satire	[ˈsæt.aɪər]	n. 풍자, 해학
573	queer	[kwɪər]	a. 기묘한, 괴상한
574	apposite	[ˈæp.ə.zɪt]	a. 적합한, 적절한
575	expedition	[ˌek.spəˈdɪʃ.ən]	n. 원정, 탐험
576	litigate	[ˈlɪt.ɪ.geɪt]	v. 제소하다, 소송하다
577	apparatus	[ˌæp.əˈreɪ.təs]	n. 기구, 기계, 장치; 조직
578	faucal	[fɔ́ːkəl]	a. 인후의
579	obscene	[əbˈsiːn]	a. 외설한, 음란한
580	astound	[əstáund]	v. 깜짝 놀라게 하다
581	psychiatric	[ˌsaɪ.kiˈæt.rɪk]	a. 정신 질환의
582	ablaze	[əˈbleɪz]	a. 빛나서; 열광하여
583	mortal	[ˈmɔː.təl]	a. 죽어야 할 운명의, 치명적인; 죽게 마련인
584	collision	[kəˈlɪʒ.ən]	n. 충돌, 대립, 상충
585	reciprocate	[rɪˈsɪp.rə.keɪt]	v. 보답하다
586	asthma	[ǽzmə]	n. 천식
587	bastard	[ˈbɑː.stəd]	n. 서자,사생아; 나쁜 놈; 잡종
588	amid	[əˈmɪd]	prep. 가운데에, ~으로 에워싸인
589	incubus	[ínkjəbəs íŋ-]	n. 악마, 악몽; 압박하는 일, 압박하는 사람
590	constituency	[kənˈstɪtʃ.u.ən.si]	n. 유권자; 선거구; 단골
591	come home to		p. 가슴에 뼈저리게 사무치다
592	put a strain on		p. ~에 압박을 가하다
593	of necessity		p. 필연적으로, 당연히
594	get to do		p. ~하게 되다
595	on exhibit		p. 전시되어, 출품되어
596	substitute A with B		p. A를 B로 대체하다
597	stand to do		p. ~할 것 같다
598	be content to do		p. 기꺼이 ~하다
599	be up for		p. 참여하다; 입후보하다
600	take with		p. 인기가 있다, 평판이 좋다

561

bellicose

[bélikòus]

a. 호전적인

bellicosely adv. 호전적으로, 투쟁적으로
bellicoseness n. 호전적임, 투쟁적임
belligerent a. 적대적인, 공격적인
antebellum a. 전쟁 전의

어원	-bel, -belli, -bella : war → '대항해서 전쟁을 일으키니 반항, 저항' * Bellona 로마 신화에 나오는 싸움의 여신
유의어	belligerent, pugnacious, aggressive, combative, hostile
반의어	peaceful, amicable, conciliatory, nonviolent, pacific
영영	Inclined to fight or be aggressive; warlike.
예문	The bellicose attitude of the politician made people uncomfortable. 그 정치인의 호전적인 태도는 사람들을 불편하게 만들었다.

562

recur

[rɪˈkɜːr]

v. 재발하다, 반복되다

recurrent a. 되풀이 되는, 재발하는
recurrence n. 재발, 재현
occur v. 발생하다
concur v. 일치하다

어원	-re : again + -car, -cur, -cour 달리다, 탈 것(L) → '다시 달려할 일이 재발' cf. curriculum 교육과정, excursion 여행, 소풍
유의어	repeat, reoccur, return, come back, persist
반의어	cease, end, stop, conclude, terminate
영영	To happen or appear again, especially at regular intervals.
예문	The problem recurred every time we tried to solve it. 그 문제는 해결하려고 할 때마다 재발했다.

563

faculty

[ˈfæk.əl.ti]

n. 학부, 교수진; 재능

facultative a. 특권을 주는 임의의
facultatively adv. 특권을 주어, 조건적으로
facility n. 시설, 설비
manufacture v. 제조하다, 생산하다

어원	-fac, -fec, -fic, -fy, -fair : make + -cul : culture → '뭔가를 만드는 문화를 배우는 학부와 교수진'
유의어	ability, skill, capability, talent, competence
반의어	disability, inability, incapacity, incompetence, ineptitude
영영	An inherent mental or physical power; an ability or aptitude.
예문	She has a faculty for learning languages quickly. 그녀는 언어를 빠르게 배우는 능력이 있다.

564

varnish

[ˈvɑː.nɪʃ]

n. 니스, 광택제 v. 니스를 바르다

unvarnished a. 니스칠하지 않은
varnishing day n. 미술 전람회 개회 전날
shoeshine n. 구두닦이

어원	-varnish : to shine → '빛나게 하기 위해 광택제를 바르다' * var바르다 nish니스를
유의어	polish, lacquer, finish, glaze, coat
반의어	strip, bare, expose, uncover, denude
영영	A liquid preparation applied to a surface for protection or decoration; also, to cover with a glossy finish.
예문	The painting was covered with a thick varnish. 그 그림은 두꺼운 니스칠이 되어 있었다.

565

savage

[sævidʒ]

a. 사나운, 야만적인

savagely adv. 잔인하게
savagery n. 잔인함, 만행
salvage n. 해난 구조 v. 구출하다
sabotage n. 방해, 파괴; 사보타주

어원	-savage : survive in woods 반 야생 → '숲에서 생존할 정도니 사납고 야만적인' * 쌔비지 모습이 사납고 야만적인
유의어	wild, untamed, ferocious, brutal, fierce
반의어	civilized, gentle, tame, domesticated, cultured
영영	Wild, untamed, or behaving violently; not civilized.
예문	The savage attack on the village shocked everyone. 마을에 대한 야만적인 공격은 모두를 충격에 빠뜨렸다.

566

province

[ˈprɒv.ɪns]

n. 지방,(행정 구역상의) 주/도

provincal a. 지방의, 주/도의
provincially adv. 지방적으로
convince v. 확신시키다
provenience n. 유래지, 발원지

어원	-pro : forward + -vinc, -vict : conquer → '전투에서 이기고 나아가 차지한 지방'
유의어	region, territory, area, domain, district
반의어	metropolis, urban area, city, megalopolis, cosmopolitan area
영영	A territory or region; an administrative division or area of expertise.
예문	The province is known for its beautiful scenery. 그 지방은 아름다운 경치로 유명하다.

567

omen

[ˈoʊ.mən]

n. 징조, 조짐

ominous a. 불길한, 흉조의
ominously adv. 불길하게
monster n. 괴물
abominate v. 혐오하다, 증오하다

어원	-omen, -omin 미래를 보여주는 물건이나 사건 → '미래를 보여주니 불길한 징조' * 오~ 맨! 불길한 징조야
유의어	sign, portent, prophecy, augury, harbinger
반의어	blessing, boon, good fortune, luck, favor
영영	A sign or event believed to foreshadow the future, often considered as a divine or supernatural message.
예문	The sudden storm was seen as an ominous sign. 갑작스러운 폭풍은 불길한 조짐으로 여겨졌다.

568

creed

[kriːd]

n. 신조, 신념, 원칙; 교의

creedal a. 교리의, 신념의, 신조의
creep v. 기어가다
credit n. 믿음, 평판
creduluous a. 너무 잘 믿는, 속기 쉬운

어원	-cre, -cred, -creed : believe 믿다(G) → '믿음의 신조와 신념'
유의어	belief, doctrine, dogma, faith, ideology
반의어	disbelief, atheism, skepticism, irreligion, unbelief
영영	A system of religious or philosophical beliefs.
예문	The creed of the religious group is based on love and forgiveness. 그 종교 단체의 신조는 사랑과 용서를 바탕으로 한다.

569

adjacent

[əˈdʒeɪ.sənt]

a. 인접한

adjacently adv. 인접하여, 가까이에
inject v. 주사하다, 주입하다
reject v. 거절하다, 거부하다
abject a. 비참한, 비열한

어원	-ad : to + -jac, -ject : throw → '가까이 던져져 근접한'
유의어	neighboring, adjoining, nearby, close, contiguous
반의어	distant, remote, far-off, separate, apart
영영	Next to or adjoining something else; neighboring.
예문	The hotel is adjacent to the shopping mall. 그 호텔은 쇼핑몰과 인접해 있다.

570

nausea

[ˈnɔː.si.ə]

n. 항해 중 고통(배멀미)

nauseous a. 구역질나는, 기분 나쁜
nauseate v. 메스껍다, 역겹다
nauseant n. 최토제, 구토약
nautical a. 선원의, 선박의

어원	-nau : navigate + -sea 바다 → '바다를 항해 중 배멀미'
유의어	queasiness, sickness, vomiting, illness, disgust
반의어	well-being, comfort, ease, contentment, satisfaction
영영	A feeling of sickness with an inclination to vomit.
예문	The smell of the food made me feel nauseous. 음식 냄새 때문에 속이 메스꺼웠다.

571

slay

[sleɪ]

v. 죽이다, 살해하다

slayer n. 죽이는 사람
slaying n. 도살, 살인, 학살
slaughter n. 도살, 대량 학살
slash v. 휙 베다, 깊숙이 베다

어원	-sl : slice 자르다 → '잘라 죽이다'
유의어	kill, murder, eliminate, slaughter, assassinate
반의어	spare, preserve, save, pardon, spare
영영	To kill in a violent or brutal manner; to greatly impress or amuse.
예문	The knight slayed the dragon and saved the princess. 기사는 용을 죽이고 공주를 구했다.

572

satire

[ˈsæt.aɪər]

n. 풍자, 해학

satirical a. 풍자적인, 해학적인
satirically adv. 풍자적으로, 해학적으로
satirize v. 풍자하다
sarcastic a. 풍자적인, 빈정대는

어원	-set, -satis : enough → '다양한 것들을 혼합하여 비꼬는 풍자'
유의어	mockery, ridicule, sarcasm, wit, lampoon
반의어	praise, admiration, approval, commendation, endorsement
영영	The use of humor, irony, or exaggeration to criticize or mock people's shortcomings or vices.
예문	The novel is a satire of modern society. 그 소설은 현대 사회를 풍자한 것이다.

573	어원	-quir, -quer, -quest, -quisit : seek 구하다, ask 묻다 (L) → '의문이 계속 생기니 괴상하고 기묘한'
queer	유의어	odd, strange, eccentric, unconventional, peculiar
[kwɪər]	반의어	normal, conventional, typical, ordinary, traditional
a. 기묘한, 괴상한	영영	Strange, odd, or unconventional; also used as a derogatory term for LGBTQ+ individuals (use with caution).
queerly adv. 이상하게, 기묘하게 queerness n. 이상함, 기묘함 request v. 요청하다 inquire v. 묻다, 조사하다	예문	The behavior of the student was queer. 그 학생의 행동은 이상했다.

574	어원	-ap : to + -pos : place → '붙어서 놓인 것이니 딱 맞는'
apposite	유의어	appropriate, fitting, relevant, apt, suitable
[ˈæp.ə.zɪt]	반의어	irrelevant, inappropriate, unsuitable, unrelated, inapplicable
a. 적합한, 적절한	영영	Relevant or appropriate in a particular context; fitting.
appositeness n. 적절함, 알맞음 apposition n. 병렬 배치, 붙어놓음 appositive a. 부가적인, 보충적인 aptitude n. 적성, 소질	예문	The apposite word for the situation is "irony". 이 상황에 적절한 단어는 "아이러니"이다.

575	어원	-ex : out + -ped : foot 발(L) → '발을 밖에 내놓은 원정 탐험대'
expedition	유의어	journey, trip, excursion, exploration, tour
[ˌek.spəˈdɪʃ.ən]	반의어	delay, hesitation, indecision, procrastination, dawdling
n. 원정, 탐험	영영	A journey or voyage undertaken for a specific purpose, often exploratory or military.
expedite v. 신속하게 처리하다 expediency n. 실용성 효율성 expeditionary a. 탐험의, 원정의 pedestrian n. 보행자	예문	The expedition to the Arctic was a success. 북극 탐험은 성공적이었다.

576	어원	-leg, -litigare : law → '법으로 소송하다'
litigate	유의어	sue, prosecute, take to court, challenge legally, bring to trial
[ˈlɪt.ɪ.geɪt]	반의어	agree, reconcile, settle, compromise, harmonize
v. 제소하다, 소송하다	영영	To engage in legal proceedings; to bring a case to court.
litigation n. 소송, 소송 절차 litigator n. 소송 당사자, 소송 변호사 litigious a. 소송적인, 소송을 좋아하는 allege v. 주장하다, 단언하다	예문	The company is litigating against its competitor. 그 회사는 경쟁사와 소송 중이다.

577	어원	* -appar : appear → '인간들 세상에 출현한 기구, 기계'
apparatus	유의어	equipment, machinery, device, instrument, tool
[ˌæp.əˈreɪ.təs]	반의어	disorganization, chaos, disorder, confusion, disarray
n. 기구, 기계, 장치; 조직	영영	A set of equipment or machinery used for a specific purpose.
apparat n. 기관, 지하 조직 appliance n. 가전제품, 기기	예문	The apparatus for measuring temperature is very accurate. 온도를 측정하는 장치는 매우 정확하다.

578	어원	-foc, -fauc : throat 목구멍, 구멍 → '목구멍인 인후의'
faucal	유의어	
[fɔ́ːkəl]	반의어	related to the throat or faucal region (no direct antonyms)
a. 인후의	영영	Related to the throat or faucal region.
fauces n. 구협, 목구멍 faucitis n. 목구멍염 suffocate v. 숨을 막다, 질식시키다 faucet n. 수도꼭지	예문	The faucal cancer is a rare type of cancer. 인후암은 희귀한 유형의 암이다.

579

obscene

[əbˈsiːn]

a. 외설한, 음란한

obscenity n. 음란물
scenario n. 극본, 대본
proscenium n. 앞 무대, 전경

어원	-ob : against + -scene → '원래 장면을 벗어나니 외설이고 음란한'
유의어	indecent, lewd, vulgar, offensive, explicit
반의어	decent, modest, proper, respectable, tasteful
영영	Offensive or morally repulsive, especially in terms of sexual content.
예문	The book was banned because of its obscene content. 그 책은 외설적인 내용 때문에 금지되었다.

580

astound

[əstáund]

v. 깜짝 놀라게 하다

astounded a. 아연실색한
astoundingly adv. 간이 떨어질 정도로
stun v. 기절시키다
stunt n. 스턴트, 곡예

어원	-as : to + -tound : thunder → '천둥 소리에 깜짝 놀라는'
유의어	amaze, astonish, surprise, stagger, bewilder
반의어	expect, anticipate, predict, foresee, comprehend
영영	To shock or greatly surprise; to fill with amazement.
예문	The news of his success astounded everyone. 그의 성공 소식은 모두를 깜짝 놀라게 했다.

581

psychiatric

[ˌsaɪ.kiˈæt.rɪk]

a. 정신 질환의

psychiatrist n. 정신과 의사
geriatrics n. 노인 의학
pediatric a. 소아과의
psychology n. 심리학

어원	-psycho : soul + -iatr, -iatry : heal → '정신을 치료하니 정신 질환의'
유의어	mental health, psychological, psychotherapeutic, psychogenic
반의어	psychological, emotional, mental health, non-psychiatric
영영	Related to the diagnosis, treatment, and study of mental disorders.
예문	The patient was admitted to the psychiatric ward. 그 환자는 정신과 병동에 입원했다.

582

ablaze

[əˈbleɪz]

a. 빛나서; 열광하여

blazing a. 불타는, 열정적인
blazed a. 불타는 듯한; 길을 표시한
emblaze v. 불태우다, 불꽃을 내다
laser n. 레이저

어원	-a : on + -blaze 불꽃 → '불꽃이 붙었으니 열광하여'
유의어	on fire, burning, flaming, ignited, alight
반의어	extinguished, smoldering, quenched, out, doused
영영	On fire; burning brightly.
예문	The house was ablaze with light. 집은 불빛으로 환했다.

583

mortal

[ˈmɔːtəl]

a. 죽어야 할 운명의, 치명적인; 죽게 마련인

mortality n. 사망자수, 사망률
mortician n. 장의사
mortify v. 굴욕감을 주다, 당황하게 만들다
mortgage n. 저당물, 담보, 보증

어원	-mort, -murder : death → '죽을 운명이니 치명적인'
유의어	deadly, fatal, lethal, human, perishable
반의어	immortal, eternal, everlasting, undying, infinite
영영	Subject to death; deadly or fatal.
예문	All humans are mortal. 모든 인간은 죽을 운명이다.

584

collision

[kəˈlɪʒ.ən]

n. 충돌, 대립, 상충

collide v. 충돌하다, 부딪히다
collateral a. 부수적인, 공동 보증의
collusion n. 공모, 결탁, 결탁 행위
corroborate v. 확증하다, 입증하다

어원	-col : together + -lis 치다 → '함께 치니 충돌'
유의어	crash, impact, accident, collision, smash
반의어	avoidance, evasion, elusion, sidestepping, circumvention
영영	A violent impact between two objects; a crash.
예문	The collision between the two cars caused a lot of damage. 두 자동차 간의 충돌로 많은 피해가 발생했다.

585

reciprocate
[rɪˈsɪp.rə.keɪt]

v. 보답하다

reciprocation n. 교환, 보복
reciprocal a. 상호의, 호혜적인
reciprocity n. 호혜(주의)
reception n. 수령, 접수

어원	-reci, -re : back + -proc, -pro : forth → '앞뒤로 오가는 호혜로 보답하다'
유의어	respond, return, counter, exchange, mutual
반의어	ignore, reject, disregard, spurn, avoid
영영	To respond to a gesture or action with a corresponding one.
예문	I will reciprocate your kindness by helping you. 당신을 도와줌으로써 당신의 친절에 보답하겠습니

586

asthma
[ǽzmə]

n. 천식

asthmatic n. 천식 환자
asthmogenic a. 천식 유발성의
asthenia n. 쇠약, 무력증
aesthetic a. 미적인 n. 미적, 미학

어원	-a : not + -sthma : sthenos 힘 → '힘 없는 상태로 숨을 쉬니 호흡기 질환' * -as : away + -th : throat → '목구멍에서 숨이 멀어져 숨이 가쁜 천식'
유의어	respiratory condition, bronchial condition, breathing disorder
반의어	well-breathed, respiratory health, healthy breathing
영영	A respiratory condition characterized by difficulty in breathing, wheezing, and coughing.
예문	He suffers from asthma and needs to use an inhaler. 그는 천식을 앓고 있어서 흡입기를 사용해야 한다.

587

bastard
[ˈbɑː.stəd]

n. 서자,사생아; 나쁜 놈; 잡종

bastardy n. 사생아임, 서출
bastardize v. ~의 질을 떨어뜨리다
abase v. 떨어뜨리다, 비하하다
ban v. 명령으로 금지하다

어원	-bas : base + -ard 극단적으로 ~하는 사람 → '기본부터 부정 출생의 자식이나 가출 아이의 뜻'
유의어	illegitimate, born out of wedlock, spurious, adulterine, baseborn
반의어	legitimate, lawful, legal, rightful, authentic
영영	Illegitimate or born out of wedlock; a derogatory term for an unpleasant person.
예문	The bastard son was not accepted by his father's family. 그 사생아는 아버지의 가족에게 인정받지 못했다.

588

amid
[əˈmɪd]

prep. 가운데에, ~으로 에워싸인

midway adv. 도중에
migrate v. 이주하다

어원	-a 하나 + -mid 중간 (E) → '가운데 혼자 에워싸인'
유의어	among, in the midst of, surrounded by, amidst, during
반의어	outside, beyond, apart from, distant from, away from
영영	In the midst of or surrounded by.
예문	The concert was held amid great excitement. 콘서트는 큰 흥분 속에서 열렸다.

589

incubus
[ínkjəbəs íŋ-]

n. 악마, 악몽; 압박하는 일, 압박하는 사람

incubate v. 부화시키다
incubation n. 부화, 잠복기
cub n. 새끼
cubby n. 아늑하고 기분 좋은 곳

어원	-in : on + -cub : lie → '위에 누운 것처럼 나를 압박하는 악몽'
유의어	burden, nightmare, oppressive force, demon, tormentor
반의어	relief, comfort, solace, ease, blessing
영영	A malevolent supernatural being, often considered as a demon causing nightmares.
예문	She had an incubus of fear that she would fail the exam. 그녀는 시험에 떨어질까 봐 두려움에 시달렸다.

590

constituency
[kənˈstɪtʃ.u.ən.si]

n. 유권자; 선거구; 단골

constitutive a. 구성적인, 구조의
constitutively adv. 구성 요소로서
constitute v. 구성하다; 설립하다; 제정하다
constitution n. 헌법; 구성

어원	-con : together + -stitu : stand → '모두를 대표해 설 사람을 뽑는 유권자'
유의어	voters, electorate, citizens, constituency, votership
반의어	opposition, dissenters, adversaries, opponents, critics
영영	A body of voters in a specified area who elect a representative to a legislative body.
예문	The politician focused on the needs of his constituency. 그 정치인은 유권자들의 요구에 집중했다.

591

come home to

p. 가슴에 뼈저리게 사무치다

poignant a. 가슴에 사무치는, 가슴 아픈
at home p. 국내에서
homegrown a. 토착의, 국내의
homemaker n. (전업) 주부

어원	home(집)에 come(와서도) 생각날 정도로 뼈저리게 사무치다
유의어	dawn on, become apparent, realize, understand, comprehend
반의어	elude, evade, escape, avoid, ignore
영영	Become fully understood or appreciated.
예문	The importance of family came home to me when I got married. 결혼을 하고 나서야 가족의 소중함을 절실히 느꼈다.

592

put a strain on

p. ~에 압박을 가하다

constrain v. 강제하다, 억제하다
restrain v. ~을 억누르다, 억제하다
distrain v. 압류하다
refrain v. 그만두다, 삼가다

어원	-strict, -strai, -strain 팽팽히 누르다 → '팽팽히 눌러 긴장시키다' * strain '힘을 주어 압박' VS constrain '다른 사람에게 억지로 강요'
유의어	burden, stress, pressure, tax, stretch
반의어	ease, relieve, lighten, alleviate, mitigate
영영	To cause stress or pressure; to burden or overtax.
예문	The long hours of work put a strain on my health. 장시간 근무는 건강에 부담을 주었다.

593

of necessity

p. 필연적으로, 당연히

necessitate v. 필요로 하다; 수반하다
necessarily adv. 어쩔 수 없이, 필연적으로
needy a. (경제적으로) 어려운

어원	-ne : not + -cess, cede 양보하다, 가다, 나아가다 → '양보할 수 없는 것이니 필연적으로 당연히'
유의어	necessarily, inevitably, by necessity, unavoidably, inherently
반의어	optionally, voluntarily, willingly, freely, by choice
영영	Out of necessity; because it is necessary.
예문	Of necessity, we had to cancel the meeting. 부득이하게 회의를 취소해야 했다.

594

get to do

p. ~하게 되다

get away from p. ~에서 벗어나다
get down to p. 시작하다, 착수하다
get nowhere p. 아무 쓸모(소용) 없다
get over p. 극복하다

어원	-get : be 상태 + -do 하다 → '하게 되는 상태'
유의어	have the opportunity to, be able to, have the chance to, get the privilege of
반의어	avoid doing, refrain from doing, neglect, bypass
영영	Have the opportunity or privilege to do something.
예문	I finally got to meet my favorite singer in person. 마침내 내가 가장 좋아하는 가수를 직접 만나게 되었다.

595

on exhibit

p. 전시되어, 출품되어

prohibit v. 금지하다, 제지하다
inhibit v. 저해하다, 억제하다

어원	-ex : out + -hib : hold → '밖에 갖고 있는 것이 전시'
유의어	on display, showcased, exhibited, presented, featured
반의어	concealed, hidden, private, withdrawn, undisclosed
영영	On display for public viewing.
예문	The painting is on exhibit at the museum. 그 그림은 박물관에 전시되어 있다.

596

substitute A with B

p. A를 B로 대체하다

substitue for p. ~의 대체물
substitution n. 대리, 대용, 대체
substitutive a. 대리가 되는, 치환의
subsist v. 살아가다; 존재하다

어원	-sub : 대신하여 + -stitu : stand → '대신하여 서게 하다'
유의어	replace A with B, exchange A for B, swap A with B, use B as a substitute for A
반의어	retain A, keep A, preserve A, maintain A, hold onto A
영영	Replace A with B; use B as an alternative for A.
예문	We substituted sugar with artificial sweetener. 우리는 설탕을 인공 감미료로 대체했다.

597

stand to do

p. ~할 것 같다

stand for p. ~을 나타내다, ~을 의미하다
stand up to p. ~에 맞서다, 저항하다
stagger v. 비틀거리다
stagnant a. 침체된, 불경기의

어원	-stand 서다 + -do 하다 → '서 있는 걸 보니 뭔가 할 것 같다'
유의어	be likely to, have a good chance of, be poised to, be in a position to
반의어	avoid, evade, shun, escape, ignore
영영	Be likely or poised to do something.
예문	He stands to lose a lot of money if the business fails. 사업이 실패하면 그는 많은 돈을 잃을 가능성이 있다.

598

be content to do

p. 기꺼이 ~하다

discontent n. 불만
table of contents p. (책 등의) 목차
contentedly adv. 만족스럽게, 기꺼이

어원	-con : together + -tain, -ten, -tin 가지다, 잡다, 담다(L) → '모두 담았으니 만족감에 기꺼이 ~하려 하는'
유의어	be satisfied to, be happy to, be pleased to, be willing to
반의어	be discontented to do, be dissatisfied to do, be displeased to do
영영	Be satisfied or willing to do something.
예문	She was content to live a simple life. 그녀는 소박한 삶을 사는 것으로 만족했다.

599

be up for

p. 참여하다; 입후보하다

be up to p. ~까지 올라오다
up to p. ~까지

어원	-up 위(E) → '위 자리까지 보며 참여하니 입후보하다'
유의어	be willing to, be ready for, be open to, be available for
반의어	be uninterested in, be unwilling for, be disinclined to, reject
영영	Be willing or available for; be enthusiastic about.
예문	He is up for election next month. 그는 다음 달에 선거에 출마할 예정이다.

600

take with

p. 인기가 있다, 평판이 좋다

take over p. 넘겨 받다; 장악하다
take possession of p. ~을 점유하다
take sides p. 편을 들다
take the liverty to do p. 실례를 무릅쓰고 하다

어원	-take 취하다 + -with → '인기를 함께 취하니 평판이 좋다'
유의어	accept, embrace, adopt, welcome, receive
반의어	reject, decline, refuse, deny, abstain from
영영	Accept or embrace; be receptive to something.
예문	marshmallows take with little kids. 마시맬로는 어린 아이들에게 인기가 있다.

Chapter 16.

601	malaria	[məlέəriə]	n. 학질, 말라리아
602	recondition	[ˌriː.kənˈdɪʃ.ən]	v. 수리하다
603	abdicate	[ˈæb.dɪ.keɪt]	v. 퇴위하다, 포기하다
604	attire	[əˈtaɪər]	v. (옷을 차려) 입히다
605	dew	[djuː]	n. 이슬
606	pension	[ˈpen.ʃən]	n. 연금; 펜션, 하숙집 v. 연금을 주다
607	prudent	[ˈpruː.dənt]	a. 사려깊은, 현명한
608	verge	[vɜːrdʒ]	n. 가장자리, 길가 v. ~에 가까워지다
609	wane	[weɪn]	v. 약해지다, 시들해지다 n. 감소, 쇠퇴
610	denote	[dɪˈnəʊt]	v. 따로 표시하다, 나타내다, 조짐을 보여주다
611	plight	[plaɪt]	n.. 역경, 곤경 v. 맹세하다
612	hitch	[hɪtʃ]	n. 급정지; 장애 v. 매다, 연결하다; 얻어 타다
613	solicit	[səˈlɪs.ɪt]	v. ~에게 간청하다; 꾀다
614	sparse	[spɑːs]	a. 드문드문한, 부족한, 희박한
615	primate	[ˈpraɪ.meɪt]	n. 영장류
616	refract	[rɪˈfrækt]	v. 굴절시키다
617	vengeful	[ˈvendʒ.fəl]	a. 복수심에 불타는
618	sequel	[ˈsiː.kwəl]	n. 속편, 후속
619	lest	[lest]	conj. ~하지 않도록
620	defer	[difɜ́ːr]	v. 따르다; 미루다, 연기하다
621	pedagogy	[ˈped.ə.gɒdʒ.i]	n. 교육학
622	senator	[sénətər]	n. 상원 의원
623	cottage	[ˈkɒt.ɪdʒ]	n. 오두막집, 시골 집
624	aftermath	[ˈɑːf.tə.mæθ]	n. 결과, 여파; 후유증
625	rhinoceros	[raɪˈnɒs.ər.əs]	n. 코뿔소
626	dogma	[ˈdɒg.mə]	n. (독단적인) 신조, 도그마
627	somnambulism	[sɒmˈnæm.bjə.lɪ.zəm]	n. 몽유병
628	longitude	[ˈlɒŋ.gɪ.tʃuːd]	n. 경도
629	disparity	[dɪˈspær.ə.ti]	n. 불일치
630	harass	[ˈhær.əs]	v. 괴롭히다
631	put A to death		p. A를 사형에 처하다
632	get the message		p. 뜻을 이해하다
633	ask after		p. ~의 안부를 묻다
634	on the grounds of		p. ~의 이유로
635	unheard-of		p. 전례가 없는, 들어본 적 없는
636	at one's disposal		p. ~의 처분에 맡겨져
637	no sooner A than B		p. A하자마자 B
638	state of the art		p. 최첨단의
639	one after the other		p. 차례로
640	to the contrary		p. 그 반대를 보여 주는, 증명하는

601

malaria

[məlέəriə]

n. 학질, 말라리아

malady n. 질병, 병폐
malediction n. 저주, 악담

어원	-mal : bad + -ari : air → '나쁜 공기로 전염된다고 믿었던 질환' * 지금은 모기에 의해 전파되는 것으로 알려짐
유의어	Jungle fever, mosquito-borne illness.
반의어	Health, wellness, vitality.
영영	A disease transmitted by mosquitoes, causing fever and chills.
예문	Malaria is a mosquito-borne disease that can cause high fever and fatigue. 말라리아는 모기에 의해 전염되는 고열 및 피로를 유발할 수 있는 질병입니다.

602

recondition

[ˌriːkənˈdɪʃən]

v. 수리하다

recondite a. 심오한, 난해한
reconnoiter v. 정찰하다

어원	-re : back + -condition 조건, 상태; 질환 → '뒤에서 상태를 살피고 수리하다'
유의어	Refurbish, renovate, overhaul.
반의어	Neglect, abandon, worsen.
영영	To renovate or restore something to a better state.
예문	We need to recondition this old car to make it run smoothly again. 이 오래된 자동차를 다시 조립하여 원활하게 작동하도록 해야 합니다.

603

abdicate

[ˈæb.dɪ.keɪt]

v. 퇴위하다, 포기하다

abdication n. 퇴위, 포기
abnegation n. 포기, 단념
abjuration n. 취소, 포기

어원	-ab : away + dict : say → '말을 하고 물러나다'
유의어	Renounce, relinquish, resign.
반의어	Ascend, inherit, claim.
영영	To formally give up a position of power or responsibility.
예문	The king decided to abdicate the throne and retire from ruling. 왕은 왕위를 포기하고 통치에서 은퇴하기로 결정했습니다.

604

attire

[əˈtaɪər]

v. (옷을 차려) 입히다

attired a. 차려 입은, 장식한
tire n. 타이어
aptitude n. 적성, 소질 재능
attorney n. 대리인, 변호사

어원	-at : to + -tire : order → '순서대로 맞춰 차려 입는'
유의어	Clothing, garments, outfit.
반의어	Undress, disrobe, nudity.
영영	Clothing or garments worn by a person.
예문	The formal attire for the event required a suit and tie. 이 행사를 위한 정장은 정장과 넥타이를 필요로 했습니다.

605

dew

[djuː]

n. 이슬

dewy a. 이슬 맺힌, 상쾌한
damp a. 축축한, 습기 있는

어원	-dew : dawn 새벽 → '새벽에 생기는 이슬'
유의어	Moisture, condensation, droplets.
반의어	Drought, dryness, aridity.
영영	Tiny drops of water that form on surfaces overnight due to condensation.
예문	The morning dew glistened on the grass as the sun rose. 아침 이슬이 해가 떠오르면서 풀 위에서 반짝였다.

606

pension

[ˈpen.ʃən]

n. 연금; 펜션, 하숙집 v. 연금을 주다

pensionary n. 연금 수령자 a. 연금의
pensionable a. 연금을 수령할 자격이되는
compensate v. 보충하다, 보상하다
dispense v. 분배하다

어원	-pens : weigh; money → '일과 삶의 무게를 달아 연금 지불', '돈을 내고 머무르는 펜션'
유의어	Retirement income, annuity, stipend.
반의어	Employment, work, labor.
영영	A regular payment made to someone, typically in retirement.
예문	After retiring, she received a monthly pension to support herself. 은퇴한 후 그녀는 자신을 지원하기 위해 매달 연금을 받았다.

607

prudent
[ˈpruːdənt]

a. 사려깊은, 현명한

prudential a. 신중한
prudence n. 사려, 분별
prudency n. 내성적임, 수줍음
preview n. 미리 보기

어원	-pr, -pro : before + -ud, -vid : see → '먼저 살피니 사려깊은'
유의어	Wise, cautious, sensible.
반의어	Foolish, reckless, careless.
영영	Acting with caution and good judgment to avoid risks.
예문	It's prudent to save money for unexpected expenses. 예기치 못한 비용을 대비하기 위해 돈을 절약하는 것이 현명하다.

608

verge
[vəːrdʒ]

n. 가장자리, 길가 v. ~에 가까워지다

verge on v. ~에 가까워지다, 근접하다
on the verge of p. 의 직전에
converge v. 한 곳에 모이다
diverge v. 갈라지다; 다르다

어원	-verge : incline → '속도가 기울어 세우는 길가가 가장자리'
유의어	Brink, edge, threshold.
반의어	Center, middle, core.
영영	The edge or border of something, often a boundary.
예문	The house was on the verge of a beautiful forest. 집은 아름다운 숲의 가장자리에 위치해 있었다.

609

wane
[weɪn]

v. 약해지다, 시들해지다 n. 감소, 쇠퇴

on the wane p. 기울기 시작하여
wainging a. 감소하는
wary a. 조심하는, 경계하는
wannabe n. 진짜가 되고 싶은 사람

어원	-wane : dwindle 사라지다 → '사라지는 것처럼 줄어들어 작아지다'
유의어	Decline, diminish, decrease.
반의어	Grow, increase, expand.
영영	To gradually decrease or diminish in intensity or size.
예문	The moon's brightness began to wane as it moved across the sky. 달의 빛이 하늘을 가로지르면서 점점 감소하기 시작했다

610

denote
[dɪˈnoʊt]

v. 따로 표시하다, 나타내다, 조짐을 보여주다

denotation n. 명시적 의미, 명확한 표시
denotative a. 표시하는, 외연적인
notion n. 개념, 생각
connote v. 암시하다, 함축하다

어원	-de : intensive + -no, -not : mark 표시하다, know 알다(L) → '따로 표시하여 나타내니 조짐을 보여주다'
유의어	Indicate, signify, represent.
반의어	Conceal, hide, obscure.
영영	To indicate or symbolize a specific meaning or concept.
예문	The red traffic light denotes that you should stop. 빨간 신호등은 멈춰야 함을 나타낸다.

611

plight
[plaɪt]

n.. 역경, 곤경 v. 맹세하다

accomplice n. 공범자
application n. 응용, 적용; 지원서

어원	-pli : weave → '일이 꼬인 상태니 곤경', '어려운 상황을 벗어 나겠다고 맹세하다'
유의어	Dilemma, predicament, situation.
반의어	Solution, resolution, success.
영영	A difficult or unfavorable situation or condition.
예문	The family found themselves in a difficult financial plight. 그 가족은 어려운 재정 상황에 처해 있었다.

612

hitch
[hɪtʃ]

n. 급정지; 장애 v. 매다, 연결하다; 얻어 타다

hitchhike v. 차를 얻어 타며 여행하다
hiccough n. 딸꾹질
hike v. 하이킹하다

어원	-hitch : hit → '줄을 고리 모양으로 만들어 홀치는 동작', '히치하이킹으로 차를 거니 급정지 후 얻어 타다'
유의어	Snag, obstacle, hindrance.
반의어	Smoothness, ease, straightforwardness.
영영	A temporary obstacle or problem that causes a delay.
예문	There was a hitch in the plan when the transportation broke down. 교통 수단이 고장 나서 계획에 일시적인 문제가 생겼다.

613

solicit

[səˈlɪs.ɪt]

v. ~에게 간청하다; 꾀다

a. solicitant 탄원하는
n. solicitor 간청자, 재촉자, 구혼자
n. solicitation 간원, 간청; 유혹
a. solicitous 열심인, 갈망하는

어원	* -sol : solve + -cit : call → '해결을 위해 부르니 간청하다, 꾀다'
유의어	Request, ask for, seek.
반의어	Discourage, dissuade, deter.
영영	To request or ask for something, often in a formal manner.
예문	She decided to solicit donations for a charity event. 그녀는 자선 행사를 위해 기부를 구하기로 결정했다.

614

sparse

[spɑːs]

a. 드문드문한, 부족한, 희박한

sparsely adv. 드물게, 희박하게
sparseness n. 희박, 빈약, 성김
interperse v. 흩뿌리다
disperse v. 흩어지게 하다, 분산시키다

어원	-spers, -spars, -sparg : scatter → '떨어져 있으니 드문드문 부족한'
유의어	Scant, meager, limited.
반의어	Abundant, plentiful, ample.
영영	Lacking in density or having very few of something.
예문	The desert landscape was vast and sparsely populated. 사막 지형은 넓고 인구가 희박하다.

615

primate

[ˈpraɪ.meɪt]

n. 영장류

primatology n. 영장류학
primatologist n. 영장류 동물학자
prime a. 최상의 n. 전성기
principal n. 교장, 학장 a. 주요한

어원	-prim, -prin, -pri : first 최고의, 첫 번째 (L) → '동물 중 으뜸이라는 영장류'
유의어	Ape, monkey, simian.
반의어	Non-primate, non-human.
영영	A group of mammals that includes humans, apes, and monkeys.
예문	Humans are considered primates within the animal kingdom. 인간은 동물 계에서 영장류로 간주됩니다.

616

refract

[rɪˈfrækt]

v. 굴절시키다

refraction n. 굴절, 굴절률
refractive a. 굴절성의, 굴절과 관련된
refractory a. 고집 센; 용해하기 어려운
refrain v. 삼가하다, 자제하다

어원	-re : again + fract : break → '방향으로 깨뜨리고 다시 굴절시키다'
유의어	Bend, deflect, deviate.
반의어	Straighten, align, direct.
영영	To bend or change the direction of light or sound waves as they pass through a medium.
예문	The glass lens refracts light, allowing us to see clearly. 유리 렌즈는 빛을 굴절시켜 우리가 명확하게 볼 수 있게 해줍니다.

617

vengeful

[ˈvendʒ.fəl]

a. 복수심에 불타는

vengeance n. 복수
avenge v. 복수하다(정의 실현)
revenge v. 복수하다(개인 원한)

어원	-veng : punish + -ful → '처벌하려 하니 복수심에 불타는'
유의어	Revengeful, vindictive, spiteful.
반의어	Forgiving, merciful, compassionate.
영영	Having a strong desire for revenge or retaliation.
예문	He had a vengeful attitude toward those who wronged him. 그는 자신을 해치는 사람들에 대해 복수심을 품었습니다.

618

sequel

[ˈsiː.kwəl]

n. 속편, 후속

sequence n. 순서, 연속
sequel to n. ~의 속편
consequence n. (직접적인) 결과
subsequence n. (간접적인) 결과

어원	-secu, -sequ, -su, -sue : follow 쫓다, 따르다 (L) → '뒤에 따라 나오는 속편이 후속'
유의어	Follow-up, continuation, outcome.
반의어	Prequel, predecessor, beginning.
영영	A continuation or follow-up to a previous event or story.
예문	The movie's sequel was even more successful than the original. 그 영화의 속편은 원작보다 더 성공적이었습니다

619

lest

[lest]

conj. ~하지 않도록

leak v. 새다, 누설하다
leper n. 나환자

어원	-lest : less → '가능성이 적으니 하지 않도록'
유의어	In case, for fear that, so that not.
반의어	Because, since, as.
영영	Used to express a precaution or warning to avoid a negative outcome.
예문	She studied diligently, lest she fail the upcoming exam. 그녀는 다가오는 시험에서 떨어지지 않도록 열심히 공부했습니다.

620

defer

[difə́:r]

v. 따르다; 미루다, 연기하다

deferment n. 연기, 유예
deferred a. 연기된, 미루어진
deferral n. 연기, 유예
preer v. 선호하다, 우선하다

어원	-de : down + -fer : carry, bring 나르다, 가져가다 → '고개를 아래로 하고 짐 들고 따르다', '날짜를 뒤로 보내다'
유의어	Postpone, delay, put off.
반의어	Expedite, advance, hasten.
영영	To delay or postpone an action or decision.
예문	We had to defer our vacation plans due to unexpected work commitments. 예상치 못한 업무 의무로 인해 휴가 계획을 미뤄야 했습니다.

621

pedagogy

[ˈped.ə.ɡɒdʒ.i]

n. 교육학

pedagogue n. 교사
pedagogical a. 교육의, 교육법의
pediatrics n. 소아과
encyclopedia n. 백과사전

어원	-ped 아이, 가르치다 + -agog, -duc 끌다 → '아이를 이끄는 교육학'
유의어	Education, teaching, instruction.
반의어	Ignorance, illiteracy, incompetence.
영영	The methods and practices of teaching and education.
예문	The school's pedagogy focuses on hands-on learning. 그 학교의 교육법은 실습 학습에 중점을 둡니다.

622

senator

[sénətər]

n. 상원 의원

senatorial a. 상원의
senatorship n. 상원 의원의 지위
senatus n. 원로원, 이사회
senior a. 고위의, 상급의; 연장자

어원	-sen : old 노인 → '로마 시대 원로원에서 유래한 상원 위원'
유의어	Legislator, lawmaker, congressperson.
반의어	Citizen, civilian, commoner.
영영	A member of a legislative body, such as the U.S. Senate.
예문	The senator proposed a new bill to address climate change. 상원의원은 기후 변화를 다루기 위한 새로운 법안을 제안했습니다.

623

cottage

[ˈkɒt.ɪdʒ]

n. 오두막집, 시골 집

cottar n. 소작 농민
caravan n. 이동식 주택, 캠핑카
cabana n. 해변가 오두막, 수영장 오두막
cabbage n. 양배추

어원	-cot : 작은집 + -age ~에 속한 것 → '작은 집에 속하는 오두막집' * 코티지 치즈 : 영국의 생치즈
유의어	Cabin, chalet, bungalow.
반의어	Mansion, palace, estate.
영영	A small, often cozy, rural house or dwelling.
예문	They spent their summer vacation in a cozy cottage by the lake. 그들은 호수 옆 아늑한 작은집에서 여름 휴가를 보냈습니다.

624

aftermath

[ˈɑːf.tə.mæθ]

n. 결과, 여파; 후유증

afterbirth n. 후산
aftertaste n. 뒷맛, 여운
after the fact p. 사건 후에
take after p. ~을 닮다

어원	-after 이후(E) + -math : meadow 풀을 베는 것 → '목초지가 베어진 후 자라는 두 번째 목초지 결과' * 'math(수학)을 풀고 난 후유증이 여파로'
유의어	Consequence, result
반의어	Antecedent, precursor, cause.
영영	The consequences or results of a significant event.
예문	The aftermath of the hurricane left widespread destruction in its wake. 허리케인의 여파로 인해 광범위한 파괴가 남았습니다.

625

rhinoceros

[raɪˈnɒs.ər.əs]

n. 코뿔소

triceratops n. 트리케라톱스
rhinal a. 코의, 비강의

어원	-rhino, -rhin : nose + -ceros : keras 뿔 → '코에 뿔이 있는 코뿔소'
유의어	Rhino, horned mammal.
반의어	Herbivore, prey, smaller animal.
영영	A large, thick-skinned herbivorous mammal with one or two horns on its snout.
예문	The rhinoceros is a critically endangered species in need of protection. 코뿔소는 보호가 필요한 위급한 멸종 위기종입니다.

626

dogma

[ˈdɒg.mə]

n. (독단적인) 신조, 도그마

dogmatic a. 독단적인
dogmatist n. 독단가, 교리주의자
heterodox a. 이단적인, 이교도의
orthodox a. 정통적인

어원	-dog 개 → '개가 끈질기게 한 주인만 쫓는 것처럼 맹목적인 신조'
유의어	Doctrine, belief, creed.
반의어	Doubt, skepticism, uncertainty.
영영	A set of firmly held beliefs or doctrines, often in a religious or ideological context.
예문	He followed the dogma of his religion with unwavering faith. 그는 불변의 신념으로 자신의 종교의 교리를 따랐습니다.

627

somnambulism

[sɒmˈnæm.bjə.lɪ.zəm]

n. 몽유병

somnambulist n. 몽유병자
somnambulistic a. 몽유병의
ambulance n. 구급차
insomnia n. 불면증

어원	-somn : sleep + -ambul 걸어다니는 → '수면 중에 걸어다니는 몽유병' * 솜누스Somnus : 잠의 신으로 밤의 여신 닉스가 혼자서 낳은 자식
유의어	Sleepwalking, noctambulism.
반의어	Wakefulness, alertness.
영영	Sleepwalking, a condition in which a person walks or performs actions while asleep.
예문	His somnambulism led him to walk in his sleep during the night. 그의 수면속걷기로 인해 그는 밤에 잠에서 걷는 일이 있었습니다.

628

longitude

[ˈlɒŋ.gɪ.tʃuːd]

n. 경도

longitudinal a. 경도의, 세로의
longitudinally adv. 세로로, 경도로
latitude n. 위도
longevity n. 장수, 수명

어원	-long, -leng,-ling : want 갈망하다, long 긴 + -tude 명접 → '지구 위에 세로로 길게 그어진 경도'
유의어	Meridian, east-west position.
반의어	Latitude, parallel, meridian.
영영	A measure of location east or west of the Prime Meridian on Earth's surface.
예문	Longitude lines run from north to south and help determine a location's east-west position. 경도선은 북에서 남으로 이어지며 위치의 동서 경도를 결정하는 데 도움을 줍니다.

629

disparity

[dɪˈspær.ə.ti]

n. 불일치

disparate a. 서로 다른, 이질적인
disparately adv. 이질적인 것들로 이뤄져
disparage v. 비방하다, 경시하다
deviation n. 편차, 일탈, 이탈

어원	-dis : away + -par : qual, peer → '같지 않으니 불일치'
유의어	Inequality, difference, imbalance.
반의어	Equality, sameness, uniformity.
영영	A significant difference or inequality between two or more things.
예문	There is a significant disparity in income levels between the rich and the poor. 부자와 가난한 사이에 소득 수준의 큰 불균형이 있습니다.

630

harass

[ˈhær.əs]

v. 괴롭히다

harassment n. 괴롭힘, 성추행
harassed a. 잔뜩 시달린, 초조한
harrowed a. 불안한, 고통스러운
harsh a. 혹독한, 가혹한

어원	-hare 토끼 + -ass 엉덩이 → '영국의 사냥개가 토끼의 엉덩이를 보고 쫓다'
유의어	Bully, torment, pester.
반의어	Assist, support, aid.
영영	To persistently bother, torment, or intimidate someone.
예문	It's important to address workplace harassment to create a safe environment. 안전한 환경을 조성하기 위해 직장 내 괴롭힘을 다뤄야 합니다.

631

put A to death

p. A를 사형에 처하다

deadly a. 치명적인
dread v. 몹시 두려워하다
drastic a. 격렬한, 과감한
drape v. (장막을) 드리우다

어원	-death : dead → '죽음에 이르게 하다'
유의어	Execute, kill, terminate.
반의어	Spare, save, rescue.
영영	To kill or execute someone, typically as a punishment.
예문	In some countries, the legal system allows for putting criminals to death as punishment for heinous crimes. 일부 국가에서는 범죄자를 악법적인 범행에 대한 처벌로 죽이는 것을 허용합니다.

632

get the message

p. 뜻을 이해하다

missile n. 미사일
missionary n. 전도사, 선교사
missive n. 편지, 공문서

어원	-get 얻다 + -message 메시지 → '메시지의 뜻을 얻었으니 이해하다'
유의어	Understand, comprehend, grasp.
반의어	Misunderstand, misinterpret.
영영	To understand or grasp the intended meaning of a communication.
예문	I hope he gets the message that we need his help urgently. 우리가 그의 도움이 급하게 필요하다는 메시지를 그가 이해했으면 좋겠다.

633

ask after

p. ~의 안부를 묻다

ask for p. 요청하다, 청구하다
askance a. 곁눈으로, 비스듬히
assail v. 공격하다, 습격하다

어원	after(이후에도) 괜찮은지 ask(안부를 묻다)
유의어	Inquire about, check on, inquire regarding.
반의어	Ignore, neglect, disregard.
영영	To inquire about someone's well-being or inquire about their condition.
예문	She called to ask after your health and well-being. 그녀는 당신의 건강과 안녕을 묻기 위해 전화했습니다.

634

on the grounds of

p. ~의 이유로

on the grounds that p. ~라는 이유로
grounded a. 근거가 있는
grounded p. ~에 기반을 둔

어원	-ground 땅; 기본, 기저 → '기저에 깔려 있는 이유로'
유의어	Based on, because of, due to.
반의어	Without cause, unjustly, unfairly.
영영	Because of or based on a particular reason or evidence.
예문	He was expelled from school on the grounds of misconduct and disruptive behavior. 그는 행동 불량과 방해적인 행동을 이유로 학교에서 퇴학당했습니다.

635

unheard-of

p. 전례가 없는, 들어본 적 없는

overhear v. 우연히 듣다, 몰래 엿듣다
heed v. 주의를 기울이다
hear out p. ~의 말을 끝까지 듣다

어원	-un : not + -hear 듣다 → '들어보지 못한'
유의어	Unprecedented, extraordinary, novel.
반의어	Known, common, typical.
영영	Something that is completely unknown or unprecedented.
예문	The level of success she achieved at such a young age was unheard-of in our industry. 그녀가 어린 나이에 달성한 성공 수준은 우리 산업에서 이례적이었습니다.

636

at one's disposal

p. ~의 처분에 맡겨져

dispose of p. ~을 처리하다
disposition n. 성향, 의향; 정리, 처분
depose v. 물러나게 하다
deposit n. 계약금; 퇴적물

어원	-de : down + -pos : put → '밑으로 내려놓고 배열 후 처리하다'
유의어	Available, within reach, accessible.
반의어	Unavailable, inaccessible, restricted.
영영	Available and ready for one's use or control.
예문	The company provided a wide range of resources at their employees' disposal. 회사는 직원들의 사용 가능한 다양한 자원을 제공했습니다.

637

no sooner A than B

p. A하자마자 B

sooner or later p. 곧, 조만간
in less than no time p. 놀라울 정도로 곧
in next to no time p. 놀라울 정도로 곧

어원	-no + -sooner 조만간 → 'B보다 우선한 A니 A하자마자 B'
유의어	Immediately, right after, promptly.
반의어	Later, subsequently, afterward.
영영	Expressing that one action immediately follows another.
예문	No sooner had he finished his breakfast than he received an urgent phone call. 그는 아침 식사를 마칠 즈음에 긴급한 전화를 받았다.

638

state of the art

p. 최첨단의

state of affairs p. 상황, 현상
overstate v. 과장하다
restate v. 새로 진술하다
make a statement p. 성명하다, 진술하다

어원	-state 상태 + -art 기술 → 기술의 현 최신 상태'
유의어	Cutting-edge, advanced, modern.
반의어	Outdated, obsolete, old-fashioned.
영영	Referring to something that is the most advanced and current in its field.
예문	The new smartphone features state-of-the-art technology and innovative design. 새로운 스마트폰은 최신 기술과 혁신적인 디자인을 갖추고 있습니다.

639

one after the other

p. 차례로

afterbirth n. 후산
after all p. 결국
after the fact p. 사건 후에
take after p. ~을 닮다

어원	-one + -after 이후(E) → '하나 이후 차례로'
유의어	Sequentially, consecutively, in succession.
반의어	Simultaneously, together, concurrently.
영영	Sequentially, with one thing happening right after the previous one.
예문	The cars in the race crossed the finish line one after the other. 경주에서 차들이 한 대씩 결승선을 통과했습니다.

640

to the contrary

p. 그 반대를 보여 주는, 증명하는

on the contrary p. 오히려, 도리어
contrary to p. ~와는 달리
controvert v. 논쟁하다, ~에 반박하다
contravene v. 반대하다, 위반하다

어원	-contr, -counter, -contra, -contro 반대쪽으로, 밖으로(L)
유의어	Contrarily, conversely, on the other hand.
반의어	Similarly, likewise, correspondingly.
영영	In contrast or opposition to what was previously stated or believed.
예문	Many people believed he would fail, but to the contrary, he succeeded against all odds. 많은 사람들은 그가 실패할 것이라고 생각했지만, 그와는 반대로 그는 모든 어려움을 이겨냈습니다.

Chapter 17.

641	reimburse	[ˌriː.ɪmˈbɜːs]	v. ~에게 변상하다, 갚다
642	hum	[hʌm]	v. 콧노래를 부르다 n. 웅웅거리는 소리 a. 활기찬
643	emit	[iˈmɪt]	v. 내뿜다, 방출하다
644	hop	[hap]	v. 깡충 뛰다
645	pedestal	[ˈped.ə.stəl]	n. 주춧돌; 기초
646	blister	[ˈblɪs.tər]	n. 물집, 수포, 발포
647	protagonist	[prəˈtæg.ən.ɪst]	n. 주연, 주인공; 주창자, 지도자
648	pending	[ˈpen.dɪŋ]	a. 아직 해결되지 않은, 보류 중인
649	etymology	[ˌet.ɪˈmɒl.ə.dʒi]	n. 어원학
650	applaud	[əˈplɔːd]	v. 박수갈채하다; 칭찬하다
651	presume	[prɪˈzjuːm]	v. 가정하다, 추측하다
652	poise	[pɔɪz]	n. 침착, 균형 v. 균형 잡히게 하다
653	feeble	[ˈfiː.bəl]	a. 허약한, 힘 없는, 희미한
654	annuity	[əˈnjuː.ə.ti]	n. 연금, 연금 수령권
655	acclaim	[əˈkleɪm]	v. 갈채를 보내다, 환호로 맞이하다 n. 환호, 갈채
656	admonish	[ədˈmɒn.ɪʃ]	v. 훈계하다, 충고하다; 경고하다, 주의시키다
657	confederate	[kənˈfed.ər.ət]	n. 동맹국, 동지; 공모자 v. 다국적으로 연맹하다
658	astonish	[əˈstɒn.ɪʃ]	v. 놀라게 하다
659	continence	[kɑ́ntənəns]	n. 절제, 금욕
660	derange	[diréindʒ]	v. 어지럽히다
661	stroll	[strəʊl]	v. 천천히 거닐다 n. 산책
662	ethnic	[ˈeθ.nɪk]	a. 민족의, 종족의
663	stalk	[stɔːk]	n. 줄기 v. 몰래 접근하다
664	delicate	[ˈdel.ɪ.kət]	a. 신중을 요하는, 민감한; 허약한; 맛있는
665	fission	[ˈfɪʃ.ən]	n. (핵·세포 등의) 분열
666	sift	[sɪft]	v. 거르다, 선별하다
667	robust	[rəʊˈbʌst]	a. 튼튼한, 강건한
668	gorgeous	[gɔ́ːrdʒəs]	a. 아주 멋진, 화려한
669	abet	[əˈbet]	v. 부추기다, 선동하다
670	apathy	[ǽpəθi]	n. 냉담, 무관심
671	be engrossed in		p.~에 몰두하다
672	be on the point of -ing		p. 막 ~하려 하다
673	in a daze		p. 멍하게
674	toss about		p. 뒤척이다
675	hand-on		p. 실전의, 실무의
676	get on with		p. ~와 잘 지내다
677	get down to		p. [진지하게 일을] 시작(착수)하다, 관심을 기울이다
678	do with		p. ~을 처리하다
679	follow through on		p. ~을 끝까지 수행하다
680	go about		p. ~을 시작하다; 방법을 찾다

641

reimburse

[ˌriːɪmˈbɜːs]

v. ~에게 변상하다, 갚다

reimbursement n. 변상, 상환
imburse v. 돈을 주다, 비용을 지불하다
burse n. 돈이나 문서를 보관하는 가방

어원	-re : again + -burs : purse → '다시 지갑에 돈을 넣어 변상하다'
유의어	Repay, refund, compensate.
반의어	Withhold, charge, keep.
영영	To repay someone for money spent or losses incurred.
예문	The company will reimburse you for any work-related expenses. 회사는 업무 관련 경비를 상환해 줄 것입니다.

642

hum

[hʌm]

v. 콧노래를 부르다 n. 웅웅거리는 소리 a. 활기찬

hummingbird n. 벌새
humor n. 유머

어원	-hum 우웅거리는 소리 → '콧노래를 부르니 활기찬'
유의어	Buzz, drone, murmur.
반의어	Silence, quiet, hush.
영영	To make a low, continuous sound, often like a buzz.
예문	The refrigerator hums softly in the background. 냉장고는 배경에서 가벼운 소리를 내며 울립니다.

643

emit

[iˈmɪt]

v. 내뿜다, 방출하다

emission n. 방사, 발산, 발행; 배설
emissive a. 발사의, 방사의
intermit v. 일시 멈추다, 중단되다
dismiss v. 해고하다

어원	-e : out + -mit, -miss, -mess : send(L) → '바깥으로 보내니 내뿜다'
유의어	Release, discharge, exude.
반의어	Absorb, conceal, suppress.
영영	To release or give off something, such as light, heat, or a smell.
예문	The factory emits pollutants into the air, causing pollution. 공장은 오염물질을 대기로 방출하여 오염을 일으킵니다.

644

hop

[hap]

v. 깡충 뛰다

hopper n. 깡충깡충 뛰는 사람
hopping a. 바쁜, ~을 돌아다니는
hip hop n. 엉덩이가 들썩이는 음악
grasshopper n. 메뚜기

어원	-hop 깡충 뛰다
유의어	Jump, leap, bounce.
반의어	Stand, stay, sit.
영영	To jump or leap with one foot, typically in a playful or energetic manner.
예문	The children happily hopped around the playground. 아이들은 기쁘게 놀이터 주위를 뛰었습니다.

645

pedestal

[ˈped.ə.stəl]

n. 주춧돌; 기초

pedestrian a. 보행의, 도보의, 평범한
bipedal a. 두 발로 걷는 n. 두발 동물
expedition n. 원정, 탐험

어원	-ped : foot 발(L) + -sta : stand → '인간의 발처럼 기초가 서 있는 것물의 기초가 되는 주춧돌'
유의어	Base, stand, foundation.
반의어	Bottom, baseless, ground-level.
영영	A base or support on which something stands or is placed to elevate it.
예문	The statue was placed on a tall pedestal in the park. 그 동상은 공원의 높은 받침대 위에 놓였습니다.

646

blister

[ˈblɪs.tər]

n. 물집, 수포, 발포

blistery a. 수포가 있는
blistering a. 물집이 생기게 하는
blastoma n. 종양
breast n. 가슴

어원	-blizzard, -blast : bhle, bhel : blow, swell → '피부에서 부풀어 오른 물집'
유의어	Bubble, pustule, sore.
반의어	Smooth, unblemished, intact.
영영	A small, raised bubble on the skin filled with fluid, typically caused by friction or heat.
예문	She developed blisters on her feet after hiking all day. 하루 종일 하이킹을 한 후 그녀는 발에 물집이 생겼습니다.

647

protagonist

[prəˈtæg.ən.ɪst]

n. 주연, 주인공; 주창자, 지도자

protein n. 단백질
antagonist n. 적대자, 반대자
prostrate v. 엎드리게 하다
properity n. 번영

어원	-prot, -proto : first + -agon : struggle → '맨 처음으로 투쟁하는 지도자'
유의어	Hero, main character, lead role.
반의어	Antagonist, villain, antagonist.
영영	The main character or leading figure in a story or narrative.
예문	The protagonist of the novel goes on a life-changing journey. 소설의 주인공은 인생을 바꾸는 여행을 떠납니다.

648

pending

[ˈpen.dɪŋ]

a. 아직 해결되지 않은, 보류 중인

pendent a. 매달린, 미결의, 드리워진
pend v. 미결인 채로 두다, 결정을 미루다
pendulum n. 진자, 추, 흔들이
pendant v. 펜던트, 목걸이

어원	-pend, -pens, -pond : hang 매달다 → '문제가 아직 매달려 있으니 아직 해결되지 않은' * pend(d,s)은 '매달리다', grav는 '고통'의 의미
유의어	Unresolved, undecided, awaiting.
반의어	Resolved, settled, decided.
영영	Not yet decided or settled; awaiting a resolution or action.
예문	The court case is still pending a verdict from the judge. 법정 소송은 아직 판사의 결정을 기다리고 있습니다.

649

etymology

[ˌet.ɪˈmɒl.ə.dʒi]

n. 어원학

etymological a. 어원론적인
etymologist n. 어원학자
etymon n. 어원, 어근
ethnic a. 민족의, 종족의

어원	-etymo 사실, 진실 (G) + -log : language → '말의 진실을 연구하는 학문'
유의어	Origin, history, derivation.
반의어	Misconception, misinformation, inaccuracy.
영영	The study of the origin and history of words and their meanings.
예문	Linguists study the etymology of words to trace their origins. 언어학자들은 어원을 연구하여 단어의 기원을 추적합니다.

650

applaud

[əˈplɔːd]

v. 박수갈채하다; 칭찬하다

applaudable a. 갈채를 보낼 만한
applaudably adv. 갈채를 보낼 만하게
applause n. 칭찬
explode v. 폭발하다

어원	-ap : to + -plaud, -plaus, -plod : clap 박수 치다 (날개 부딪치는 소리) → '~에게 박수를 치다' * 로마인들은 좋은 일이 있으면 새를 날려서 축하
유의어	Clap, cheer, commend.
반의어	Boo, jeer, criticize.
영영	To show approval or praise by clapping hands or expressing approval.
예문	The audience applauded loudly after the outstanding performance. 관객들은 훌륭한 공연 뒤에 큰 박수를 쳤습니다.

651

presume

[prɪˈzjuːm]

v. 가정하다, 추측하다

presumably adv. 아마도, 생각하건데
presumed a. 당연한 것으로 생각되고 있는
sum n. 액수, 총액 v. 더하다; 요약하다
consume v. 소비하다

어원	-pre : before + -sum : take → '미리 취해보는 생각이니 가정'
유의어	Assume, suppose, conjecture.
반의어	Doubt, question, dispute.
영영	To assume or believe something to be true without conclusive evidence.
예문	Don't presume that I agree with everything you say. 내가 당신의 말에 모든 것에 동의한다고 가정하지 마세요.

652

poise

[pɔɪz]

n. 침착, 균형 v. 균형 잡히게 하다

poised a. 태세를 갖춘, 준비가 된
position n. 자리, 위치, 직책
propose v. 제안하다, 청혼하다

어원	-poise, -posit : place → '위치 균형을 맞추니 침착'
유의어	Composure, balance, stability.
반의어	Unbalance, instability, unsteadiness.
영영	A state of balance, stability, or composure, both physically and mentally.
예문	She maintained her poise even in stressful situations. 그녀는 스트레스 상황에서도 평형을 유지했습니다.

653

feeble
[ˈfiː.bəl]

a. 허약한, 힘 없는, 희미한

feebly adv. 나약하게, 무기력하게
feebleness n. 약함, 허약함, 무력함
enfeeble v. 약하게 하다
infant n. 유아, 어린 아기, 아기

어원	* -fee : feed + -able → '먹여야만 하는 입장이니 허약하고 힘 없는'
유의어	Weak, frail, delicate.
반의어	Strong, powerful, robust.
영영	Lacking strength, vigor, or power; weak or frail.
예문	The feeble old man needed assistance to walk. 연약한 노인은 걷기 위해 도움이 필요했습니다.

654

annuity
[əˈnjuː.ə.ti]

n. 연금, 연금 수령권

annuitant n. 연금 수령인, 연금 생활자
annals n. 연대기
annually adv. 해마다, 매년

어원	-ann ,-enn : annus=year(L) → '연마다 받는 연금'
유의어	Pension, allowance, stipend.
반의어	Lump sum, one-time payment, single payment.
영영	A regular payment made at fixed intervals, often as part of a retirement plan.
예문	She receives a monthly annuity from her retirement plan. 그녀는 은퇴 계획에서 매월 연금을 받습니다.

655

acclaim
[əˈkleɪm]

v. 갈채를 보내다, 환호로 맞이하다 n. 환호, 갈채

acclamation n. 환호, 갈채
acclamatory a. 환호의, 갈채의
exclaim v. 외치다
reclaim v. 되찾다

어원	-ac : to + -claim : cry → '~를 향해 소리치며 환호와 갈채를 보내다'
유의어	Praise, applause, recognition.
반의어	Criticism, condemnation, disapproval.
영영	Enthusiastic approval, praise, or recognition for something.
예문	The actor's performance received critical acclaim from reviewers. 배우의 연기는 평론가들로부터 칭찬을 받았습니다.

656

admonish
[ədˈmɒn.ɪʃ]

v. 훈계하다, 충고하다; 경고하다, 주의시키다

admonishment n. 훈계, 설득, 경고
monitor n. 감시자, 관찰자
premonish v. 미리 경고하다, 예고하다

어원	-ad : to + -mon, -moni : advise * '~에게 moster가 나타났다고 경고하다'
유의어	Warn, reprimand, scold.
반의어	Praise, commend, laud.
영영	To caution or warn someone firmly or criticize them for their actions.
예문	The teacher admonished the students to complete their homework on time. 선생님은 학생들에게 과제를 제때에 끝내라고 경고했습니다.

657

confederate
[kənˈfed.ər.ət]

n. 동맹국, 동지; 공모자 v. 다국적으로 연맹하다

confederation n. 다국적 연방, 다자간 연합
federal a. 연방의
conference n. 협의

어원	-con : together + -fed : trust → '서로 믿으니 공모자'
유의어	Ally, partner, accomplice.
반의어	Opponent, rival, enemy.
영영	A person or group that is allied with another for a common purpose.
예문	The two countries entered into a confederate alliance for mutual defense. 두 나라는 상호 방어를 위한 동맹을 체결했습니다.

658

astonish
[əˈstɒn.ɪʃ]

v. 놀라게 하다

astounded a. 아연실색한
astoundingly adv. 간이 떨어질 정도로
stun v. 기절시키다
stunt n. 스턴트, 곡예

어원	-as : to + -ton, -toun, -stun : thunder 놀라게 하다 → '천둥 소리처럼 놀라게 하다' syn. astound
유의어	Amaze, astound, surprise.
반의어	Expect, foresee, anticipate.
영영	To greatly surprise or amaze someone.
예문	Her incredible talent never failed to astonish the audience. 그녀의 놀라운 재능은 관객을 항상 놀라게 했습니다.

659

continence

[kάntənəns]

n. 절제, 금욕

container n. 용기, 그릇
abstain n. 삼가다, 그만두다

어원	-con : together + -tin, -ten : hold → '마음 속에 모든 욕심을 잡아 두니 절제와 금욕'
유의어	Self-control, restraint, moderation.
반의어	Indulgence, excess, unrestraint.
영영	Self-restraint, especially in resisting impulses or desires.
예문	Practicing continence is important for maintaining good health. 절제를 실천하는 것은 건강을 유지하는 데 중요합니다.

660

derange

[diréindʒ]

v. 어지럽히다

deranged a. 미친, 혼란된
derangement n. 교란, 혼란, 광기
range n. 범위, 다양성
ranch n. 목장

어원	-de : off + -range 범위 → '정상 범위를 벗어나도록 어지럽히다'
유의어	Disturb, disrupt, disarrange.
반의어	Arrange, organize, order.
영영	To disturb or disarrange the normal functioning or order of something.
예문	The sudden change in routine seemed to derange him. 갑작스러운 루틴 변화가 그를 혼란스럽게 한 것 같았다.

661

stroll

[stroʊl]

v. 천천히 거닐다 n. 산책

strolling a. 순회 공연하는, 떠돌아다니는
take a stroll p. 산책하다
stroller n. 유모차; 천천히 거니는 사람
pedestrian n. 보행자

어원	-st : street + -roll 회전 → '거리를 굴러다니듯 천천히 거닐다'
유의어	Walk, amble, saunter.
반의어	Rush, sprint, hasten.
영영	To walk in a leisurely or relaxed manner.
예문	They decided to take a leisurely stroll through the park. 그들은 공원을 여유롭게 산책하기로 결정했습니다.

662

ethnic

[ˈeθ.nɪk]

a. 민족의, 종족의

ethnicity n. 민족(집단)
ethnocentric a. 자기 민족 중심적인
ethic n. 도덕, 윤리
ethanol n. 에탄올

어원	-eth 도덕, 윤리 → '도덕, 윤리가 공존하는 민족'
유의어	Racial, cultural, national.
반의어	Non-ethnic, mixed, diverse.
영영	Relating to a particular racial, cultural, or national group.
예문	The neighborhood is known for its diverse ethnic communities. 이 동네는 다양한 민족 공동체로 유명합니다.

663

stalk

[stɔːk]

n. 줄기 v. 몰래 접근하다

stalker n. 스토커
stalk about p. 거드럭거리면서 걷다
stem from p. ~에서 비롯되다
thorn n. 가시

어원	-stalk : stem 줄기 / -st : street + -alk : walk with long stride → '긴 보폭으로 몰래 접근하다'
유의어	Base, origin, source.
반의어	Originate, generate, spawn.
영영	The main structural part of a plant that supports leaves, flowers, and fruit.
예문	The stem of the flower is green and supports the petals. 꽃의 줄기는 녹색이며 꽃잎을 지지합니다.

664

delicate

[ˈdel.ɪ.kət]

a. 신중을 요하는, 민감한; 허약한; 맛있는

delicately adv. 정교하게, 섬세하게
delicacy n. 섬세함
delicious a. 맛있는
delight n. 기쁨, 즐거움

어원	-delic 부드러운 → '부드럽고 약해 신중을 요하는', '부드럽다 못해 가냘퍼 우아한'
유의어	Fragile, dainty, sensitive.
반의어	Sturdy, robust, resilient.
영영	Fragile, easily damaged, or requiring careful handling.
예문	Be careful with the delicate glassware; it can break easily. 섬세한 유리제품은 쉽게 깨질 수 있으니 조심하세요.

665

fission

[ˈfɪʃ.ən]

n. (핵·세포 등의) 분열

fissile a. 분열성의, 분열할 수 있는
fissure n. 균열, 갈라진 틈
deficient a. 결핍된, 부족한
diffuse v. 확산하다, 분산시키다

어원	-fi 쪼개다, 자르다 → '원자핵이 분열하여 더 작은 원자핵과 중성자를 생성하는 과정'
유의어	Split, division, separation.
반의어	Fusion, amalgamation, unification.
영영	The splitting of an atomic nucleus into two or more smaller nuclei, accompanied by the release of energy.
예문	Nuclear reactors use controlled fission reactions to generate power. 원자로는 에너지를 생성하기 위해 통제된 핵분열 반응을 사용합니다.

666

sift

[sɪft]

v. 거르다, 선별하다

sifting n. 체질한 것
sifter n. 체질하는 사람
discern v. 식별하다, 분간하다
concern v. 관여하다; 걱정하다

어원	-sift 체로 거르다 * -si : sink → '가라 앉으면서 걸러지다'
유의어	Filter, strain, separate.
반의어	Clump, combine, mix.
영영	To separate or filter out particles or substances using a sieve or similar device.
예문	She used a sieve to sift the flour and remove lumps. 그녀는 덩어리를 제거하기 위해 가루를 체로 걸렀습니다.

667

robust

[rəʊˈbʌst]

a. 튼튼한, 강건한

robustness n. 건강한 상태, 강건함
robbustious a. 건장한, 건강한
corroborate v. 확증하다, 입증하다
robber n. 강도, 약탈자

어원	-rob : strong / 강탈하다, 약탈하다 → 'robot 로봇처럼 튼튼하고 강건한'
유의어	Strong, sturdy, healthy.
반의어	Weak, frail, delicate.
영영	Strong, healthy, and vigorous.
예문	Regular exercise can lead to a robust and healthy body. 정기적인 운동은 튼튼하고 건강한 신체로 이끌 수 있습니다.

668

gorgeous

[ɡɔ́ːrdʒəs]

a. 아주 멋진, 화려한

gorgeously adv. 아주 매력적으로
gorg n. 협곡 v. 게걸스럽게 먹다
gorgon n. 고르곤; 무서운 여자; 끔찍한 여자

어원	gorgias '아름다운 외모와 매혹적인 목소리를 가졌던 그리스 신화의 고르시아스' * Gorgonzola 고르곤졸라 치즈의 맛처럼 매력적인
유의어	Beautiful, stunning, magnificent.
반의어	Plain, unattractive, homely.
영영	Extremely beautiful or attractive.
예문	The sunset over the ocean was absolutely gorgeous. 바다 위의 일몰은 정말 아름다웠습니다

669

abet

[əˈbet]

v. 부추기다, 선동하다

abetment n. 선동, 교사
abettor n. 선동자
bait n.미끼, 유혹

어원	-a : to + -bet : bait 미끼 → '미끼로 유인하다'
유의어	Aid, assist, support.
반의어	Hinder, obstruct, impede.
영영	To assist, support, or encourage someone in carrying out a wrongdoing.
예문	He was accused of abetting the thief in the robbery. 그는 도둑을 강도에 부추긴 혐의로 기소되었습니다.

670

apathy

[ǽpəθi]

n. 냉담, 무관심

apathetic a. 무관심한, 냉담한
apathetically adv. 무관심하게, 냉담하게 sympathy n. 동정, 공감
antipathy n. 반감, 혐오

어원	-a, -an : without + -path : feeling → '느낌이 없는'
유의어	Indifference, disinterest, apathetic.
반의어	Enthusiasm, interest, passion.
영영	A lack of interest, enthusiasm, or concern; indifference.
예문	The apathy of the students toward the class was concerning to the teacher. 학생들의 수업에 대한 무관심은 선생님에게 걱정이었습니다.

671

be engrossed in

p. ~에 몰두하다

engross v. 마음을 빼앗다
grocery n. 식료품, 식품점
gross a. 중대한 n. 총

어원	-en : in + -gross : large 큰 → '큰 일에 빠지게 만드니 집중시키다'
유의어	Be absorbed in, be immersed in, be captivated by.
반의어	Be indifferent to, be disinterested in, ignore.
영영	To be deeply absorbed or completely focused on something.
예문	She was engrossed in a captivating novel all weekend. 그녀는 주말 내내 매료되는 소설에 몰두했습니다.

672

be on the point of -ing

p. 막 ~하려 하다

at one point in time p. 어떤 시점에서
point of view p. 관점
point out p. 가리키다, 지적하다
at some point p. 어느 시점에서, 언젠가

어원	막 시작하려는 point(지점)에 이르렀다
유의어	Be about to, be on the verge of, be close to.
반의어	Be distant from, be far from, be unprepared for.
영영	To be very close to doing something or experiencing a particular situation.
예문	They were on the point of leaving for their vacation when the phone rang. 그들은 휴가를 떠날 준비를 하려던 순간 전화벨이 울렸다.

673

in a daze

p. 멍하게

dazzlement n. 눈부심
bedazzle v. 압도하다, 현혹하다
dizzy a. 어지러운, 아찔한
daze n. 멍한 상태 v. 멍하게 하다

어원	* -daze : dazzle 눈부시다 → '눈이 부셔 어지러우니 멍한 상태'
유의어	Confused, bewildered, disoriented.
반의어	Clear-minded, alert, focused.
영영	In a confused or bewildered state.
예문	After the long flight, she wandered around the airport in a daze. 긴 비행 후 그녀는 공항을 멍하니 돌아다녔다.

674

toss about

p. 뒤척이다

toss v. 뒤흔들다, 내던지다
touch v. 만지다, 접촉하다

어원	-toss 흔들다 + -about 이리저리 → '이리저리 흔들며 뒤척이다'
유의어	Agitate, shake, jolt.
반의어	Settle, stabilize, steady.
영영	To move or handle something roughly or in a disorderly manner.
예문	The stormy sea tossed the boat about violently. 폭풍우 치는 바다가 배를 격렬하게 흔들었다.

675

hand-on

p. 실전의, 실무의

on one hand p. 한편으로는
second-hand p. 간접적으로
hand down p. ~을 물려주다
hand out p. 나눠주다

어원	-hand 손 + -on 접촉 → '직접 손을 써야 하니 실전의'
유의어	Hands-on, practical, interactive.
반의어	Theoretical, theoretical, uninvolved.
영영	Involving practical experience or direct involvement.
예문	The training program includes hands-on experience in the field. 이 교육 프로그램은 현장에서의 실제 경험을 포함합니다.

676

get on with

p. ~와 잘 지내다

get away from p. ~에서 벗어나다
get down to p. 시작하다, 착수하다
get nowhere p. 아무 쓸모(소용) 없다
get over p. 극복하다

어원	-get 얻다 + -on 접촉 → '붙어 지낼 정도로 신뢰를 얻으니 잘 지내다'
유의어	Proceed, continue, advance.
반의어	Halt, pause, stop.
영영	To proceed or continue with something.
예문	Let's get on with the project and finish it by the deadline. 프로젝트를 진행하고 마감일까지 완료합시다.

677

get down to

p. [진지하게 일을] 시작(착수)하다, 관심을 기울이다
get in p. (대학 등에) 입학 허가를 받다
get on with p. ~와 잘 지내다
get to do p. ~하게 되다
get around p. 돌아다니다

어원	get down(식탁을 떠나) to(일로 가서) 진지하게 임하니 착수하다
유의어	Begin, start, undertake.
반의어	Avoid, dodge, evade.
영영	To start or begin doing something seriously or with determination.
예문	It's time to get down to studying for the upcoming exams. 다가오는 시험 공부를 진지하게 시작할 때입니다.

678

do with

p. ~을 처리하다

to do with p. ~와 관계가 있는
do away with p. 폐지하다, 없애다
do one's part in p. 에서 자신의 몫을 다하다
do over p. ~을 다시 하다, 꾸미다

어원	-do 하다
유의어	Manage, handle, deal with.
반의어	Neglect, disregard, ignore.
영영	To handle or manage a situation or problem.
예문	He didn't know how to do with the unexpected situation. 그는 예상치 못한 상황을 어떻게 다뤄야 할지 모르고 있었다.

679

follow through on

p. ~을 끝까지 수행하다

follower n. 추종자
following a. 다음의
fellow n. 동료, 녀석

어원	* -follow 따라가다 + -through ~을 통하여 → '~을 통해서 끝까지 따라가며 일을 끝내다'
유의어	Complete, carry out, execute.
반의어	Abandon, abort, quit.
영영	To carry out or complete a task or plan.
예문	It's important to follow through on your commitments. 약속을 이행하는 것이 중요합니다.

680

go about

p. ~을 시작하다; 방법을 찾다

go along with p. ~에 동조하다, 찬성하다
go for p. ~을 좋아하다, ~를 찾다
go hand in hand p. ~와 관련이 있다
go off p. (알람·경보 등이) 울리다

어원	-go 가다 + -about 이것저것 → '이것저것 시작하며 방법을 찾다'
유의어	Proceed, undertake, engage in.
반의어	Halt, stop, cease.
영영	To approach or undertake something in a particular way or manner.
예문	They needed to go about their daily tasks despite the challenges. 그들은 어려움에도 불구하고 일상적인 일을 할 필요가 있었습니다.

Chapter 18.

681	rap	[ræp]	v. 가볍게 두드리다; 비난하다 a. 황홀해 하는
682	aggrieve	[əˈgriːv]	v. 고통을 주다, 괴롭히다
683	concur	[kənˈkɜːr]	v. 의견이 일치하다
684	prick	[prɪk]	v. 찌르다, 자극하다
685	pupil	[ˈpjuː.pəl]	n. 학생; 눈동자(동공)
686	shabby	[ˈʃæb.i]	a. 누추한, 초라한
687	sabotage	[sæbətɑːʒ]	v. 고의로 방해하다, 파괴하다
688	abstain	[æbˈsteɪn]	v. 삼가다, 그만두다
689	puddle	[ˈpʌd.əl]	n. 웅덩이
690	relish	[ˈrel.ɪʃ]	n. 맛, 즐거움 v. 즐기다
691	interlock	[ˌɪn.təˈlɒk]	v. 맞물리다, 연결하다
692	glaze	[gleɪz]	v. 유리를 끼우다; 유약을 칠하다 n. 유약
693	drudgery	[ˈdrʌdʒ.ər.i]	n. 고된 일 a. 힘들고 단조로운
694	priest	[priːst]	n. 성직자
695	timescale	[ˈtaɪm.skeɪl]	n. (어떤 일에 소요되는) 기간
696	hinder	[ˈhɪn.dər]	v. 가로막다, 방해하다
697	distress	[dɪˈstres]	n. 고통, 괴로움, 고뇌; 곤궁, 빈곤
698	granule	[ˈgræn.juːl]	n. 알갱이, 작은 입자
699	dissimulate	[dɪˈsɪm.jə.leɪt]	v. 숨기다, 시치미떼다, 가장하다
700	complacent	[kəmˈpleɪ.sənt]	a. 만족해 하는, 자기 만족의
701	placid	[ˈplæs.ɪd]	a. 평온한
702	naive	[naɪˈiːv]	a. 순진해 빠진, 경험이 없는
703	repress	[rɪˈpres]	v. 억제하다, 진압하다
704	commotion	[kəˈməʊ.ʃən]	n. 소요, 소동
705	refuge	[ˈref.juːdʒ]	n. 도피(처), 피난(처)
706	intrinsic	[ɪnˈtrɪn.zɪk]	a. 고유한, 본질적인, 내적인
707	digress	[daigrés]	v. 벗어나다
708	weep	[wiːp]	v. 울다, 슬퍼하다
709	forbear	[fɔːˈbeər]	v. 참다, 삼가다
710	meteor	[ˈmiː.ti.ɔːr]	n. 유성, 별똥별
711	across the table		p. 얼굴을 맞댄, 직접적인
712	ask a favor of		p. ~에게 부탁을 하다
713	in the ratio of		p. ~의 비율로
714	associate A with B		p. A를 B와 관련시키다
715	from square one		p. 처음부터
716	correspond to N		p. ~과 일치하다, ~에 상응하다
717	make at		p. ~을 향해 나아가다; 공격하다
718	speak of the devil		p. 호랑이도 제 말하면 온다
719	behave oneself		p. 바르게 행동하다, 행동을 삼가다
720	come to terms with		p. ~와 타협하다

681

rap

[ræp]

v. 가볍게 두드리다; 비난하다 a. 황홀해 하는

rapper n. 노커, 수다쟁이, 가수
raptor n. 랩터, 맹금, 육식조류
rapid a. 빠른

어원	-rap : rapere (짧은 시간 안에) 빼앗다 → '짧은 시간에 빼앗으려면 몰두해야 하는' * rap 랩(음악) → '속사포처럼 빠른 랩'
유의어	strike, knock, hit
반의어	caress, stroke, pat
영영	To strike sharply.
예문	He gave a sharp rap on the door to get their attention. 그들의 주의를 끌기 위해 문에 날카로운 두드림을 가했다.

682

aggrieve

[əˈɡriːv]

v. 고통을 주다, 괴롭히다

aggrieved a. 고통을 받은, 분개한
aggrievedly adv. 분개하여, 억울해 하며
aggress v. 공격하다, 시비를 걸다
grievance n. 불만

어원	-ag : to + -grieve 슬프게 하다 → '~를 슬프게 고통을 주다'
유의어	harm, injure, hurt
반의어	comfort, console, soothe
영영	To cause distress or suffering.
예문	He gave a sharp rap on the door to get their attention. 그들의 주의를 끌기 위해 문에 날카로운 두드림을 가했다.

683

concur

[kənˈkɜːr]

v. 의견이 일치하다

concurrent a. 동시에 일어나는
concurrence n. 동의, 일치
recur v. 재발하다, 반복되다
incur v. 초래하다

어원	-con : together + -cour, -cur : run → '의견이 동시에 나오며 일치하니 동의'
유의어	agree, coincide, coincide with
반의어	disagree, dispute, dissent
영영	To agree or coincide.
예문	He gave a sharp rap on the door to get their attention. 그들의 주의를 끌기 위해 문에 날카로운 두드림을 가했다.

684

prick

[prɪk]

v. 찌르다, 자극하다

pricky a. 가시가 많은, 성가신
pricking n. 따끔하게 찌르기
picky a. 까다로운
pungent a. 신랄한

어원	-pick, -punc, -pung : prick 찌르다 → '마음을 찌르니 자극'
유의어	puncture, jab, pierce
반의어	soothe, dull, blunt
영영	To puncture or pierce.
예문	Be careful with that cactus; its needles can prick your skin. 그 선인장을 다룰 때 조심하세요; 그것의 가시가 피부를 찌를 수 있습니다.

685

pupil

[ˈpjuːpəl]

n. 학생; 눈동자(동공)

pupilary a. 동공의, 학생의
puppet n. 꼭두각시
pure a. 순수한

어원	-pupil, -puppa 작은 아이 → '작은 아이니 유독 커보이는 동공'
유의어	student, learner, scholar
반의어	teacher, instructor, educator
영영	A student or the dark center of the eye.
예문	The teacher observed the pupil's progress in mathematics. 선생님은 학생의 수학 공부 진행 상황을 관찰했다.

686

shabby

[ˈʃæb.i]

a. 누추한, 초라한

shabbily adv. 부적절하게, 초라하게
shab n. 추잡한 것, 구두쇠
shed n. 헛간 v. 깎다
shave v. 깎다, 면도하다

어원	-shab : scab 딱지, 피부병 → '피부병으로 행색이 누추한' * -sha : shape '모양이 누추하고 초라한'
유의어	run-down, dilapidated, decrepit
반의어	stylish, elegant, chic
영영	Worn-out or run-down.
예문	The old couch in the corner looked shabby and worn. 구석에 있는 오래된 소파는 초라하고 낡아 보였다.

687

sabotage

[sǽbətàːʒ]

v. 고의로 방해하다, 파괴하다

saboteur n. 파괴 행위를 하는 사람
sabot n. 나막신

어원	-sabot 나무 신발 (F) → '나무 신발을 신고 중세 유럽 농민들이 영주의 수확물을 짓밟은 것' * 비밀리에 적의 주요 시설들을 파괴하는 것 포함
유의어	undermine, subvert, sabotage
반의어	assist, support, aid
영영	To undermine or disrupt.
예문	It was clear that someone had tried to sabotage the company's computer system. 누군가가 회사의 컴퓨터 시스템을 파괴하려고 시도한 것이 분명했다.

688

abstain

[æbˈsteɪn]

v. 삼가다, 그만두다

abstinence n. 절제
abstinent a. 절제하는
obtain v. 얻다
detain v. 억류하다

어원	-ab : away + -tain, -ten, -tin 가지다, 잡다, 담다(L) → '나를 잡고 있던 욕망을 멀리 하고 절제하니 삼가다'
유의어	refrain, withhold, avoid
반의어	indulge, partake, engage
영영	To refrain or withhold.
예문	He decided to abstain from voting on the controversial issue. 그는 논란이 되는 문제에 대한 투표를 삼가기로 결정했다.

689

puddle

[ˈpʌd.əl]

n. 웅덩이

plaque n. 판, 표지만
placard n. 공포문, 게시판

어원	-puddle 물 웅덩이 → '못된 물이 늪지던 곳' * pool 풀장보다 작은 puddle 물 웅덩이
유의어	pool, pond, small pool of water
반의어	dry, drain, evaporate
영영	A small pool of water.
예문	After the rain, there were puddles of water all over the road. 비 후에 도로 곳곳에 물 웅덩이가 있었다.

690

relish

[ˈrel.ɪʃ]

n. 맛, 즐거움 v. 즐기다

relishable a. 맛있는, 재미있는
relief n. 안도, 안심
elf n. 요정
elicit v. 이끌어 내다, 유도하다

어원	-re : again + -li : leave 놓다 → '맛의 즐거움을 놓고 다시 즐기는 모든 쾌감'
유의어	enjoy, savor, appreciate
반의어	loathe, despise, detest
영영	To enjoy or savor.
예문	She always relished the opportunity to try new and exotic foods. 그녀는 항상 새로운 이국적인 음식을 시도하는 기회를 매우 즐겼다.

691

interlock

[ˌɪn.təˈlɒk]

v. 맞물리다, 연결하다

interlocutory a. 대화의, 문답의
interlocution n. 대화, 문답, 회화
locker n. 사물함
unlock v. 잠금을 해제하다

어원	-inter : between + lock 잠그다 → '서로 잠그니 맞물리다'
유의어	intertwine, connect, mesh
반의어	disconnect, separate, unhook
영영	To connect or mesh together.
예문	The gears in the machine are designed to interlock smoothly. 기계 내의 기어는 부드럽게 서로 맞물리도록 설계되었다.

692

glaze

[gleɪz]

v. 유리를 끼우다; 유약을 칠하다 n. 유약

glazing n. 창유리; 유리 공사
glazed a. 유리로 덮인, 빛나는
glasses n. 안경
glacier n. 빙하

어원	-glass → '유리처럼 투명한 막을 바르다'
유의어	enamel, veneer, coating
반의어	uncover, reveal, expose
영영	To cover with a smooth, shiny coating.
예문	The chef used a sweet glaze to coat the pastry. 요리사는 빵에 달콤한 도금을 입혔다.

693

drudgery

[ˈdrʌdʒ.ər.i]

n. 고된 일 a. 힘들고 단조로운

drudge n. 노동자, 노예
drudgerous a. 지루하고 힘든
drag v. 질질 끌다, 끌어내다
drastic a. 격렬한, 과감한

어원	-drudg : drag along heavy → '무거운 것을 끄니 고된 일' * drug(마약)을 먹고 싶을 정도로 고된 일
유의어	toil, labor, grind
반의어	leisure, pleasure, enjoyment
영영	Tedious or unpleasant work.
예문	His job involved a lot of drudgery, with repetitive tasks and long hours. 그의 일은 반복적인 업무와 긴 근무 시간이 포함된 힘들게 느껴지는 작업을 포함하고 있었다.

694

priest

[priːst]

n. 성직자

priesthood n. 성직자, 사제
priestly a. 성직자의, 성직자적인
pray v. 기도하다
preach v. 설교하다, 전도하다

어원	-pray, -pri 기도 + -est 사람 → '기도하는 사람이 성직자'
유의어	clergyman, cleric, minister
반의어	layperson, secular, noncleric
영영	A religious leader or clergyman.
예문	The priest conducted the wedding ceremony in the church. 신부는 교회에서 결혼식을 진행했다.

695

timescale

[ˈtaɪm.skeɪl]

n. (어떤 일에 소요되는) 기간

scale n. 규모; 계급 ; 저울; 비늘

어원	-time + -scale 저울 → '시간을 저울로 재는 것처럼 소요되는 기간' * 라틴어 scala = ladder에서 유래
유의어	timeframe, schedule, timetable
반의어	instantaneous, immediate, momentary
영영	A schedule or timeframe.
예문	The timescale for completing the project was extended by two weeks. 프로젝트 완료를 위한 시간표가 2주 연장되었다.

696

hinder

[ˈhɪn.dər]

v. 가로막다, 방해하다

hindrance n. 방해, 장애물
unhindered a. 방해 없는, 제지받지 않는
behind prep. 뒤의

어원	-hin : behind → '뒤에 두고 계속 방해하다'
유의어	impede, obstruct, block
반의어	facilitate, assist, promote
영영	To impede or obstruct.
예문	Bad weather can hinder the progress of construction projects. 나쁜 날씨는 건설 프로젝트의 진행을 방해할 수 있다.

697

distress

[dɪˈstres]

n. 고통, 괴로움, 고뇌; 곤궁, 빈곤

distressful a. 고통스러운, 괴로운
distressingly adv. 괴롭게도, 고통스럽게도
strict a. 엄격한
strangle v. 목졸라 죽이다

어원	-di : away + -strict, -stress, -stig 팽팽히 누르다 → '팽팽하게 당겼던 것이 끊어진 고통'
유의어	anguish, suffering, misery
반의어	comfort, ease, solace
영영	Extreme suffering or anguish.
예문	The news of the accident caused great distress to the family. 사고 소식은 가족에게 큰 고통을 더했다.

698

granule

[ˈgræn.juːl]

n. 알갱이, 작은 입자

granular a. 알갱이 모양의, 입자상의
granulate v. 알갱이 형태로 만들다
granola n. 씨리얼
grain n. 낟알, 곡물

어원	-grain, -gran : seed 알갱이 * '그래놀라'는 씹히는 알갱이 맛이 있는 씨리얼
유의어	particle, grain, tiny piece
반의어	lump, clump, mass
영영	A small particle or tiny grain.
예문	The sugar is in the form of fine granules. 설탕은 작은 알갱이 형태로 되어 있다.

699

dissimulate

[dɪˈsɪm.jə.leɪt]

v. 숨기다, 시치미떼다, 가장하다

dissimulation n. 위장, 위선
dissimulator n. 감추는 사람
simulation n. 모의 실험, 가장
association n. 연합, 결연, 협회

어원	-dis : not + -simil, -simul : imitate → '모방하지 못하고 숨기다'
유의어	pretend, feign, dissemble
반의어	reveal, expose, unveil
영영	To hide true feelings or intentions.
예문	She tried to dissimulate her disappointment with a forced smile. 그녀는 억지 웃음으로 실망을 숨기려고 노력했다.

700

complacent

[kəmˈpleɪ.sənt]

a. 만족해 하는, 자기 만족의

complacency n. 자기만족, 만족감
complacently adv. 현실에 안주하여
placate v. 달래다
complaisant a. 공손한, 고분고분한

어원	-com : intensive + -plac, -pla : please → '완전히 즐거운'
유의어	self-satisfied, smug, content
반의어	discontented, dissatisfied, unhappy
영영	Overly self-satisfied.
예문	He became complacent after achieving his first major success. 그는 첫 번째 큰 성공을 거두고 나서 만족스러워졌다.

701

placid

[ˈplæs.ɪd]

a. 평온한

placable a. 진정시키기 쉬운
placidly adv. 평온하게, 조용하게
placate v. 달래다
complacent a. 만족스러운

어원	-plac, -pla : please → '기분 좋게 달래니 평온한'
유의어	calm, tranquil, peaceful
반의어	agitated, turbulent, disturbed
영영	Calm and peaceful.
예문	The lake was placid, reflecting the calmness of the morning. 호수는 아침의 고요함을 반영하여 차분했다.

702

naive

[naɪˈiːv]

a. 순진해 빠진, 경험이 없는

naively adv. 단순히
naivete n. 순진, 순진한 행위
natal a. 태어난, 출생의
nasty a. 끔찍한, 고약한, 더러운

어원	-na, -nat, -gna : born 낳다, 태어나다 → '태어난 아기처럼 순진한'
유의어	innocent, gullible, inexperienced
반의어	sophisticated, worldly, experienced
영영	Lacking experience or sophistication.
예문	Being so naive, she easily fell for their tricks. 너무 순진해서 그들의 속임수에 쉽게 넘어갔다.

703

repress

[rɪˈpres]

v. 억제하다, 진압하다

repression n. 억압, 저지
repressive a. 억압적인, 탄압적인
downpress v. 억압하다
depress v. 낙담시키다

어원	re : back + -press 누르다 → '뒤에서 눌러 억제하다'
유의어	suppress, control, restrain
반의어	express, release, reveal
영영	To suppress or control.
예문	He had to repress his anger and maintain a calm demeanor during the meeting. 그는 회의 중에 분노를 억누르고 침착한 태도를 유지해야 했다.

704

commotion

[kəˈmoʊ.ʃən]

n. 소요, 소동

commotional a. 소란의, 소동의
promote v. 촉진하다, 장려하다, 승진시키다
demote v. 강등하다, 강제로 내리다
make a commotion p. 소동을 일으키다

어원	-com : together + -mot : move → '함께 움직이는 소동'
유의어	turmoil, uproar, disturbance
반의어	calm, tranquility, stillness
영영	A noisy disturbance.
예문	There was a commotion in the crowd as they rushed to see the celebrity. 그 들은 유명인을 보러 달려가며 군중 속에서 소란이 있었다.

705

refuge
[ˈref.juːdʒ]

n. 도피(처), 피난(처)

refugee n. 난민, 망명자, 피난민
refuse v. 거절하다, 반대하다
refute v. 반박하다, 논박하다

어원	-re : back + -fuge 도망치다 → '뒤로 도망치는 곳이 피난처'
유의어	shelter, sanctuary, haven
반의어	exposure, vulnerability, danger
영영	A place of safety.
예문	The forest provided a refuge for many endangered species. 숲은 많은 멸종 위기에 처한 종들을 위한 피난처를 제공했다.

706

intrinsic
[ɪnˈtrɪn.zɪk]

a. 고유한, 본질적인, 내적인

intrinsicality n. 본질적인 성격, 내재성
intrinsically adv. 내재적으로, 본질적으로
intrigue n. 음모 v. 음모를 꾸미다

어원	-intrin : in + -sic : secus 본성, 본질 → '본성 안에 내재된 것이니 본질적이고 내적인'
유의어	inherent, innate, essential
반의어	extrinsic, external, acquired
영영	Essential or inherent.
예문	The beauty of the artwork lies in its intrinsic details. 이 작품의 아름다움은 내재적인 세부사항에 있다.

707

digress
[daigrés]

v. 벗어나다

digression n. 여담; 탈선
transgress v. 넘다, 벗어나다; 위반하다
regress v. 되돌아가다, 퇴행하다, 퇴보하다
aggress v. 공격하다, 시비를 걸다

어원	-di : away + -gress : go → '떨어져 가니 벗어나다'
유의어	deviate, wander, diverge
반의어	stay on topic, remain focused, stick to the point
영영	To deviate from the main topic.
예문	He tends to digress during conversations, often going off on tangents. 그는 대화 중에 주제를 벗어나기 쉽고 종종 본질에서 벗어난다.

708

weep
[wiːp]

v. 울다, 슬퍼하다

bewailingly adv. 비통해하며, 애통해하며
bewailment n. 비통, 애통
wail v. 울부짖다, 통곡하다
bewail v. 통곡하다

어원	-wa, -we : -wab 부르다, 울다, 물뿜하다 → '부르며 울부짖다' syn. wail, bewail, lament, mourn
유의어	cry, sob, shed tears
반의어	laugh, chuckle, giggle
영영	To cry or shed tears.
예문	She couldn't help but weep when she heard the sad news. 그녀는 슬픈 소식을 듣자마자 울음을 참을 수 없었다.

709

forbear
[fɔːˈbeər]

v. 참다, 삼가다

forbearance n. 삼가, 절제
forbearing a. 참을성 있는, 자제력 있는
bear v. 운반하다, 견디다; 애를 낳다 n. 곰

어원	-for : far + -bear 견디다 → '멀리하는 고통도 견디며 참다'
유의어	abstain, refrain, resist
반의어	act, indulge, engage
영영	To refrain or abstain.
예문	He had to forbear from making sarcastic comments in a serious meeting. 그는 진지한 회의에서 비꼬는 말을 하지 않아야 했다.

710

meteor
[ˈmiː.ti.ɔːr]

n. 유성, 별똥별

meteoroid n. 유성체
meteorology n. 기상학
method n. 방법, 방식; 질서
metaphor n. 은유

어원	-met, -meth, -meta 변화하는 (G) → '가만히 있지 않고 움직이는 별'
유의어	shooting star, meteoroid, celestial body
반의어	stationary object, immovable, fixed
영영	A celestial body.
예문	They saw a bright meteor streak across the night sky. 그들은 밤하늘을 가로질러 빛나는 유성을 보았다.

711

across the table

p. 얼굴을 맞댄, 직접적인

end table p. 소파 옆에 붙이는 작은 탁자
tablet n. 알약; 현판
taboo n. 금기 a. 금제의
tabor n. 작은 북

어원	-across 가로 질러 + -table 테이블 → '테이블로 가로 질러 얼굴을 맞대고'
동의어	face to face, opposite, in front of
반의어	on the same side, next to, beside
영영	On the opposite side of a table.
예문	They discussed the contract terms across the table. 그들은 계약 조건을 상대 편 테이블을 사이에 두고 논의했다.

712

ask a favor of

p. ~에게 부탁을 하다

in favor of p. ~ 제안에 찬성하는
favored a. 선호하는
favorable a. 호의적인
unfavorable a. 호의적이지 않은

어원	-ask 부탁하다 + -fav, -fev : burn → '마음이 탈 정도로 따뜻한 호의를 부탁하다'
동의어	request assistance from, seek help from
반의어	grant a favor to, assist willingly, offer help to
영영	Request assistance.
예문	She decided to ask a favor of her neighbor to help with the gardening. 정원 일을 돕기 위해 이웃에게 부탁하기로 결정했다.

713

in the ratio of

p. ~의 비율로

rating n. 평점, 등급, 평가
ratio n. 비율
at the rate of p. ~의 비율로
ration n. 배급, 배급량

어원	-rat, -reas 생각하여 평가하다[E] → '생각하여 평가하는 비율'
동의어	in proportion to, relative to, according to
반의어	out of proportion to, unevenly, disproportionately
영영	In proportion to.
예문	The ingredients should be mixed in the ratio of 2:1 for the recipe to work. 레시피가 작동하려면 재료를 2:1의 비율로 섞어야 합니다.

714

associate A with B

p. A를 B와 관련시키다

associate with p. ~와 교제하다, 사귀다
associated a. 관련된, 지지하는
association n. 연상, 연관성
dissociated v. 분리시키다

어원	-as : to + -soc 결합 + -with → '~에 일을 결부짓는 것이 연관시키다'
동의어	link A to B, connect A with B, relate A to B
반의어	disconnect A from B, separate A from B, dissociate A from B
영영	Connect A to B.
예문	Many people associate the smell of freshly baked bread with comfort and home. 많은 사람들이 따뜻함과 집을 신선하게 구운 빵의 향기와 연관시킵니다.

715

from square one

p. 처음부터

어원	-quare : quarter 4 → '4개의 동일한 변을 가진 정사각형이 출발점'
동의어	from the beginning, from scratch, starting over
반의어	from an advanced stage, from the middle, from the end
영영	From the beginning.
예문	After the computer crashed, he had to start his project from square one. 컴퓨터가 다운된 후, 그는 프로젝트를 다시 처음부터 시작해야 했다.

716

correspond to N

p. ~과 일치하다, ~에 상응하다

correspond with p. ~와 일치하다
corresponding a. 상응하는, 대응하는
correspondent n. 기자, 특파원
spontaneous a. 자발적인, 자연스러운

어원	-cor : together + -respond : 응답하다 → '서로 모두 응답하니 일치하다'
동의어	match, equate to, parallel
반의어	differ from, deviate from, disagree with
영영	Match or agree with.
예문	Your actions should correspond to your words. 당신의 행동은 당신의 말과 일치해야 합니다.

717

make at

p. ~을 향해 나아가다; 공격하다

make attempt to do p. ~하려고 노력하다
make clear p. 분명히 하다
make end meets p. 간간히 연명하다
make public p. 알리다, 공표하다

어원	-make 만들다 + -at 지점 → '공격 지점을 만들고 나아가다'
유의어	attempt, try, endeavor
반의어	abstain from, avoid, refrain from
영영	Attempt or try.
예문	She tried to make at least some progress in her studies. 그녀는 공부에서 최소한 어느 정도의 진전을 만들려고 노력했다.

718

speak of the devil

p. 호랑이도 제 말하면 온다

speak badly of p. 험담하다, 헐뜯다
spokesman n. 대변인
spear n. 창

어원	-div : deva 신 * devil 악마 → '악마도 제 말하면 온다'
유의어	mention someone who then appears, talk about someone who arrives unexpectedly
반의어	avoid mentioning someone, keep quiet about someone
영영	Mention someone who appears unexpectedly.
예문	Speak of the devil, and he shall appear. 악마에 관해 말하면 악마가 나타난다.

719

behave oneself

p. 바르게 행동하다, 행동을 삼가다

well-behaved p. 얌전한, 품행이 바른
behavior n. 행동, 처신
hay n. 건초
haven n. 항구, 정박소

어원	-be : toward, near 더 가까이 + -have : hold + -oneself → '더 가까이 두고 살게 하며 가르치니 바르게 행동하다'
유의어	conduct oneself, act appropriately, act in a socially acceptable manner
반의어	misbehave, act inappropriately, break the rules
영영	Act appropriately.
예문	He was told to behave himself during the formal dinner. 그에게 공식적인 만찬 중에는 제대로 행동하라고 했다.

720

come to terms with

p. ~와 타협하다

in terms of p. ~의 관점에서
term n. 용어, 학기
terms n. 요금; 계약, 조항, 조건
terms of the acquisition p. 인수 조항

어원	-come 이르다 + -terms 계약 + -with ~와 → '~와 계약 합의에 이르니 타협하다'
유의어	accept, reconcile with, make peace with
반의어	resist, reject, refuse
영영	Accept a difficult situation.
예문	It took her a while to come to terms with the loss of her beloved pet. 그녀는 사랑하는 애완동물의 손실을 받아들이는 데 시간이 걸렸다.

Chapter 19.

721	shrub	[ʃrʌb]	n. 가시, 관목
722	malice	[ˈmæl.ɪs]	n. 악의, 원한
723	dissonance	[ˈdɪs.ən.əns]	n. 부조화음, 불협화음, 불일치
724	penetrate	[ˈpen.ɪ.treɪt]	v. 관통하다, 침투하다
725	dormant	[ˈdɔː.mənt]	a. 휴면기의, 잠복 중인
726	pregnable	[prégnəbl]	a. 공략할 수 있는, 취약점이 있는
727	eradicate	[ɪˈræd.ɪ.keɪt]	v. 뿌리째 뽑다, 근절하다
728	prognosis	[pragnóusis]	n. 예지, 예측
729	parable	[ˈpær.ə.bəl]	n. 우화, 비유담
730	salute	[səˈluːt]	v. 경례하다, 경의를 표하다 n. 경례
731	conduce	[kənˈdʒuːs]	v. 도움이 되다, 공헌하다
732	omnibus	[ˈɒm.nɪ.bəs]	n. 승합버스
733	anomy	[ǽnəmìː]	n. 무질서
734	tidy	[ˈtaɪ.di]	a. 깔끔한, 단정한
735	turmoil	[tə́ːrmɔil]	n. 혼란, 소란
736	retrieve	[ritríːv]	v. 만회하다, 회복하다
737	irrupt	[irʌpt]	vi. 침입하다
738	impede	[ɪmˈpiːd]	v. 방해하다
739	confute	[kənˈfjuːt]	v. 논박하다
740	induce	[ɪnˈdjuːs]	v. 설득하여 ~하게 하다; 야기하다
741	nasty	[ˈnɑː.sti]	a. 끔찍한, 고약한, 더러운
742	trespass	[ˈtres.pəs]	v. 불법 침해하다
743	contingent	[kənˈtɪn.dʒənt]	a. ~을 조건으로 하는; 우연한
744	petty	[ˈpet.i]	a. 사소한, 하찮은, 옹졸한
745	timber	[ˈtɪm.bər]	n. 건축 밖 용도의 재목; 수목, 목재, 대들보
746	desist	[dɪˈsɪst]	v. 단념하다, 그만두다
747	malevolent	[məˈlev.əl.ənt]	a. 사악한
748	pervert	[pəˈvɜːt]	v. 타락시키다, 왜곡하다; 악용하다
749	despair	[dispέər]	n. 절망 v. 절망하다
750	abominate	[əˈbɒm.ɪ.neɪt]	v. 혐오하다, 증오하다
751	carbon footprint		p. 탄소 발자국
752	in a crow line		p. 가장 가까운 직선거리로
753	round the clock		p. 24시간 내내
754	collect on		p. (채무) 회수하다
755	do A up		p. A 단추를 채우다, 잠그다; 포장하다; 개조하다
756	shed light on		p. 해명하다, ~을 비추다
757	carry weight		p. 중요하게 여기다
758	in view of		p. ~을 고려하여
759	let out		p. 방출하다; 빌려주다
760	run for		p. ~에 입후보하다, 출마하다

721

shrub

[ʃrʌb]

n. 가시, 관목

shrubbery n. 관목, 키 작은 나무
shrubby a. 관목의, 관목 모양의
ambush n. 매복, 급습
shrive v. 참회시키다, 고해하다, 자백하다

어원	* -sha, -shi, -she, -sho : cut → '키가 작고 가지치기를 많이 하는 나무'
유의어	bush, shrubbery, underbrush
반의어	tree, sapling, plant
영영	A small woody plant with multiple branches.
예문	The garden was adorned with colorful shrubs and flowers. 정원은 다양한 관목과 꽃으로 장식되어 있었다.

722

malice

[ˈmæl.ɪs]

n. 악의, 원한

malicious n. 악성 a. 악의 있는, 심술궂은
maliciously adv. 악의를 가지고, 심술궂게
malefactor n. 죄인, 악인
malevolent a. 사악한

어원	-mal, -malice, malus : evil 추한, 나쁜 (L) +-ice 명접 → '나쁜 마음의 악의를 갖고 있는 원한'
유의어	spite, hatred, malevolence, animosity
반의어	goodwill, benevolence, kindness
영영	A desire to harm or ill will toward others.
예문	Her actions were driven by malice, as she tried to harm her coworker's reputation. 그녀의 행동은 악의에 기반하여, 동료의 평판을 손상시키려고 시도했다.

723

dissonance

[ˈdɪs.ən.əns]

n. 부조화음, 불협화음, 불일치

dissonant a. 조화되지 않는, 불협화의
dissonantly adv. 불협화음을 내어
consonant n. 자음
resonant a. 울리는

어원	-dis : away + -son : sound → '음이탈이 나니 불협화음이고 부조화음'
유의어	discord, disagreement, conflict, disharmony
반의어	harmony, agreement, concord
영영	Lack of harmony or agreement, often in ideas or music.
예문	The dissonance between their opinions made it difficult to reach a consensus. 그들의 의견 사이의 불화로 합의에 도달하기 어려웠다.

724

penetrate

[ˈpen.ɪ.treɪt]

v. 관통하다, 침투하다

penetration n. 관통, 침투
penetrable a. 돌파할 수 있는
penetrant n. 침입자, 침투물
penalize v. 처벌을 하다

어원	-penet : pierce into 뚫고 들어가다 → '뚫고 들어가니 관통하다' * penalty 페널티킥으로 골망을 관통
유의어	infiltrate, pierce, enter, permeate
반의어	withdraw, exit, evacuate
영영	To enter or pierce something.
예문	The sharp knife easily penetrated the soft fruit. 날카로운 칼이 부드러운 과일을 쉽게 관통했다.

725

dormant

[ˈdɔː.mənt]

a. 휴면기의, 잠복 중인

dormancy n. 휴면 상태, 잠복 상태
dormitory n. 기숙사
dormitive n. 수면제
dove n. 비둘기, 평화

어원	-dormit 잠자다 → '겨울잠을 자니 휴면기의'
유의어	inactive, latent, quiescent, asleep
반의어	active, awake, alert
형정	Inactive or temporarily not growing.
예문	During the winter, many plants go dormant and don't grow. 겨울 동안 많은 식물들이 휴면 상태에 들어가 성장하지 않는다.

726

pregnable

[prégnəbl]

a. 공략할 수 있는, 취약점이 있는

impregnable a. 난공불락의, 확고한
prehension n. 파악, 잡기, 포착
pregnant a. 임신한

어원	-preg, -prehend : grasp + -able → '잡아서 취할 수 있으니 공략할 수 있는'
유의어	vulnerable, susceptible, open to attack
반의어	impregnable, invulnerable, secure
형정	Vulnerable and easily attacked.
예문	The fortress was considered impregnable due to its high walls and strong defenses. 그 요새는 높은 벽과 강력한 방어 때문에 점령하기 어렵다고 여겨졌다.

727

eradicate

[ɪˈræd.ɪ.keɪt]

v. 뿌리째 뽑다, 근절하다

eradication n. 근절
eradicable a. 근절시킬 수 있는
eradicative a. 근절시키는
radish n. 무(뿌리 식물)

어원	-e, ex : out + -radic : root → '뿌리째 뽑으니 근절하다'
유의어	eliminate, exterminate, obliterate
반의어	preserve, protect, maintain
영영	Completely eliminate or destroy something.
예문	The government launched a campaign to eradicate the disease from the country. 정부는 그 나라에서 그 병을 근절하기 위한 캠페인을 시작했다.

728

prognosis

[pragnóusis]

n. 예지, 예측

prognostic a. 예후의 n. 예상,— 조짐
prognosticate v. ~을 예언하다, 예지하다
prognostication n. 예지, 전조, 예언
diagnose v. 진단하다

어원	-pro : before + -gno : know → '미리 아는 것이니 예지나 예측'
유의어	forecast, prediction, diagnosis, outlook
반의어	uncertainty, unpredictability, ambiguity
영영	A prediction, especially about a disease's outcome.
예문	The doctor gave a positive prognosis for the patient's recovery. 의사는 환자의 회복에 대한 긍정적인 예후를 제시했다.

729

parable

[ˈpær.ə.bəl]

n. 우화, 비유담

parabolical a. 비유담의, 우화적인
parade n. 퍼레이드, 열병, 행진
paradox n. 역설, 패러독스, 모순

어원	-para : beside 나란히 + -bl : throw → '인간과 나란한 의미를 던지는 식물 동물 이야기'
유의어	allegory, story, fable, tale
반의어	reality, fact, non-fiction
영영	A simple story teaching a moral lesson.
예문	The teacher used a parable to illustrate the importance of honesty. 선생님은 정직의 중요성을 설명하기 위해 우화를 사용했다.

730

salute

[səˈluːt]

v. 경례하다, 경의를 표하다 n. 경례

salutation n. 인사말
salubrious a. 건강에 좋은, 유익한
salubrity n. 건강함, 건강에 좋음
salud n. 건배

어원	-salut 편안한 상태 → '편안하냐고 묻는 인사가 경례'
유의어	greet, hail, welcome, acknowledge
반의어	insult, offend, disrespect
영영	A gesture expressing respect or acknowledgment.
예문	The soldier gave a crisp salute to his commanding officer. 그 병사는 지휘관에게 깔끔한 경례를 했다.

731

conduce

[kənˈdʒuːs]

v. 도움이 되다, 공헌하다

conducive a. 도움이 되는, 공헌하는
induce v. 설득하여 ~하게 하다; 야기하다
seduce v. 부추기다; 매혹시키다
conduct v. 행하다, 지휘하다

어원	-con : together + -duc : lead → '모두를 끌어가는데 도움이 되니 공헌하다'
유의어	contribute, lead to, result in, promote
반의어	hinder, obstruct, impede
영영	To contribute to a particular result.
예문	A healthy diet and regular exercise can conduce to a longer life. 건강한 식사와 규칙적인 운동은 더 긴 삶을 이끌어 낼 수 있다.

732

omnibus

[ˈɒm.nɪ.bəs]

n. 승합버스

omnipotent a. 전능한
omnivorous a. 잡식성의
omnipresent a. 편재하는, 어디에나 존재하는
omniscient a. 모든 것을 아는

어원	-omni, -omn 전부(L) + -bus → '모두 나르는 버스'
유의어	comprehensive, all-inclusive, general, inclusive
반의어	specific, limited, exclusive
영영	Comprehensive or all-inclusive.
예문	The omnibus bill contained a wide range of legislative proposals. 종합 법안은 다양한 입법 제안을 포함하고 있었다.

733

anomy

[ǽnəmìː]

n. 무질서

anomaly n. 이상, 기형, 비정상
anomalism n. 변칙, 이상
anomalously adv. 변칙적으로, 이례적으로
metronome n. 메트로놈, 박절기

어원	-a : not + -nem 율법 + -sis 명접 → '율법이 없으니 무질서' * 네메시스(Nemesis)는 그리스의 율법과 복수의 여신
유의어	lawlessness, disorder, chaos, normlessness
반의어	order, norm, stability
영영	Lawlessness or social instability.
예문	The breakdown of social norms can lead to a state of anomy in a society. 사회적 규범의 붕괴는 사회의 무질서 상태로 이어질 수 있다.

734

tidy

[ˈtaɪ.di]

a. 깔끔한, 단정한

tidy up p. ~을 깔끔하게 정리하다
tidiness n. 깔끔함
tide n. 조수(밀물과 썰물)
tiny a. 아주 작은

어원	* -tid : time → '시간이 잘 맞춰진 질서니 깔끔한'
유의어	neat, organized, orderly, clean
반의어	messy, disorganized, cluttered
영영	Neat, organized, or orderly.
예문	She always keeps her room tidy and organized. 그녀는 항상 방을 깨끗하고 정리정돈되게 유지한다.

735

turmoil

[tə́ːrmɔil]

n. 혼란, 소란

in turmoil p. 혼란에 빠진
turbulence n. 격동, 격변; 난기류
turbid a. 무질서한, 어수선한

어원	-turn → '계속 도니 혼란'
유의어	chaos, confusion, disorder, upheaval
반의어	calm, order, tranquility
영영	A state of confusion or chaos.
예문	The political turmoil in the country led to uncertainty and unrest. 그 나라의 정치적 격동으로 불확실성과 불안이 생겼다.

736

retrieve

[ritríːv]

v. 만회하다, 회복하다

retrieval n. 회복, 되찾음
retrievable a. 회복할 수 있는
retriever n. 사냥개

어원	-re : again + -triev 되찾다[F] → '다시 원래 모습을 되찾으니 만회하고 회복하다'
유의어	recover, regain, get back
반의어	relinquish, give up, surrender
영영	To recover something lost.
예문	He managed to retrieve his lost wallet after retracing his steps. 그는 자신의 분실한 지갑을 자신의 발자취를 따라 찾아냈다.

737

irrupt

[irʌpt]

vi. 침입하다

irruption n. 침입, 돌입, 난입
irruptive a. 침입하는, 관입성의
interrupt v. 방해하다, 중단하다
abrupt a. 돌연한, 갑작스러운

어원	-in : in + -rupt : break → '안으로 깨고 들어가니 침입하다'
유의어	burst in, invade, rush in, storm
반의어	retreat, withdraw, recede
영영	To burst in suddenly.
예문	The sudden irruption of laughter broke the silence in the room. 갑작스러운 웃음 소리가 방안의 침묵을 깨뜨렸다.

738

impede

[ɪmˈpiːd]

v. 방해하다

impediment n. 장애물, 방해물
impeditive a. 방해하는, 어렵게 만드는
impedancer n. 저항
impel v. 재촉하다

어원	-im, -in : in + -ped : foot → '발부터 집어 넣어 방해하다'
유의어	hinder, obstruct, block, delay
반의어	assist, facilitate, help
영영	To hinder or obstruct.
예문	Traffic congestion can impede the flow of vehicles on the highway. 교통 정체는 고속도로의 차량 흐름을 방해할 수 있다.

739

confute

[kənˈfjuːt]

v. 논박하다

confutation n. 반박, 논박
confutable a. 논파할 수 있는
confutative a. 논파하는

어원	-con : together + -fut : beat → '모든 의견을 때리니 논박하다'
유의어	refute, disprove, contradict, rebut
반의어	confirm, prove, validate
영영	To prove something false.
예문	The scientist was able to confute the previous theory with new evidence. 과학자는 새로운 증거로 이전의 이론을 반박할 수 있었다.

740

induce

[ɪnˈdjuːs]

v. 설득하여 ~하게 하다; 야기하다

induced a. ~의 원인의
inducement n. 유인, 권유, 동기
conduce v. 도움이 되다, 공헌하다
seduce v. 부추기다, 매혹시키다

어원	-In + -duc : lead → '조직 안으로 들어오도록 설득하니 위험을 야기'
유의어	cause, bring about, persuade, prompt
반의어	discourage, deter, dissuade
영영	To persuade or bring about.
예문	The warm tea helped to induce a feeling of relaxation. 따뜻한 차는 편안함을 유도하는 데 도움이 되었다.

741

nasty

[ˈnɑːsti]

a. 끔찍한, 고약한, 더러운

nastily adv. 심술궂게, 비열하게
nastiness n. 불쾌함, 악의
natal a. 태어난, 출생의
naïve a. 순진한

어원	-na, -nat, -gna : born + * -ty : dirty → '태어날 때부터 더러워 끔찍한'
유의어	unpleasant, disgusting, vile, repulsive
반의어	pleasant, agreeable, nice
영영	Unpleasant or offensive.
예문	His nasty comments upset everyone in the room. 그의 불쾌한 발언은 방 안의 모든 사람을 불안하게 했다.

742

trespass

[ˈtres.pəs]

v. 불법 침해하다

trespasser n. (가택) 침입자
impasse n. 교착, 난국, 답보
compass n. 나침반 v. 순회하다, 둘러싸다
tremendous a. 엄청난, 막대한; 멋진

어원	-tres, -trans : across + -pass → '건너서 들어가려 하니 불법 침입'
유의어	encroach, intrude, violate, transgress
반의어	obey, respect, adhere
영영	Unlawfully enter or encroach.
예문	Trespassing on private property is illegal and can result in fines. 사유지 침입은 불법이며 벌금을 부과할 수 있다.

743

contingent

[kənˈtɪn.dʒənt]

a. ~을 조건으로 하는; 우연한

contingency n. 비상사태
contingently adv. 여부에 따라, 경우에 따라
contagious a. 전염성의
contiguous a. 인접한, 연속된

어원	-con : together + -ting : touch → '다른 일에 붙어 사건에 따라 결정되니 우연한'
유의어	dependent, conditional, subject to, reliant on
반의어	definite, certain, fixed
영영	Dependent on conditions; a group with a common goal.
예문	The success of the project is contingent on securing adequate funding. 프로젝트의 성공은 충분한 자금 확보에 의존한다.

744

petty

[ˈpet.i]

a. 사소한, 하찮은, 옹졸한

pettiness n. 사소함, 하찮음
petit a. 소규모의, 작은
repetition n. 반복, 되풀이
compete v. 경쟁하다

어원	-petit : small (F) * '뽀로로'에 나오는 패티가 작은 → '작아 보이는 일이니 사소하고 하찮은'
유의어	small, trivial, minor, insignificant
반의어	significant, important, substantial
영영	Of little importance or trivial.
예문	Don't let petty disagreements ruin your friendship. 사소한 불화로 인해 친구관계가 파괴되지 않게 하라.

745

timber

[ˈtɪm.bər]

n. 건축 밖 용도의 재목; 수목, 목재, 대들보

timbered a. 목재로 만들어진, 나무로 된
timberland n., 나무거 우거진 땅, 삼림지역
lumber n. 목재, 잡동사니
timbre n. 음색, 음질

어원	-timber : tree + -trim 사르나 → '10피트 이상 되는 나무를 잘라 만든 재목' * lumber 가공하지 않은 목재
유의어	wood, lumber, logs, timberland
반의어	metal, concrete, stone
영영	Wood for construction.
예문	The carpenters used high-quality timber to build the new house. 목수들은 새 집을 지을 때 고품질 목재를 사용했다.

746

desist

[dɪˈsɪst]

v. 단념하다, 그만두다

어원	-de : stop + -sist : system 설치하다 → '설치하는 것을 멈추니 단념하다'
유의어	cease, stop, halt, abstain
반의어	continue, persist, endure
영영	To stop or cease.
예문	The protesters were asked to desist from blocking the road. 시위대에게 도로 차단을 그만두라고 요청했다.

747

malevolent

[məˈlev.əl.ənt]

a. 사악한

malevolence n. 악의, 증오, 악심
malevolently adv. 악의를 가지고, 심술궂게
malefactor n. 죄인, 악인
malfeasance n. 위법 행위

어원	-male : bad + -vol : will 의지 → '나쁜 의지를 가진'
유의어	malicious, evil, hostile, harmful
반의어	benevolent, kind, friendly
영영	Having harmful intent.
예문	The malevolent witch cast a spell on the princess. 악의적인 마녀가 공주에게 주문을 걸었다.

748

pervert

[pəˈvɜːt]

v. 타락시키다, 왜곡하다; 악용하다

perverted a. 이상의, 변태의, 그릇된
perversity n. 사악, 고집이 셈
subvert v. 전복시키다, 뒤엎다, 파괴하다
perverse a. 심술궂은, 사악한

어원	-per : 완전히 + -vers : turn → '완전히 뒤바뀐 방향으로만 가니 왜곡하고 타락시키다'
유의어	corrupt, distort, twist, deviate
반의어	uphold, preserve, protect
영영	To distort or corrupt; also, a deviant person.
예문	He was arrested for attempting to pervert the course of justice. 그는 사법 과정을 왜곡하려고 시도하여 체포되었다.

749

despair

[dispέər]

n. 절망 v. 절망하다

desperate a. 필사적인, 절실한
desperation n. 자포자기, 절망
desperate a. 절망적인, 자포자기의
desperado n. 무법자; 자포자기식의 사람

어원	-de : down + -sper, -spar, -spair 희망 → '희망을 꺼지게 하니 절망'
유의어	hopelessness, desperation, discouragement, gloom
반의어	hope, optimism, confidence
영영	A feeling of hopelessness.
예문	In moments of despair, it's important to seek support from friends and family. 절망적인 순간에는 친구와 가족의 지원을 찾는 것이 중요하다.

750

abominate

[əˈbɒm.ɪ.neɪt]

v. 혐오하다, 증오하다

abomination n. 혐오
abominable a. 혐오스러운, 혐악한
hold A in abomination v. A를 아주 싫어하다
omen n. 징조, 조짐

어원	-ab : away + -omin, -omen 징조 → '불길한 징조를 느끼고 혐오하다'
유의어	detest, loathe, hate, abhor
반의어	love, adore, cherish
영영	To intensely detest.
예문	She abominated the idea of cruelty to animals. 그녀는 동물에 대한 잔인함을 혐오했다.

751

carbon footprint

p. 탄소 발자국

carbohydrate n. 탄수화물
carbon emission p. 탄소 배출
carbonic acid p. 석탄산
charcoal n. 숯, 목탄

어원	-carb : carbon 탄소 + footprint 발자국 → '이산화탄소의 총량' * coal 석탄 → 탄소 덩어리
유의어	environmental impact, carbon emissions, ecological footprint
반의어	eco-friendly, green, sustainable
영영	Impact of carbon emissions.
예문	Calculating your carbon footprint helps you understand your environmental impact. 탄소 발자국을 계산하면 환경 영향을 이해하는 데 도움이 된다.

752

in a crow line

p. 가장 가까운 직선거리로

crew n. 승무원, 선원
crowed n. 군중
overcrowd v. 너무 많이 들이다
crown n. 왕위, 왕권

어원	-crow 까마귀 * 배가 방향을 잃었을 때 까마귀를 풀어 놓으면 육지 쪽으로 날아감
유의어	as the crow flies, directly, in a straight line
반의어	indirect, circuitous, roundabout
영영	In a straight line.
예문	The nearest store is just in a crow line from here, about a mile away. 가장 가까운 가게는 여기서 직선거리로 약 1마일 떨어져 있다.

753

round the clock

p. 24시간 내내

clone n. 복제 생물, 클론
cliff n. 절벽, 낭떠러지
close to one's heart p. ~에게 소중한
draw to a close p. 끝나가다

어원	-round 원, 주변 + -clock 시계 → '시계가 계속 원을 그리며 도니 24시간 내내
유의어	continuously, constantly, nonstop
반의어	part-time, intermittent, occasional
영영	Continuously, 24/7.
예문	The hospital provides care round the clock, 24 hours a day. 병원은 24시간 내내 365일 동안 치료를 제공한다.

754

collect on

p. (채무) 회수하다

collective a. 집단의, 단체의
collar n. 칼라, 깃, 목걸이
colleague n. 동료
elide v. 생략하다, 무시하다

어원	-col : together + -lec, -lect, -leg, -lig : gather 모으다 → '모두 한데 모으다' * -op(t) 둘 중 하나를 선택 VS -lec(t) : 보다 넓은 범위에서 취사선택
유의어	claim, demand payment, retrieve payment, collect money owed
반의어	refund, reimburse, repay
영영	Demand payment for a debt.
예문	I need to collect on the payment for the services I provided. 제공한 서비스에 대한 대금을 수금해야 한다.

755

do A up

p. A 단추를 채우다, 잠그다; 포장하다; 개조하다

that'll do p. 그거면 됐어.
do away with p. 폐지하다, 없애다
do's and don'ts p. 지켜야할 사항들
do over p. ~을 다시 하다, 꾸미다

어원	-do 하다 + -up 끝까지 → '끝까지 단추를 채우다'
유의어	renovate, refurbish, redecorate, fix up
반의어	dismantle, disassemble, take apart
영영	Renovate or decorate.
예문	They decided to do up their old house with a fresh coat of paint. 그들은 오래된 집을 새로 칠해서 개조하기로 결정했다.

756

shed light on

p. 해명하다, ~을 비추다

shabbily adv. 부적절하게, 초라하게
shab n. 추잡한 것, 구두쇠
shed n. 헛간 v. 깎다 v. 비추다
shave v. 깎다, 면도하다

어원	-shed 비추다 + -light 빛 → '빛을 비추어 밝히는 것처럼 해명하다'
유의어	clarify, illuminate, explain, reveal
반의어	obscure, cloud, confuse
영영	Provide clarification.
예문	The new documentary sheds light on the hidden history of the region. 새로운 다큐멘터리는 그 지역의 숨겨진 역사를 밝혀 준다.

757

carry weight

p. 중요하게 여기다

carry on p. 계속 수행하다
carry out p. ~을 수행하다
carry away p. 넋을 잃게 하다
miscarry v. 유산하다

어원	-carry 나르다 + -weight 무게 → '무게감을 갖고 수행하니 중요하게 여기다'
유의어	have influence, hold sway, be significant, be important
반의어	lack influence, be inconsequential, be unimportant
영영	Have influence or importance.
예문	Her opinion on the matter carries a lot of weight among the team members. 그녀의 의견은 팀원들 사이에서 많은 영향력을 가진다.

758

in view of

p. ~을 고려하여

with a view toward p. ~할 목적으로
view A as B p. A를 B로 간주하다
viewpoint n. 관점
overview n. 개요, 개관

어원	-vis, -vid : view → '보는 관점을 고려하여'
유의어	considering, taking into account, in light of, given
반의어	disregarding, ignoring, neglecting
영영	Considering a fact or circumstance.
예문	In view of recent developments, we need to revise our strategy. 최근의 발전을 고려하여, 우리는 전략을 수정해야 한다.

759

let out

p. 방출하다; 빌려주다

let down p. 기대를 저버리다
let go p. (걱정 근심 등을) 떨쳐버리다
let up p. (강도가) 약해지다
let in p. 들여보내다

어원	-let 허락하다 + -out 바깥 → '바깥으로 나가는 걸 허락하니 방출'
유의어	release, allow to leave, set free, permit to go
반의어	confine, imprison, incarcerate
영영	Release or allow to leave.
예문	The teacher will let out the students early today because of the holiday. 선생님은 오늘 휴일 때문에 학생들을 일찍 보내 줄 것이다.

760

run for

p. ~에 입후보하다, 출마하다

run away from p. ~을 피하려 하다
run behind p. ~보다 뒤떨어지다
run into p. 우연히 만나다
run out p. (시간·돈 등이) 다 되다, 다 떨어지다

어원	-run 달리다 + -for 목적 → '목적을 위해서 뛴다고 하니 입후보하다'
유의어	compete for, vie for, campaign for, seek reelection for
반의어	withdraw from, drop out, resign from
영영	Participate in a political campaign.
예문	She decided to run for public office to make a positive impact on her community. 그녀는 지역사회에 긍정적인 영향을 미치기 위해 공직에 출마하기로 결정했다.

Chapter 20.

761	vanguard	[ˈvæn.gɑːd]	n. 선봉, 선두
762	diagonal	[daɪˈæg.ən.əl]	a. 대각선의, 사선의
763	extricate	[ˈek.strɪ.keɪt]	v. 구출시키다, 탈출시키다
764	devour	[diváuər]	v. 게걸스레 먹다; 삼켜버리다; 파괴하다
765	refute	[rɪˈfjuːt]	v. ~을 논박하다, 반박하다
766	untimely	[ʌnˈtaɪm.li]	a. 제 때가 아닌; 너무 이른
767	intrigue	[ɪnˈtriːg]	v. 호기심을 불러일으키다; 모의하다 n. 음모
768	deviate	[ˈdiː.vi.eɪt]	v. 벗어나다, 빗나가다
769	horticultural	[ˌhɔː.tɪˈkʌl.tʃər.əl]	a. 원예(학)의
770	racism	[ˈreɪ.sɪ.zəm]	n. 민족 차별주의, 인종 차별
771	sanitary	[ˈsæn.ɪ.tər.i]	a. 위생의, 위생적인
772	dissect	[daɪˈsekt]	v. 해부하다, 분석하다
773	terrain	[təˈreɪn]	n. 지형, 지역, 지세
774	tremendous	[trɪˈmen.dəs]	a. 엄청난, 막대한; 멋진
775	trivial	[ˈtrɪv.i.əl]	a. 변변치 않은, 사소한
776	retract	[rɪˈtrækt]	v. 취소하다, 철회하다
777	malfunction	[mælfəˈŋkʃən]	n. 기능 불량, 오작동
778	irrigate	[ˈɪr.ɪ.geɪt]	v. 물을 대다, 관개하다
779	aggregate	[ˈæg.rɪ.gət]	v. 모으다, 모이다; 합계가 ~이 되다 n. 합계, 총액
780	abbreviate	[əbríːvièit]	v. 생략하다, 축약하다
781	contemn	[kəntém]	v. ~를 경멸하다
782	intricate	[ˈɪn.trɪ.kət]	a. 뒤얽힌, 복잡한
783	disquiet	[dɪˈskwaɪət]	v. ~을 불안하게 하다; 불안
784	placate	[pləˈkeɪt]	v. 달래다
785	breast	[brest]	n. 가슴
786	anthropology	[ˌæn.θrəˈpɒl.ə.dʒi]	n. 인류학
787	advocate	[ˈæd.və.keɪt]	v. 옹호하다, 옹호자(변호사)
788	arrogant	[ˈær.ə.gənt]	a. 거만한, 오만한
789	attorney	[əˈtɜː.ni]	n. 대리인, 변호사
790	antagonist	[æntǽgənist]	n. 적대자, 반대자
791	rule out		p. 배제하다, 제외시키다
792	be in the way		p. 방해가 되다
793	out of tune		p. 음이 맞지 않는
794	bring on		p. ~을 야기하다, 초래하다
795	come into effect		p. 효력이 발생하다
796	to the core		p. 깊숙이, 핵심까지
797	of name		p. 이름난
798	look back on		p. 회상하다
799	all at once		p. 갑자기, 동시에
800	word got around		p. 소문이 돌았다

761

vanguard

[ˈvæn.ɡɑːd]

n. 선봉, 선두

vantage n. 우세, 유리
servant n. 하인, 노예
relevant a. 관련 있는, 의의가 있는
vanity n. 허영심

어원	-vant 앞 + -guard 방어 → '앞을 방어하는 선봉이 선두'
유의어	forefront, leading edge, avant-garde
반의어	Rear, back, last
영영	The leading position in a movement, field, or group.
예문	She was at the vanguard of the feminist movement. 그녀는 여성주의 운동의 최전방에 있었습니다.

762

diagonal

[daɪˈæɡ.ən.əl]

a. 대각선의, 사선의

diagonalize v. 대각선화하다
pentagon n. 오각형
diagram n. 도표, 도해
diagnosis n. 진단

어원	-dia : across + -gon 각, 십자가(G) → '각과 각 사이를 가로지르는 대각선의'
유의어	slanting, oblique, askew
반의어	Vertical, horizontal, straight
영영	A straight line joining two opposite corners of a square, rectangle, or other straight-sided shape.
예문	Draw a diagonal line from the top left to the bottom right. 왼쪽 위에서 오른쪽 아래로 대각선을 그려보세요.

763

extricate

[ˈek.strɪ.keɪt]

v. 구출시키다, 탈출시키다

extricable a. 구출할 수 있는, 해결할 수 있는
inextricable a. 풀리지 않는, 해결할 수 없는
intrigue v. 호기심을 불러 일으키다, 모의하다
extrinsic a. 외부로부터의, 비본질적인

어원	-ex : out + -tric : perplexities → '난처한 상황에서 나오게 하니 구출'
유의어	free, liberate, disentangle
반의어	Entangle, ensnare, complicate
영영	To free or release from a difficult or tangled situation.
예문	Firefighters worked hard to extricate the trapped passengers from the wreckage. 소방대원들은 잠긴 승객들을 잔해에서 구출하기 위해 열심히 노력했습니다.

764

devour

[díváuər]

v. 게걸스레 먹다; 삼켜버리다; 파괴하다

devouring a. 게걸스레 먹는
flavour n. 풍미, 맛
voracious a. 게걸스러운
devout a. 독실한, 경건한

어원	-de : down + -vor : eat → '떨어진 음식을 게걸스럽게 먹다'
유의어	consume, gulp down, eat up
반의어	Abstain, nibble, savor
영영	To eat something hungrily and quickly.
예문	The hungry lion would devour its prey within minutes. 배고픈 사자는 먹잇감을 몇 분 내로 씹어 삼키곤 했습니다.

765

refute

[rɪˈfjuːt]

v. ~을 논박하다, 반박하다

refutation n. 논박, 반박
refutable a. 논박할 수 있는
irrefutable a. 반박할 수 없는
refuge n. 피난처

어원	-re : again + -fut : beat → '계속 말로 때리며 논박하다'
유의어	rebut, disprove, contradict
반의어	Confirm, support, affirm
영영	To prove something to be false or incorrect.
예문	The scientist presented evidence to refute the theory. 과학자는 그 이론을 반박하기 위한 증거를 제시했습니다.

766

untimely

[ʌnˈtaɪm.li]

a. 제 때가 아닌; 너무 이른

untimeliness n. 시기 상조
timely a. 적시의, 시기 적절한
tide n. 조수
overtime n. 초과 근무

어원	-un : not (E) + -timely 시기 적절한 → '시기 적절하지 않으니 시기 상조'
유의어	premature, inopportune, early
반의어	Timely, punctual, appropriate
영영	Occurring or done at an inappropriate or inconvenient time.
예문	Her untimely death shocked everyone. 그녀의 일찍 가신 죽음은 모두를 깜짝 놀라게 했습니다.

767	어원	-in + -trig : 엉키다 → '안에 뒤엉켜 있는 음모, 계략'
intrigue	유의어	plot, scheme, conspiracy
[ɪnˈtriːg]	반의어	Simplicity, straightforwardness, honesty
	영영	A secret or underhanded scheme or plot, often for political or personal gain.
v. 호기심을 불러일으키다; 모의하다 n. 음모		
intriguing a. 아주 흥미로운 intriguingly adv. 흥미롭게 intrigue against p. ~에 대해 음모를 꾸미다 intrigue the eye p. 눈을 끌다	예문	The spy's intrigue involved a complex web of espionage. 스파이의 음모는 복잡한 스파이 활동의 미묘한 망을 포함하고 있었습니다.

768	어원	-de : away + -via, vey, voy : way → '길을 멀리 벗어나다'
deviate	유의어	diverge, stray, veer
[ˈdiː.vi.eɪt]	반의어	Conform, comply, adhere
	영영	To depart from an established course or norm.
v. 벗어나다, 빗나가다		
deviant a. 벗어난, 일탈적인 deviation n. 탈선, 일탈 demerit n. 단점, 결점 devitalize v. ~의 활력을 빼앗다	예문	Try not to deviate from the original plan. 원래 계획에서 벗어나지 않도록 노력해보세요.

769	어원	-horti : hortus 정원(L) + -cultura 경작 → '정원을 경작하니 원예학의'
horticultural	유의어	gardening, cultivation, horticulture
[ˌhɔː.tɪˈkʌl.tʃər.əl]	반의어	Non-gardening, non-agricultural, urban
	영영	Relating to the art or science of cultivating gardens and plants.
a. 원예(학)의		
horticulture n. 원예학 horticulturist n. 원예가 horticulturally adv. 원예로 a host of p. 다수의	예문	He studied horticultural techniques to improve his garden. 그는 정원을 더 좋게 만들기 위해 원예 기술을 연구했습니다.

770	어원	-rad, -rac 뿌리, 혈통, 근본 / 흐름 → '뿌리 다른 인종 차별' * radish 무(뿌리 식물)
racism	유의어	racial discrimination, prejudice, bias
[ˈreɪ.sɪ.zəm]	반의어	Equality, tolerance, inclusivity
	영영	believing that one race is superior to others, leading to unfair treatment based on race.
n. 민족 차별주의, 인종 차별		
racial a. 인종의, 종족의 racist n. 인종차별주의자 radical a. 급진적인, 파괴적인 radically adv. 완전히, 철저히	예문	Society should work to eliminate racism and promote equality. 사회는 인종 차별을 없애고 평등을 촉진하기 위해 노력해야 합니다.

771	어원	-saint 건강 → '건강을 위해 위생적인'
sanitary	유의어	clean, hygienic, sterile
[ˈsæn.ɪ.tər.i]	반의어	Dirty, unclean, unsanitary
	영영	Relating to conditions affecting public health, especially as a result of cleanliness and hygiene.
a. 위생의, 위생적인		
sanitation n. 위생시설 sanitize v. 위생 처리하다 sanitizer n. 세정제, 살균제 sterilize v. 살균하다; 불임 시술을 하다	예문	It's essential to maintain sanitary conditions in a food processing facility. 식품 가공 시설에서 위생 상태를 유지하는 것이 중요합니다.

772	어원	-dis : apart + -sect : cut → '잘라서 따로 나누다'
dissect	유의어	analyze, examine, scrutinize
[daɪˈsekt]	반의어	Assemble, construct, integrate
	영영	To methodically analyze or examine something in detail.
v. 해부하다, 분석하다		
dissected a. 절개한 dissecting a. 해부의, 절개용의 dissector n. 해부자, 해부 기구 insect n. 곤충	예문	In biology class, we dissected a frog to study its anatomy. 생물 수업에서 개구리를 해부하여 해부학을 공부했습니다.

773

terrain

[təˈreɪn]

n. 지형, 지역, 지세

Mediterranean a. 지중해의
subterranean a. 지하의
territory n. 영토, 지역
extraterrestrial a. 지구 밖의, 외계의

어원	-terr : land 땅
유의어	ground, landscape, topography
반의어	Sky, air, atmosphere
영영	The physical features and nature of a tract of land.
예문	The rugged terrain of the mountain made hiking challenging. 산의 울퉁불퉁한 지형 때문에 하이킹이 어려웠습니다.

774

tremendous

[trɪˈmen.dəs]

a. 엄청난, 막대한; 멋진

tremendously adv. 엄청나게
tremble v. 떨다, 흔들리다
trendy a. 최신 유행의
trespass v. 불법 침해하다

어원	-trem 떨다 → '떨 정도로 엄청난'
유의어	enormous, colossal, gigantic
반의어	Tiny, small, minuscule
영영	Extremely large, great, or powerful.
예문	The impact of the earthquake was tremendous, causing widespread damage. 지진의 영향은 엄청난데, 광범위한 피해를 초래했습니다.

775

trivial

[ˈtrɪv.i.əl]

a. 변변치 않은, 사소한

triviality n. 하찮음
trivialize v. 하찮아 보이게 만들다
trilogy n. 3부작
trifle n. 약간 하찮은 것

어원	-tri : three + -via : way → '삼거리에 오고 가는 사람들의 하찮은 이야기' * od, ob 길 ex. obvious '길(vi=way) 위에 있는 것과 같이 명백한'
유의어	unimportant, insignificant, minor
반의어	Significant, important, crucial
영영	Of little value or importance; insignificant.
예문	Don't waste your time on trivial matters; focus on what's important. 하찮은 일에 시간을 낭비하지 마세요. 중요한 것에 집중하세요.

776

retract

[rɪˈtrækt]

v. 취소하다, 철회하다

retractioni n. 철회
detract v. 떨어뜨리다, 손상시키다
distract v. 산만하게 하다
distribute v. 분배하다, 배포하다

어원	-re : back + -tract : draw → '다시 의견을 가져가니 취소하고 철회하다'
유의어	withdraw, take back, revoke
반의어	Extend, prolong, maintain
영영	To withdraw or take back something that has been said or done.
예문	The newspaper had to retract its false story and issue an apology. 신문은 거짓 기사를 철회하고 사과를 발표해야 했습니다.

777

malfunction

[mælfəˈŋkʃən]

n. 기능 불량, 오작동

malfunctioning a. 제 기능을 발휘하지 않는
dysfunction n. 악기능, 역기능
functions n. 함수
functionally a. 직무상, 기능상

어원	-mal : bad(L) +-fun : feasance 이행 * dysfunction 치명적 고장 VS malfunction 덜 치명적 고장
유의어	failure, breakdown, glitch
반의어	Function, work, operate
영영	A failure or defect in a machine or system.
예문	The malfunction of the computer caused a delay in the project. 컴퓨터의 고장으로 인해 프로젝트가 지연되었습니다.

778

irrigate

[ˈɪr.ɪ.geɪt]

v. 물을 대다, 관개하다

irrigation n. 관개 수로
irrigable a. 물을 댈 수 있는
irrigative a. 관개의
irritate v. 짜증나게 하다

어원	-ir, -in : into + -rig, -riv : water → '안으로 물을 대는 것이 관개'
유의어	water, hydrate, moisten
반의어	Dehydrate, dry, drain
영영	To supply water to land or crops to help growth, typically using pipes or channels.
예문	Farmers use irrigation systems to water their crops. 농부들은 농작물을 관개하기 위해 관개 시스템을 사용합니다.

779

aggregate

[ˈæg.rɪ.gət]

v. 모으다, 모이다; 합계가 ~이 되다 n. 합계, 총액

aggregation n. 집합, 집성
aggregative a. 집합하는; 사교적인
aggregately adv. 모두 합하여
aggregates n. 골재

어원	-ag : to + -greg : flock 무리짓다 → '떼지어 모이다', '모이는 숫자가 합계'
유의어	total, combine, accumulate
반의어	Separate, disperse, distribute
영영	To collect or gather into a mass or whole; a total or sum.
예문	The aggregate sales figures for the month reached a new record. 이번 달의 누적 판매량은 새로운 기록을 세웠습니다.

780

abbreviate

[əbríːvièit]

v. 생략하다, 축약하다

abbreviation n. 생략, 단축
breviate v. 요약하다, 축약하다
breviary n. 기도문서
briefing n. 브리핑

어원	-ab : to + -brev : short → '짧게 만들려고 축약하고 생략하다' cf. briefing(브리핑) : 간단한 정보를 전달하는 회의
유의어	shorten, condense, truncate
반의어	Elongate, extend, expand
영영	To shorten or condense a word or phrase.
예문	Please abbreviate the long names in the document. 문서에서 긴 이름들을 축약해 주세요.

781

contemn

[kəntém]

v. ~를 경멸하다

contempt n. 경멸, 멸시
contemptible a. 경멸할 만한
contemptuous a. 경멸하는, 업신여기는
temper n. 성질

어원	-con : intensive + -temn : despise → '매우 경시하며 경멸'
유의어	despise, scorn, disdain
반의어	Respect, admire, esteem
영영	To treat with contempt; despise.
예문	It's not right to contemn others based on their appearance or background. 외모나 배경에 따라 다른 사람들을 멸시하는 것은 올바르지 않습니다.

782

intricate

[ˈɪn.trɪ.kət]

a. 뒤얽힌, 복잡한

trick n. 속임수
intricacy n. 복잡한 일
intrinsic a. 고유한, 본질적인
extrinsic a. 외부로부터의 비본질적인

어원	-in : in + -tric, -trig : obstacle → '장애물이 많아 복잡한'
유의어	complex, complicated, convoluted
반의어	Simple, straightforward, uncomplicated
영영	Very complicated or detailed; having many interconnected parts.
예문	The intricate design of the artwork impressed the viewers. 작품의 복잡한 디자인은 관람객들을 감동시켰습니다.

783

disquiet

[dɪˈskwaɪət]

v. ~을 불안하게 하다; 불안

disquietude n. 불안함
disquieting a. 불안한
disquietingly adv. 불안하게
disrupt v. 붕괴시키다, 방해하다

어원	-dis : away + -quiet 평온한 → '평온함에서 거리가 멀어지게 하니 불안하게 하다'
유의어	disturb, unsettle, agitate
반의어	Calm, peace, tranquility
영영	A feeling of anxiety or unease; to make someone feel uneasy or anxious.
예문	The disquiet in the city grew as the protests continued. 시내에서 시위가 계속되면서 불안함이 커져갔습니다.

784

placate

[pləˈkeɪt]

v. 달래다

placable a. 달래기 쉬운, 달랠 수 있는
placation n. 진정시킴, 회유
complacent a. 만족해 하는, 자기 만족의
placid a. 평온한

어원	-plac, -pla : please → '기분 좋게 달래다'
유의어	appease, pacify, mollify
반의어	Provoke, aggravate, incite
영영	To make someone less angry or hostile by making concessions or soothing gestures.
예문	He offered an apology to placate his upset friend. 그는 분노한 친구를 달래기 위해 사과를 했습니다.

785

breast

[brest]

n. 가슴

breastfeed v. 모유 수유하다
breaststroke n. 접영
blast n. 돌풍, 센 바람
blister n. 물집, 수포, 발포

어원	-blizzard, -blast : bhle, bhel : blow, swell → '바람이 들어간 것처럼 부푼 가슴'
유의어	chest, bosom, bust
반의어	Back, rear
영영	The front part of a person's body between the neck and the stomach; also, a woman's mammary gland.
예문	She held her baby close to her breast. 그녀는 아기를 가슴에 가까이 끌어안았습니다.

786

anthropology

[ˌæn.θrəˈpɒl.ə.dʒi]

n. 인류학

anthropologist n. 인류학자
anthropological a. 인류학의
anthropologist n. 인류학자
anterior a. 이전의

어원	-anthrop 사람, 인류 + -logy 학문 → '인류를 연구하는 학문'
유의어	study of humanity, social science, ethnology
반의어	Zoology, geology, physics
영영	The scientific study of humanity, including its origins, behavior, and cultures.
예문	Anthropology explores the diversity of human cultures and societies. 인류학은 인간 문화와 사회의 다양성을 탐구합니다.

787

advocate

[ˈæd.və.keɪt]

v. 옹호하다, 옹호자(변호사)

advocacy n. 지지, 옹호 변호
advocacy group p. 시민 단체
evoke v. 불러 일으키다, 환기시키다
revoke v. ~을 취소하다, 무효로 하다

어원	-ad : to + -voc, -vok, -vow : voice 목소리 → ~를 향한 목소리니 옹호하다 * provoke '앞에서 소리를 쳐서 상대방을 자극하여 화나게 하다'
유의어	champion, support, endorse
반의어	Oppose, protest, object
영영	To publicly support or recommend a particular cause, policy, or action.
예문	She was a strong advocate for environmental protection. 그녀는 환경 보호를 강력하게 지지하는 사람이었습니다.

788

arrogant

[ˈær.ə.gənt]

a. 거만한, 오만한

arrogance n. 오만, 거만, 자만
arrogantly adv. 거만하게
arrogate v. 침해하다, 가로채다, 사칭하다
interrogate v. 심문하다, 조사하다

어원	-ar : to + -rog : ask → '남의 것을 강제로 요구하니 거만한' * 'arrow(화살)을 잘 쏘니 거만한'
유의어	haughty, conceited, proud
반의어	Humble, modest, meek
영영	Having an exaggerated sense of one's own importance or abilities; showing excessive pride.
예문	His arrogant attitude made it difficult to work with him. 그의 거만한 태도로 인해 그와 일하기 어려웠습니다.

789

attorney

[əˈtɜː.ni]

n. 대리인, 변호사

attorn v. 양도하다
attribute v. ~탓으로 돌리다
atttribute A to B b. A를 B탓으로 돌리다
attire v. 옷을 차려 입히다

어원	-at : to + -torn : turn → '대신 일을 수행하도록 하는 사람'
유의어	lawyer, counsel, legal representative
반의어	Client, defendant, plaintiff
영영	A person legally appointed to act on behalf of another, typically in legal matters.
예문	The attorney will represent you in court. 변호사가 법정에서 당신을 대표할 것입니다.

790

antagonist

[æntǽgənist]

n. 적대자, 반대자

antagonism n. 적의, 적대감
antagonistic a. 적대적인, 적대하는
antagonistically adv. 반대하여
agony n. 고통

어원	-anti : against + -agon : struggle → '반대편에서 싸우는 적대자'
유의어	adversary, opponent, foe
반의어	Ally, supporter, friend
영영	A person or character who opposes or is in conflict with the protagonist in a story or situation.
예문	In the story, the antagonist opposes the main character. 이 이야기에서 악역은 주인공에게 반대합니다.

791	어원	-rul, -rule 다스리다 + -out 벗어난 → '다스림에서 벗어나게 하나 배제하다'
rule out	유의어	exclude, eliminate, dismiss
	반의어	Include, consider, allow
p. 배제하다, 제외시키다	영영	To eliminate as a possibility; to exclude.
rule out of p. ~에서 제외시키다 rule out foul play p. 부정 행위를 하다 rule out any possibility p. 어떤 가능성도 배제하다	예문	Let's rule out any possible errors before drawing conclusions. 결론을 내리기 전에 가능한 모든 오류를 제외해 봅시다.

792	어원	-in 안 + -the way 길 → '길 안에 뭔가 있으니 방해가 되다'
be in the way	유의어	obstruct, hinder, impede
	반의어	Assist, facilitate, support
p. 방해가 되다	영영	To obstruct or hinder someone or something.
all the way p. 줄곧, 내내 make one's way p. 나아가다 in a big way p. 대규모로	예문	Your backpack is in the way; please move it. 가방이 방해가 되고 있어요. 제발 옮겨 주세요.

793	어원	-out of 벗어난 + -ton, -tun : sound 소리 (L) → '톤이 벗어나니 음이 맞지 않는'
out of tune	유의어	off-key, dissonant, discordant
	반의어	In tune, harmonious, melodious
p. 음이 맞지 않는	영영	Not in harmony or not working correctly.
tone n. 음색; 어조, 말투 tune out p. ~을 듣지 않다 tune in p. 귀 기울이다, ~을 이해하다 tune in to p. ~에 맞추다	예문	The guitar sounds out of tune; it needs to be tuned. 기타가 튜닝이 안 맞는 것 같아요. 조율이 필요합니다.

794	어원	-bring 가져오다 + -on : about → '~에 관한 사건을 가져오니 야기하다'
bring on	유의어	induce, provoke, cause
	반의어	Prevent, stop, deter
p. ~을 야기하다, 초래하다	영영	To cause or initiate something, often negative.
bring A to bear p. A에 집중하다 bring oneself to p. ~할 마음이 생기다 bring to the table p. ~을 제공하다, 제시하다 bring up p. 기르다, 교육하다	예문	The spicy food always brings on a craving for cold water. 매운 음식은 항상 차가운 물을 원하게 만듭니다.

795	어원	-come to 이르다 + -effect 결과 → '결과에 이르렀으니 효력을 발생하다'
come into effect	유의어	take effect, start, begin
	반의어	Expire, end, terminate
p. 효력이 발생하다	영영	To become operational or start having an impact.
in effect p. 사실상; 유효한 effective a. 효과적인 effectively adv. 유효하게, 효과적으로 go into effect p. 시행되다	예문	The new law will come into effect next month. 새로운 법은 다음 달에 효력을 발휘합니다.

796	어원	-cord, -cour, -cor : heart 마음, 심장 → '심장처럼 가장 중요한 핵심'
to the core	유의어	thoroughly, completely, entirely
	반의어	Superficially, partly, incompletely
p. 깊숙이, 핵심까지	영영	Completely, thoroughly, in every respect.
hard core p. 핵심적인 accord v. 일치하다, 조화되다 in accord with p. ~와 부합하여, 일치하여 encore n. 앙코르	예문	She is dedicated to her job to the core. 그녀는 직업에 완전히 헌신하고 있습니다.

797

of name

p. 이름난

nameless a. 이름 없는
namely adv. 다시 말해서, 즉
nameplate n. 명찰; 표찰, 문패
namesake n. 동명인

어원	-name 이름
유의어	named, titled, called
반의어	Nameless, unnamed, anonymous
영영	Titled or bearing a specific name.
예문	The book is of the name 'The Adventures of Sherlock Holmes.' 이 책의 이름은 '셜록 홈즈의 모험'입니다.

798

look back on

p. 회상하다

look after p. 돌보다
be on the lookout for p. ~을 찾고 있다
look over p. 전체를 훑어보다
look through p. ~을 훑어보다

어원	-look 보다 + -back 뒤 → '뒤돌아 보며 회상하다'
유의어	reminisce, recall, remember
반의어	Forget, disregard, ignore
영영	To recall or reflect upon past events or experiences.
예문	As I look back on my childhood, I have fond memories. 어린 시절을 회상하면 나에겐 좋은 추억들이 있습니다.

799

all at once

p. 갑자기, 동시에

for this once p. 이번만은
once and again p. 여러 번 되풀이하여
once and for all p. 최종적으로
let alone p. ~은 고사하고

어원	all(모든 것이) at once(즉시) 나오니 갑자기, 동시에
유의어	simultaneously, suddenly, instantly
반의어	Gradually, sequentially, one by one
영영	Simultaneously or suddenly.
예문	The unexpected news hit us all at once. 예상치 못한 소식이 우리 모두에게 동시에 전해졌습니다.

800

word got around

p. 소문이 돌았다

word of mouth p. 구두의, 말로 전하는
wording n. 표현(법), 용어
foreword n. 머리말
wordsmith n. 문장가, 카피라이터

어원	-word 말, 단어 (E) + -get around 돌아다니다 → '말이 도는 걸 보니 소문이 났다'
유의어	information spread, news circulated, rumor went out
반의어	Conceal, keep secret, hide
영영	Information or news spread among people.
예문	Word got around that they were getting married. 그들이 결혼한다는 소문이 돌았습니다.

Chapter 21.

801	impoverish	[impɑ́vəriʃ]	v. 가난하게 하다, 고갈시키다
802	despise	[dɪˈspaɪz]	v. 경멸하다
803	transient	[ˈtræn.zi.ənt]	a. 무상한, 일시의, 덧없는; 단기 투숙객, 부랑자
804	imperil	[impérəl]	v. 위태롭게 하다
805	resonant	[rézənənt]	a. 울리는, 울려 퍼지는
806	univocal	[juːnívəkl]	a. 뜻이 하나인, 모호하지 않은
807	interpret	[ɪnˈtɜː.prɪt]	v. 통역하다, 해석하다, 이해하다, 설명하다
808	expedient	[ikspíːdiənt]	a. 편리한, 편의의
809	ornament	[ɔ́ːrnəmənt]	n. 장식품
810	branch	[bræntʃ]	n. 나뭇가지; 지점, 지사
811	coincide	[ˌkəʊ.ɪnˈsaɪd]	v. 동시에 일어나다; 일치하다
812	precedent	[ˈpres.ɪ.dənt]	n. 선례, 판례, 전례
813	depreciate	[dipríːʃièit]	v. 가치를 떨어뜨리다
814	meteorology	[ˌmiː.ti.əˈrɒl.ə.dʒi]	n. 기상학
815	clarify	[ˈklær.ɪ.faɪ]	v. 명확하게 하다, 정화하다
816	cohere	[kouhíər]	v. 붙다, 응집하다; 일관성있다
817	transcribe	[trænˈskraɪb]	v. 베끼다, 필기하다
818	con	[kan]	n. 속임수; 사기 v. 사기를 치다
819	cohabit	[kənvóuk]	v. 동거하다, 양립하다
820	dislodge	[dɪˈslɒdʒ]	v. 빼내다, 쫓아내다
821	behold	[bɪˈhəʊld]	v. 보다, 바라보다
822	benumb	[binʌm]	v. 무감각하게 하다, 얼게 하다
823	intangible	[ɪnˈtæn.dʒə.bəl]	a. 무형의; 모호한
824	mislead	[ˌmɪsˈliːd]	v. 현혹시키다, 속이다
825	engulf	[ɪnˈgʌlf]	v. 삼켜버리다
826	transcend	[trænsénd]	v. 넘다, 초월하다
827	constellation	[ˌkɒn.stəˈleɪ.ʃən]	n. 별자리, 성좌; 모임
828	misplace	[ˌmɪsˈpleɪs]	v. 잘못 놓다, 잊어버리다 n. 불운, 불행
829	convoke	[kənvóuk]	v. 불러 모으다, 소집하다
830	converge	[kənˈvɜːdʒ]	v. 한 곳에 모이다
831	status quo		p. 현상 유지
832	be equal to N		p. ~와 동일하다
833	jump the queue		p. 새치기하다
834	in a bid to do		p. ~하기 위하여, ~을 겨냥하여
835	while away		p. 시간을 보내다
836	hold one's tongue		p. 입을 다물다
837	call A in question		p. A를 의심하다
838	too much for		p. ~을 감당하기에 너무한
839	go on errands		p. 심부름하다
840	by no means		p. 결코 ~이 아닌

801

impoverish

[impάvəriʃ]

v. 가난하게 하다, 고갈시키다

pauperism n. 가난한 삶, 빈곤
pauperize v. 가난하게 만들다
pauperization n. 가난화, 빈곤화
poverty n. 가난

어휘	-im, -in : in + -pover : poor → '가난에 들어가도록 고갈시키다'
유의어	Deplete, drain, exhaust
반의어	Enrich, prosper, wealthify
영영	To make someone or something poor or destitute.
예문	The war impoverished many people in the country. 전쟁은 그 나라의 많은 사람들을 가난하게 만들었다.

802

despise

[dɪˈspaɪz]

v. 경멸하다

inspect v. 검사하다, 조사하다
suspect v. 의심하다; 용의자
despond vi. 낙심하다
conspicuous a. 눈에 띄는, 현저한

어휘	-de : down + -spi : look → '밑으로 내려다보며 경멸하다'
유의어	Detest, loathe, abhor
반의어	Admire, respect, esteem
영영	To have a strong feeling of dislike or contempt for someone or something.
예문	She despises people who are lazy. 그녀는 게으른 사람들을 경멸한다.

803

transient

[ˈtræn.zi.ənt]

a. 무상한, 일시의, 덧없는; 단기 투숙객, 부랑자

transience n. 일시적임, 무상
transition n. 변천, 전이
transitory a. 일시의, 순간의
transit n. 통과, 횡단

어휘	-tran, -trans : across + -i, it : go → '건너서 획 지나가니 일시적인'
유의어	Fleeting, temporary, brief
반의어	Permanent, lasting, enduring
영영	Something that is temporary or short-lived, not lasting.
예문	His happiness was transient. 그의 행복은 일시적이었다.

804

imperil

[impérəl]

v. 위태롭게 하다

implore v. 애원하다, 간청하다
peril n. 위험(성)
extemporize v. 즉흥적으로 하다
extension n. 확장, 연장

어휘	-im, -in : in + -peril 위험 → '위험에 빠지게 하니 위태롭게 하다'
유의어	Endanger, jeopardize, risk
반의어	Protect, safeguard, secure
영영	To put someone or something in danger or at risk.
예문	The reckless driving imperiled the lives of others. 무모한 운전은 다른 사람들의 생명을 위태롭게 했다.

805

resonant

[rézənənt]

a. 울리는, 울려 퍼지는

dissonant a. 조화되지 않는, 불협화의
dissonantly adv. 불협화음을 내어
consonant n. 자음
sonata n. 소나타(이탈리아어)

어휘	-re : again + -son 소리 (L) → '다시 소리가 나는 것이니 울리는'
유의어	Vibrant, reverberating, echoing
반의어	Muted, quiet, silent
영영	Producing a deep, clear, and continuous sound; also, having a strong impact or influence.
예문	The sound of the church bells was resonant in the night air. 교회의 종소리는 밤 공기 속에서 울려 퍼졌다.

806

univocal

[ju:nívəkl]

a. 뜻이 하나인, 모호하지 않은

unisex a. 남겨 공통의
unitable a. 결합할 수 있는
unity n. 단일, 통일체
reunification n. 재결합

어휘	-uni, -una : an, one 하나(L) + -voc : speak '말할 때 뜻이 하나여서 모호하지 않은'
유의어	Unambiguous, clear, unequivocal
반의어	Ambiguous, vague, unclear
영영	Having only one possible meaning; unambiguous.
예문	His univocal message was clear to everyone. 그의 명백한 메시지는 모두에게 분명했다.

807

interpret

[ɪnˈtɜː.prɪt]

v. 통역하다, 해석하다, 이해하다, 설명하다

interpreter n. 통역관
interpretation n. 통역, 해석, 이해
misinterpretation n. 오해
interlock v. 맞물리다, 연결하다

어원	-inter : between + -pret : price → '사이에서 가격을 정하는 해석이 통역'
유의어	Explain, elucidate, construe
반의어	Misinterpret, misunderstand, misrepresent
영영	To explain the meaning of something, often in a specific context.
예문	The teacher interpreted the student's drawing. 선생님은 학생의 그림을 해석해주었다.

808

expedient

[ikspíːdiənt]

a. 편리한, 편의의

expedite v. 신속하게 처리하다
expediency n. 실용성 효율성
expeditionary a. 탐험의, 원정의
pedestrian n. 보행자

어원	-ex : out + -ped, patch : foot → '족쇄로 옥죄는 발을 밖으로 빼서 편한'
유의어	Pragmatic, practical, advantageous
반의어	Inconvenient, impractical, disadvantageous
영영	A convenient and practical means to achieve a specific purpose.
예문	The government's decision to raise taxes was expedient. 세금 인상을 결정한 정부의 결정은 편의주의적이었다.

809

ornament

[ɔ́ːrnəmənt]

n. 장식품

ornate a. 많이 꾸며진, 과하게 갖춘
ornamental a. 관상용의
adorn v. 꾸미다, 장식하다
adorable a. 사랑스러운

어원	-orn 새 깃털; 꾸미다, 갖추다 + -ment 명접 → '새 깃털처럼 화려하게 꾸민 장식품'
유의어	Decoration, embellishment, adornment
반의어	Eyesore, eyesore, blemish
영영	An attractive decoration or embellishment.
예문	The Christmas tree was ornamented with lights and decorations. 크리스마스 트리는 조명과 장식으로 꾸며졌다.

810

branch

[brænʧ]

n. 나뭇가지; 지점, 지사

branches n. 지조
branch off p. 갈라지다, 다른 길로 접어들다
branch out p. 시작하다; 가지가 나오다
bracnh off in all directions p. 사방으로 갈라지다

어원	* -bra : brace 팔 → '나무의 팔처럼 생긴 나뭇가지'
유의어	Offshoot, division, subsidiary
반의어	Main, trunk, root
영영	A division or offshoot of something larger, such as a tree or organization.
예문	The bank has many branches in different cities. 은행은 여러 도시에 많은 지점을 가지고 있다.

811

coincide

[ˌkəʊ.ɪnˈsaɪd]

v. 동시에 일어나다; 일치하다

coincide with p. ~와 부합하다, 일치하다
coincidence n. 우연의 일치
coincident a. 일치하는, 동시에 일어나는
adhere v. 부착하다, 고수하다

어원	-co, -com : together + -in : upon + cid : fall → '같이 위로 동시에 떨어지는 일'
유의어	Align, synchronize
반의어	Differ, conflict, disagree
영영	To happen at the same time or to align in terms of events or positions.
예문	My birthday and my sister's birthday coincide. 내 생일과 여동생의 생일은 같다.

812

precedent

[ˈpres.ɪ.dənt]

n. 선례, 판례, 전례

precede v. ~보다 먼저 일어나다
unprecedented a. 선례 없는, 전례 없는
precedence n. 우선(함)
cease to do p. ~이 아니게 되다

어원	-pre, -pri : before (L) + -cede, -ceed, -cess,- ceas : go → '먼저 가서 겪으니 선례'
유의어	Example, model
반의어	Break, deviation, anomaly
영영	An earlier event or decision that serves as an example or guide for future actions.
예문	The court's decision set a precedent for future cases. 법원의 판결은 향후 사건들에 대한 선례가 되었다.

813

depreciate

[diprí:ʃièit]

v. 가치를 떨어뜨리다

depreciation n. 가치 절하
depreciative a. 경멸적인, 비하하는
depreciator n. 비평하는 사람, 경멸하는 사람
appreciate v. 진가를 인정하다

어원	-de : down + -ap : to + -prec, -pric, -priz : price 가격(L) → '어떤 것의 가치를 인정할 줄 모르니 가치를 떨어뜨리다'
유의어	Devalue, diminish, decrease in value
반의어	Appreciate, increase in value, rise
영영	To decrease in value over time.
예문	The value of the currency depreciated against the dollar. 통화 가치가 달러 대비 하락했다.

814

meteorology

[ˌmiː.ti.əˈrɒl.ə.dʒi]

n. 기상학

meteorological a. 기상학의
meteoroid n. 유성체
method n. 방법, 방식; 질서
metaphor n. 은유

어원	-met, -meth, -meta 변화하는 (G) + -logy 학문 → '가만히 있지 않고 움직이는 별을 보고 기상 관측'
유의어	Weather science, atmospheric science, climatology
반의어	Geology, biology, astronomy
영영	The study of the Earth's atmosphere and weather.
예문	Meteorology is the study of the atmosphere and weather. 기상학은 대기와 날씨를 연구하는 학문이다.

815

clarify

[ˈklær.ɪ.faɪ]

v. 명확하게 하다, 정화하다

clarity n. 명확성, 깨끗함
clarifying n. 정화
clarify one's position p. 입장을 분명히 하다
declare v. 단언하다, 공언하다

어원	-clar : clean + -fy : make → '깨끗하게 만드는 것이 명확하게'
유의어	Elaborate, elucidate, explain
반의어	Confuse, obscure, complicate
영영	To make something clear or easier to understand.
예문	The manager clarified the rules of the game. 매니저는 게임의 규칙을 명확하게 설명했다.

816

cohere

[kouhíər]

v. 붙다, 응집하다; 일관성있다

coherence n. 부착(성), 응집(성)
coherent a. 일관된, 융통성이 있는
cohesive a. 단결된, 화합하는
cohesiveness n. 응집성

어원	-co, -com : together + -her, -here, -hes : cling, stick → '서로 붙어 있는'
유의어	Stick together, adhere, bond
반의어	Disperse, scatter, separate
영영	To stick or hold together in a unified way.
예문	The ideas in the report do not cohere well. 보고서의 아이디어는 일관성이 없다.

817

transcribe

[trænˈskraɪb]

v. 베끼다, 필기하다

transcript n. 필사, 사본
transcription n. 복사, 녹음
transcend v. 넘다, 초월하다
transact v. 취급하다, 거래하다

어원	-tran, -trans : beyond + -scrib, -script : write → '넘겨 본 것으로 쓰니 베끼다'
유의어	Record, copy, document
반의어	Delete, erase, obliterate
영영	To write down or type out a copy of spoken or written material.
예문	She transcribed the speech from the recording. 그녀는 녹음된 연설을 베껴 적었다.

818

con

[kan]

n. 속임수; 사기 v. 사기를 치다

contrast n. 대조, 대비
in contrast p. 대조적으로
pros and cons p. 찬반양론, 장단점

어원	-contra : against + -st : stand → '반대 입장에 서서 사기를 치다'
유의어	Swindle, deceive, trick
반의어	Honest, fair, upright
영영	To deceive or trick someone, often for personal gain.
예문	The con artist tricked people out of their money. 사기꾼은 사람들을 속여 돈을 빼앗았다.

819

cohabit

[kənvóuk]

v. 동거하다, 양립하다

cognate a. 동족의, 친족의
congnition n. 인식
cohere v. 동거하다, 양립하다
cohesion n. 응집력

어원	-co : together + -habit 살다 → '같이 사니 동거하다'
유의어	Live together, coexist, reside together
반의어	Separate, disperse, part ways
영영	To live together in the same residence, typically referring to unmarried couples.
예문	They have been cohabiting for five years. 그들은 5년째 동거하고 있다.

820

dislodge

[dɪˈslɒdʒ]

v. 빼내다, 쫓아내다

lodging n. 숙박
lodgings n. 하숙집
lobby n. 로비
loom v. 어렴풋이 보이다, 다가오다

어원	-dis : away + -lodge 머무르다 → '머무르는 이들을 멀리 쫓아내다'
유의어	Remove, eject, oust
반의어	Secure, fasten, fix in place
영영	To forcibly remove or displace from a position or location.
예문	The firefighters were able to dislodge the car from the tree. 소방관들은 나무에 박힌 차를 빼낼 수 있었다.

821

behold

[bɪˈhəʊld]

v. 보다, 바라보다

beholden a. 신세를 진, 은혜를 입은
beholder n. 구경꾼
behead v. 목 베다, 참수하다
on behalf of p. ~을 대표하여, ~을 대신하여

어원	-be : completely + -hold 유지하다 → '온전히 관심을 갖고 바라보다'
유의어	See, witness, observe
반의어	Ignore, overlook, disregard
영영	To see or observe something, often with a sense of wonder or amazement.
예문	I beheld a beautiful sunset over the ocean. 나는 바다 위로 아름다운 일몰을 보았다.

822

benumb

[binʌm]

v. 무감각하게 하다, 얼게 하다

numb a. 감각이 없는, 멍한
numbness n. 무감각함, 마비
number n. 숫자
denumber v. 제거하다, 수를 뺏다

어원	-be : make + -numb 부감각한 → '무감각하게 만들다' * numb(-num : take → '놈(num)한테 감각을 빼앗겨 멍한')
유의어	Numb, paralyze, stun
반의어	Stimulate, invigorate, awaken
영영	To make someone or something numb or insensitive.
예문	The cold weather benumbed my fingers. 추운 날씨에 손가락이 마비되었다.

823

intangible

[ɪnˈtæn.dʒə.bəl]

a. 무형의; 모호한

intact a. 완전한, 손상되지 않은
contingent a. 우연한
entire a. 전체의, 완전한
intergrate A with B p. A와 B를 통합시키다

어원	-in : not + -tang : touch + -ible 할 수 있는 → '만질 수 없으니 무형의'
유의어	Insubstantial, immaterial, non-physical
반의어	Tangible, concrete, physical
영영	Something that cannot be touched or physically perceived; often refers to abstract concepts.
예문	The intangible benefits of exercise include improved mood and reduced stress. 운동의 무형적인 이점으로는 향상된 기분과 스트레스 감소가 있다.

824

mislead

[ˌmɪsˈliːd]

v. 현혹시키다, 속이다

misleading a. 잘못된 인식을 주는
misnomer n. 틀린 이름
misplace v. 잘못 놓다, 잊어버리다
misrepresent v. 잘못 말하다, 거짓 설명하다

어원	-mis : wrong + -lead 이끌다 → '잘못 이끌어 현혹시키다'
유의어	Deceive, misinform, misguide
반의어	Guide, direct, inform
영영	To give someone incorrect or false information, leading them to believe something that is not true.
예문	The advertisement misled consumers into thinking the product was better than it actually was. 광고는 소비자들이 제품이 실제보다 더 좋다고 오해하게 만들었다.

825

engulf

[ɪnˈgʌlf]

v. 삼켜버리다

guts n. 배짱, 용기
gutless a. 소심한, 용기 없는
gutted a. 내부가 파괴된, 갈아엎힌
gutter 배수구, 하수구

어원 * -en : in + -gu : gut 장
→ '장 안에 음식을 넣으니 삼켜버리다'

유의어 Swallow, consume, immerse
반의어 Release, free, liberate

영영 To completely surround or immerse something.

예문 The fire engulfed the entire building.
불이 건물 전체를 집어삼켰다.

826

transcend

[trænsénd]

v. 넘다, 초월하다

transcendent a. 초월적인, 탁월한
transcendental a. 초월한, 뛰어난
transcendentalism n. 초월주의
transaction n. 거래; 처리

어원 -tran, -trans : beyound + -scend : climb
→ '넘어서 오르니 초월하다'

유의어 Surpass, exceed, go beyond
반의어 Fall short of, lag behind, be inferior to

영영 To go beyond the limits or boundaries of something.

예문 The artist's work transcends the boundaries of traditional art.
예술가의 작품은 전통적인 예술의 경계를 초월한다.

827

constellation

[ˌkɒn.stəˈleɪ.ʃən]

n. 별자리, 성좌; 모임

stella a. 별의
satellite n. 위성, 인공위성
asteroid n. 소행성; 불가사리

어원 -con : together + -stella : star
→ '별들이 모여있는 별자리 모임'

유의어 Configuration, arrangement, pattern
반의어 Disarray, disorder, chaos

영영 A group of stars forming a recognizable pattern in the sky.

예문 The constellation Orion is visible in the winter sky.
겨울철 하늘에서는 오리온자리가 보인다.

828

misplace

[ˌmɪsˈpleɪs]

v. 잘못 놓다, 잃어버리다 n. 불운, 불행

misleading a. 잘못된 인식을 주는
misnomer n. 틀린 이름
mislead v. 현혹시키다, 속이다
misrepresent v. 잘못 말하다, 거짓 설명하다

어원 -mis : bad + -place : put
→ '잘못 위치를 잡아 잃어버리다'

유의어 Lose, mislay
반의어 Locate, find, keep track of

영영 To lose or put something in the wrong location.

예문 I misplaced my keys and can't find them.
열쇠를 잃어버려서 찾을 수가 없어요.

829

convoke

[kənvóuk]

v. 불러 모으다, 소집하다

advocacy n. 지지, 옹호 변호
invocation n. 기도, 기원
evoke v. 불러 일으키다, 환기시키다
revoke v. ~을 취소하다, 무효로 하다

어원 -con : together + -vok, -voc : call
→ '모두 불러 모으다'

유의어 Summon, call, assemble
반의어 Cancel, adjourn, disband

영영 To call together or summon for a meeting or assembly.

예문 The president convoked the emergency meeting.
대통령은 긴급 회의를 소집했다.

830

converge

[kənˈvɜːdʒ]

v. 한 곳에 모이다

verge on v. ~에 가까워지다, 근접하다
on the verge of p. 의 직전에
verge n. 가장자리, 길가
diverge v. 갈라지다; 다르다

어원 -con : together + -verg : incline
→ '모두 한 곳으로 뜻이 기우니 한 곳으로 모이다'

유의어 Meet, intersect, come together
반의어 Diverge, separate, move apart

영영 To come together or meet at a common point.

예문 The lines converge at the point.
선들이 그 지점에서 모인다.

831

status quo

p. 현상 유지

status n. 상태, 지위, 자격, 신분
statue n. 상, 조각상
stature n. 키, 신장
steeep a. 가파른

어원	-stat : stand → '서 있는 상태를 유지'
유의어	Existing state, current situation, the way things are
반의어	Change, alteration, transformation
영영	The existing state or condition of things; the current situation.
예문	The workers voted to maintain the status quo. 노동자들은 현상 유지를 찬성하는 투표를 했다.

832

be equal to N

p. ~와 동일하다

eqaully adv. 마찬가지로, 동시에
eqaulize v. 동등하게 하다
inequality n. 불평등, 불공평
equation n. 방정식, 등식

어원	-equ, -equi, -ident : same 같은(L)
유의어	Match, correspond to, be equivalent to
반의어	Differ from, fall short of, not match N
영영	To be of the same value or amount as N.
예문	This machine is equal to any other machine in the market. 이 기계는 시장에 있는 다른 어떤 기계와도 동등하다.

833

jump the queue

p. 새치기하다

queue-jumping p. 새치기
queue up for a bus p. 줄지어 버스를 기다리다
queuejumper n. 새치기하는 사람
queer a. 기묘한, 괴상한

어원	jump 뛰어 들다 + -queue 줄 → '줄 사이에 뛰어드니 새치기하다'
유의어	Cut in line, skip ahead, bypass others in a line
반의어	Wait one's turn, stand in line, queue up
영영	To skip ahead in a line or queue without waiting one's turn.
예문	Don't jump the queue. You have to wait your turn. 새치기 하지 마세요. 순서를 기다려야 합니다.

834

in a bid to do

p. ~하기 위하여, ~을 겨냥하여

bid n. 입찰; v. 값을 매기다; 명령하다
bidder n. 가격 제시자
forbid v. 금하다
abide v. 참다, 머무르다

어원	-bid : 입찰 → '~하기 위하여 입찰하다'
유의어	In an effort to, with the aim of, to achieve
반의어	Without trying to, without attempting to
영영	In an attempt to or with the goal of achieving a particular objective.
예문	The company reduced its prices in a bid to increase sales. 회사는 매출을 늘리기 위한 노력으로 가격을 인하했다.

835

while away

p. 시간을 보내다

whilst c. ~하는 동안에
meanwhile adv. 그 동안에
worthwhile a. 가치 있는
awhile adv. 잠시, 잠깐

어원	-while ~동안에 + -away 떨어져 → '~동안에 현실과 떨어져 시간을 보내다'
유의어	Pass, spend, occupy (time)
반의어	Be productive, make the most of, utilize (time)
영영	To pass the time idly or in an enjoyable manner.
예문	She while away her time reading books. 그녀는 책을 읽으며 시간을 보낸다.

836

hold one's tongue

p. 입을 다물다

get hold of p. ~을 구하다, 손에 넣다
hold A in check p. A를 억제하다
hold on p. 붙잡고 있다, 잠시만
hold out p. ~을 내밀다

어원	-hold 잡다 + tongue 혀 → '혀를 잡고 입을 다물다'
유의어	Stay silent, keep quiet, refrain from speaking
반의어	Speak up, voice one's opinion, express oneself
영영	To remain silent or refrain from speaking.
예문	I held my tongue when I saw the mistake. 나는 실수를 봤을 때 침묵했다.

837

call A in question

p. A를 의심하다

call after p. ~을 따라 이름짓다
call back p. ~을 취소하다
call A into question p. A에게 의의를 제기하다
call off p. 취소하다, 중지하다

어원	-call 말하다 + -question 의문 → '의문을 갖고 말하니 으시ㅣㅁ하다'
유의어	Challenge, doubt, question the validity of A
반의어	Accept A unquestioningly, believe A without doubt
영영	To doubt or question the validity or truth of A.
예문	Some people called the president's decision in question. 일부 사람들은 대통령의 결정에 이의를 제기했다.

838

too much for

p. ~을 감당하기에 너무한

much of a p. 대단한
too much like hard work p. 손이 많이 가는
too much of a good thing p. 좋은 것도 한 두번

어원	-much, -major, -master, -mayor, -magni, -majes, -maxim : great → '너무 부담이 큰'
유의어	Overwhelming for, too difficult for, more than can be handled by
반의어	Manageable for, within one's capabilities, not overwhelming for
영영	Overwhelming or too difficult for.
예문	The task was too much for me to do alone. 그 일은 혼자서 감당하기에는 너무 힘들었다.

839

go on errands

p. 심부름하다

errand of mercy p. 고통을 덜어 주는 여행
errand agency p. 심부름대행업
fool's errand p. 헛걸음, 헛고생

어원	-go 가다 + - errand 심부름 → '심부름 가다'
유의어	Run errands, do chores, perform tasks outside the home
반의어	Stay at home, rest, relax
영영	To run short tasks or chores outside the home.
예문	I have to go on errands for my mother. 어머니 심부름을 가야 해요.

840

by no means

p. 결코 ~이 아닌

by means of p. ~에 의하여, ~의 도움으로
by the time p. ~할 즈음에
by the same token p. 같은 이유로
by chance p. 어쩌다가, 우연히

어원	-no + -means 수단 → '어떤 수단도 쓰지 않으니 결코 ~이 아닌'
유의어	Absolutely not, under no circumstances, not at all
반의어	Definitely, certainly, absolutely
영영	Absolutely not, under no circumstances.
예문	By no means should you give up your dream. 결코 꿈을 포기해서는 안 된다.

Chapter 22.

841	undue	[əndu¹]	a. 어울리지 않는, 지나친, 과도한; 불법의, 부당한
842	proceeds	[ˈprəʊ.siːdz]	n. 수익금
843	analogy	[ənælədʒi]	n. 유추, 유사성; 비유
844	ramp	[ræmp]	n. 경사로, 램프 v. 덤벼들다; 달려들다
845	immerse	[imə́ːrs]	v. 잠기게 하다, 담그다; 몰두시키다
846	transaction	[trænˈzæk.ʃən]	n. 처리, 취급; 거래, 매매
847	rejuvenate	[ridʒúːvənèit]	v. 다시 활기를 띠게 하다
848	disembodied	[ˌdɪs.ɪmˈbɒd.id]	a. 현실에서 유리된, 실체 없는
849	impracticable	[ɪmˈpræk.tɪ.kə.bəl]	a. 실행 불가능한, 다닐 수 없는
850	extrinsic	[ikstrínsik]	a. 외부로부터의, 비본질적인
851	comprehensive	[ˌkɒm.prɪˈhen.sɪv]	a. 포괄적인, 함축적인
852	evade	[ɪˈveɪd]	v. 피하다, 벗어나다
853	deplore	[diplɔ́ːr]	v. 한탄하다, 비판하다
854	transparent	[trænˈspær.ənt]	a. 투명한;솔직한; 명쾌한, 이해하기 쉬운
855	recession	[rɪˈseʃ.ən]	n. 불황, 침체, 불경기, 후퇴, 위기
856	intimidate	[intímədèit]	v. 위협하다, 협박하다
857	restrain	[rɪˈstreɪn]	v. ~을 억누르다, 억제하다
858	perverse	[pəˈvɜːs]	a. 외고집의, 심술궂은, 사악한
859	averse	[əˈvɜːs]	a. 싫어하는
860	pervade	[pərvéid]	v. ~에 온통 퍼지다, 가득차다
861	embark	[ɪmˈbɑːk]	v. 승선하다; 기업에 투자하다
862	overhaul	[ouˈvərhɔɪl]	v. 점검하다; 따라잡다
863	pragmatic	[prægmǽtik]	a. 실용적인
864	unassuming	[əˌnəsuˈmiŋ]	a. 잘난체 하지 않는, 겸손한
865	dissemble	[disémbl]	v. 숨기다, 가장하다
866	indelicate	[indélikət]	a. 조잡한, 천한
867	lumber	[ˈlʌm.bər]	n. 잡동사니; 목재; 느릿느릿 움직이다
868	revoke	[rivóuk]	v. ~을 취소하다, 무효로 하다
869	evoke	[ɪˈvəʊk]	v. 불러일으키다, 환기시키다
870	patent	[ˈpeɪ.tənt]	v. 특허를 받다 n. 특허, 특허권
871	cannot too		p. 아무리 ~해도 지나치지 않다
872	not so much A as B		p. A라기 보다는 B
873	at the mercy of		p. ~에 좌우되어, ~에 마음대로 되어
874	in pledge		p. 담보로
875	in the interests of		p. ~을 위해
876	sit out		p. ~이 끝나기를 기다리다; (활동에서) 빠지다
877	in no way		p. 결코 ~하지 않다
878	exact to the life		p. 실물 그대로의
879	be down on		p. ~을 싫어하다
880	hold good		p. 유효하다

841

undue

[əndu']

a. 어울리지 않는, 지나친, 과도한; 불법의, 부당한

due to p. ~때문에
duly adv. 정식으로, 정당하게
duty free p. 면세의
undue influence p. 부당 압박

어원	-un : not + due 책임 → '책임을 넘겨 지나치니 불법'
유의어	Excessive, unwarranted, unjustifiable.
반의어	Justified, Appropriate
영영	More than necessary or appropriate.
예문	She faced undue criticism for her actions. 그녀는 그녀의 행동에 대해 과도한 비판을 받았다.

842

proceeds

['prəʊ.siːdz]

n. 수익금

proceed v. 진행하다
procedure n. 절차; 방법
proclivity n. 경향, 기질
processor n. 처리기, 처리장치

어원	-pro : forth + -cess, -ced, -ceed : go → '앞으로 가기 위해 진행하니 판매 수익까지'
유의어	Earnings, income, revenue, profits.
반의어	Expenses, Losses
영영	Money obtained from an event or activity.
예문	The proceeds from the charity event will go to a good cause. 자선 행사의 수익금은 좋은 목적에 기여될 것이다.

843

analogy

[ənǽlədʒi]

n. 유추, 유사성; 비유

analogical a. 유추적인
analogous a. 유사한
analogize v. 유추하다
elocution n. 웅변술

어원	-ana 위 + -log : speech → '원래 개념 위에서 하는 말이니 유추와 비유'
유의어	Comparison, similarity, likeness, correlation.
반의어	Dissimilarity, Unlikeness
영영	A comparison between two things for explanation.
예문	He used an analogy to explain the complex scientific concept. 그는 복잡한 과학 개념을 설명하기 위해 유사성을 사용했다.

844

ramp

[ræmp]

n. 경사로, 램프 v. 덤벼들다; 달려들다

rampage n. 난동
rampant a. 사납게 날뛰는
rampantly adv. 난폭하게
rampart n. 누벽, 성벽

어원	-ramp 경사로; 동물이 웅크렸다 달려드는 모습
유의어	Incline, slope, gradient, ascent.
반의어	Decline, Downturn
영영	An inclined surface or slope.
예문	The wheelchair-accessible ramp made it easier for people with disabilities to enter the building. 휠체어 이용자용 경사로는 장애인들이 건물에 들어가기 더 쉬워졌다.

845

immerse

[imə́ːrs]

v. 잠기게 하다, 담그다; 몰두시키다

immersive n. 몰입, 본능
immersive technology p. 몰입 기술
immersion n. 몰입, 몰두
merge v. 합병하다, 융합하다

어원	-im, -in : in + -mers : dip → '~안에 잠기게 하니 담그다'
유의어	Submerge, soak, engross, involve deeply.
반의어	Emerge, Surface
영영	To involve oneself deeply in a particular activity or interest.
예문	She likes to immerse herself in a good book on the weekends. 주말에 좋은 책에 몰두하는 것을 좋아한다.

846

transaction

[trænˈzæk.ʃən]

n. 처리, 취급; 거래, 매매

transact v. 취급하다, 거래하다
transcript n. 필사, 사본
transcription n. 복사, 녹음
transcend v. 넘다, 초월하다

어원	-tran, -trans : across + -act → '의견이 오가며 거래 후 행동으로 처리'
유의어	Deal, exchange, trade, negotiation.
반의어	Non-deal, Inaction
영영	An instance of buying or selling.
예문	The financial transaction was completed smoothly. 금융 거래는 원활하게 완료되었다.

847

rejuvenate

[ridʒúːvənèit]

v. 다시 활기를 띠게 하다

juvenile a. 젊은
rejuvenation n. 회춘, 회복
subjuvene a. 어린, 미성숙한
prejuvenescence n. 청소년기 이전

어원	-re : again + -juven : young → '다시 젊은 시절 활기를 띠게 하다'
유의어	Renew, revitalize, refresh, regenerate.
반의어	Age, Wither
영영	To make someone or something look or feel younger or more lively.
예문	A relaxing vacation can rejuvenate your mind and body. 편안한 휴가는 마음과 몸을 활기차게 만들 수 있다.

848

disembodied

[ˌdɪs.ɪmˈbɒd.id]

a. 현실에서 유리된, 실체 없는

antibody n. 항체
embody v. 구체화 하다; 포함하다
embodiment n. 구체화, 형상화
reembody v. 재구성하다

어원	-dis : away + -em, -en : in + -body 실체 → '~안에 실체를 만든 것과 거리가 머니 실체 없는'
유의어	Incorporeal, ethereal, ghostly, spirit-like.
반의어	Incarnate, Embodied
영영	Separated from or existing without a body.
예문	The disembodied voice on the phone made her feel uneasy. 전신이 없는 전화 상의 목소리가 그녀를 불안하게 만들었다.

849

impracticable

[ɪmˈpræk.tɪ.kə.bəl]

a. 실행 불가능한, 다닐 수 없는

impractical a. 실용적이지 않는, 비현실적인
put into practice p. ~을 실행에 옮기다
progmatic a. 실용적인

어원	-in : not + -prac, -pract 꾸준히 하다 (G) → '꾸준히 하지 않으면 실행 불가능한'
유의어	Infeasible, unworkable, unattainable, impossible.
반의어	Feasible, Practical
영영	Not feasible or practical to do.
예문	Crossing the river at this point is impracticable due to the strong current. 강한 흐름 때문에 이 지점에서 강을 건너는 것은 실행하기 어렵다.

850

extrinsic

[ikstrínsik]

a. 외부로부터의, 비본질적인

extricable a. 구출할 수 있는, 해결할 수 있는
extricate v. 구출시키다, 탈출시키다
inextricable a. 풀리지 않는, 해결할 수 없는
intrigue v. 모의하다

어원	-extrin : ouside + -sic : following → '바깥에서 따라오니 외부로부터'
유의어	External, outward, foreign, unrelated.
반의어	Intrinsic, Inherent
영영	Not part of the essential nature of someone or something; coming from the outside.
예문	His motivation was extrinsic, as he was only doing it for the reward. 그의 동기는 외부적이었으며 보상을 위해서만 그 일을 했다.

851

comprehensive

[ˌkɒm.prɪˈhen.sɪv]

a. 포괄적인, 함축적인

comprehend v. 이해하다
comprehension n. 이해, 이해력
comprehensible a. 이해할 수 있는
apprehend v. 체포하다, 이해하다

어원	-com : together + -prehen, -pren, -pregn, -pris : seize → '모든 개념을 잡았으니 포괄적으로 이해'
유의어	Thorough, complete, all-encompassing, exhaustive.
반의어	Limited, Narrow
영영	Complete and including everything that is necessary.
예문	The report provides a comprehensive analysis of the company's financial performance. 이 보고서는 회사의 재무 성과에 대한 포괄적인 분석을 제공한다.

852

evade

[ɪˈveɪd]

v. 피하다, 벗어나다

invasion n. 침략
pervade v. ~에 온통 퍼지다, 가득차다
vapor n. 증기
vapid a. 맛이 없는; 지루한

어원	-e, ex : out + -vad : go → '상황 밖으로 피하다'
유의어	Avoid, elude, escape, dodge.
반의어	Confront, Face
영영	Escape or avoid, especially by cleverness or trickery.
예문	He tried to evade answering the difficult question. 그는 어려운 질문에 대답을 회피하려고 했다.

853

deplore

[diplɔ́ːr]

v. 한탄하다, 비판하다

implore v. 애원하다, 간청하다
peril n. 위험(성)
extemporize v. 즉흥적으로 하다
extension n. 확장, 연장

어원	-de : intensive + -plor : weep, cry 울다, 외치다 → '너무 슬프게 울며 한탄하다'
유의어	Condemn, lament, regret, bemoan.
반의어	Praise, Celebrate
영영	To feel or express strong disapproval of something.
예문	Many people deplore the violence in the city and call for peace. 많은 사람들이 도시의 폭력을 비난하고 평화를 요구한다.

854

transparent

[trænˈspær.ənt]

a. 투명한;솔직한; 명쾌한, 이해하기 쉬운

transparence n. 투명, 명백
transparency n. 투명성, 투명도
translucent a. 반투명의
apparent a. 또렷한, 명백한

어원	-trans : through + -par : appear → '투과시켜 보이니 투명한'
유의어	Clear, see-through, obvious, lucid.
반의어	Opaque, Hidden
영영	Allowing light to pass through so that objects can be distinctly seen.
예문	The glass is transparent, allowing you to see through it clearly. 유리는 투명하며 명확하게 그 뒤를 볼 수 있다.

855

recession

[rɪˈseʃ.ən]

n. 불황, 침체, 불경기, 후퇴, 위기

recess n. 휴식; 후미진 곳
recessive a. 지배되지 않은
process v. 처리하다, 진행하다
recede v. 물러나다; 희미해지다

어원	-re : back + -cede, -cess : go → '뒤에 후미진 곳으로 후퇴하는 것 같은 침체'
유의어	Economic downturn, slump, decline, depression.
반의어	Boom, Growth
영영	A period of temporary economic decline.
예문	The economic recession led to job losses and financial difficulties for many people. 경기 침체로 많은 사람들이 일자리를 잃고 재정적 어려움을 겪었다.

856

intimidate

[intímədèit]

v. 위협하다, 협박하다

timid a. 겁 많은, 소심한
timidity n. 소심함
intimidation n. 위협, 협박
timbre n. 음색

어원	-in : make + -timid : fear → '겁 먹게 만드니 위협하다'
유의어	Bully, frighten, threaten, coerce.
반의어	Comfort, Reassure
영영	Frighten or overawe someone, especially to make them do what one wants.
예문	His aggressive behavior was meant to intimidate others. 그의 공격적인 행동은 다른 사람들을 위협하기 위한 것이었다.

857

restrain

[rɪˈstreɪn]

v. ~을 억누르다, 억제하다

constrain v. 강제하다, 억제하다
restraint n. 억제, 제지
distrain v. 압류하다
refrain v. 그만두다, 삼가다

어원	-re : against + -strain, -string, -stric : draw tight → '대항해서 팽팽히 당기며 억누르다'
유의어	Control, inhibit, limit, hold back.
반의어	Release, Liberate
영영	Prevent someone or something from doing something; keep under control.
예문	She had to restrain her anger in the meeting. 그녀는 회의에서 분노를 억제해야 했다.

858

perverse

[pəˈvɜːs]

a. 외고집의, 심술궂은, 사악한

perversity n. 외고집
perversely adv. 비뚤어져, 뒤틀려, 뒤집혀서
pervert v. 타락시키다, 왜곡하다
subvert v. 전복시키다, 뒤엎다, 파괴하다

어원	-per : 완전히 + -vers : turn → '완전히 뒤바뀐 방향으로만 가니 외고집이고 심술궂은'
유의어	Stubborn, contrary, wayward, obstinate.
반의어	Compliant, Obedient
영영	Showing a deliberate desire to behave in an unreasonable or unacceptable way.
예문	His perverse sense of humor often offended people. 그의 비뚤어진 유머 감각은 종종 사람들을 불쾌하게 했다.

859

averse

[ə'vɜːs]

a. 싫어하는

avert v. (불행한 일을) 피하다, 막다
aversion n. 혐오, 반감, 기피
vertigo n. 현기증
subvert v. 전복시키다, 뒤집다

어원	-ad : to + -verse : turn → '반대로 돌려 말하니 싫어하는'
유의어	Reluctant, unwilling, disinclined, resistant.
반의어	Keen, Enthusiastic
영영	Having a strong dislike of or opposition to something.
예문	She is averse to taking risks in her investments. 그녀는 투자에서 리스크를 감수하기를 싫어한다.

860

pervade

[pərvéid]

v. ~에 온통 퍼지다, 가득차다

pervation n. 충만; 보급
pervasive a. 넘치는
invasion n. 침략
evanescent a. 사라지는, 덧없는

어원	-per 완전히 통해서 (L) + -vad : go → '사방으로 퍼져가는'
유의어	Permeate, saturate, fill, spread throughout.
반의어	Vacate, Leave
영영	(of a quality) to be present and apparent throughout.
예문	The aroma of freshly baked bread pervaded the entire kitchen. 막 만들어진 빵의 향기가 부엌 전체에 스며들었다.

861

embark

[ɪm'bɑːk]

v. 승선하다; 기업에 투자하다

embark on p. ~에 나서다
embed v. 꽂아 넣다, 깊이 박다
emanate v. 발산하다, 방출하다
emaciate v. 여위게 하다

어원	-em, -en : in + -bark 돛단배 → '돛단배 안에 탔으니 승선'
유의어	Begin, commence, start, initiate.
반의어	Disembark, Withdraw
영영	Begin a course of action, especially one that is important.
예문	They are about to embark on a long journey around the world. 그들은 세계 일주 장기 여행을 떠나려고 하고 있다.

862

overhaul

[ou'vərhɔ‚l]

v. 점검하다; 따라잡다

haulage n. 운송, 운반
hauling n. 끌어당기기, 운반
haul v. 끌다, 운반하다
hale v. 잡아끌다

어원	-over : above + -haul : drag 잡아 끌다 → '너머까지 운반하여 따라잡다'
유의어	Revamp, renovate, modernize, refurbish.
반의어	Neglect, Ignore
영영	Take apart in order to examine and repair if necessary.
예문	The mechanic had to overhaul the engine to get the car running again. 차를 다시 작동시키려면 정비사가 엔진을 오버홀해야 했다.

863

pragmatic

[prægmætik]

a. 실용적인

pragmatism n. 실용주의
pragmatize v. 현실화하다, 합리화하다
pragmatically adv. 실용적으로
put into practice p. ~을 실행에 옮기다

어원	-prac, -pract 꾸준히 하다 (G) → '꾸준히 하니 실제적이고 실용적인 능력이'
유의어	Practical, realistic, sensible, practical-minded.
반의어	Idealistic, Impractical
영영	Dealing with things sensibly and realistically in a way that is based on practical rather than theoretical considerations.
예문	His pragmatic approach to problem-solving often yielded effective solutions. 그의 실용적인 문제 해결 방식은 종종 효과적인 해결책을 낳았다.

864

unassuming

[ə‚nəsu'miŋ]

a. 잘난체 하지 않는, 겸손한

assume v. ~인 체하다, 가정하다
assumedly adv. 아마
presume v. 가정하다, 추측하다
resume v. 다시 시작하다; n 이력서

어원	-un : not + -assume ~인 체하다 → '가진 척 하지 않으니 겸손한'
유의어	Modest, humble, unpretentious, low-key.
반의어	Pretentious, Arrogant
영영	Not pretentious or arrogant; modest.
예문	Despite his talent, he remained unassuming and humble. 그의 재능에도 불구하고 그는 겸손하고 주제넘지 않았다.

865	어원	-dis : away + -semble : seen → '원래의 이미지와 떨어져 보이는'
dissemble	유의어	Pretend, feign, hide, mask.
[disémbl]	반의어	Reveal, Disclose
v. 숨기다, 가장하다	영영	Conceal or disguise one's true feelings or beliefs.
ensemble n. 앙상블, 합창 resemble v. 닮다, 비슷하다 assemble v. 모으다; n. 조립 resent v. ~에 분개하다, 원망하다	예문	He tried to dissemble his true intentions, but we could see through his lies. 그는 진정한 의도를 감추려고 했지만, 우리는 그의 거짓말을 희미하게 볼 수 있었다.

866	어원	-in : not + -delicate 우아한 → '우아하지 못하니 거칠고 상스러운'
indelicate	유의어	Vulgar, crude, impolite, offensive.
[indélikət]	반의어	Tactful, Sensitive
a. 조잡한, 천한	영영	Lacking in sensitivity or good taste.
delicately adv. 정교하게, 섬세하게 delicacy n. 섬세함 delicious a. 맛있는 delight n. 기쁨, 즐거움	예문	Making indelicate jokes in a formal setting is considered inappropriate. 정식 행사나 격식 있는 상황에서 무례한 농담을 하는 것은 부적절하다.

867	어원	-lumber 목재, 잡동사니 * timber 건축 가공 재목
lumber	유의어	Timber, wood, logs, lumberyard.
['lʌm.bər]	반의어	Glide, Move Smoothly
n. 잡동사니; 목재; 느릿느릿 움직이다	영영	Move in a slow, heavy, awkward way.
timbered a. 목재로 만들어진, 나무로 된 timberland n., 나무거 우거진 땅, 삼림지역 lumbar a. 요추의 timbre n. 음색, 음질	예문	The lumber was used to build a new house. 목재는 새 집을 짓는 데 사용되었다.

868	어원	-re : back + -voke : call → '반대편을 외치니 취소하다'
revoke	유의어	Annul, cancel, rescind, withdraw.
[rivóuk]	반의어	Reinstate, Uphold
v. ~을 취소하다, 무효로 하다	영영	Put an end to the validity or operation of a decree, decision, or promise.
advocacy n. 지지, 옹호 변호 convoke v. 불러 모으다, 소집하다 provoke v. 자극하여 화나게 하다 invoke v. 빌다, 기원하다	예문	The judge decided to revoke the defendant's bail. 판사는 피고인의 보석을 철회하기로 결정했다.

869	어원	-e : out + -voc, -vok, -vow : voice 목소리 / call 부르다 → '밖으로 특정한 사람이나 목적을 위하여 목소리를 낸다'
evoke	유의어	Summon, elicit, bring forth, evoke emotions.
[ɪ'vəʊk]	반의어	Suppress, Quell
v. 불러일으키다, 환기시키다	영영	Bring or recall a feeling, memory, or image to the conscious mind.
advocacy n. 지지, 옹호 변호 advocacy group p. 시민 단체 provoke v. 자극하여 화나게 하다 revoke v. ~을 취소하다, 무효로 하다	예문	The movie's soundtrack was designed to evoke strong emotions in the audience. 영화의 사운드트랙은 관객들에게 강한 감정을 불러일으키도록 디자인되었다.

870	어원	-patent : open 공개(L) → '내 기술임을 공개' * 14세기 영국의 국왕은 특허권을 부여할 때 개봉된 상태로 수여
patent	유의어	Copyright, intellectual property, exclusive right, trademark.
['peɪ.tənt]	반의어	Hidden, Secret
v. 특허를 받다 n. 특허, 특허권	영영	Easily recognizable; obvious.
patented a. 개인이나 그룹에 의해 창안된 patently adv. 명백히, 틀림없이 patents n. 전용권, 독점권 patentable a. 특허를 받을 수 있는	예문	He received a patent for his innovative invention. 그는 그의 혁신적인 발명품에 대한 특허를 받았다.

871

cannot too

p. 아무리 ~해도 지나치지 않다

cannot but do p. ~하지 않을 수 없다
cannot enough p. 아무리 ~해도 부족하다
cannot bear to p. 차마 ~할 수 없다
cannot away with p. ~을 참을 수 없다

어원	-cannot 할 수 없다 + -too 너무 → '너무 ~해도 할 수 없으니 지나치지 않다'
유의어	Cannot emphasize enough, cannot stress enough.
반의어	Can Only Just, Barely Can
영영	Expresses the impossibility of overdoing something.
예문	You cannot too carefully consider your options before making a decision. 결정하기 전에 선택사항을 지나치게 신중하게 고려해야 한다.

872

not so much A as B

p. A라기 보다는 B

and so on p. 등등
not so much as p. ~조차 않다
so far p. 지금까지
so so p. 그저 그렇다

어원	not so much A(A까지 많지는 않으니) B
유의어	More B than A, not primarily A but B.
반의어	More A than B
영영	Used to express that B is more applicable or relevant than A.
예문	His success was not so much due to luck as it was to hard work and dedication. 그의 성공은 행운보다는 열심히 일하고 헌신적이었기 때문이었다.

873

at the mercy of

p. ~에 좌우되어, ~에 마음대로 되어

in mercy p. 불쌍히 여겨, 봐주어
merchant n. 상인
commerce n. 상업, 무역

어원	-marc, -merc : reward / trade + -y 명접 → '보상을 베푸니 이에 의해 좌우되어'
유의어	Vulnerable to, under the control of, subject to.
반의어	Independent of, Free from
영영	Completely in the power or under the control of someone or something.
예문	The sailors were at the mercy of the stormy sea. 선원들은 폭풍 바다의 자비에 맡겨져 있었다.

874

in pledge

p. 담보로

pledge n. 약속, 맹세, 담보
pledge to p. ~을 서약하게 하다
pledge one's word p. 명예를 걸고 약속하다
compromise v. 화해하다, 양보하다

어원	-pledge > promise → '담보를 맹세로 약속하다'
유의어	As collateral, as security, as a guarantee.
반의어	Freed, Unpledged
영영	Something given or held as security for the fulfillment of a promise or obligation.
예문	He offered his car as collateral in pledge for the loan. 그는 대출을 위해 자동차를 담보로 제공했다.

875

in the interests of

p. ~을 위해

interests n. 이익
in the best interest of p. ~을 위해 최선인
disinterest n. 이해 관계가 없음, 무관심
uninterested a. 무관심한, 냉담한

어원	-in 안 + -interests 이익 → '안에 품을 이익을 위해'
유의어	For the benefit of, for the sake of, in favor of.
반의어	Against the interests of, Detrimental to
영영	For the benefit or good of something or someone.
예문	The new policies were implemented in the interests of public safety. 새로운 정책은 공공 안전을 위해 시행되었다.

876

sit out

p. ~이 끝나기를 기다리다; (활동에서) 빠지다

deposit n. 착수금 v. 두다, 침전시키다
transit n. 수송, 통과
sit-in p. 연좌농성

어원	sit(앉아서) out(끝나기를) 기다리다
유의어	Abstain, refrain, not participate, skip.
반의어	Participate, Join In
영영	To choose not to participate in an activity or event.
예문	She decided to sit out the dance party and relax at home. 그녀는 댄스 파티를 빠져나와 집에서 편하게 쉬기로 결정했다.

877

in no way

p. 결코 ~하지 않다

all the way p. 줄곧, 내내
make one's way p. 나아가다
be in the way p. 방해가 되다

어원	-in 안 + -no way 길이 없다 → '길이 없으니 결코 ~하지 않다'
유의어	Not at all, absolutely not, in no manner.
반의어	Completely, Entirely
영영	Absolutely not; under no circumstances.
예문	His actions were in no way acceptable. 그의 행동은 결코 허용할 수 없는 것이었다.

878

exact to the life

p. 실물 그대로의

exactly adv. 정확히, 틀림없이
exactness n. 정확성

어원	-exact 정확한 + -life 생명 → '정확히 생명체 그대로의'
유의어	Precise, accurate, lifelike, true to reality.
반의어	Inaccurate, Unrealistic
영영	Extremely realistic or accurate in detail.
예문	The artist's portrait was so detailed that it seemed exact to the life. 화가의 초상화는 너무 상세해서 생동감 있게 느껴졌다.

879

be down on

p. ~을 싫어하다

on charge of p. ~의 죄목으로
on demand p. 요구만 있으면 (언제든지)
on pain of p. ~을 각오하고
on reserve p. 예약중인

어원	-down 아래 + -on ~에 관한 → '~에 대한 마음이 가라 앉으니 싫어하다'
유의어	Be critical of, disapprove of, have a negative opinion of.
반의어	Be fond of, Approve
영영	To be critical, negative, or hostile towards someone or something.
예문	He's always been down on that restaurant because of one bad experience. 그는 항상 그 식당을 한 번의 나쁜 경험 때문에 싫어해 왔다.

880

hold good

p. 유효하다

get hold of p. ~을 구하다, 손에 넣다
hold A in check p. A를 억제하다
hold on p. 붙잡고 있다, 잠시만
hold one's tongue p. 입을 다물다

어원	-hold 잡다 + -good 좋은 → '좋은 마음을 갖고 있으니 아직 유효하다'
유의어	Remain valid, still apply, continue to be true.
반의어	Be invalid, Not Apply
영영	To remain valid, true, or applicable.
예문	The rules and regulations still hold good despite the changes. 규칙과 규정은 여전히 유효하다.

Chapter 23.

881	surname	[ˈsɜː.neɪm]	n. 성
882	proceed	[prəˈsiːd]	v. 진행하다 n. 판매 또는 거래의 수익
883	transition	[trænˈzɪʃ.ən]	n. 변천, 전이
884	hollow	[ˈhɒl.əʊ]	a. 속이 빈, 움푹 꺼진; 분지
885	disjoint	[disdʒɔ́int]	v. 해체하다, (관절을) 삐게 하다
886	sophisticated	[səˈfɪs.tɪ.keɪ.tɪd]	a. 세련된, 경험 많은; 정교한, 복잡한
887	beguile	[bigáil]	v. 속이다; 즐겁게 하다
888	plumber	[ˈplʌm.ər]	n. 배관공
889	misrepresent	[mìsreprizént]	v. 잘못 말하다, 거짓 설명하다
890	dialect	[ˈdaɪ.ə.lekt]	n. 사투리, 방언
891	concourse	[kɑ́nkɔːrs]	n. 집합, 군중; 중앙 광장, 홀
892	augment	[ɔːgmént]	n. 증강 v. 증강시키다
893	humility	[hjuːˈmɪl.ə.ti]	n. 겸손
894	desperado	[ˌdes.pəˈrɑː.dəʊ]	n. 무법자; 자포자기식으로 사는 사람
895	reciprocal	[risíprəkəl]	a. 상호의, 호혜적인
896	extemporize	[ikstémpə-ràiz]	v. 즉흥적으로 하다, 즉석에서 하다
897	decipher	[dɪˈsaɪ.fər]	v. 해독하다
898	feign	[fein]	v. ~인 체하다, 위조하다
899	declaim	[dikléim]	v. 연설하다, 낭독하다; 비난하다
900	resentment	[rɪˈzent.mənt]	n. 분개, 분노
901	coherent	[kəʊˈhɪə.rənt]	a. 일관된, 통일성이 있는, 논리적인
902	dreadful	[drédfəl]	a. 지독한, 굉장히 무서운
903	implore	[ɪmˈplɔːr]	v. 애원하다, 간청하다
904	latitude	[ˈlæt.ɪ.tʃuːd]	n. 위도; 허용범위
905	zealot	[zélət]	n. 열광자, 광신자
906	incense	[ínsens]	n. 향, 냄새 v. 격분시키다
907	harry	[ˈhær.i]	v. 약탈[침략]하다, 끊임없이 괴롭히다
908	surveillance	[sərvéiləns]	n. 감시, 감독, 관찰
909	herbivore	[ˈhɜː.bɪ.vɔːr]	n. 초식동물
910	pious	[ˈpaɪ.əs]	a. 독실한, 경건한
911	all but		p. 사실상, 거의
912	take sides		p. 편을 들다
913	hit the ceiling		p. 노발대발하다, 분통을 터뜨리다
914	once and for all		p. 최종적으로, 마지막으로 한 번만 더
915	concentrate A on B		p. A를 B에 집중시키다
916	hang up		p. 전화를 끊다
917	take over		p. 맡다, 넘겨 받다; 점거하다, 장악하다, 인수하다
918	no more than		p. 단지 ~에 지나지 않는, ~일 뿐인
919	no less than		p. 꼭 ~만큼, ~와 마찬가지로; ~못지 않게
920	go up		p. (가격, 기온 등이) 오르다

881

surname

[ˈsɜːˌneɪm]

n. 성

first name p. 세례명의
by name p. 별명, 명칭

어원	-sur : super + -name → '이름보다 우선하는 성'
유의어	last name, family name
반의어	given name, first name
영영	Family name.
예문	My surname is Smith. 제 성은 스미스입니다.

882

proceed

[prəˈsiːd]

v. 진행하다 n. 판매 또는 거래의 수익

proceeds n. 수익금
procedure n. 절차; 방법
proclivity n. 경향, 기질
processor n. 처리기, 처리장치

어원	-pro : forth + -cess, -ced, -ceed : go → '앞으로 가기 위해 진행하니 판매 수익까지'
유의어	advance, continue, move forward
반의어	halt, stop, cease
영영	To continue or move forward.
예문	Please proceed with the presentation. 발표를 진행해 주세요.

883

transition

[trænˈzɪʃ.ən]

n. 변천, 전이

transience n. 일시적임, 무상
transitional a. 변천하는
transitory a. 일시의, 순간의
transit n. 통과, 횡단

어원	-tran, -trans : across + -i, it : go → '다른 상태로 가로질러 가는 변천'
유의어	change, shift, conversion
반의어	stasis, stability, sameness
영영	A change from one state or condition to another.
예문	The transition from summer to fall is my favorite time of the year. 여름에서 가을로의 전환은 제가 가장 좋아하는 시기입니다.

884

hollow

[ˈhɒl.əʊ]

a. 속이 빈, 움푹 꺼진; 분지

hollowly adv. 공허하게
hollowness n. 구덩이, 멍한 모양, 공허
plug the holes p. 구멍을 막다
holy a. 신성한

어원	-hole 구덩이, 구멍 → '구덩이 처럼 속이 빈'
유의어	empty, vacant, void
반의어	solid, full, filled
영영	Empty or having a space inside.
예문	The tree had a hollow trunk. 그 나무는 비어 있는 줄기가 있었습니다.

885

disjoint

[disdʒɔ́int]

v. 해체하다, (관절을) 삐게 하다

disjointed a. 연결이 안 되는, 흐트러진
joint a. 관절, 공동의
junction n. 접합, 교차점
conjunction n. 결합, 접속사

어원	-dis : not + -join, -junc, -junct 합치다(L) → '합치지 못하게 해체하다' * join, junc(t) '다른 것이 만나 합침' VS ser(t) '밀어 넣어서 합침'
유의어	separate, disconnect, disunite
반의어	unite, connect, join
영영	To disconnect or separate.
예문	The puzzle pieces are disjoint and do not fit together. 이 퍼즐 조각들은 분리되어 있어 서로 맞지 않습니다.

886

sophisticated

[səˈfɪs.tɪˌkeɪ.tɪd]

a. 세련된, 경험 많은; 정교한, 복잡한

sophistic a. 궤변적인
sophisticate v. 세련되게 하다, 정교하게 하다
sophist n. 궤변학자
sophomore n. 2학년

어원	-soph, -sophia : wise → '지혜로 토론하는 궤변학자처럼 현명하고 세련된'
유의어	refined, cultured, elegant
반의어	simple, unsophisticated, basic
영영	Elegant and advanced.
예문	The restaurant has a sophisticated atmosphere. 그 레스토랑은 세련된 분위기를 갖고 있습니다.

887

beguile
[bigáil]

v. 속이다; 즐겁게 하다

guileful a. 교활한
guileless a. 악의 없는, 순진한
guilty a. 죄책감이 드는, 유죄의
guilty look p. 죄책감을 느끼는 표정

어원	-be : do + -guile 기만 → '남을 기만하는 행동이니 속이다'
유의어	deceive, charm, enchant
반의어	inform, enlighten, clarify
영영	To charm or deceive.
예문	The magician can beguile the audience with his tricks. 그 마술사는 그의 마술로 관객들을 속일 수 있습니다.

888

plumber
[ˈplʌm.ər]

n. 배관공

plumb n. 추 v. 재다; 납으로 봉하다
plumbum n. 납
plum n. 자두

어원	-plumb 끈에 매달린 납 덩어리 / 납 원소 기호 : Pb → '납을 가지고 일하는 사람'
유의어	pipefitter, plumbing technician
반의어	customer, homeowner
영영	A professional who works with pipes and plumbing.
예문	We need to call a plumber to fix the leaky faucet. 우리는 물이 새는 수도꼭지를 고치기 위해 배관공을 불러야 합니다.

889

misrepresent
[mìsreprizént]

v. 잘못 말하다, 거짓 설명하다

misleading a. 잘못된 인식을 주는
misnomer n. 틀린 이름
mislead v. 현혹시키다, 속이다
misplace v. 잘못 놓다, 잊어버리다 n. 불운

어원	-mis : bad + -represent 말하다
유의어	distort, falsify, misstate
반의어	represent accurately, portray truthfully
영영	To present falsely or inaccurately.
예문	It is not right to misrepresent the facts in a report. 보고서에서 사실을 잘못 나타내는 것은 옳지 않습니다.

890

dialect
[ˈdaɪ.ə.lekt]

n. 사투리, 방언

dialectal a. 방언의, 방언 특유의
dialectology n. 방언학
dialectic a. 변증적인
dialectics n. 변증법

어원	-dia : across + -lec, -lect, -leg, -lig : read 읽다(L) → '먼 거리를 가로지르면 다르게 읽는 사투리와 방언'
유의어	regional language, vernacular, accent
반의어	standard language, common speech
영영	A regional or local form of a language.
예문	There are many dialects spoken in different regions of the country. 나라의 다른 지역에서는 많은 방언이 사용됩니다.

891

concourse
[kánkɔːrs]

n. 집합, 군중; 중앙 광장, 홀

concurrent a. 동시에 일어나는
concurrence n. 동의, 일치
recur v. 재발하다, 반복되다
incur v. 초래하다

어원	-con : together + -cour, -cur : run → '동시에 몰려드는 군중의 집합' cf. discourse 담화, 연설 / excursion 소풍, 산책 / incur 초래하다
유의어	gathering, assembly, crowd
반의어	dispersion, scattering, disbandment
영영	A large gathering or crowd.
예문	The train station's concourse was crowded with commuters. 기차역의 집합 장소는 통근자들로 북적였습니다.

892

augment
[ɔːgmént]

n. 증강 v. 증강시키다

augmented a. 증강된, 늘어난
augur n. 점쟁이 v. 점치다
augmented reality p. 증강현실(AR)
aggro n. 난폭, 도발, 싸움

어원	* -aug : aggro 어그로; 도발 → '어그로로 도발해서 싸움을 증강시키다'
유의어	increase, enhance, boost
반의어	decrease, reduce, diminish
영영	To increase or enhance.
예문	We need to augment our workforce to meet the increased demand. 우리는 증가한 수요를 충족시키기 위해 우리 노동력을 늘려야 합니다.

893

humility

[hjuːˈmɪl.ə.ti]

n. 겸손

humiliation n. 굴욕, 수치심
humiliate v. 굴욕감을 주다
humble a. 겸손한
humid a. 습한, 습기가 많은

어원	-hum, -humili : earth 땅 → '땅에 가까운 겸손'
유의어	modesty, meekness, humbleness
반의어	arrogance, pride, conceit
영영	Modesty or humbleness.
예문	His humility is one of his most admirable qualities. 그의 겸손함은 그의 가장 칭찬받는 덕목 중 하나입니다.

894

desperado

[ˌdes.pəˈrɑː.dəʊ]

n. 무법자; 자포자기식으로 사는 사람

desperate a. 필사적인, 절실한
desperation n. 자포자기, 절망
desperate a. 절망적인, 자포자기의
despair n. 절망 v. 절망하다

어원	-de : down + -sper, -spar, -spair 희망 → '절망적이기에 자포자기식으로 사는 무법자'
유의어	outlaw, renegade, bandit
반의어	law-abiding citizen, civilian
영영	An outlaw or criminal.
예문	The town sheriff was determined to catch the desperado. 마을의 보안관은 그 무법자를 잡기로 결심했습니다.

895

reciprocal

[risíprəkəl]

a. 상호의, 호혜적인

reciprocation n. 교환, 보복
reciprocate v. 보답하다
reciprocity n. 호혜(주의)
reception n. 수령, 접수

어원	-reci, -re : back + -proc, -pro : forth → '앞뒤로 오가는'
유의어	mutual, shared, corresponding
반의어	one-sided, unilateral, non-reciprocal
영영	Mutual or shared.
예문	The two countries have a reciprocal trade agreement. 두 나라는 상호적인 무역 협정을 가지고 있습니다.

896

extemporize

[ikstémpə-ràiz]

v. 즉흥적으로 하다, 즉석에서 하다

extemporization n. 즉흥, 즉흥적 작품
temporary a. 시간적인, 일시의
contemporary a. 같은 시대의, 현대의
temptation n. 유혹

어원	-ex : out + -tempo : time → '준비할 시간 없이 하니 즉흥적으로 하다'
유의어	improvise, ad-lib, make up
반의어	plan, prepare, rehearse
영영	To improvise or speak without preparation.
예문	He can extemporize a speech on any topic. 그는 어떤 주제에 대해서도 즉흥적으로 스피치를 할 수 있습니다.

897

decipher

[dɪˈsaɪ.fər]

v. 해독하다

cipher n. 암호
declaim v. 연설하다, 낭독하다
debris n. 쓰레기, 잔해
decomposition n. 해체

어원	-de : off + -cipher 암호로 쓰다 → '암호의 가치가 떨어지게 해독'
유의어	decode, interpret, translate
반의어	encode, encrypt, confuse
영영	To decode or interpret.
예문	It took me a while to decipher the ancient writing. 나는 고대 문자를 해독하는 데 시간이 걸렸습니다.

898

feign

[fein]

v. ~인 체하다, 위조하다

feign v. ~인 체하다, 위조하다
feigned a. 가장한
faint a. 기절한, 희미한
configure v. 구성하다

어원	-fei : feint 거짓 페인트 공격 → '거짓으로 ~인 체하다'
유의어	fake, pretend, simulate
반의어	reveal, show, display
영영	To pretend or fake.
예문	She tried to feign surprise when she received the surprise party. 그녀는 서프라이즈 파티를 받을 때 놀람을 가장하려고 노력했습니다.

899

declaim

[dikléim]

v. 연설하다, 낭독하다; 비난하다

claim v. 주장하다
claimable a. 요구할 수 있는
exclaim v. 외치다
proclaim v. 선언하다

어원	-de : completely + -calim 주장하다 → '완벽한 주장으로 열변을 토하다'
유의어	recite, deliver, proclaim
반의어	mumble, whisper, mutter
영영	To speak or recite loudly.
예문	The actor declaimed his lines with great passion. 배우는 큰 열정으로 대사를 고함쳤습니다.

900

resentment

[rɪˈzent.mənt]

n. 분개, 분노

resent v. ~에 분개하다, 원망하다
resentment at p. ~에 분함
resentful a. 화난, 분개한
resentfully adv. 분개하여

어원	-re : back + -sent : feel → '뒤에서 느끼는 분노'
유의어	bitterness, indignation, grudge
반의어	contentment, satisfaction, acceptance
영영	Bitterness or anger.
예문	She harbored resentment towards her co-worker for a long time. 그녀는 오랜 시간 동안 동료에 대한 원한을 품었습니다.

901

coherent

[koʊˈhɪə.rənt]

a. 일관된, 통일성이 있는, 논리적인

coherence n. 부착(성), 응집(성)
cohere v. 붙다, 응집하다; 일관성 있다
cohesive a. 단결된, 화합하는
cohesiveness n. 응집성

어원	-co : together + -here : stick → '이성과 행동이 함께 달라 붙을 정도로 논리적인'
유의어	logical, consistent, cohesive
반의어	incoherent, confused, disjointed
영영	Logical and consistent.
예문	His argument was clear and coherent. 그의 주장은 명확하고 일관성 있었습니다.

902

dreadful

[drédfəl]

a. 지독한, 굉장히 무서운

dread v. 몹시 두려워하다
dreadfully adv. 몹시 두려워하여
dreary a. 음울한, 따분한
drape v. (장막을) 드리우다

어원	-dra : drive + -ful : full → '가득 몰아치니 지독하게 무서운'
유의어	terrible, horrifying, frightening
반의어	pleasant, delightful, enjoyable
영영	Extremely bad or terrible.
예문	The storm caused dreadful damage to the town. 폭풍은 마을에 무시무시한 피해를 줬습니다.

903

implore

[ɪmˈplɔːr]

v. 애원하다, 간청하다

imploring a. 애원하는, 탄원의
imploration n. 애원, 간청, 탄원
deplore v. 한탄하다, 비판하다
peril n. 위험(성)

어원	-im, -in : in + -plor : cry → '마음 안에서 울며 애원하니 간청'
유의어	beseech, beg, plead
반의어	demand, command, order
영영	To beg or plead.
예문	She implored him to forgive her for the mistake. 그녀는 그에게 실수를 용서해 달라고 간청했습니다.

904

latitude

[ˈlæt.ɪ.tʃuːd]

n. 위도; 허용범위

latitudinal a. 위도의, 위도상의
latitudinally adv. 위도상으로

어원	-lat 넓은 + -tude 명접 → '넓은 지구의 너비는 가로로 위도'
유의어	freedom, flexibility, leeway
반의어	restriction, limitation, confinement
영영	Freedom or flexibility.
예문	The ship's latitude was recorded in the navigation log. 선박의 위도가 항해일지에 기록되었습니다.

905

zealot

[zélət]

n. 열광자, 광신자

zeal n. 열정
zealous a. 열성적인
zealously adv. 열성적으로, 열광적으로
zealotry n. 광기

어원	-zeal 열정 * 스타크래프트 '질럿'처럼 복종하는 무리
유의어	fanatic, extremist, enthusiast
반의어	moderate, centrist, apathetic
영영	A fanatical and devoted person.
예문	He was a political zealot who never wavered in his beliefs. 그는 자신의 신념에서 결코 흔들리지 않는 정치적 열성자였습니다.

906

incense

[ínsens]

n. 향, 냄새 v. 격분시키다

incendiary a. 방화하는, 선동적인
incensed a. 분개한, 격노한
incentive a. 자극적인, 고무적인

어원	-in : in + -cen, -can, -candere : glow → '불빛을 내며 타는 향의 냄새'
유의어	infuriate, enrage, anger
반의어	please, satisfy, appease
영영	To infuriate or anger.
예문	The room was filled with the sweet smell of incense. 그 방은 향로의 달콤한 냄새로 가득 찼습니다.

907

harry

['hær.i]

v. 약탈[침략]하다, 끊임없이 괴롭히다

harried a. 몹시 곤란을 겪는
harrowed a. 불안한, 고통스러운
harass v. 괴롭히다
harsh a. 혹독한, 가혹한

어원	-har : -harm, -har 해를 끼치다 → '해를 끼치는 것이니 괴롭히다'
유의어	harass, torment, pester
반의어	assist, help, support
영영	To harass or torment.
예문	The persistent paparazzi continued to harry the celebrity. 끈질긴 퍼파라치는 유명인을 계속 괴롭혔습니다.

908

surveillance

[sərvéiləns]

n. 감시, 감독, 관찰

surveil v. 감시하다, 감시하에 두다
surveillant a. 감시하는 n. 감시자, 감독자
surge v. 밀어닥치다, 쇄도하다; 급등하다

어원	-sur : over + veill : watch → '위에서 지켜보다 감시하다'
유의어	monitoring, observation, scrutiny
반의어	privacy, seclusion, confidentiality
영영	Monitoring or observation.
예문	The security cameras provided constant surveillance of the building. 보안 카메라는 건물을 지속적으로 감시했습니다.

909

herbivore

['hɜːbɪˌvɔːr]

n. 초식동물

herbivorous a. 초식성의
herbivory n. 초식성임
omnivore n. 잡식동물
insectivore n. 곤충식동물

어원	-herb 풀, 약초, 허브 + -vore : eat → '풀 먹고 사는 동물'
유의어	plant-eater, vegetarian, grazer
반의어	carnivore, omnivore
영영	An animal that eats plants.
예문	Elephants are herbivores and mainly eat plants. 코끼리는 초식 동물이며 주로 식물을 먹습니다.

910

pious

['paɪ.əs]

a. 독실한, 경건한

piety n. 경건, 신앙심
piously adv. 경건하게, 신앙심 깊게
copiously adv. 엄청난 양으로, 방대하게
purification n. 정화, 정제

어원	-pious : pius 경건한 * -pi : pure → '순수한 마음으로 신을 찬양하는'
유의어	devout, religious, godly
반의어	impious, irreverent, sacrilegious
영영	Devoutly religious.
예문	She was a pious woman who attended church every Sunday. 그녀는 매주 교회에 참석하는 신앙심 깊은 여성이었습니다.

911

all but

p. 사실상, 거의

all-around p. 다재다능한
all the more p. 그만큼 더
all the same p. 그럼에도 불구하고
all too p. 완전 너무, 너무나, 정말

어원	-al 모두, 전부 (E) + -but → '모두는 아니지만 사실상 거의'
유의어	nearly, almost, practically
반의어	completely, entirely, wholly
영영	Almost or nearly.
예문	She was all but certain of the outcome. 그녀는 결과에 대해 거의 확신했습니다.

912

take sides

p. 편을 들다

take over p. 넘겨 받다; 장악하다
take possession of p. ~을 점유하다
take up p. ~을 맡다
take the liverty to do p. 실례를 무릅쓰고 ~하다

어원	-take 취하다 + -sides 편 → '내 편을 취하니 편을 들다'
유의어	choose, support, align with
반의어	remain neutral, stay impartial
영영	To support one party or viewpoint.
예문	It's not always easy to take sides in a conflict. 갈등에서 편을 드는 것은 항상 쉽지 않습니다.

913

hit the ceiling

p. 노발대발하다, 분통을 터뜨리다

hit the books p. 열심히 공부하다
become a hit p. 히트를 치다
hit a plateau p. 정체기에 들다
ceiling n. 천장

어원	ceiling(천장)을 hit(칠) 정도의 분노니 노발대발하다
유의어	explode, rage, become furious
반의어	remain calm, stay composed
영영	To become very angry.
예문	When he heard the news, he hit the ceiling in anger. 그가 그 소식을 듣자마자 분노하여 화를 냈습니다.

914

once and for all

p. 최종적으로, 마지막으로 한 번만 더

all at once p. 갑자기, 동시에
once and again p. 여러 번 되풀이하여
for this once p. 이번만은
let alone p. ~은 고사하고

어원	-on : one(E) + for all 전부 → '한 번만 더, 그리고 끝'
유의어	finally, conclusively, ultimately
반의어	temporarily, for the time being
영영	Finally and conclusively.
예문	Let's settle this matter once and for all. 이 문제를 일단영원히 해결합시다.

915

concentrate A on B

p. A를 B에 집중시키다

concentrate on p. 집중하다
concentrated a. 집주적인, 농축된
concentration n. 집중; 농축
concentration camp p. 강제 수용소

어원	-con : together + -cent 가운데 → '모두 가운데로 집중하다'
유의어	focus A on B, center A around B
반의어	disperse A from B, divert A from B
영영	To focus A on B.
예문	Please concentrate your efforts on completing the project. 프로젝트를 완료하기 위해 노력을 집중해 주세요.

916

hang up

p. 전화를 끊다

hang on p. 기다리다
hang around p. 서성거리다, 배회하다
hanger n. 옷걸이
hanging n. 교수형

어원	-hang 걸다 → '옛날 전화기는 수화기를 고리에 걸어야 끊겼다'
유의어	terminate, end, disconnect
반의어	answer, pick up, continue the call
영영	To end a telephone call.
예문	I accidentally hung up the phone before finishing the conversation. 대화를 끝내지 않고 전화를 실수로 끊었습니다.

917

take over

p. 맡다, 넘겨 받다; 점거하다, 장악하다, 인수하다

take place p. 일어나다, 발생하다
take possession of p. ~을 점유하다
take sides p. 편을 들다
take the liverty to do p. 실례를 무릅쓰고 ~하다

어원	-take 취하다 + -over → '취해서 넘겨 받으니 차지하다'
유의어	assume control, seize, acquire
반의어	relinquish, surrender, give up control
영영	To assume control or responsibility.
예문	She will take over as the new manager of the department. 그녀가 부서의 새로운 매니저로 인수할 것입니다.

918

no more than

p. 단지 ~에 지나지 않는, ~일 뿐인

more of p. ~중에 많이, 더, 더 많이
more often than not p. 대개, 흔히
no less than p. 꼭 ~만큼, ~와 마찬가지로

어원	-no more + -than → '~이상 하지 않으니 단지 ~일 뿐인' * only
유의어	only, just, merely
반의어	more than, greater than
영영	Only and not exceeding.
예문	The price should be no more than $50. 가격은 $50을 넘지 않아야 합니다.

919

no less than

p. 꼭 ~만큼, ~와 마찬가지로; ~못지 않게

more of p. ~중에 많이, 더, 더 많이
more often than not p. 대개, 흔히
no more than p. 단지 ~에 지나지 않는, ~일 뿐인

어원	-no less + -than → '~보다 덜 하지 않으니 최소한' * at least
유의어	at least, minimum of, not fewer than
반의어	fewer than, under, below
영영	At least and a minimum of.
예문	The event attracted no less than 500 attendees. 그 이벤트는 최소 500명의 참석자를 끌어들였습니다.

920

go up

p. (가격, 기온 등이) 오르다

go with p. 받아들이다; 어울리다
go through p. 통과되다, 성사되다, 해결되다
go over p. 점검하다, 검토하다
go out of one's way p. 굳이 뭔가를 하다

어원	-go 가다 + up 위로 → '위로 가는 것이니 오르다'
유의어	ascend, rise, climb
반의어	descend, go down, lower
영영	To ascend or rise.
예문	The temperature is expected to go up in the afternoon. 오후에 기온이 올라갈 것으로 예상됩니다.

Chapter 24.

921	disclaim	[diskléim]	v. 부인하다
922	malign	[məláin]	a. 유해한, 악성인
923	neologism	[niːɑ́lədʒizm]	n. 새로운 말, 신어
924	embellish	[imbéliʃ]	v. 아름답게 하다, 장식하다, (이야기를) 꾸미다
925	dismay	[dɪˈsmeɪ]	v. 당황하게 하다, 실망하게 하다
926	arbitrary	[ˈɑːbɪtrər.i]	a. 제멋대로인, 변덕스러운
927	recourse	[rɪˈkɔːs]	n. 의지가 되는 것, 의지가 되는 사람
928	reminiscent	[rèmənísnt]	a. 생각나게 하는, 연상시키는
929	antithesis	[æntíθəsis]	n. 정반대, 대립; 대조
930	ambush	[ǽmbuʃ]	n. 매복, 급습
931	disdain	[disdéin]	v. 경멸하다, 거부하다
932	congestion	[kənˈdʒes.tʃən]	n. (교통) 혼잡, (인구) 밀집
933	affront	[əfrʌnt]	v. 모욕하다
934	devise	[dɪˈvaɪz]	v. 궁리하다, 고안하다
935	spare	[speər]	v. ~을 면해 주다, 당하지 않게 하다
936	reposit	[ripɑ́zit]	v. ~을 저장하다, 보존하다
937	stagnant	[ˈstæɡ.nənt]	a. 침체된, 불경기의
938	succumb	[səkʌm]	vi. 지다, 굴복하다
939	foster	[ˈfɒs.tər]	v. 양육하다, 기르다, 촉진하다, 육성하다
940	incriminate	[inkrímənèit]	v. 고발하다
941	quarrel	[ˈkwɒr.əl]	v. 싸우다, 언쟁을 벌이다; 말다툼, 불만
942	condone	[kəndóun]	v. 용서하다
943	discreet	[dɪˈskriːt]	a. 신중한, 조심스러운
944	dissent	[disént]	vi. 의견을 달리하다 n. 불찬성, 이의
945	succor	[sʌkər]	v. 도움, 원조; ~을 도와주다
946	interlude	[íntərlùːd]	n. (잠깐의) 시기; 막간극, 간주
947	allude	[əˈluːd]	v. 언급하다, 암시하다
948	elusiveness	[ilúːsivnis]	n. 모호함, 난해함
949	jolt	[dʒoult]	n. 놀람 v. 갑자기 거칠게 움직이다, 충격을 주다
950	collapse	[kəˈlæps]	v. 무너지다, 붕괴하다 n. 붕괴, 와해
951	be concerned with		p. ~에 관심이 있다
952	on hold		p. 보류된
953	by means of		p. ~에 의하여, ~의 도움으로
954	work on		p. 애쓰다
955	come down with		p. (별로 심각하지 않은 병에) 걸리다, 들리다
956	to a person		p. 만장일치로
957	get off the ground		p. 순조롭게 출발하다
958	let alone		p. ~은 고사하고
959	go through		p. 통과되다, 성사되다, 해결하다
960	stem from		p. ~에서 비롯되다

921

disclaim
[diskléim]

v. 부인하다

discard v. 버리다, 포기하다
discomfit v. 좌절시키다; 당황하게 하다
discompose v. ~을 교란하다, 당황케 하다
disarrange v. 어지럽히다, 혼란시키다

어원	-dis : not + -claim 주장하다 → '주장의 반대니 부인하다'
유의어	renounce, reject, abandon, give up
반의어	assert, claim, own, acknowledge
영영	to formally deny or reject (a claim, right, or responsibility)
예문	He disclaimed any involvement in the project's failure. 그는 프로젝트 실패와 아무런 연관이 없다고 부인했습니다.

922

malign
[məláin]

a. 유해한, 악성인

malignant a. 악의에 찬, 악성인
malignity n. 악성, 깊은 원한
malignancy n. 악영향, 악의, 악성
malice n. 악의, 원한

어원	-mal, -male : bad(L) +-gn, -gen : birth → '안 좋은 성질로 나온 것이니 유해한'
유의어	slander, defame, vilify, criticize
반의어	praise, compliment, endorse, support
영영	to speak ill of someone, especially in a way that is unfair or untrue
예문	She tried to malign her opponent's reputation during the election. 그녀는 선거 중에 상대편의 평판을 비방하려고 했습니다.

923

neologism
[ni:ɑ́lədʒizm]

n. 새로운 말, 신어

paleolith n. 구석기
neolith n. 신석기
nematode n. 선충; 기생충
neural a. 신경의

어원	-ne, -neo : new 새로운 (G) + -log : language → '새로운 말이니 신어'
유의어	novelty, innovation, invention, new term
반의어	conventional, established, traditional, familiar
영영	a new word or phrase, especially one that has been created recently
예문	"Selfie" is a neologism that became popular in recent years. "셀피"는 최근 몇 년 동안 유행한 신조어입니다.

924

embellish
[imbéliʃ]

v. 아름답게 하다, 장식하다, (이야기를) 꾸미다

embellishment n. 장식, 수식, 윤색
unembellished a. 꾸밈없는, 수수한
belle n. 미인, 미녀

어원	-em, -en : in + -bel : beuty → '아름다움을 넣어 장식하다'
유의어	adorn, decorate, beautify, enhance
반의어	simplify, strip, diminish, reduce
영영	to make something more attractive or interesting by adding details or decoration
예문	She liked to embellish her stories to make them more interesting. 그녀는 이야기를 더 흥미롭게 만들기 위해 그것을 장식하는 것을 좋아했습니다.

925

dismay
[dɪˈsmeɪ]

v. 당황하게 하다, 실망하게 하다

in dismay p. 낙심하여
act dismay p. 당황한 체하다
undismayed a. 낙담하지 않은, 동요하지 않은
dismayingly adv. 경악하게 만들어

어원	-dis : away + -may 가능성 → '가능성이 사라져 크게 실망시키다'
유의어	alarm, terrify, panic, horrify
반의어	delight, please, satisfy, gratify
영영	to fill someone with fear, worry, or sadness
예문	The sudden news of the accident filled them with dismay. 사고의 갑작스러운 소식으로 그들은 경악했습니다.

926

arbitrary
[ˈɑːbɪtrəri]

a. 제멋대로인, 변덕스러운

arbitrate v. 중재하다, 조정하다
arbitral a. 조정의, 중재의
arbitrage n. 중개 매매
arbitrable a. 조정할 수 있는, 중재할 수 있는

어원	-ar : to + -bit, -baet : go → '가고 싶은 쪽으로만 가니 제멋대로인'
유의어	random, capricious, unpredictable, unreasonble
반의어	rational, logical, systematic, methodical
영영	based on personal preference or whim, rather than on reason or evidence
예문	The decision seemed arbitrary and unfair to many. 결정은 많은 사람들에게 임의적이고 불공평하게 보였습니다.

927	어원	-re : back + -cour, -cur : run → '뒤에서 달릴 수 있도록 힘을 주는'
recourse	유의어	resort, fallback, alternative, resource
	반의어	none, no alternative, no resource, no fallback
[rɪˈkɔːs]	영영	a source of help or support, especially when there are no other options
n. 의지가 되는 것, 의지가 되는 사람		
recourseful a. 능숙한, 대처력이 있는 recur v. 재발하다, 반복되다 resource n. 수단, 자원 discursive a. 산만한, 두서 없는	예문	They had no recourse but to file a formal complaint. 그들은 공식적인 불만을 제기할 대책이 없었습니다.
928	어원	-re : again + -min, -men : mind → '다시 생각이 떠오르게 하니 연상시키는'
reminiscent	유의어	evocative, suggestive
	반의어	non-reminiscent, unreminiscent, forgetful, unmindful
[rèmənísnt]	영영	reminding you of something or someone, or suggesting that something or someone is similar to something or someone else
a. 생각나게 하는, 연상시키는		
reminisce v. ~을 추억하다, 회상에 잠기다 in reminiscence p. 회고하여 reminiscential a. 생각나게 하는. 연상시키는	예문	The old house was reminiscent of her childhood. 그 오래된 집은 그녀의 어린 시절을 회상시켰습니다.
929	어원	-anti : against + -thes : put → '반대로 넣으니 정반대로 대립'
antithesis	유의어	opposition, contrast, contradiction
	반의어	thesis, agreement, unity, conformity
[æntíθəsis]	영영	the opposite or contrast of something
n. 정반대, 대립; 대조		
antinomy n. 모순; 이율 배반 antipodes n. 대척지 antagonist n. 적대자, 반대자 antidote n. 해독, 소독	예문	His cheerful personality is the antithesis of her gloomy demeanor. 그의 쾌활한 성격은 그녀의 어두운 태도의 대조입니다.
930	어원	-am, -in : in + -bush 덤불 → '덤블 안에 숨어 매복 후 급습'
ambush	유의어	trap, snatch, surprise, attack
	반의어	open, overt, public, in the open
[æmbuʃ]	영영	to attack someone suddenly and unexpectedly, usually when they are not expecting it
n. 매복, 급습		
ambusher n. 매복자, 복병 from ambush p. 매복했다가 lie in ambush p. 매복 하다 fall into ambush p. 복병을 만나다	예문	The soldiers were ambushed by the enemy in the forest. 병사들은 숲에서 적에게 습격을 받았습니다.
931	어원	-dis : away + -dain , -dign : worth → '남의 가치를 멀리 떨어뜨리다'
disdain	유의어	scorn, contempt, disregard, ignore
	반의어	respect, admire, esteem, honor
[disdéin]	영영	to feel contempt or scorn for someone or something
v. 경멸하다, 거부하다		
disdain for p. ~에 대한 경멸 disdainfully adv. 업신여기며, 무시하여 disdainful of p. ~을 경멸하여 dignity n. 위엄, 존엄	예문	She looked at him with disdain after his rude comment. 그녀는 그의 무례한 말 뒤에 경멸의 눈초리로 그를 바라봤습니다.
932	어원	-con : together + -gest : carry → '모든 이를 실어 나르느라 생긴 혼잡'
congestion	유의어	jam, traffic, crowd, overcrowding
	반의어	clear, free, unobstructed, vacant
[kənˈdʒes.tʃən]	영영	a state of being very crowded or blocked, especially in a road, railway, or airport
n. (교통) 혼잡, (인구) 밀집		
congest v. 혼잡하게 하다 congested a. 혼잡한, 밀집한 congestive a. 울혈성의, 충혈의 conjecture v. 추측하다	예문	Traffic congestion is a common problem in big cities. 교통 혼잡은 대도시에서 흔한 문제입니다.

933

affront

[əfrʌnt]

v. 모욕하다

affront to p. ~에 대한 모욕
affrontive a. 모욕적인, 불쾌한
confront v. 맞서다, 대항하다

어원	-af : to + -front 앞 → '앞에서 면박을 주니 모욕하다'
유의어	insult, offense, indignity, disrespect
반의어	compliment, praise, flatter, gratify
영영	an insult or disrespectful treatment
예문	His behavior at the meeting was seen as an affront to the team's efforts. 회의에서의 그의 행동은 팀의 노력에 대한 모욕으로 여겨졌습니다.

934

devise

[dɪˈvaɪz]

v. 궁리하다, 고안하다

device n. 고안, 방책; 기기, 장치
devisee n. 유산 수령자
devolve v. 양도하다, 양도되다

어원	-de : completely + -vis 보다 → '직접 눈으로 보며 궁리하더니 고안하다'
유의어	invent, contrive, design, plan
반의어	copy, imitate, replicate, reproduce
영영	to plan or invent something, especially a clever or original idea
예문	They had to devise a new strategy to win the game. 게임을 이기기 위해 그들은 새로운 전략을 고안해야 했습니다.

935

spare

[speər]

v. ~을 면해 주다, 당하지 않게 하다

spare tyre p. 임시 타이어
span n. 기간, 폭
spatial a. 공간의, 공간적인

어원	-spare : not plentiful → '여분의 것을 주어 당하지 않게 하다'
유의어	save, economize, preserve, protect
반의어	waste, expend, consume, use up
영영	to save or keep something for future use
예문	He always carries spare batteries for his flashlight. 그는 항상 손전등을 위한 여분의 배터리를 가지고 다닙니다.

936

reposit

[ripάzit]

v. ~을 저장하다, 보존하다

repository n. 보존 용기; 저장소
reposition n. 저장, 보존, 보관
preposition n. 전치사
reprieve v. 형집행을 연기하다

어원	-re : again + -pos : place → '다시 찾아볼 수 있도록 놓아두니 저장하다'
유의어	deposit, store, lay down, set aside
반의어	remove, take away, withdraw, confiscate
영영	to put something somewhere for safekeeping
예문	You can reposit your belongings in the locker. 당신은 사물을 사물함에 보관할 수 있습니다.

937

stagnant

[ˈstæɡ.nənt]

a. 침체된, 불경기의

stagnancy n. 정체, 침체, 불경기
stagger v. 비틀거리다
staggering a. 충격적인, 믿기 어려운
stand up to p. 용감하게 맞서다

어원	-stag : stage → '무대 위 배우처럼 벗어나지 못하고 침체된'
유의어	sluggish, inactive, still, motionless
반의어	active, dynamic, vigorous, brisk
영영	not moving or developing, and therefore lacking freshness or vitality
예문	The company's growth has been stagnant for the past few years. 이 회사의 성장은 지난 몇 년 동안 침체되어 있습니다.

938

succumb

[səkʌm]

vi. 지다, 굴복하다

succumb to p. ~에 지다
succumb to disease p. 병으로 쓰러지다
succumb to temptation p. 유혹에 넘어가다

어원	-su : sub + -cumb : lie → '밑에 엎드려 굴복하다'
유의어	surrender, yield, give in, collapse
반의어	resist, withstand, endure, survive
영영	to give in to something, especially because you are too weak or tired to continue fighting against it
예문	Despite his efforts, he eventually succumbed to his illness. 그의 노력에도 불구하고, 그는 결국 그의 병에 굴복했습니다.

939

foster

[ˈfɒs.tər]

v. 양육하다, 기르다, 촉진하다, 육성하다

fosterer n. 수양 부모, 양육하는 사람
fosterage n. 수양 자식 제도
fosterling n. 수양 아들, 수양 자녀
forgage v. 먹을 것을 찾아다니다

어원	-food, -feed, -fost 음식 → '잘 먹여 길러 성장을 촉진하다'
유의어	nurture, cultivate, promote, encourage
반의어	hinder, impede, obstruct, block
영영	to encourage the growth or development of something
예문	The organization aims to foster creativity in young artists. 이 기관은 젊은 예술가들의 창의력을 육성하기 위해 노력합니다.

940

incriminate

[inkrímənèit]

v. 고발하다

crime n. 범죄, 범행
criminal a. 범죄의
discriminate v. 차별하다, 구별하다

어원	-in 안 + -crimin : crime → '죄 안에 넣으니 죄를 씌우다'
유의어	blame, accuse, charge, implicate
반의어	exonerate, clear, vindicate, acquit
영영	to prove someone guilty of a crime
예문	His fingerprints on the weapon could incriminate him. 무기 위의 그의 지문은 그를 유죄로 취급할 수 있습니다.

941

quarrel

[ˈkwɒr.əl]

v. 싸우다, 언쟁을 벌이다; 말다툼, 불만

quarrel with p. ~와 언쟁하다
quarrel over p. ~에 대해 언쟁하다
quarrel breaks out p. 말다툼이 일어나다
quarrel over trifles p. 사소한 일로 다투다

어원	* quick 빨리 → '빨리 말로만 언쟁을 벌이다'
유의어	argue, dispute, conflict, discord
반의어	agree, harmonize, reconcile, pacify
영영	to argue or fight with someone
예문	They had a quarrel over the division of the inheritance. 그들은 유산 분배에 대한 다툼을 가졌습니다.

942

condone

[kəndóun]

v. 용서하다

condonation n. 용서, 묵과
pardonable a. 용서할 수 있는
donation n. 기부금, 기증
condolence n. 애도, 조의

어원	-con : intensive + -don : give → '완전한 용서를 주다'
유의어	forgive, overlook, tolerate, excuse
반의어	condemn, criticize, reprove, disapprove
영영	to forgive someone for something wrong they have done
예문	It's important not to condone unethical behavior. 비윤리적인 행동을 용납하지 않는 것이 중요합니다.

943

discreet

[dɪˈskriːt]

a. 신중한, 조심스러운

discrete a. 분리된, 별개의
discretion n. 결정권, 분별
discretely adv. 별개로, 따로따로
excrete v. 배설하다

어원	-dis : away + -creet, -cret, -cern, -cri : separate → '따로 구별할 때는 신중하고 조심스럽게'
유의어	prudent, cautious, circumspect, careful
반의어	indiscreet, imprudent, reckless, careless
영영	careful and considerate in one's speech or actions, so as to avoid causing offense or revealing private information
예문	He gave her a discreet nod to signal that the plan was on. 그는 그 계획이 진행 중이라는 신호를 내리기 위해 조용히 고개를 끄덕였습니다.

944

dissent

[disént]

vi. 의견을 달리하다 n. 불찬성, 이의

dissenter n. 반대자
dissentient a. 의견을 달리하는
dissension n. 의견 차이, 불화
consensus n. (의견의) 일치, 합의

어원	-dis : not + together + -sens, -sent : feel → '반대로 느끼니 이의를 말하다'
유의어	disagree, oppose, protest, critique
반의어	agree, consent, concur, assent
영영	to disagree with an opinion or decision
예문	There was dissent among the team members regarding the project's direction. 프로젝트 방향에 대한 팀원들 간의 의견 불일치가 있었습니다.

945

succor

[sʌkər]

v. 도움, 원조; ~을 도와주다

succorance n. 의존, 양육 원조
succor the needy p. 가난한 사람을 돕다
succorable a. 원조할 수 있는
succorant a. 의존하는, 양육을 의존하는

어원	-suc, -sub : under + -cor, -cur → '밑에 있는 사람들을 도와 주기 위해 달려가는'
유의어	aid, help, support, relief
반의어	harm, hurt, injure, damage
영영	to provide help or support to someone in need
예문	The Red Cross provides succor to disaster victims. 레드 크로스는 재난 피해자에게 도움을 제공합니다.

946

interlude

[íntərlùːd]

n. (잠깐의) 시기; 막간극, 간주

allude v. 언급하다, 암시하다
collude v. 공모하다, 결탁하다
prelude v. 전주, 서곡
elude v. 교묘히 피하다, 빠져 나오다

어원	-inter : between + -lud : play → '극 사이 잠깐의 시기'
유의어	pause, break, intermission, interval
반의어	continuation, progression, sequence, unbroken flow
영영	a short break or pause between parts of a performance or piece of writing
예문	The music served as a peaceful interlude in the middle of the chaos. 그 음악은 혼돈 가운데서의 평화로운 간주 역할을 했습니다.

947

allude

[əˈluːd]

v. 언급하다, 암시하다

allusion n. 암시
allusive a. 암시적인
allusively adv. 넌지시, 암시적으로
allude to p. ~을 넌지시 언급하다, 비치다

어원	-al : to + -loud : play → '~에게 장난치듯 얘기하며 암시'
유의어	refer, hint, suggest, imply
반의어	specify, state, mention, point out
영영	to refer to something indirectly, without giving it a direct mention
예문	She didn't directly address the issue but alluded to it in her speech. 그녀는 문제를 직접 다루지 않았지만 연설에서 그것을 암시했습니다.

948

elusiveness

[ilúːsivnis]

n. 모호함, 난해함

elude v. 교묘히 피하다
elusive a. 정의하기 어려운, 찾기 힘든
elusively adv. 찾기 힘들게
delusive a. 기만적인, 망상적인

어원	-e, -ex : out + -lud : play → '교묘하게 놀리니 모호하고 난해함'
유의어	evasiveness, ambiguity, vagueness, obscurity
반의어	clarity, transparency, explicitness, directness
영영	the quality of being difficult to understand or catch
예문	The elusiveness of the criminal made it difficult for the police to catch him. 범죄자의 피하는 행동은 경찰이 그를 잡기 어렵게 했습니다.

949

jolt

[dʒoult]

n. 놀람 v. 갑자기 거칠게 움직이다, 충격을 주다

jolty a. 동요가 심한, 덜거덕덜거덕 흔들리는
joltingly adv. 거칠게 흔들리며
joltless a. 동요가 없는
jolt into p. 갑자기 하다

어원	-jolt : knock → '거칠게 두드리니 놀람'
유의어	shock, impact, shake
반의어	smooth, steady, uneventful, tranquil
영영	a sudden and strong shock or impact
예문	The sudden jolt of the earthquake woke everyone up. 지진의 갑작스러운 충격 때문에 모두 깨어났습니다.

950

collapse

[kəˈlæps]

v. 무너지다, 붕괴하다 n. 붕괴, 와해

collapsible a. 접을 수 있는
lapse v. 끝나다 n. 배교(종교를 배신)
elapse v. 경과하다
relapse v. 되돌아가다; 퇴보

어원	-co, -com : completely + -lap : fall → '완전히 떨어지면서 무너지다'
유의어	fall, breakdown, ruin, breakdown
반의어	stand, erect, stable, upright
영영	to fall down or suddenly become weak or ineffective
예문	The building's collapse was a result of poor construction. 건물의 붕괴는 부실한 건설의 결과였습니다.

951

be concerned with

p. ~에 관심이 있다

concerning prep. ~에 관한
be concerned about p. 걱정하다
concern oneself with p. ~에 관여하다

어원	-con : together + -cern, -cert, -crimin, -cri : sift 거르다 → '체로 쳐서 거를 정도로 자세히 관심을 갖다, 걱정하다'
유의어	be interested in, be involved in, deal with, take care of
반의어	be unconcerned with, ignore, neglect, disregard
영영	to pay attention to or worry about something or someone
예문	This research project is concerned with environmental sustainability. 이 연구 프로젝트는 환경 지속 가능성과 관련이 있습니다.

952

on hold

p. 보류된

on business p. 사업차, 볼 일이 있어
on duty p. 근무 중인
on foot p. 걸어서
on no account p. 무슨 일이 있어도

어원	-on 상태+ -hold 보류 → '보류 상태인'
유의어	waiting, pending, in abeyance, in suspense
반의어	active, ongoing, in progress, underway
영영	waiting for something to happen or to be completed
예문	The project is currently on hold due to funding issues. 자금 문제로 인해 현재 프로젝트가 대기 중에 있습니다.

953

by means of

p. ~에 의하여, ~의 도움으로

by no means p. 결코 ~가 아닌
by the same token p. 같은 이유로
by the time p. ~할 즈음에
by chance p. 어쩌다가, 우연히

어원	-mean : middle 중간, 보통의, 평균의 → '중간에서 ~수단에 의하여'
유의어	through, with the help of, by dint of, in virtue of
반의어	without, devoid of, apart from, aside from
영영	using something to achieve a particular end
예문	She communicated with her team by means of video conferences. 그녀는 비디오 회의를 통해 팀과 의사소통했습니다.

954

work on

p. 애쓰다

work out p. 운동하다; 해결하다; 계산하다
worked up p. 흥분한, 화난
workmanship n. 솜씨, 기술, 기량

어원	-work, -erg, -urg, -ag 일, 일하다 + -on 계속 → '계속 노력하니 애쓰다'
유의어	concentrate on, focus on, devote oneself to, strive for
반의어	neglect, ignore, postpone, procrastinate
영영	to spend time doing something in order to improve or complete it
예문	They need to work on improving their customer service. 그들은 고객 서비스를 개선하기 위해 노력해야 합니다.

955

come down with

p. (별로 심각하지 않은 병에) 걸리다, 들리다

come up with p. ~을 떠올리다
come up p. 발생하다, 생기다
come to do p. ~하게 되다
come to one's senses p. 정신이 들다

어원	-come 오다 + -down 아래 + -with → '등급이 떨어지는 병에 걸리다'
유의어	contract, catch, suffer from, acquire
반의어	recover from, overcome, resist, fight off
영영	to become ill or sick
예문	He came down with a severe case of the flu. 그는 강한 독감에 걸렸습니다.

956

to a person

p. 만장일치로

in person p. 직접
personnel n. 인원, 직원; 인사과
impersonal a. 냉담한
personality n. 개성, 성격

어원	-to + -person → '한 사람의 의견으로 모아지니 만장일치'
유의어	to someone, for someone, in someone's name, on behalf of someone
반의어	to everyone, to all, indiscriminately, impartially
영영	specifically for or to someone
예문	The team, to a person, supported the manager's decision. 팀 구성원 모두가 매니저의 결정을 지지했습니다.

957

get off the ground

p. 순조롭게 출발하다

get by p. 그럭저럭 살아나가다
get into trouble p. ~을 어려움에 빠뜨리다
get A out of the way p. A를 치우다
get out p. 생산하다

어원	-get off 이륙하다 + -ground 땅 → '일단 땅에선 떴으니 순조로운 출발'
유의어	start, begin, initiate, launch
반의어	fail, collapse, stagnate, falter
영영	to start successfully
예문	The new business struggled to get off the ground in its first year. 새로운 사업은 첫 해에 시작하기 어려웠습니다.

958

let alone

p. ~은 고사하고

all at once p. 갑자기, 동시에
once and again p. 여러 번 되풀이하여
for this once p. 이번만은
let up p. 약해지다, 느슨해지다

어원	-let + -alone 혼자 → '따로 두는 건 말할 것도 없이'
유의어	not to mention, to say nothing of, far from, much less
반의어	include, take into account, consider, factor in
영영	not to mention; to say nothing of
예문	He couldn't afford a new car, let alone a luxury one. 그는 새 차를 살 여유가 없었는데, 더군다나 고급차는 말할 것도 없었습니다.

959

go through

p. 통과되다, 성사되다, 해결하다

go with p. 받아들이다; 어울리다
go up p. (가격, 기온 등이) 오르다
go over p. 점검하다, 검토하다
go out of one's way p. 굳이 뭔가를 하다

어원	-go 가다 + through 통하여 → '통한 것이니 통과 됐고 해결하다'
유의어	experience, undergo, pass through, go through hell
반의어	avoid, escape, bypass, sidestep
영영	to experience or undergo something
예문	She had to go through a difficult period of adjustment after moving to a new country. 그녀는 새로운 나라로 이사한 후 어려운 적응 기간을 겪어야 했습니다.

960

stem from

p. ~에서 비롯되다

stem n. 줄기 v. 기인하다, 비롯되다
stalk n. 줄기 v. 몰래 접근하다
thorn n. 가시

어원	-st : stand → '꼿꼿이 서 있어야 하는 줄기' → '모든 열매는 줄기를 통해서 비롯되다'
유의어	originate from, arise from, result from, derive from
반의어	end, terminate, conclude, finish
영영	to originate from or result from something
예문	Many social issues stem from economic inequality. 많은 사회적 문제는 경제적 불평등에서 유래합니다.

Chapter 25.

961	cacophony	[kəˈkɒf.ə.ni]	n. 불협화음
962	decent	[ˈdiː.sənt]	a. 제대로 된, 적절한, 알맞은, 품위 있는
963	abject	[æbdʒekt]	a. 비참한, 비열한
964	reconcile	[rékənsàil]	v. 조정하다, 화해시키다; 만족시키다
965	elucidate	[ilúːsədèit]	v. 밝히다, 명료하게 설명하다
966	implicit	[implísit]	a. 내재적인, 암시적인
967	dubious	[djúːbiəs]	a. 의심스런; 애매한
968	adept	[ədépt	ædept]	a. 숙련된, 능숙한 n. 전문가, 달인
969	amicable	[ǽmikəbl]	a. 우호적인
970	ambient	[ǽmbiənt]	a. 주위의, 주변의
971	traduce	[trədjúːs]	v. 비방하다, 중상하다
972	betray	[bɪˈtreɪ]	v. 배반하다, 저버리다
973	desecrate	[désikrèit]	v. 신성을 모독하다
974	aberrant	[əbérənt]	a. 정도를 벗어난, 변태적인
975	nexus	[néksəs]	n. 유대, 관계
976	delinquent	[dɪˈlɪŋ.kwənt]	a. 비행의, 태만한; 체납된, 연체된, 미불의
977	impeccable	[impékəbl]	a. 결함없는, 완벽한
978	sedentary	[sédntèri]	a. 주로 앉아서 지내는
979	fallacy	[ˈfæl.ə.si]	n. 잘못된 생각, 오류, 허위
980	devout	[diváut]	a. 독실한, 경건한
981	procrastinate	[prəˈkræs.tɪ.neɪt]	v. 질질 끌다, 지체하다
982	incursion	[inkáːrʒən]	n. 침략, 습격
983	abridge	[əbrídʒ]	v. 요약하다, 단축시키다
984	extort	[ikstɔ́ːrt]	v. 강탈하다, 강요하다
985	retort	[ritɔ́ːrt]	v. 보복하다, 반박하다
986	abrasive	[əbréisiv, əbréiziv]	a. 연마의; 귀에 거슬리는 n. 연마재
987	affiliate	[əfílièit]	v. 가입하다, 제휴하다 n. 계열사, 자회사
988	agile	[ǽdʒəl]	a. 민첩한
989	collude	[kəlúːd]	v. 공모하다, 결탁하다
990	explicit	[ɪkˈsplɪs.ɪt]	a. 분명한, 명백한, 솔직한, 명시적인
991	in the light of		p. ~의 관점에서
992	come across as		p. ~이라는 인상을 주다
993	all the same		p. 그래도, 그럼에도 불구하고, 역시
994	as a matter of fact		p. 실제로, 사실은
995	get the better of		p. ~을 이기다, 능가하다
996	at a loss		p. 어쩔 줄을 모르는
997	on the whole		p. 대체로, 전체적으로 볼 때
998	dwell on		p. ~에 대해 곰곰이 생각하다
999	turn in		p. ~을 제출하다; 되돌려주다; 잠자리에 들다
1000	take A into account		p. A를 고려하다

961	어원	-caco 추한 나쁜 + -phone : sound → '추한 소리'
cacophony [kəˈkɒf.ə.ni] n. 불협화음	유의어	Dissonance, discord, noise
	반의어	Harmony, melody, tranquility
	영영	A harsh, unpleasant mixture of sounds.
symphony n. 교향곡 cacography n. 악필 caca n. 응가	예문	The cacophony of car horns and sirens in the city was deafening. 도시에서 차 경적과 사이렌의 불협화음이 귀에 찌르는 소리였다.

962	어원	-dec 딱 들어맞는+ -ent 형용사 → '딱 들어맞으니 적절한'
decent [ˈdiː.sənt] a. 제대로 된, 적절한, 알맞은, 품위 있는	유의어	Respectable, proper, honorable
	반의어	Indecent, improper, unacceptable
	영영	Respectable, morally upright, or satisfactory.
decently adv. 적절하게, 알맞게 decency n. 예의, 품위 있는 행동 indecently adv. 부적절하게 indecency n. 부적절함	예문	He always dressed in a decent manner for formal occasions. 그는 항상 격식 있는 자리에서 품위 있는 방식으로 옷을 입었다.

963	어원	-ab : away + -jac, -ject : throw → '멀리 버려지니 비참한'
abject [æbdʒekt] a. 비참한, 비열한	유의어	Miserable, wretched, degraded
	반의어	Noble, dignified, respectable
	영영	Miserably low in condition or quality; extremely unfortunate.
abjection n. 비굴, 비천함, 비겁 inject v. 주사하다, 주입하다 reject v. 거절하다, 거부하다 adjacent a. 인접한	예문	The poor orphan lived in abject poverty and despair. 불우한 고아는 천하태평하고 절망 속에서 살았다.

964	어원	-re : again + -con : together + -cil : call → '다시 모두 불러 조정하다'
reconcile [rékənsàil] v. 조정하다, 화해시키다; 만족시키다	유의어	Harmonize, resolve, settle
	반의어	Conflict, estrange, divide
	영영	To restore friendly relations or resolve differences.
reconcile oneself to p. ~을 감수하다 reconciliation n. 화해, 조화 reconcilable a. 화해시킬 수 있는 irreconcilable a. 화해할 수 없는, 대립되는	예문	After their argument, they tried to reconcile and mend their friendship. 그들은 다툰 뒤에 화해하고 친구 사이를 회복하려고 노력했다.

965	어원	-e, -ex : out + -lucid : light
elucidate [ilúːsədèit] v. 밝히다, 명료하게 설명하다	유의어	Clarify, explain, illuminate
	반의어	Confuse, obscure, mystify
	영영	To make something clear or explain it thoroughly.
elucidation n. 설명, 해명 luxury n. 사치, 쾌락 luster n. 광택 deluxe a. 고급의	예문	The teacher used diagrams and examples to elucidate the complex concept. 선생님은 복잡한 개념을 명확하게 설명하기 위해 다이어그램과 예제를 사용했다.

966	어원	-im : in + -pli, -ply, -ploy, -ploit, -plex : weave 짜다 → '안에 의미가 엮여 있어 내포하다, 암시하다'
implicit [implísit] a. 내재적인, 암시적인	유의어	Implied, inferred, understood
	반의어	Explicit, clear, definite
	영영	Implied or understood without being directly expressed.
implicitly adv. 내재적으로, 암시적으로 implicate v. 관련시키다, 연관시키다 implication n. 드러나지 않은 영향, 암시 implications n. 결과, 영향	예문	Although he didn't say it explicitly, his implicit approval was evident. 그가 명확하게 말하지는 않았지만, 그의 암묵적인 승인은 분명했다.

967	어원	-bi, -du, -duo : two(L) → '두 개의 가능성을 두고 의심하는'
dubious [djúːbiəs] a. 의심스런; 애매한	유의어 반의어	Suspicious, uncertain, questionable Trustworthy, certain, reliable
	영영	Doubtful, uncertain, or suspicious.
dubiously adb. 의심스럽게, 괴상하게 dubiosity n. 의심, 의혹 dubiousness n. 의심함, 수상쩍음 doubt v. 의심하다	예문	Her dubious explanation raised doubts about her story's truthfulness. 그녀의 수상한 설명은 그녀 이야기의 진실성에 대한 의심을 불러일으켰다.
968	어원	-ad : to + -ept : grasp 잡다 → '그 방향으로 완전히 잡아서 이해한'
adept [ədépt | ǽdept] a. 숙련된, 능숙한 n. 전문가, 달인	유의어 반의어	Skilled, proficient, capable Inept, unskilled, clumsy
	영영	Highly skilled or proficient in a particular activity or field.
adeptly adv. 능숙하게 adept in p. ~에 능숙한 adeptness n. 능숙함 adapt to p. ~에 적응하다	예문	She is an adept pianist and can play complex pieces flawlessly. 그녀는 숙련된 피아니스트로, 복잡한 곡을 완벽하게 연주할 수 있다.
969	어원	-amic, -amor, -amat, -enamor, -emy, -imic : love 사랑 [L] → '사랑하니 우호적인' cf. amor fati 운명을 사랑하라
amicable [ǽmikəbl] a. 우호적인	유의어 반의어	Friendly, harmonious, peaceful Hostile, antagonistic, unfriendly
	영영	Characterized by friendliness and goodwill.
amor fati p. 운명을 사랑하라 amiable a. 호감을 주는, 친절한 amicably adv. 우호적으로 amiability n. 상냥함, 온화	예문	Despite their differences, they reached an amicable agreement. 그들은 갈등이 있음에도 불구하고 친근한 합의를 이뤘다.
970	어원	-amb, -ambi 양쪽; 주위 (L) → '양쪽을 보며 주위를 살피는'
ambient [ǽmbiənt] a. 주위의, 주변의	유의어 반의어	Surrounding, atmospheric, environmental Stagnant, motionless, still
	영영	Relating to the surrounding environment or atmosphere.
ambience n. 분위기, 환경 amphibian n. 양서류 ambition n. 야망 ample a. 충분한	예문	The ambient lighting in the restaurant created a cozy atmosphere. 식당의 주변 조명은 아늑한 분위기를 조성했다.
971	어원	-tra, -trans : across + duc : lead → '선을 넘어서까지 끌어서 비방하다'
traduce [trədjúːs] v. 비방하다, 중상하다	유의어 반의어	Defame, slander, malign Praise, commend, honor
	영영	To slander or maliciously defame someone's character.
traducement n. 비방, 중상 traducer n. 중상하는 사람 traitor n. 배신자 turncoat n. 변절자	예문	Spreading false rumors about someone is a cruel way to traduce their reputation. 누군가에 대한 거짓 소문을 퍼뜨리는 것은 그들의 평판을 훼손시키는 잔인한 방법이다.
972	어원	-be : intensive + -trad, -tray, -trai : hand over 넘겨주다 → '다 넘겨주니 신의를 저버리고 배반'
betray [bɪˈtreɪ] v. 배반하다, 저버리다	유의어 반의어	Deceive, disloyal, backstab Loyalty, faithfulness, honesty
	영영	To be disloyal or reveal secrets or trust.
betrayal n. 배신, 밀고, 내통 traducer n. 중상하는 사람 traitor n. 배신자 turncoat n. 변절자	예문	Trust is easily broken when someone you thought was loyal betrays you. 충실하다고 생각했던 사람이 배신하면 신뢰는 쉽게 깨진다.

973

desecrate

[désikrèit]

v. 신성을 모독하다

desecration n. 신성 모독
desecrator n. 모독자
consecrate v. 신성하게 하다, 봉헌하다
execrate v. 저주하다, 비난하다

어원	-de : down + -secra : sacred 신성한 → '신성한 것을 모독하는'
유의어	Profane, violate, defile
반의어	Reverence, sanctify, respect
영영	To violate or treat something sacred with disrespect.
예문	Vandals broke into the church and attempted to desecrate the altar. 범죄자들이 교회에 침입하고 제단을 더럽히려고 시도했다.

974

aberrant

[əbérənt]

a. 정도를 벗어난, 변태적인

aberration n. 탈선; 이상
aberrancy n. 일탈, 이상
abolish v. 폐지하다, 없애다

어원	-ab : away + -err, -error : wander → '정상으로부터 멀리 벗어났으니 변태적인'
유의어	Abnormal, deviant, atypical
반의어	Normal, typical, conventional
영영	Departing from the normal or typical.
예문	His aberrant behavior at the party surprised everyone; he's usually very reserved. 그가 파티에서 보인 이상한 행동은 모두를 놀라게 했으며, 그는 일반적으로 매우 내성적이다.

975

nexus

[néksəs]

n. 유대, 관계

annex v. 부가하다; 합병하다
annexure n. 합병 v. 합병하다
annexation n. 합병, 부가
connect with p. ~와 친해지다, ~을 이해하다

어원	-nex, - nect : bind → '묶여 있는 관계가 유대'
유의어	Connection, link, relationship
반의어	Disconnection, separation, detachment
영영	A connection or central point linking different things.
예문	The nexus between education and economic development is well-established. 교육과 경제 발전 사이의 연결 관계는 잘 알려져 있다.

976

delinquent

[dɪˈlɪŋ.kwənt]

a. 비행의, 태만한; 체납된, 연체된, 미불의

delinquency n. 비행, 체납금, 범죄
delinquently adv. 비행을 저질러
relinquish v. 포기하다, 양도하다
relic n. 유물, 유적

어원	-de : off + -linq, -lict : leave → '정상 날짜에서 떨어지니 연체된'
유의어	Offender, lawbreaker, criminal
반의어	Law-abiding, responsible, obedient
영영	Failing to fulfill a duty or obligation, especially in legal terms.
예문	The delinquent youth was sent to a rehabilitation center for his criminal activities. 범죄 행위로 인해 문제가 있는 청소년은 회복 센터로 보내졌다.

977

impeccable

[impékəbl]

a. 결함없는, 완벽한

impeccably adv. 완벽하게, 나무랄 데 없이
impeccability n. 완전무결
impeccant a. 죄 없는, 결백한
impecunious a. 가난한

어원	-im, -in : not + -pecc : sin(L) → '죄가 없으니 완벽한'
유의어	Flawless, perfect, faultless
반의어	Flawed, imperfect, faulty
영영	Flawless or faultless in every aspect.
예문	Her impeccable manners and etiquette impressed everyone at the formal event. 그녀의 흠잡을 데 없는 예절과 에티켓은 격식 있는 행사에 참석한 모든 이들을 감동시켰다.

978

sedentary

[sédntèri]

a. 주로 앉아서 지내는

sedentarily adv. 눌러 앉아서
sedentariness n. 앉아 있음, 앉아 일함

어원	-sid, -sed : sit → '앉아만 있는'
유의어	Inactive, stationary, sitting
반의어	Active, mobile, dynamic
영영	Inactive or characterized by prolonged sitting.
예문	A sedentary lifestyle with little physical activity can lead to health problems. 신체 활동이 적은 생활 방식은 건강 문제를 일으킬 수 있다.

979

fallacy

[ˈfæl.ə.si]

n. 잘못된 생각, 오류, 허위

fallen a. 떨어진, 타락한
fallacious a. 불합리한
fallout n. 후유증
fall for it p. 속아 넘어가다

어원	-fals, -fal, -fail, -faul : deceive 속이다 / wrong 잘못된(L) / fall 떨어지다
유의어	Falsehood, misconception, error
반의어	Truth, fact, reality
영영	A false or mistaken belief or idea.
예문	Believing that all politicians are corrupt is a fallacy; there are honest ones too. 모든 정치인이 부패한 것으로 믿는 것은 오류이며, 정직한 정치인도 있습니다.

980

devout

[diváut]

a. 독실한, 경건한

devoutly adv. 독실하게, 경건하게
vow v. 다짐하다, 천명하다
votary a. 열성적인
devour v. 게걸스레 먹다; 파괴하다

어원	-de : down + -vot, -vout : vow → '엎드려 절하는 신앙이니 독실한'
유의어	Pious, religious, faithful
반의어	Irreligious, atheistic, secular
영영	Deeply religious or committed to a belief or practice.
예문	She is a devout believer who attends church every Sunday. 그녀는 매주 교회에 참석하는 신앙심 깊은 신자입니다.

981

procrastinate

[prəˈkræs.tɪ.neɪt]

v. 질질 끌다, 지체하다

procrastination n. 지연, 꾸물거림
procrastinator n. 꾸물거리는 사람
prodigal a. 낭비하는, 방탕한
prodigious a. 거대한, 막대한

어원	-pro : forth + -crastin : tomorrow → '내일까지 앞으로 쭉 미루다'
유의어	Delay, postpone, dawdle
반의어	Act promptly, prioritize, expedite
영영	To delay or postpone tasks intentionally.
예문	Don't procrastinate; start working on your assignments right away. 미루지 마세요. 과제를 즉시 시작하세요.

982

incursion

[inkɔ́:rʒən]

n. 침략, 습격

incursive a. 침입하는, 침략적인
inculcate v. 되풀이하여 가르치다
incumbent a. 의무인, 재직 중인
indecisive a. 우유부단한

어원	-in : in + -cur : run → '성 안으로 달려 침략' * in(안)에 curse(저주)를 내리고 침략
유의어	Invasion, intrusion, attack
반의어	Retreat, withdrawal, departure
영영	An invasion or aggressive entry into a territory or domain.
예문	The military launched a surprise incursion into enemy territory. 군대가 적 영토로의 놀란 침입을 시작했습니다.

983

abridge

[əbrídʒ]

v. 요약하다, 단축시키다

briefing n. 간단한 정보를 전달하는 회의
abridgement n. 요약, 요약본
unbridged a. 요약되지 않은; 완본인

어원	-ab : to + -brev : short → * bridge 다리를 세워 시간을 단축시키다
유의어	Shorten, condense, compress
반의어	Expand, lengthen, amplify
영영	To shorten or condense something, typically a text.
예문	The editor had to abridge the lengthy manuscript to fit it into the magazine. 편집자는 잡지에 맞게 긴 원고를 요약해야 했습니다.

984

extort

[ikstɔ́:rt]

v. 강탈하다, 강요하다

extortion n. 강탈, 강요
extortionate a. 터무니 없는, 부당한
retort v. 복복하다, 반박하다
distort v. 왜곡하다

어원	-ex : out + -tort → '비틀어서 밖으로 소유물이 나오게 하니 강탈'
유의어	Blackmail, coerce, demand
반의어	Give willingly, offer, concede
영영	To obtain something through force or threats.
예문	The criminal tried to extort money from the business owner by making threats. 범죄자는 협박을 가하며 사업주부터 돈을 갈취하려고 시도했습니다.

985

retort

[ritɔ́:rt]

v. 보복하다, 반박하다

retorted a. 뒤로 구부러진
retortion n. 비틀어 젖히기; 보복
extort v. 강탈하다, 강요하다
distort v. 왜곡하다

어원	-re : back + -tort 비틀다 → '반대로 비트니 보복'
유의어	Reply, answer, counter
반의어	Agree, concur, accept
영영	A sharp or witty reply in response to a remark or criticism.
예문	She couldn't resist making a sharp retort to his rude comment. 그녀는 그의 무례한 댓글에 날카로운 대답을 참지 못했습니다.

986

abrasive

[əbréisiv, əbréiziv]

a. 연마의; 귀에 거슬리는 n. 연마재

abrade v. 마멸시키다
abrasion n. 마멸
abrasively adv. 연마하여, 쓸려, 거칠게
abrasiveness n. 마손성, 마멸성, 거침

어원	-ab : away + -ras, -rad, -rod, -rub : scrape → ' 떨어지도록 문지르며 닳게 하는'
유의어	Rough, harsh, irritating
반의어	Smooth, gentle, mild
영영	Rough or harsh in manner or texture.
예문	His abrasive attitude made it difficult for him to maintain friendships. 그의 거친 태도로 인해 그는 친구 관계를 유지하기 어려웠습니다.

987

affiliate

[əfílièit]

v. 가입하다, 제휴하다 n. 계열사, 자회사

affiliation n. 관계, 소속, 협력, 제휴
filicide n. 자식 살해
filial a. 자식의
affiance v. ~을 약혼시키다

어원	-af : to + -fil : son → '아들로 받아들이는 것처럼 가입시키다'
유의어	Associate, partner, member
반의어	Disassociate, disconnect, separate
영영	To officially join or associate with a group or organization.
예문	The local chapter of the charity is affiliated with a national organization. 이 지역의 자선단체 지부는 국가 기관과 제휴되어 있습니다.

988

agile

[ædʒəl]

a. 민첩한

agility n. 명민함, 민첩성
agiliely adv. 날렵하게, 민첩하게, 기민하게
cagily adv. 말을 안 하고, 비밀스럽게
fragile a. 취약한, 깨지기 쉬운

어원	-ag : act + -ile ~하기 쉬운<형접> → '행동하기 쉽게 민첩한'
유의어	Nimble, quick, flexible
반의어	Clumsy, slow, rigid
영영	Quick and nimble in movement or thinking.
예문	Cats are known for their agile and graceful movements. 고양이는 그들의 민첩하고 우아한 움직임으로 유명합니다.

989

collude

[kəlú:d]

v. 공모하다, 결탁하다

collusion n. 공모, 결탁, 음모
collusive a. 공모한, 미리 짠, 담합에 의한
in collusion with p. ~와 결탁하여
elude v. 교묘히 피하다, 빠져나오다

어원	-co, -com : together + -lud : play → '다른 이와 함께 하는'
유의어	Conspire, cooperate, scheme
반의어	Oppose, compete, confront
영영	To conspire or cooperate secretly for a dishonest purpose.
예문	The two companies were accused of colluding to fix prices. 두 회사는 가격을 조작하기 위해 공모한 혐의를 받았습니다.

990

explicit

[ɪkˈsplɪs.ɪt]

a. 분명한, 명백한, 솔직한, 명시적인

explicitly adv. 명시적으로, 솔직하게
explicate v. 해명하다
explicitness n. 분명하, 명쾌함, 솔직함
replicate v. 복제하다; 모사하다

어원	-ex : out + -pli, -ply, -ploy, -ploit, -plex : fold(E) → '접었던 사실을 밖으로 꺼내니 분명한, 솔직한'
유의어	Clear, specific, unambiguous
반의어	Ambiguous, unclear, vague
영영	Clearly and directly stated, leaving no room for ambiguity.
예문	The contract contains explicit terms and conditions that both parties must follow. 계약에는 양측 모두가 따라야 하는 명확한 조항과 조건이 포함되어 있습니다.

991

in the light of

p. ~의 관점에서

in the long run p. 결국, 결국에는
in the mood for p. ~하고 싶은
stand in the way p. 방해가 되다
in the first place p. 우선, 애당초

어원	-in 안 + -light 불빛 → '시야 안에서 불을 밝힌 관점에서는'
유의어	Considering, given, taking into account
반의어	Despite, regardless of, irrespective of
영영	Considering or taking into account.
예문	In the light of recent developments, we need to reconsider our strategy. 최근의 개발을 고려할 때, 우리는 전략을 재고해야 합니다.

992

come across as

p. ~이라는 인상을 주다

come across p. 우연히 발견하다
come in handy p. 쓸모가 있다
come on p. 시작하다; ~이 닥쳐오다
come out ahead p. 결국 이득을 보다

어원	-come 오다 + -across + -as ~로서 → '오가며 ~라는 인상을 주다'
유의어	Seem, appear, give the impression of
반의어	Conceal, hide, mask
영영	To give the impression of being a certain way.
예문	She may come across as shy, but she's actually very outgoing once you get to know her. 그녀는 수줍어 보일 수 있지만, 실제로는 그녀를 알게되면 매우 외향적입니다.

993

all the same

p. 그래도, 그럼에도 불구하고, 역시

all-around p. 다재다능한
all the more p. 그만큼 더
all but p. 사실상, 거의
all too p. 완전 너무, 너무나, 정말

어원	-all : always + -same 같은 → '항상 같으니 그럼에도 불구하고 역시'
유의어	Nevertheless, nonetheless, still
반의어	Different, distinct, unique
영영	Nevertheless or regardless.
예문	Despite the differences in their opinions, they decided to work together all the same. 의견 차이에도 불구하고, 그들은 어쨌든 함께 일하기로 결정했습니다.

994

as a matter of fact

p. 실제로, 사실은

a matter of course p. 당연지사
in a matter of p. 불과 ~만에
make matters worse p. 상황을 더 악화시키다

어원	-matter 문제 + -fact 사실 → '사실 문제는'
유의어	In fact, actually, in reality
반의어	Falsehood, untruth, fabrication
영영	In reality or truth.
예문	As a matter of fact, I have already completed the project ahead of schedule. 사실, 저는 일정보다 먼저 프로젝트를 완료했습니다.

995

get the better of

p. ~을 이기다, 능가하다

get A out of the way p. A를 치우다
get something out p. ~을 생산하다
get to the point p. 핵심에 이르다
get the hang of p. ~에 익숙해지다

어원	-get 얻다 + -better 더 나은 → '더 나은 상태를 얻은 것이니 능가해서 이긴 것이다'
유의어	Overcome, defeat, conquer
반의어	Succumb to, be defeated by, lose to
영영	To overcome or defeat.
예문	Don't let your emotions get the better of you; stay calm and rational. 감정을 제어하지 못하게 두지 마세요. 차분하고 이성적으로 유지하세요.

996

at a loss

p. 어쩔 줄을 모르는

at all cost p. 기어코, 무슨 수를 써서라도
at an angle p. 비스듬히
at first glance p. 처음에는, 언뜻 보기에는
at a distance p. 멀리서

어원	loss(자신을 잃은) at(지점에서) 어쩔 줄을 모르는
유의어	Confused, puzzled, uncertain
반의어	Knowledgeable, informed, certain
영영	Confused or uncertain about what to do.
예문	When faced with a difficult decision, she was often at a loss for what to do. 어려운 결정을 해야 할 때, 그녀는 종종 어떻게 해야 할지 모르겠었습니다.

997

on the whole

p. 대체로, 전체적으로 볼 때

on the same page p. 같은 생각을 하다
as a rule p. 대체로, 전체적으로 볼 때
on charge of p. ~의 죄목으로
on pain of p. ~을 각오하고

어원	-on 상태 + -whole 전체 → '전체적으로 보니 대체로'
유의어	Generally, overall, in general
반의어	Partially, in part, incompletely
영영	Generally or overall.
예문	On the whole, the conference was a success, with only a few minor issues. 전체적으로, 회의는 성공적이었으며 몇 가지 작은 문제만 있었습니다.

998

dwell on

p. ~에 대해 곰곰이 생각하다

dwelling n. 거주, 주거지
dweller n. 거주자, 주민
dwindle v. 줄어들다, 감소하다

어원	-d : away + -well : spring or turn, move → '움직임을 멈추고 곰곰이 생각하다'
유의어	Obsess over, fixate on, linger on
반의어	Disregard, ignore, overlook
영영	To think or talk about something at length.
예문	Don't dwell on your past mistakes; focus on the present and future. 과거 실수에 생각을 많이 하지 마세요. 현재와 미래에 집중하세요.

999

turn in

p. ~을 제출하다; 되돌려주다; 잠자리에 들다

in return p. ~에 대한 보상으로
by turns p. 차례로
turn down p. 거절하다
turn out p. ~임이 판명되다

어원	-tour, turn 뒤집다, 회전하다 (L) * role '같은 자리를 회전' VS tour, turn '방향을 바꿈'
유의어	Submit, hand over, deliver
반의어	Keep, retain, possess
영영	To submit or hand over something, often a task or assignment.
예문	Please turn in your homework by the end of the week. 이번 주 끝까지 숙제를 제출해 주세요.

1000

take A into account

p. A를 고려하다

account for p. 설명하다
account n. 계산, 회계; 책임
accountability n. 책임(성)
accounting n. 경리, 회계, 회계학

어원	-ac, -ad : add + -count 세다 → '계속 수를 세면서 고려하다'
유의어	Consider, factor in, include A in the calculation
반의어	Disregard A, exclude A, ignore A
영영	To consider or include A in the decision or analysis.
예문	When making a decision, it's important to take all factors into account. 결정을 할 때에는 모든 요소를 고려하는 것이 중요합니다.

무지개보카 고등 중급

발 행 | 2024년 3월 4일
저 자 | 김동원
펴낸이 | 한건희
펴낸곳 | 주식회사 부크크
출판사등록 | 2014.07.15(제2014-16호)
주 소 | 서울특별시 금천구 가산디지털1로 110 SK트윈타워 A동 305호
전 화 | 1670-8316
이메일 | info@bookk.co.kr

ISBN | 979-11-410-7473-9

www.bookk.co.kr
ⓒ 김동원 2024